RETHINKING COLLECTION
DEVELOPMENT AND
MANAGEMENT

RETHINKING COLLECTION DEVELOPMENT AND MANAGEMENT

Becky Albitz, Christine Avery, and Diane Zabel, Editors

LIBRARIES UNLIMITED

AN IMPRINT OF ABC-CLIO, LLC
Santa Barbara, California • Denver, Colorado • Oxford, England

Library of Congress Cataloging-in-Publication Data

Rethinking collection development and management / Becky Albitz,
Christine Avery, and Diane Zabel, editors.
    pages cm
  Includes bibliographical references and index.
  ISBN 978-1-61069-305-9 (pbk. : acid-free paper) —
  ISBN 978-1-61069-306-6 (ebook)   1. Collection management (Libraries)
2. Collection development (Libraries)   3. Acquisitions (Libraries)   4. Library
materials—Conservation and restoration.   I. Albitz, Becky, editor of compilation.
II. Avery, Christine, 1954– editor of compilation.   III. Zabel, Diane,
editor of compilation.
  Z687.R48   2014
  025.2'1—dc23   2013038447

ISBN: 978-1-61069-305-9
EISBN: 978-1-61069-306-6

18   17   16   2   3   4   5

This book is also available on the World Wide Web as an eBook.
Visit www.abc-clio.com for details.

Libraries Unlimited
An Imprint of ABC-CLIO, LLC

ABC-CLIO, LLC
130 Cremona Drive, P.O. Box 1911
Santa Barbara, California 93116-1911

This book is printed on acid-free paper ∞
Manufactured in the United States of America

CONTENTS

PART II: ACQUISITIONS

PART III: ACCESS, COOPERATIVE EFFORTS,
SHARED COLLECTIONS

PART IV: PRESERVATION AND SPECIAL COLLECTIONS

ACKNOWLEDGMENTS

The old saying "if you want something done, ask a busy person to do it" comes to mind as we take this opportunity to thank our many contributors. Our authors are all highly accomplished in their various fields and as a result are very busy indeed. We are all the more grateful for the care and thought that went into these chapters as we know the time spent by each individual was precious, but given generously.

In addition, we would like to extend a special thank you to John Swinton, who kindly agreed on short notice to index this volume. Becky, in particular, says, "thanks, Dad!"

INTRODUCTION

Collection development and management have changed dramatically during the past 25 years. The fact that management has become the predominant word in this activity illustrates a shift in focus from the physical selection, acquisition, and preservation of the object to providing access to a variety of content, no matter who owns the materials or what the packaging is. This shift becomes more evident when the table of contents to Evans' second edition of *Developing Library and Information Center Collections*, published in 1987, is compared to this volume's chapter titles. On the surface they appear similar—both address topics such as selection, weeding, cooperative collection development, and preservation—foundation activities of collection building and maintenance. *Rethinking Collection Development and Management*, however, redefines collection-related activities for the 21st century—expanding the definitions of each of these activities to take into account the critical issues facing the profession. These include technological innovations, licensing rather than purchase of content, funding restrictions, physical space limitations, and a pervasive culture of assessment. All of these pressures create a climate that encourages cooperation and creativity, both of which are evident in our contributors' approaches to a variety of collections challenges. Our goal is not to supersede the classic collection development texts, as they continue to provide valuable context to future library and information science professionals. Rather, our hope is to examine these same issues in light of our current environment so that these same professionals have both a theoretical and practical foundation upon which to build their collections skills.

A unique feature of this book is its first chapter. In addition to the factors discussed previously, one that is often mentioned is the publishing environment. Publishing and the mission and goals of publishers are often portrayed as inherently in conflict with the values of the library profession. Publishers, however, are a critical part of the information ecosystem, and an understanding of the pressures they face in order to remain viable will assist the library professional in working effectively with his or her publisher counterparts. Robert W. Boissy provides such an overview and establishes an excellent foundation upon with to build our discussion about collections.

The next six chapters broadly examine the role of the subject librarian in selection and assessment of library materials. John M. Budd provides an overview of the current collection-related topics and trends in the library and information science curriculum. In a provocative chapter that examines the past, current, and future role of collection development in the large research library, Mark Sandler considers the value, broadly speaking, of local collection building and the future role of the subject specialist. In the public library setting, collections librarians must work closely with librarians and staff in other units in order to provide optimum service to their communities. Laurel Tarulli examines the dynamics between and among public and technical services staff, and how this relates to collections. Although it is easy to forget about library materials once licensed or purchased, a collections librarian is continuously evaluating collections and assessing their ongoing value. Nadine P. Ellero and Juliet T. Rumble discuss strategies in evaluating subscription databases—a critical activity considering the money devoted to these resources and the ever-changing availability of alternative ways to expose library content to our users. Finally, as mentioned earlier, physical space is an issue for the vast majority of libraries, as well as the need to keep collections accurate and relevant. Two chapters on collection weeding, one from an academic library perspective (David A. Tyckoson) and the other from the public library view (Merle Jacob, Sue O'Brien, and Bonnie Reid), discuss a collection management activity that addresses both currency and overcrowding.

Part II focuses on content we acquire, how we acquire it, and the tools we use to evaluate materials before we purchase or license them. Rather than focus on the acquisition of traditional print monographs and serials, this book applies acquisition practices to newly developed and less pervasive forms of information. Because eBooks in public and academic libraries are very different, both in content and how that content is delivered, two chapters address this content type, with Christopher Baker speaking to the public library experience and Michael Levine-Clark raising eBook issues for academic libraries. E-journal packages known as the Big Deal are one common way journal content is marketed to the academic community. Jeffrey D. Carroll offers an overview of the history of the Big Deal, how such an agreement can become financially unsustainable, and some models that may replace the Big Deal moving forward. Print books, of course, are still acquired, but one type of book—the self-published monograph—is becoming more common as desktop publishing and online distribution are available to individuals. James LaRue examines this previously shunned type of publication, suggesting that they do have a place in our libraries. And deg farrelly explores one of the newest formats, and one of the most difficult to license, deliver to users, and manage—streaming video.

How we locate and acquire materials has changed as well. While book and material reviews are still common selection tools, Neal Wyatt explores other resources that offer guidance to collections librarians. In other cases explored here, librarians have partially ceded content selection to other constituents. Kathy Tezla and Victoria Morse first relate the history of collection development at Carleton College, where the teaching faculty play a central role in title selection and collection building, and then discuss, from the faculty perspective, the practical implications of this collection development model. In Robert Alan's chapter on demand-driven acquisitions, the development of an eBook collection at Penn State University based on the actual use of a title prior to purchase places the onus of developing that collection on the user. One way to acquire popular materials or materials with a limited shelf life is through leasing rather than purchase. This method allows the library to make multiple copies of a high-demand title available while not investing the collections budget in purchasing, cataloging, housing, and preserving them. Anne Behler writes about developing a leased popular content collection for an academic library while Kathleen Sullivan discusses the value of such a collection for public libraries. Finally, Sian Brannon examines the pros and cons of four acquisition models used in public libraries: centralized, decentralized, outsourcing, and hybrid.

Getting the best information resources possible into our users' hands is a central value all librarians share. How one accomplishes this, however, varies. Part III examines a variety of options that can be employed to bring users and content together. Linda R. Musser and Christopher H. Walker explore the continued value of the traditional online catalog in accomplishing this goal. Logan Macdonald takes a different approach in his discussion of Anythink, a word-based system that has taken the place of the Dewey Decimal System. The catalog in many institutions is now just one tool used to locate information resources of all types. Libraries have implemented discovery services such as Summon in order to retrieve results from licensed resources, from print holdings, and from resources the institution does not even license. The introduction of such a product can have implications for collection development and management, which Jody Condit Fagan and Meris A. Mandernach consider in their contribution.

Providing our users with access to information is not dependent upon our having ownership of the physical manifestation of that information. Within libraries we have a long-standing philosophy that no single institution can possibly own, pay for, or store all of the information a user might need at any given time. Thus, cooperative relationships between and among a variety of different types of libraries must exist for us to accomplish our primary mission of providing access. Beyond interlibrary loan—the foundation upon which libraries share information—a number of other strategies are available for libraries to leverage cooperative arrangements to efficiently and effectively serve their constituencies. Kim Armstrong looks at the valuable role consortia play in academic library collection development. Another approach to cooperatively sharing materials is through the establishment of floating collections. Multibranch libraries or libraries located closely together that borrow frequently from each other agree to locally house any book borrowed from another library until needed at the home institution. Wendy Bartlett describes how such a collaborative collection management program has worked within the Cuyahoga County Public Library System, while Karen Greever describes the floating collection implementation between Kenyon and Denison Colleges. Once monographs reach the stage in their life cycle that they are no longer in high demand but could be of potential interest in the future, many libraries choose to move these titles to a storage facility. Some are located close to the owning institution; others are housed in remote facilities in different cities or even states. More important than the physical storage facility, however, is the development of shared print retention and disposition strategies among libraries. Such programs allow partner institutions to dispose of titles knowing that a critical number of copies have been retained and are available if needed. Robert H. Kieft discusses the impetus behind the development of these programs, how they have been implemented, and the implications thereof.

A central responsibility of library and information science professionals is to preserve and make available the record of human knowledge. Part IV of this book speaks directly to this imperative by engaging in discussions about preservation of nonunique content as well as the importance of the library in collecting and preserving one-of-a-kind or rare items. Steven K. Galbraith introduces this section in his chapter that articulates the value of special collections to a library's identity and importance. L. Suzanne Kellerman then guides the reader through the process she has developed to identify and manage digitization projects, which both preserve and make available rare and fragile materials. Jacob Nadal discusses the concept of a unified preservation strategy for research materials based on current print and digital initiatives. Finally, all of our hard work in developing physical collections, be they in print or in digital form but housed on local servers, will be for not if we are not prepared to respond to unplanned circumstances. Whether the unexpected event is a natural disaster, mold outbreak, or fire, having a disaster preparedness plan in place will enable a library to approach recovery in a systematic fashion. Thomas F. R. Clareson addresses this critical issue in his chapter.

REFERENCE

Evans, G. Edward. 1987. *Developing Library and Information Center Collections.* 2nd ed. Littleton, CO: Libraries Unlimited.

PART I

SELECTION AND ASSESSMENT

1

FORCES SHAPING SCHOLARLY PUBLISHING

Robert W. Boissy

INTRODUCTION

The scholarly publishing industry has been in a state of self-analysis since the Internet and linking technology upended its environment. It is as if publishers began to produce online versions of their journals and books before comprehending where such actions would lead, and then they woke up and got nervous. The Internet's momentum was self-perpetuating—any attempts to mold, guide, shape, or obstruct its progress were futile. The inevitability of the migration of all future scholarly publishing to some online format draws a natural parallel with that point in history when publishing emerged from the scriptoriums and was transformed by another piece of technology—the printing press. We should remind ourselves about the mid-15th century when Johannes Gutenberg introduced this history-altering mechanism. Andrew Pettegree (2010, 29) describes it nicely in his work *The Book in the Renaissance*:

> The Gutenberg Bible was an immediate sensation. . . . But recouping the purchase price from a mass of individual customers or intermediary agents was inevitably a slow process; too slow to save Gutenberg's partnership with Fust. As soon as the Bible was published, Fust sued for return of his loans. Gutenberg could not pay. The case went to court, and Gutenberg lost. To meet his obligations he was forced to surrender his only substantial asset, his printing shop. . . . Gutenberg faded from the scene. He would not be the last printer to learn that large complex projects carry the greatest risk, as well as the greatest renown. Although the Bible was a technical triumph, it effectively ended Gutenberg's active career as a printer.

So, does Gutenberg's experience offer anything to modern scholarly publishers who are fully engaged with the electronic medium? Do not trust your partners? Cultivate advanced sales? Develop better sales and marketing strategies?

Or perhaps just take on projects you can afford in this new environment until you can finance outright more elaborate projects. The student of history must go beyond the interesting tale of Johannes Gutenberg, and view the bigger picture. The lesson from the 15th century is that a new technical environment for distribution of knowledge and entertainment that radically increases both the volume and exposure of content will likely lead to (1) *a change in the valuation of that content* and (2) *the creation of markets that were not foreseen*. The following remarks on the forces shaping modern scholarly publishing should be considered in light of these two basic transformative factors.

OPEN ACCESS PUBLISHING

Of all the developments in scholarly publishing since the mid-1990s that have shaped valuation and markets, the open access model, or open access movement if you prefer, has had the greatest impact. Open access should therefore be defined before further commentary. To paraphrase the Bethesda Statement on Open Access Publishing, from June 20, 2003, an open access publication is a complete work in a standard electronic format, made freely available online to the public immediately upon initial publication, with permission for liberal use in exchange for proper attribution.[1] In some sense, the logic of open access arrived with the Internet, though proponents were still needed to shepherd the process along.[2] Today we see ongoing, if not always comfortable, progress with both newer and long-standing publishers increasing their open access offerings, alongside other open access content made available by individuals, libraries, and disciplinary groups. All of these efforts owe a debt of gratitude to the Creative Commons Organization, which has carefully charted the options and terminology necessary to promote and support open use of intellectual property.[3] The question publishers ask themselves is if we are to be viable contributors to open access publishing, how will we survive financially? How do we avoid Gutenberg's fate? One answer is instituting processing fees to authors or research funding organizations. The size of such fees and the commercial viability of publishing based on a fee system has been studied and openly debated.[4] It is also notable that while some researchers are quite vocal in their promotion of open access, the vast majority are more concerned with (1) their own access to the content they require and (2) the ability of a journal or book to improve their chance for tenure, promotion, and other recognition (Hunter 1998; Warlick and Vaughan 2007). Another option for scholarly publishers interested in moving forward with open access, awkwardly enough, is advertising. Scholarly publishing held advertising at arm's length, as the principal clientele for academic content has been academic librarians, who believe their subscription payments should preclude the need for advertising (Esposito 2008). But in an attempt to balance production and distribution costs with the increasing pressure to expand open access content, publishers must consider every method to defray

costs. In sum, no matter which method or methods publishers employ to manage the open access model of publishing, manage they must, as open access is
the strongest active force shaping developments in scholarly publishing today.

USER-CENTERED ACQUISITION

A second important factor shaping scholarly publishing is the rise of the
user-centered assignment of quality: perhaps another element of the information ecology that logically emerged along with the Internet. Electronic content
can be readily found, sampled, and used online, and that use can be counted.
When you can count use reliably, one may tend to equate higher use with
higher quality. Even though publishers, librarians, and researchers know that
popularity is not a substitute for scholarly integrity, accuracy, or comprehensiveness, there has been a growing trend to trust popularity over intellectual
review and selection since we entered the world of online scholarship. For
many librarians, the conflation of use with quality reaches its logical conclusion with demand-driven or patron-driven acquisition programs, in which an
electronic book is added to a library's permanent collection only after someone has used it. What librarians do not realize is that ceding selection to end
users directly influences publishers, fundamentally changing the nature of
editorial work.[5] Editors receive the message that content need not be so carefully selected based on assessments of academic rigor or excellence in a niche
area, but must rather be assessed in terms of potential popularity with the
larger population of potential readers. In other words, just look to the data on
what content is being used the most, and produce more of it. We must be wary
of this development to the extent that it leads us away from better scholarship.
This development can be welcomed, however, to the extent that user preferences can be married to a distribution system that continues to make rigorous,
high-quality content available.

OTHER QUALITY MEASURES

A related measurement of quality is the impact factor, a well-known measure that correlates value with the number of times content is cited.[6] Impact
factor is such an established measurement of quality that it is now often viewed
both inside and outside of publishing as confining. Consequently, new quality
measures have been floated to complement impact factor, some universal and
some local. Today we see many academic institutions assessing journal collections based on local faculty participation on editorial boards or as editors.
Another metric is the number of times local faculty publish in or cite a particular journal. Other measures include eigenfactor and the usage factor proposed
by UKSG (formerly the United Kingdom Serials Group).[7] The eigenfactor
takes the approach of ranking journals based on whether they are cited by
other influential journals, and also how long users spend online with articles.

The UKSG usage factor is a compilation of COUNTER (Counting Online Usage of Networked Electronic Resources) compliant usage data to get at universal popularity of a journal. One measure stresses intellectual selectivity and influence, and another stresses universal appeal. Balanced against all measurements of usefulness and quality stands both the individual editor, making choices about what is good enough and deserves to be published, and the individual librarian, who sometimes still gets to select individual journals and books based on whether they will further the mission of his or her institution. As will be discussed by others contributing to this volume, there are pressures moving against the act of intermediated individual intellectual selection as both editors and librarians have traditionally practiced. For editors, the sheer mass of content to be assessed threatens selection. For librarians, it is the preponderance of database products, bundles, and patron-driven acquisitions that has altered content selection.

DIGITAL TECHNOLOGY

Another important factor shaping scholarly publishing is the inevitable and insatiable demand for enhanced technology to improve the user experience and educational impact of, and research outcomes with, scholarly content.[8] Most publishers' initial response to the demand for digitized content has been to digitize all their content backward and forward in time, using the most convenient format available—PDF (portable document format). If the market for scholarly publishing content was stable in its acceptance of the PDF, some financial pressure might be relieved. The market, however, seems to call for more sophisticated content delivery and manipulation options all the time, partially driven by the parade of ever more sophisticated consumer electronics. The pressure has mounted to go beyond a database of PDFs to something more sophisticated—to include, at the very least, search engine optimization for better discovery of content. Applications for specific reading devices are proliferating, and semantic linking of content to other similar content augments the well-understood reference-linking infrastructure already in place. Data sets, interactive tables, three-dimensional images that can be manipulated, supplemental content, and video content are all part of mainstream publishing now. The ability to give feedback and commentary, and make both private and public annotations has transformed what it means to publish. What was once a set and final document may be an ongoing dialogue. And, beyond the technology itself, the increasingly technical nature of scholarly publishing has transformed the staff skills publishers need, whether production and distribution are managed in-house or outsourced. Today publishers must respond to market demands pushing them to adopt the many technical wonders available to augment publishing on the Internet. The largest publishers are able to make technical advances based on their economies of scale, but smaller publishers struggle to keep the technical aspects of their product offerings current.

INCREASING VOLUME OF SCHOLARLY CONTENT

The increasing volume of scholarly content available to publish is often cited as a factor pressing publishers to increase output and raise prices accordingly. The question is whether publication of more and more research is contributing to the well-being of scholarship (Bauerlein et al. 2010). Certainly there are more scholarly authors than ever before, and the amount of published content has risen dramatically through the 20th and into the 21st century. Publishers differ on the amount of content they appraise and accept for publication, but most would agree that manuscript flow has been steady over the past decades. What has changed is the increasing percentage of content contributed from Eastern countries as compared to the Western countries. Will this change the nature of scholarly publishing? Yes, probably, though the effect is not immediately apparent. A large-scale study would be needed to evaluate trends in disciplinary preferences, applied versus theoretical content, and so forth. For the short term, publishers have found it important to invest in services that aid English-as-a-second-language scholars and to provide advice on navigating the publishing process.

THE CHALLENGE OF DUAL DELIVERY

Duel delivery models for scholarly content also challenge publishers who are trying to save money and streamline workflow. Is there still pressure to publish in print? To some extent, pressure to keep a print option open remains. This has disappointed those who see 100 percent electronic publishing as the ultimate goal for convenience and cost savings. However, much as we hear about retail sales of eBooks outpacing print books, there is still a large market for print books, although the market for printed scholarly books has diminished. For this reason, print-on-demand or print-when-ordered options are still available from even the most electronic of electronic publishers. This demand-driven approach to printing eliminates warehousing, wholesaling, returns, and much financial uncertainty, even if it sacrifices typeset hardbound editions with color images for soft-cover gray-scale editions.

PRESSURE TO PUBLISH FASTER

No analysis of the challenges facing modern publishing would be complete without mentioning the urgency to publish content more quickly. Research is done not only to advance human understanding of the nature of the physical universe but also the career and notability of the researcher. Researchers, like artists, want their work to be widely viewed, appreciated, and experienced. But unlike art, research is almost always incremental, building on recent findings to advance knowledge in a discipline. For this reason timing is critical, and publishers have been under ever-increasing pressure in the Internet era to publish scientific findings quickly. This pressure to release content quickly has led publishers to post articles online prior to the release of the journal issue. The journal issue had its roots in print convenience and logistics, and is largely a holdover in the electronic world. The journal article is now the focus of modern science. Even books, once thought to be the steady and thoughtful summary review tool for science, are now being published through a much faster cycle than before. Book chapters are becoming more like journal articles in their speed of production, importance in the discovery layer, and tendency to stand on their own. Both journal articles and book chapters are now sold on their own through a variety of established and experimental models, reflecting the increasing granularity of reader interest. The logical endpoint of granularity is the specific unit of scholarly content that answers a question, bolsters an argument, or suggests an alternative. The logical endpoint of speed in dissemination of scholarly findings is disintermediated communication between and among researchers, which is simultaneously (1) happening all the time and (2) not an efficient way to keep track of scholarly advances for a wider audience. For now, publishers can best answer the call for speedy publishing by making their print and electronic versions available simultaneously, so that overworked librarians can make their format choices confidently and efficiently.

BUNDLING

Some publishers have felt the need to organize their e-journal and/or eBook content into bundles, offering a volume discount and a low per-unit price. E-journals are typically sold through library consortium licenses. eBooks are more typically sold in packages direct to individual libraries, though there are variant models for both e-journals and eBooks. In his 2005 work *Books in the Digital Age*, John B. Thompson (2005, 368–69) identified two ideas publishers fostered in relation to making eBooks a viable product. First, he notes that *"the principal market for scholarly book content in electronic form is likely to be institutional rather than individual."*[9] This statement is not surprising— no publisher will realize a profit selling scholarly eBooks to individuals when academic librarians have been the primary curators of scholarly books for centuries. Thompson (2005, 368–69) also states, "The best way to maximize the added value of delivering scholarly book content online is *to treat individual books as part of a scholarly corpus or database which has scale, selectivity and focus."*[10] He goes on to point out the utility of a collection of information for searching and cross-referencing. Thompson's points mirror the thinking of commercial publishers, and this approach to content dissemination has benefits for authors as well. Even a librarian at a well-funded institution would select only certain titles from any imprint based on an assessment of topical relevance for his or her institution. But selling a bundle of content to a library exposes more of a publisher's authors to an institution's researchers, encourages multidisciplinary investigation, and attracts authors to an imprint that might have gone unnoticed due to the specialized nature of its title list. Even with the most analytical of selection workflows in place, bibliographers find it difficult to predict the journals and books that researchers will use (Collection Development Executive Committee 2010). Selection is, after all, an attempt at intellectual premonition. One common anecdotal finding is that neither publishers nor librarians could anticipate the e-journals and eBooks that would be utilized as part of a package or bundle of content. It is fair to say that the pushback from librarians against bundling has been equal to the push from publishers to sell bundles. Similarly, the preference to have either bibliographers or library users select content has been equally as strong as any publisher's desire to expose large groupings of its portfolio to readers.

PITFALLS

There is a tendency, particularly among nonscientists, to romanticize or idealize science as a pure pursuit. But science is as vulnerable to politics, pet projects, cronyism, least publishable unit thinking, and inertia as any other human endeavor. The natural ebb and flow of scientific discovery happens within a lattice of funding, reviewing, and the hierarchy of authority. What is published can sometimes have as much to do with a researcher's positioning of his or her study and methodology in relation to some current context as it does with the inherent quality of the research itself. In other words, one of the important factors in determining what publishers publish is what authors offer, and how well the author positions his or her work in relation to other influential works of the day.

EFFICIENCY

Finally, there has always been and will always be pressure on publishers to cut costs, streamline processes, lower prices, and generally make every aspect of publishing less expensive. For commercial publishers this will always be done within the context of making a profit. But cost cutting is never easy and can sometimes be in direct conflict with a quality publisher's primary goal, which is to produce high-quality content worthy of its intellectual reputation. Hence there is a tension between outsourcing to cut costs and close oversight to control product quality. In the electronic world, this struggle continues.

CONCLUSION

This reflection was not put together in isolation. Besides the input of numerous editors and other colleagues at my company, I have the pleasure of providing implementation and promotional support to academic librarians from the Northeast and Mid-Atlantic regions of the United States. So my days are spent listening to how publishing can be made better by librarians who are not shy with their feedback. As a librarian myself, I understand the motivation to provide excellent information services. For hundreds of years, publishers could enjoy a comfortable arm's length relationship with libraries, and libraries in their turn could focus on building excellent information collections that by themselves would attract readers and researchers. Now this cushion of managing print logistics has been significantly removed and we share the challenge that comes with the Internet—to provide a rich, organized, and useful information environment for researchers, mostly of online content but partly still in print, while staying within our economic means. This situation is likely to require publishers to become a bit more like libraries with respect to service values, and to require libraries to become a bit more like publishers with respect to marketing orientation. Scholarly publications must be made affordable and libraries must market what they acquire. This is a challenging message. So be it.

NOTES

1. As befits its content, the full Bethesda Statement is available online at http://www.earlham.edu/~peters/fos/bethesda.htm. All other definitions since this benchmark statement are mostly gloss.

2. Stevan Harnad is the most well-known advocate for open access scholarship. See his Web site http://openaccess.eprints.org for the latest discussions in this area.

3. See http://creativecommons.org/ for more on the various licensing options open to creators of intellectual property these days.

4. For a refresher on the environment of article processing fees, see David J. Solomon and Bo-Christer Björk, *A Study of Open Access Journals Using Article Processing Charges,* available online at http://www.openaccesspublishing.org/apc2/preprint.pdf.

5. There has been so much written and presented about patron-driven acquisitions. I mention one recent article for those feeling the need to catch up. Erin S. Fisher and Lisa Kurt, "Exploring Patron-Driven Access Models for E-journals and E-Books," *The Serials Librarian* 62 (2012): 1–4, http://www.tandfonline.com/doi/abs/10.1080/0361526X.2012.652913.

6. See http://thomsonreuters.com/products_services/science/free/essays/impact_factor/ for a recent explanation of the impact factor.

7. See http://www.eigenfactor.org/about.php for an introduction to the eigenfactor and its use in bibliographic research; See both the UKSG Web site (http://www.uksg.org/usagefactors) and the COUNTER Web site (http://www.projectcounter.org/usage_factor.html) for more on usage factor.

8. While one does not normally cite a whole conference, it seems appropriate here. The annual O'Reilly Tools of Change Conference would be the place to go to catch up on the latest in publishing technology and experiments in publishing. http://www.toccon.com/.

9. Italics are the author's.

10. Italics are the author's.

REFERENCES

Bauerlein, Mark, Mohamed Gad-el-Hak, Wayne Grody, Bill McKelvey, and Stanley W. Trimble. 2010. "We Must Stop the Avalanche of Low Quality Research." *The Chronicle of Higher Education*, June 13. http://chronicle.com/article/We-Must-Stop-the-Avalanche-of/65890/.

Collection Development Executive Committee Task Force on Print Collection Usage. 2010. *Report*. Cornell University Library, November 22. http://staffweb.library.cornell.edu/system/files/CollectionUsageTF_ReportFinal11-22-10.pdf.

Esposito, Joseph J. 2008. "Open Access 2.0: Access to Scholarly Publications Moves to a New Phase." *JEP: The Journal of Electronic Publishing* 11 (2).

Hunter, Karen. 1998. "Electronic Journal Publishing: Observations from Inside." *D-Lib Magazine*, July/August. http://www.dlib.org/dlib/july98/07hunter.html.

Pettegree, Andrew. 2010. *The Book in the Renaissance*. New Haven: Yale University Press.

Thompson, John B. 2005. *Books in the Digital Age*. Cambridge, UK: Polity Press.

Warlick, Stephanie E., and K. T. L. Vaughan. 2007. "Factors Influencing Publication Choice: Why Faculty Choose Open Access." *Biomedical Digital Libraries* 4 (1). http://www.bio-diglib.com/content/4/1/1.

2

THE GHOSTS IN THE STACKS: COLLECTION DEVELOPMENT PRACTICE PAST, PRESENT, AND FUTURE IN ACADEMIC RESEARCH LIBRARIES

Mark Sandler

Library collection development is the decision-making process by which libraries seek to accumulate and disseminate useful resources over time. With or without formal collection policy statements, libraries of all types strive to rationalize their content purchasing decisions by relating their acquisitions to organizational goals. Collection building, we would like to think, is intentional, aimed at fulfilling certain *a priori* needs or purposes. These collection-building purposes will obviously vary by library type and the user community that any individual library is committed to serve. The general point of this chapter, however, is that collection development for any library is—or should be—goal-driven, and there should be some accountability for the extent to which collection expenditures achieve their intended purposes.

This chapter focuses on the collection development activities of large research libraries, but many of the challenges faced by the large academics are, in one form or another, being visited upon other library types as well. Past and current patterns of library collection development and collection management raise several important questions about how libraries think about their collection development responsibilities:

- What are the goals, stated or otherwise, that library collection development seeks to achieve?
- How do we assess whether those goals are being achieved?
- How have the goals of collection development changed with changes in the ecosystem of scholarly communication?
- How is the work of collection development being carried out?
- What does the future hold for library collection development and management?

COLLECTION DEVELOPMENT GOALS

Most academic libraries proffer that the goal of their collection development efforts is to support campus research and instruction. Such vague goal language, however, does not allow research libraries to adequately assess if they are accomplishing their stated intention to advance either research or instruction. For any given library to evaluate its collection development program, much tighter measures would be required to direct staff efforts or to determine if their acquisition program is fulfilling expectations (Tenopir 2012a; Anderson 2011).

Most business textbooks teach that organizational goals should be specific, measurable, and time-bound (Mager 1997). Following such leads, orienting goal statements for research library collection efforts would take the following form:

- Increase circulation of legacy print holdings by 5 percent in 2014.
- Increase the chapter downloads from purchased or licensed eBooks by 10 percent in 2014.
- In the fall semester, induce 20 humanities faculty members to assign the use of licensed historical corpora in undergraduate term papers.
- Reduce the ratio of collection management costs to content costs by 3 percent.
- In two years' time, increase the number of community (noncampus) uses of special collections by 5 percent.
- Over the course of the 2014 academic year, increase undergraduate citation of specialized research journals by 7 percent.
- By 2015, reduce the loss, theft, or damage to 19th-century collections by 10 percent.

While the substance of these examples should be ignored, their form is intended to show that collection development officers and library directors could be doing more to manage their campus investments in scholarly resources, and the costs associated with building and maintaining those library collections.

In theory, this kind of goal setting and program assessment seems obvious. In practice, however, management at this level is almost entirely absent from past and present-day library oversight of collection development activity (Yi 2013).

Picking Up the Tab

Much of the difficulty that libraries face in articulating collection development goals is a reflection of a lack of overall goals for academic research libraries. As tax supported—or tuition supported—lending exchanges, the value of library collections or services is not typically determined or reinforced by the consumers of collections and services. A third-party payer system at work in developing library collections and services attempts to intuit the value provided by the library for campus users, when neither the library nor its users have an incentive to limit collection expenditures. While third-party funders exist in many other spheres, there are often sophisticated systems in place for assessing the value provided to end users, and some co-pay strategy that would inhibit overuse or abuse (Aron-Dine, Einav, and Finklestein 2013). Libraries and their funders have placed few such governors on the acquisitiveness of library subject specialists, campus faculty, donors, and library directors.

Shoppers and Learners

In most respects, libraries are a distribution channel for knowledge in the way that retail outlets—grocery stores, clothing stores, and so forth—are distribution channels for other goods and services. Taking the grocery model, storekeepers aspire to stock their shelves with saleable merchandise, some intended to meet known needs of consumers—for example, milk, bread—and some that might tempt consumers to acquire and spend more than intended— for example, Hostess Twinkies or M&Ms (Hitt 1996). A retailer's goal is to maximize profits by selling as much inventory as possible, as quickly as possible, and for as much money as the consumer market will bear. People coming into a store to simply browse, stay warm, use the restrooms, read magazines, and leave will likely be treated courteously to the extent that they are perceived as potential purchasers. In most cases, however, retailers are not simply trying to drive up their gate count by attracting browsers to their space. Rather, they are attempting to generate revenues by selling shoppers products: preferably more than the customer initially intended by driving up impulse purchases through clever product placements, sales, and other time-tested marketing techniques.

Unlike retail stores, libraries, without incentives for sales or profits, are more inclined than storekeepers to stock their shelves with purportedly high-quality products that are deemed good for their constituents, as opposed to popular items that are more likely to capture users' attention or unleash their consumptive urges. In other words, academic libraries are not in the business of profiting from the baser needs of their users. They endeavor, instead, to build a prescriptive inventory of items that they consider to be intellectually nourishing, even if that means that potential users might not show up in large numbers, and will not load up their shopping carts with intellectual staples or treats. Collection development librarians do not share the grocer's imperative to sell and sell fast. Instead, they are more inclined to invest in the edifying and enduring, as opposed to the popular choices du jour.

In this sense, collection librarians are perhaps more like museum curators than storekeepers. For storekeepers—at least those storekeepers still in business—their inventory reflects the preferences of their customers rather than their own personal tastes or preferences. Successful retailers fill their scarce shelf space with the items that customers expect and want. In contrast, museum curators and administrators are more likely to make acquisitions based on their own aesthetic sensibilities; the sensibilities of known art critics; the perception that some pieces or artists complement and reinforce earlier acquisitions; or the goal of advancing thematic commitments for an institution—for example, local artists or local themes. This less-than-market-driven approach to collection building is certainly understandable for educational institutions charged with shaping young—and not so young—minds, or challenging banal social preferences with more evolved or acquired tastes.

As educational and cultural institutions, museums and libraries are understandably prescriptive about the opportunities they provide for learning and enrichment. Neither of them, however, is very systematic about defining or measuring such learning events, relying instead on gate counts or foot traffic, on the apparent assumption that mere proximity to learning opportunities can translate to actual learning. Although both museums and libraries are good at acquiring the tools of learning—for example, collections—neither seems unduly troubled by their inability to demonstrate when learning outcomes have been achieved by their users. While retailers work day and night to convert browsers into shoppers, museums and libraries are remarkably laissez-faire about converting their visitors to learners.

Circling back to the driving question of this section, the collection development goals for large academic libraries are surprisingly ill-defined considering the amount of money expended, the intellect of their users, and the management savvy of library and campus administrators. It does not do much good to say that the goal of collection building is to support the research and instructional needs of the campus, if (1) we do not know much about those needs; (2) we do not understand the relationship between library resources and the fulfillment of acknowledged needs; and (3) we have not considered whether there might be more efficient or effective ways of satisfying campus needs than by funding the development of a large and locally managed library collection.

Does Size Matter?

If an academic research library is spending something on the order of $7, $10, or $15 million per year to purchase scholarly resources—and perhaps an equivalent amount on operations to select, acquire, process, store, promote, circulate, and preserve those print and electronic resources—it is not unreasonable to think they would have pretty compelling data about the dividends being returned on these investments (Oakleaf 2010; Montgomery and King 2002). By default or design, libraries, as a community, have been slow to develop such measures of the value of their collections (Neal 2011). Later in this chapter I discuss the increased reliance upon usage statistics for managing electronic resources, but usage alone does not really address the issues of value, which would more directly link campus or user goal attainment to library expenditures (Tenopir 2012b).

In earlier times—by which is meant *print times*—libraries might have been more inclined to conflate the size of a collection with its quality. Historically, libraries used collection size—that is, volume count, current subscriptions, and so forth—as the best indicators of the value they were producing—or the latent value that could be unleashed in the hands of the right user. Such measures made particular sense in the print world of scholarly communication, where campuses that were located out of shouting distance from the centers of leading-edge scholarship (i.e., London, Paris, Boston, etc.) relied upon large, standalone libraries to connect local scholars with the ideas and research of their colleagues from around the world. In the 19th-century world of limited real-time channels of communication, books and journals housed at arm's length, connected far-flung scholars to the major contributors and contributions of their disciplines. If a professor of philosophy in the 1860s were to take a position in Athens (Georgia, Ohio, or Greece), access to a large, proximate book stock would be essential to maintain contact with worldwide scholarly communities.

Skipping ahead 150 years, most agree that it no longer makes sense to tout collection size as a surrogate for library effectiveness (Franklin 2005). The Association of Research Libraries (ARL) members should be actively working to develop meaningful benchmarks and best practices that could shine a light on the meaning and significance of collection efficacy in a world of increasingly distributed collection resources (Lib-Value n.d.). While they are at it, the research library community could also seek to measure the efficiency of their collection building programs—that is, the level of campus collection use in relation to the cost of building those collections (Franklin 2005).

If large is no longer beautiful when it comes to library collections, then some characteristic or combination of characteristics are still leading most universities to believe and say that they possess an *excellent* library collection. An excellent collection, in the parlance of a research library, likely means that the tens of thousands of books they add each year are written in a manner that approximates a scholarly format, and cover a broad array of topics approached from an equally broad array of cultural and theoretical perspectives. The notion of an excellent collection undoubtedly connotes library shelves crammed with some combination of outstanding, good, and mediocre scholarly output, even if that output exceeds consumer demand, or if the subject matter, language, or level of discourse is a poor fit for the interests of the campus user community.

Measures of Collection Efficacy

Of course, there are other ways to assess collection excellence than the size, breadth or diversity of accumulated library holdings. One such measure is use: use relative to the overall size of the collection, use relative to the size of the campus, or use relative to the dollars invested. By focusing on collection use as a measure of excellence, we might find that the libraries at liberal arts colleges or smaller regional campuses have a greater claim to collection excellence than their counterparts at top-tier research universities. And, by refining our measures of collection use we might be able to draw more meaningful comparisons among research libraries themselves. In retrospect, one can certainly question the complacency of library directors, collection development officers, and bibliographers about the staggering investments their libraries and campuses made in un- and under-utilized library materials (Gammon and O'Neil 2011; Kent 1979). A grocer or shopkeeper would act with urgency to reduce investments in inventory that is not selling, and yet library collection officers accept with complacency that a significant proportion of their book inventory will not be read.

If students and faculty members are rejecting library offerings in the tens of thousands and millions, it might be time to reconsider the marketing strategy of libraries, or to question the competence of library book buyers. Cramming more and more unwanted books into a finite space can hardly pass muster as a rational business strategy, or as an effective means for advancing scholarly communication. Granted, libraries buy what publishers sell, and publishers sell what scholars write, so the overall supply chain of books is not the creation of libraries. Libraries, however, have stoked the flames of authorship and publishing by shoveling cash into that market for decades, providing necessary capital when there was no evident reader interest—neither in academic nor trade markets—that would sustain a publisher or incentivize an author. In the name of collection excellence, academic research libraries became buyers of last resort, taking it upon themselves to ensure that every book was granted an inch-and-a-half of shelf space, if not a reader as Ranganathan (1931) had once suggested.

THE ELECTRONIC PIVOT

Just about everything I have said about library collections so far applied to collection structures built to support large, on-site print collections in the geographically dispersed academic research libraries of a bygone era. To what extent have the issues characterizing print collection development been attenuated—or exacerbated—with today's campus reliance on electronic resources? Volumes—in print or electronic form—could be written about the impacts of digital resources on campus scholarship and research libraries, so in the space of a chapter we can merely enumerate a few highlights and try to identify fruitful directions for more in-depth analysis. Some of the many changes that have rocked the collection development world are as follows:

- The tendency to purchase electronic content in bundles or large aggregations as opposed to individual titles.
- The attention paid to the platforms upon which the content is made accessible, and the licensing terms governing that access.
- The option to lease access to content as opposed to purchasing and owning it.
- The proliferation of nontraditional publishing and dissemination options for scholarly content.
- The extent—and quality—of available content on the free Web, as opposed to that purchased or licensed by libraries.
- The extraordinary amount of retrospective born print content being marketed to libraries, including science journal backfiles.
- The proliferation of digital information formats, including numeric data, spatial data, audio and video files, art images, medical illustration and simulations, and so forth.
- Investments in local digitization initiatives or mass digitization partnerships like the Google library scanning program.
- Content decision making compounded by format decision making—that is, print, electronic, or both.
- The emergence of Amazon and the popularity of eBooks in the trade market.
- Greater centralization of library budgets and library decision making.
- The systematic monitoring of usage that is possible with electronic resources.
- Stronger collection-building roles for regional consortia, and even national coordinated purchasing strategies.

In the space available to us here, I will focus on just a few of these themes that address the issues raised earlier about the mission of research libraries going forward. In particular, I will highlight the ubiquity of electronic information, the assault on expertise, and the emphasis on usage as an indicator of value.

Think Local, Buy Global

Electronic content is at once everywhere and nowhere—it has lost any spatial connectedness or locale. The shoving match between libraries and publishers about sending article PDFs in response to interlibrary loan (ILL) requests is a good example of this: a hypothetical user in Timbuktu could gain access to an article from an American research library in about the time it would take a student in a dormitory to access the same article in print form from a library at the heart of campus. As annoying as ILL has been to publishers in the print era, there were clearly disincentives to lenders and borrowers to supply or rely upon the shipping of physical items. These barriers can be totally circumvented in the electronic world where the only limitation on transmission of information is the speed of light. This is obviously threatening to commercial publishers who are struggling mightily, not only against the sharing ways of libraries, but also with the open sharing norms of tens of millions of academic authors and users worldwide.

While the difficulty of spatially bounding electronic content is a challenge to the potential earnings of commercial publishers or rights holders, it also presents a significant potential challenge to thousands of academic libraries at thousands of colleges and universities nationwide. If Harvard, MIT, or Stanford can teach courses to tens of thousands of dispersed students online, then we can begin to envision a world where the libraries at Harvard, MIT, or Stanford could supply content as needed to students anywhere. And, if not these libraries, we could envision online providers of higher education moving into this space—as have the University of Phoenix and the Open University in the United Kingdom—or the development of scholarly content stores by less library-like suppliers such as Apple, Google, or Amazon. It is understood there are valid academic concerns regarding such utopian or dystopian predictions about new distribution channels for scholarly information, but these are raised here to make the fairly incontrovertible point that in a world of electronic information resources, a couple of thousand locally developed, locally managed, and locally delivered print and electronic hybrid library collections could be usurped by a nationally or globally developed and distributed collection of electronic academic resources.

While no local academic library of any consequence has shut its doors in the age of the Internet, nor disbanded its collection development programs, there have been evident trends for nationalization of eResource decision making or licensing in countries across Europe, Asia, Latin America, and Canada. While this pattern of national dealing is not as advanced within the United States, we have seen glimpses of scaled-up selection in Ohio, California, and the Midwest. ARL, Lyrasis, and the Center for Research Libraries have all been exploring the potential for national purchasing agreements, reinforcing the contention that the nature of electronic resources makes it possible—and perhaps desirable—to envision different structures for acquiring, housing, and distributing library content in an electronic age than the structures put in place for meeting the needs of scholars in a world of print books and journals.

Some—perhaps many—might challenge the notion that national deal-making could adequately reflect and support local research, scholarship, and curriculum needs on any given campus. Since all campuses are not alike, it cannot be the case that a globally conceived collection would be a good fit for the needs of any particular user community. Libraries have long celebrated the customization of their collections such that differences from one to the next are justified in terms of calibrating the mix of resources to align with campus demand. While customization to address local needs is a theoretically compelling argument for local control of collection development, in practice we know that local control of decision making has not always resulted in the desired results of collection relevance. Defenders of the status quo should be asked to address some or all of the following:

- Is there a point at which the costs of customization outweigh the benefits?
- Is there a point at which hiring thousands of librarians to avoid buying unwanted material undermines the available funds to purchase desirable content?
- For similar universities in terms of mission, structure, status, and budgets, how much variance might one expect in their associated library needs?
- Given that libraries are currently funded to build collections locally, how confident can we be that the resultant collections actually satisfy the campus needs they are intending to support?

While collection decision making based on local priorities might sound like a good idea, when pitted against the best practices or modal decisions of a hundred peer libraries, reasonable campus administrators might question the preference for supporting the prerogatives of an individual selector versus the wisdom of the crowd.

What's the Use?

More so than they had in the print world, collection librarians do pay attention to usage statistics for electronic resources. In the case of journal usage, user downloads are routinely monitored and used to (1) demonstrate the value of library licensed content; (2) cancel low-use journal titles, or in some cases whole databases; or (3) threaten publishers with cancellations or otherwise point to low-use content to gain some advantage in price negotiations. Mostly, usage statistics are used to trim already selected or acquired content as opposed to informing selection in the first place. While it is true that usage cannot be measured if readers do not have access to the content in question, it is most often the case that users somewhere have access, and data from these other libraries could be considered before a new subscribing or purchasing library makes a commitment. Such meta-analysis of library use would clearly steer toward consensus decision making, de facto establishing a national collection that undergirds the work of scholarship everywhere.

To employ usage statistics prior to purchase, libraries or publishers would need to contribute data to some regularly updated service for gathering usage reports, contextualized with information about the reporting institutions. Knowing that certain titles receive low usage at 10 peer universities could be valuable baseline data for a purchase or licensing decision, although could be trumped if there are known program differences among the universities reporting data and the one considering a particular title or product. Despite the potential utility of such interlibrary meta-analysis, libraries have not chosen to invest in tools to share usage statistics, or otherwise calculate the statistical probability of use prior to purchase. While much of the needed information is already available to publishers, aggregators, and discovery services, developing predictive systems to analyze library content usage is apparently not in their business interests, and perhaps not in the interest of libraries either.

Beyond the general limitations of deploying usage statistics in prospective library decision making, the collection development community has not done a good job of norming usage patterns by discipline, or campus status (i.e., faculty, graduate, or undergraduate student), and, in fact, does not track on such user data. Whereas advertisers are very interested in the demographics of users who are viewing their ads on TV or in magazines, libraries have shown no such interest in parsing usage statistics by more or less valued communities of users. This issue harkens back to the failure of libraries to set goals for their collections, but most would agree that not all uses or downloads are of equivalent value to the campus, just like not all TV viewers are of equal value to a Mercedes dealership that purchases ad time.

Probabilities of content use could be accurately calculated by taking into account the characteristics of a user community, and numerous factors about the content itself, including variable descriptors regarding the author, publisher, discipline, topic, theoretical perspective, language, format, length, reviewer comments, and other factors that might emerge over time as predictive. Publishers routinely make these calculations as a matter of course in deciding upon a business case for any given manuscript, and library selectors do as well in making purchase decisions. What is being suggested here, however, is that these intuitive calculations of potential value could be replaced by much more sophisticated and objective predictive tools by taking advantage of the large number of data points that make up the collective library holdings, student bodies, and research communities at U.S. universities (Silver 2012).

Were libraries to embrace more sophisticated systems for predicting the likely use of particular titles, it would inevitably weaken the continued control that local library subject specialists might exercise over collection development decisions. On the other hand, tools that would enhance the desired outcomes of library acquisitions would ultimately strengthen the perception of library (King et al. 2005). With improved tools for collection decision making, responsibility for collection development could be shifted to library staff with little or different training. For that matter, formulaic approaches to collection building based on sophisticated computer algorithms could provide the underpinnings for a national stocking service for libraries, akin to way that retail outlets from the largest box stores to 7-Eleven convenience stores manage their inventory and stock their shelves (Chanil 2010). While there is understandable discomfort at treating scholarly journals and monographs as if they were chips and beef jerky, it is hard to imagine that more data-driven, crowd-sourced, and real-time strategies for managing collections will not emerge: strategies that ultimately shift the locus of collection building beyond the purview of the local library and its cadre of collection development specialists.

THE ROLE OF BIBLIOGRAPHERS

Limiting ourselves for the moment to collection building in the print world, bibliographers had all the incentives to over-purchase for their libraries and audience, using size and diversity of their past acquisitions to argue for ever more funds to purchase greater quantities of little-used material. If activity is the measure of the professional performance of a bibliographer, then the more one acquired—including pursuit of obscure offerings once the readily available sources of content were exhausted—the better the assessment of their performance. In the world of bigger is better, dozens of library bibliographers at a given institution, or in a given discipline nationally, had every incentive to try to outdo each other in bibliographic gluttony. Needless to say, there are not many business analogies for the kinds of perverse incentives that characterized the work strategies adopted by research library bibliographers post-World War II.

While bibliographers of prior decades might have made a habit of over-buying, they were acting in good faith to fulfill the expectations codified in their institutional job descriptions and collection development policies. The drive and ability of these bibliographers to build large and often idiosyncratic collections were traits rewarded by their managers, peers, and campus constituents. In retrospect, we can see that there are indeed negative consequences of overconsumption that haunt libraries to this day. Research libraries are now burdened with the obligation to manage an accumulated glut of little-used legacy print collections that demand staff attention and occupy valuable space (Courant and Nielsen 2010). In addition, this legacy of aggressive acquisitiveness and spending on the journal front has set burdensome expectations for continued library expenditures at historically established levels.

All this is to say that, in the absence of goals or measures for defining the quality or fitness of a collection, it is pretty much impossible to assess the performance of those responsible for developing and managing it. This stands in marked contrast to the way commercial organizations manage their account managers or sales representatives where goals are clear-cut and success is easily determined. I will say more about this topic in the next section.

Library Liaisons

A scan of the current Web sites of ARL libraries surfaces a lot of language about the outreach and liaison roles of library subject specialists, to an extent replacing older job descriptions that focused on their back-office functions as selectors (Mack 2010). In fact, current library norms suggest that administrators want their subject specialists spending more time interpreting the library for users, and much less time picking and choosing books and journals. The library liaison movement has been evolving for several decades, but subject-related service roles are clearly now the norm for collection development job descriptions. Liaison roles usually include such activities as providing new resource updates, advanced reference service, classroom instruction, research consultation, tours and graduate orientation, assistance with faculty recruitment, and support for making decisions about publishing rights and data management (Hahn 2009; Williams 2009; Logue 2007; Latta 1992).

While the concept of library subject specialists providing expert consultation to faculty and advanced students makes sense in theory, it is not clear that the concept has taken hold in practice. For one thing, there have been, and continue to be, pockets of resistance on the library side. Many library selectors and bibliographers who were hired at a different time, and with different expectations, have not embraced the newer service roles, or are not well suited to carrying them out. Thus, the experience of liaison support on most campuses is uneven at best, and, overall, might be said to skew to the negative side of a performance continuum.

Beyond the limiting factors of librarian aptitude for liaison roles, there is little evidence to suggest that the concept has taken hold with faculty or students. Studies of user expectations for their libraries suggest that faculty care more about the purchasing role of librarians than the services they might offer to provide (Schonfeld, Housewright, and Wulfson 2013). This does not mean that some faculty members on some—or perhaps most—campuses do not value the support of their library colleagues. That, however, is not the attitudinal norm, nor is seeking support from a library liaison anywhere close to a normative faculty behavior. It is likely the case that faculty do not recognize the subject expertise of their library colleagues, nor do they value many of the services being promoted.

While execution of the liaison concept is limited by both librarian aptitude and faculty attitude, the most serious hurdle to success is how these programs are managed. The library has assembled an array of goods and services that it believes would be desirable to the market it serves—campus faculty and students. Uptake of the library's offerings, however, is less than ideal. Given this disconnect, how can libraries increase market uptake? The typical answer to this common challenge is to (1) make the goods and services being offered more appealing, more convenient, or more affordable; or (2) elevate market awareness through promotion and sales. While most library liaison programs attempt to position their professional staff as expert colleagues to the faculty— or perhaps service-oriented support staff—a more effective model might be to organize the cadre of library liaisons as a sales force, trained and incentivized to breakdown market resistance. While our first instinct might be to say that this would not work in an academic culture, it has to be recognized that textbook publishers have unleashed legions of sales representatives to interact with faculty on a more-or-less regular basis, and we can only assume that such investments in sales pays dividends.

Were a sales management strategy applied to library liaison work, we would expect to see some very different library strategies in place for hiring, managing, and evaluating staff. There is literature on sales aptitude, suggesting that certain personality traits and skills can predict sales success. These predictive traits can vary widely, in part due to the variation in sales models or strategies in place. So, for example, some companies that emphasize a problem-solving approach to sales might seek applicants who have skills such as relationship building, memory, empathy, and customer service, while another company whose sales program relies upon cold calls might seek out candidates who score higher on traits associated with convincing or closing, including assertiveness, fluency, doggedness, and the ability to withstand rejection. There are dozens of different approaches to sales, and therefore dozens of notions of the kinds of individuals that adapt well to particular models. The general point being made here is that libraries might be well served to give more weight to the appropriate sales characteristics in their hiring decisions.

Were library liaison roles modeled on sales, we would expect a whole different management and reward structure in place for library staff. Most sales workers are incentivized by commissions, and managed with the assistance of activity trackers and organizers like Salesforce.com. As for incentives, it is understood that in a campus library setting there can be no one-to-one application of commissions based on sales revenue, especially since there is no sales revenue from which to draw commissions. Ironically, sales success in a library setting would not beget additional salary, but additional work (i.e., instruction sessions, reference consultations, etc.). Nonetheless, if library collections and services were more ubiquitously and highly valued across a campus, one could expect that library funding would increase, including resources directed to librarian salaries.

As for the management of library outreach, systems like Salesforce.com— the industry leader in this space—are best known for their Customer Relationship Management modules, including measures of sales effort (i.e., emails, calls, visits, time spent), customer responses, and forecasts of the likelihood of converting a contact into an active customer (Salesforce.com n.d.). If faculty departments were viewed as a sales territory, and faculty were viewed as customers, then libraries and their liaisons could be much more intentional about their efforts to optimize uptake of library resources and services. As currently managed, however, it is not the case that library liaisons have sales skills, nor the tools and direction needed to succeed at what they are being asked to do. And, in those cases where success *is* apparent, either by luck or the sheer perseverance of uncommonly self-motivated librarians, there are no structures in place to recognize and reward those successes.

FUTURE PROSPECTS FOR COLLECTION DEVELOPMENT

Library collection development in academic settings has evolved from models that emphasized faculty control, to bookish bibliographers, to more service-oriented library liaisons. Where is this evolution likely to lead over the next decade? First and foremost, it is likely that attention will be given to reducing the costs of collection development, not only by continuing to challenge the unsustainable costs of content charged by commercial publishers, but also by addressing the equally unsustainable staffing costs that libraries currently commit to this work. One can readily foresee that the 19th-century idea of maintaining thousands of locally shaped collections across the United States—or world—will give way to aggregated digital collections that can be developed and stored once, yet distributed everywhere. Whatever one might think about the track record of local collection development librarians in acquiring useful scholarly resources, we expect that local collection management will be supplanted by national strategies because the distributed alternatives are no longer affordable.

If collection development does scale up to national and global selection—and many instances of this are already in place—that means that our libraries will need to give much greater attention to the transition of staff time from the back-office functions of selection and collection management to an emphasis on managing the outreach efforts of library liaisons or outreach librarians. Organizing and managing these staff roles will need to evolve with the overall changing functions of libraries in a rapidly changing academic culture. Faculty liaisons—or what we might prefer to view as *customer development and service librarians*—will measure their performance by the number and quality of the faculty contacts they are able to cultivate and convert to valued users of library services.

Students, too, need to be converted to customers by librarians. For students, however, we would deploy different sales and marketing strategies. Since students are both greater in number and more transient than faculty members, relationships, cultivated by the library, would necessarily be less personal than those forged with the faculty. Successful strategies are most likely to be centrally conceived, implemented, and disseminated via online channels such as social media sites, and a variety of mobile applications. In other words, different sales and marketing strategies would need to be developed to address the needs and habits of different library customers, and different library staff skills and attention would need to be directed to each constituency.

What then do we foresee as the future role of collection development librarians? First, no matter how strong the relationship between library liaisons and their campus constituents, sales success requires a good product at the right price; price here refers to the effort required to access library resources and services. We know that what faculty members most expect from their libraries is access to needed resources. As argued earlier, traditional collection development approaches have not proven particularly adept at predicting the resources that will be needed by local scholars, and that the computer profiling and algorithms of companies like Google and Amazon might achieve better results if applied to the challenge of anticipating library user needs. Customer profiling and referral services could be managed in Amsterdam, New York, or Mountain View, so the idea that a local cadre of collection specialists is required to surface researcher interests is just not defensible in an age of Web-scale computing.

Second, as current scholarly resources—published or otherwise—are almost entirely produced in digital form, the idea that libraries must predict and acquire resources in advance of demand will likely be superseded by emerging business models that will allow users to access needed content instantaneously, regardless of whether that need had been anticipated by a library or dissemination service. iTunes may or may not correctly predict a customer's next album purchase, but that is not really an impediment to the service's ability to provide immediate access to a selection that strays from predicted patterns.

Third, the current emphasis that libraries place on subject specialty for selection and management of scholarly resources will likely be replaced by more generic skills of relationship building—librarian or otherwise. As collections go global—both in development and in access—relationships and most services will remain local, customized, and individual. Call it sales, outreach, or collegiality, the future of libraries will depend upon the ability of their staff to be as appealing to users as the resources and services they represent.

Fourth, the current distinctions between ownership, subscription, and access will almost certainly recede in significance, as discovery and access transcend local collecting practices. The 19th- and 20th-century conventions of building thousands of scholarly collections at arm's length to scholars in remote locales will inevitably be replaced by central discovery and retrieval strategies.

Fifth, even though there are legitimate concerns about the long-term archiving of so-called scholarly record, it does not make much sense to think that a thousand libraries need to be deciding what they will and will not preserve for the ages; or that tens of thousands of library subject selectors, working, as they do, in geographic and disciplinary silos, will ultimately develop a coordinated strategy for efficiently and assuredly fulfilling this needed archiving function. If archiving maintains its place as a priority for libraries, publishers, and scholars, we can be confident that one or several national or global strategies will be developed at scale.

At the margins, we can foresee some individual library attention given to building, servicing, and preserving highly specialized collections like local history, campus ephemera, or gray literature. Collection development at this level might take on the roles currently fulfilled by archivists in special collections. For mainstream, published scholarship, however, we can only assume that a business form equivalent to Amazon, iTunes, or NetFlix will obviate the need for thousands of locally and idiosyncratically developed library collections. This does not portend the end of research libraries, but it does suggest that they need to redirect their efforts from selecting and warehousing an ever-expanding universe of content to helping their constituents navigate that universe of scholarly content as it is being aggregated elsewhere.

CONCLUSION

The specter haunting research libraries is that their practices for building collections in the past missed the mark—often by a wide margin—and that has visited upon them a considerable burden to manage large, deteriorating, and little-used legacy collections into the future. Add to this the near inevitable eventuality that library collection work will increasingly face disintermediation from more nationally and globally developed services for content provision, we can foresee that local library collection work will be relegated to the dustbin of history. Research libraries everywhere are now struggling to unshackle themselves from the bounds imposed by their little-used print collections. At the same time, they have been slow to embrace the analytical tools or strategies that would justify their continued primacy as gatekeepers for maintaining access to legacy print holdings, while securing access to some, but not all, born digital collections going forward.

This chapter suggests that legions of locally oriented and managed library subject specialists will inevitably be replaced by more rational and cost-effective strategies for matching users to the content they need. Going forward, this will likely involve sophisticated computer algorithms for predicting demand, if indeed, prediction is even necessary in a world where digital content can be transferred in real time from central or distributed servers to any user, without limitations that stem from their locale or preferred medium of communication. Authors, publishers, libraries, retailers, and readers will all need to adapt to new business models for incentivizing, funding, and disseminating scholarly information.

While it is predicted here that the local collection development roles of librarians might be short-lived, there is a need for continued campus outreach—even increased and more effective outreach. As educational in-stitutions, campuses need to impart and reinforce lessons about accessing scholarly information in a rapidly changing landscape of exponentially in-creasing authorship, rapidly emerging and receding channels of dissemina-tion, concentration of content provision for some kinds of content, while the dissemination of other bodies of continually upgraded and updated platform enhancements, and shifting social and legal conventions surrounding the use of scholarly content. Libraries are not wrong to emphasize their campus ser-vice roles, although they might be trying to fulfill these roles with the wrong people being managed in the wrong way. Librarianship, as a profession, does not necessarily encompass the skills of marketing or sales as a profession. Just as librarians would take umbrage if a publisher encouraged students to direct their advanced reference questions to an online chat service they provide, perhaps we should reconsider if existing library staff—or the new staff being hired in the image of the old staff—are in the best position to build the kinds of relationships with campus users that our libraries should aspire to develop going forward.

REFERENCES

Anderson, Rick. 2011. "The Crisis in Research Librarianship." *Journal of Academic Librari-anship* 37 (4): 1–2.

Aron-Dine, Aviva, Liran Einav, and Amy Finklestein. 2013. "The RAND Health Insurance Experiment, Three Decades Later." *Journal of Economic Perspectives* 27 (1): 197–222.

Chanil, Debra. 2010. "Top 25 Wholesalers." *Convenience Store News*, October 4. Available at: http://www.csnews.com/article-top_25_wholesalers-1196.html.

Courant, Paul N., and Matthew Nielsen. 2010. "On the Cost of Keeping a Book." *The Idea of Order: Transforming Research Collections for 21st Century Scholarship*, 81–105. Washington, DC: Council on Library and Information Resources.

Franklin, Brinley. 2005. "Use Measures for Electronic Resources: Theory and Practice." Paper presented at the Annual Meeting of the American Library Association, Chicago, IL, June. Available at: http://digitalcommons.uconn.edu/libr_pres/15/.

Gammon, Julia, and Edward T. O'Neil. 2011. *OhioLINK—OCLC Collection and Circula-tion Analysis Project*. Dublin, OH: OCLC.

Hahn, Karla. 2009. "Introduction: Positioning Liaison Librarians for the 21st Century." *Research Library Issues,* No. 265. Washington, DC: Association for Research Libraries. Available at: http://www.arl.org/bm~doc/rli-265-hahn.pdf.

Hitt, Jack. 1996. "The Theory of Supermarkets," *New York Times Magazine* (March 10). Available at: http://www.nytimes.com/1996/03/10/magazine/the-theory-of-supermarkets .html?pagewanted=all&src=pm.

Kent, Allen. 1979. *Use of Library Materials: The University of Pittsburgh Study*. New York: Marcel Dekker.

King, Donald W., Sarah Aerni, Fern Brody, Matt Herboson, and Amy Knapp. 2005. *The Use and Outcomes of University Library Print and Electronic Collections*. Pittsburgh, PA: University of Pittsburgh.

Latta, Gail, ed. 1992. *Liaison Services in ARL Libraries*. SPEC Kit 189. Washington, DC: Association of Research Libraries.

Lib-Value Project, n.d. *LIBValue: Value, Outcomes, and Return on Investment of Academic Libraries*. Available at: http://libvalue.cci.utk.edu/node/.

Logue, Susan. 2007. *Liaison Services*. SPEC Kit 301. Washington, DC: Association of Research Libraries.

Mack, Daniel. 2010. *Behavioral Performance Guidelines for Subject Specialists/Liaison Librarians in the Department of Reference, Collections and Research*. University Park, PA: The Pennsylvania State University Libraries. Available at: http://www.libraries.psu.edu/content/dam/psul/up/groups/documents/Behavioral%20performance%20guidelines%20for%20subject%20specialists%20liaison%20librarians%20may%202010.pdf.

Mager, Robert F. 1997. *Goal Analysis*. 3rd ed. Belmont, CA: Fearon Publishers, Lear Siegler, Inc.

Montgomery, Carol Hansen, and Donald W. King. 2002. "Comparing Library and User Related Costs of Print and Electronic Journal Collections: A First Step Towards a Comprehensive Analysis." *D-Lib Magazine* 8 (10). Available at: http://www.dlib.org/dlib/october02/montgomery/10montgomery.html.

Neal, James G. 2011. *Stop the Madness: The Insanity of ROI and the Need for New Qualitative Measures of Academic Library Success*. Philadelphia, PA: ACRL 2011.

Oakleaf, Megan. 2010. *Value of Academic Libraries: A Comprehensive Research Review and Report*. Chicago, IL: Association of College and Research Libraries. Available at: www.acrl.ala.org/value/.

Ranganathan, S.R. 1931. *The Five Laws of Library Science*. Madras, India: Madras Library Association.

"Salesforce.com." n.d. *Wikipedia: The Free Encyclopedia*. Wikimedia Foundation, Inc. Available at: http://en.wikipedia.org/wiki/Salesforce.com.

Schonfeld, Roger C., Ross Housewright, and Kate Wulfson. 2013. *Ithaka S+R U.S. Faculty Survey 2012*. New York: Ithaka S+R. Available at: http://www.sr.ithaka.org/research-publications/us-faculty-survey-2012.

Silver, Nate 2012. *The Signal and the Noise*. New York: Penguin.

Tenopir, Carol. 2012a. "Beyond Usage: Measuring Library Outcomes and Value." *Library Management* 33 (1/2): 5–13.

Tenopir, Carol. 2012b. "COUNTER at 10: Evolving Measures of Journal Impact, Value and Utility." Paper presented at The 2012 Charleston Conference, Charleston, SC, November 7–10.

Williams, Karen. 2009. "A Framework for Articulating New Library Roles." *Research Library Issues,* No. 265. Washington, DC: Association for Research Libraries. Available at: http://www.arl.org/bm~doc/rli-265-williams.pdf.

Yi, Zhixian. 2013. "Setting Goals for Change in the Information Age: Approaches of Academic Library Directors in the USA." *Library Management* 34 (1/2): 5–19.

3

WHO DOES WHAT?
BUILDING RELATIONSHIPS
BETWEEN TECHNICAL AND
PUBLIC SERVICES STAFF

Laurel Tarulli

How many times have you been told it must be nice to read all day because you are a librarian? For many professionals working in the library, or those of you whose titles include the term librarian, our friends, family, and community often make this assumption. While this conjures up images of cozy reading nooks or large, wooden reference desks with stacks of books around us for our enjoyment, it is a traditional and antiquated view of librarians. And although we likely all enjoy a cozy reading nook, this type of reading is not part of a librarian's professional activities. We can also use the example of the stereotypical librarian, whose closet is bursting with tweeds, sensible shoes, and sweater sets. There is also that common and often frustrating assumption that all staff employed by the library are librarians. Although we can spend the day listing all of these misconceptions, the fact is, our profession is riddled with stereotypes, generalizations, and assumptions. Many of these are based on traditional views of libraries, while others are born out of a lack of communication, a lack of desire to delve deeper into the profession, static practices and theories within librarianship, and apathy.

Within our profession and among each other, there are also generalizations, assumptions, and stereotypes. While attending library school, we assume that the social and outgoing individuals will become public-service professionals, whereas the studious and quiet will find themselves tucked in the backroom of libraries, never dealing with the public and happy to spend their years in the company of books and other inanimate collections. When we find ourselves in the workplace, these assumptions also continue. Rather than a cohesive workplace, many larger libraries continue to operate an organization comprised of silos, assuming traditional roles and applying traditional job descriptions. While many managers will argue that despite the silos, staff in technical services and public services work together and often share responsibilities, it is the very nature of the language we use that places a label (and meaning) on how we practice librarianship and our specific roles within the organization.

Before moving forward, however, it is important to define the meaning of technical services and the departments found therein. Technical services is the name used for the department that traditionally houses cataloging, collection development, and processing and receiving. Information technology (IT) often also falls within this department. It is interesting to note that while IT falls under the umbrella of technical services in many libraries, Web site design and maintenance does not. Although not within the scope of this chapter, it would be interesting to explore why these two departments are not more closely intertwined, and whether a closer relationship should be addressed between these two areas of service. Selecting, purchasing, and receiving are functions that exist within the realm of collection development. However, how those services are organized varies from library to library. The collection development department may rely on vendors for selection of items, librarians within the system, or make all purchasing decisions within the department. Cataloging, in the most traditional capacity, provides description and access for the purchased items. However, with more items arriving within libraries already cataloged and prepared for the shelves, this service and its function are changing. This is addressed in more detail within this chapter. And finally, the processing department not only prepares new material for the shelves but also often takes part in the weeding and mending process. For those who work in technical services, we understand that none of the tasks we perform stand alone and that many of these duties rely on partnerships among department members. As such, it is hard to create black-and-white definitions for each service. For example, the collection development manager seeks a cataloger's assistance regarding the collection placement of an item, while the processer consults with both to determine how best to make a three-piece item shelf-ready. It is the building of a larger relationship within the library that this chapter seeks to examine.

This chapter explores the nature of the divide between technical services and public services staff. While consideration is given to why this divide exists, the emphasis is on how we can breach the divide and start building relationships that will strengthen our profession, professional practices, the operations of the library and, by extension, the services that we offer to our communities. Important consideration needs to be given to the following questions:

- Why does the divide exist and why do we continue to practice in professional silos?
- What are the benefits of working in an environment with fewer silos and less hierarchy?
- How can we start the collaboration process and begin building meaningful and beneficial relationships?

SEPARATE BUT EQUAL

In her book, *Civilizing Rituals*, Carol Duncan presents the idea that the way we build museums, the materials we use, the descriptions for the artwork and all other elements of a structure or an exhibit influence how we behave, think, and interpret. The same can be applied to libraries. Rather than focusing on libraries on a large scale (which is beyond the realm of this chapter), let's examine how this can be applied and evaluated when applied to public services and technical services staff. The title of this chapter gives some indication of the bias of terminology that may be the cause, or result, of the silos that generally exist between technical services and public services staff. Does the term public service not apply to technical services? Do those backroom staff, largely responsible for collection development, collection access (cataloging), Web resources, and IT, not provide public service to both staff and customers? While changing the roles of technical services has evolved from a paper-based, backroom-specific operation to a broader, virtual one, it seems as if the terminology used in our profession continues to color our perception of the roles and responsibilities found within. However, this is not only a back-room issue. Frontline staff are also dealing with the effects of traditional name branding. The familiar reference desk is being renamed throughout libraries to reflect the new demands of users and the attempt to turn a traditional service with preexisting assumptions into an applicable and desired service. We can conclude that the name we give to a department or service within the library influences how our managers, vendors, we, and ultimately our customers view the service. In an effort to create an impression of equality within this chapter, the term public service is applied to all areas of librarianship. The terms frontline and backroom staff are used to differentiate between the traditional technical and public services terms.

Unfortunately, the terms we choose to label our departments and services are not the only possible barriers that we face within the profession. Physical proximity, or lack thereof, may also impact the relationships we develop between frontline and backroom staff. The physical layouts and design of libraries have contributed to an unspoken but existing rift between frontline work in libraries and backroom activities. Traditionally, if backroom services, such as cataloging or collection development, were housed within the library, they were either located in the basement or tucked away in an out-of-the-way and often less-desirable space. Even today, if these services remain housed in libraries, the space tends to be limited, the offices dark, and the furniture old. This is in direct opposition to many newly renovated libraries that reflect open spaces, light, and state-of-the-art furniture. While many public library spaces even include windows rather than opaque walls to invite customers into the workings of the library, backroom staff continue to operate behind closed doors. The negative impact of this closed-door policy is twofold. The customers and frontline staff are unable to observe and interact with backroom professionals, and vice versa. And today, the movement to relocate backroom staff from the physical library to an offsite location may increase the risks of sustaining our fragile collaborations and relationships.

The distance, created by physical proximity as well as by terminology, may have created the barrier that exists between backroom and frontline public services staff, or it may just be the result thereof. It is important to understand that if these situations exist in libraries, they may continue to strain or inhibit a healthy, thriving relationship between these two areas of public service and thus we need to determine how best to overcome these limitations to promote a collaborative environment.

ROBBING PETER TO PAY PAUL

When we attend library school, we are united by our interest in joining the library profession. As a team of soon-to-be professionals, we work in groups to discuss current issues facing libraries; we collaborate on projects and talk about emerging trends. We are comrades and colleagues.

Unfortunately, when we enter the practicing profession, we tend to follow our interests and grow apart from each other. Whether we choose reference, cataloging, youth services, or readers' services, we follow our passion and feel that the area we have chosen is vital to the services that libraries provide. Because of this passion and dedication to our own area of librarianship, some professionals believe that their interests and their services are more important to the running of the library than another area of librarianship. As a group of professionals, we no longer look at the importance of librarianship as a whole, but divide it into smaller parts, which results in an us versus them mentality. Unfortunately, the result of focusing solely on our special areas of the profession deteriorates relationships and the collaborative environment we enjoyed while attending university and at the early stages of our career.

This problem is further exacerbated by budget cuts and library closures. We often become even more divided, seeking ways to devalue another library service in an effort to save our own positions. In essence, we are attempting to rob one area of librarianship to sustain another. While we do not intentionally do this, and writing it down on paper makes us appear calculating, it is a reality in many library situations. We are all facing budget cuts, limited resources, and an increasing amount of pressure to justify our existence. Added to this, our community is demanding more services and competitive expectations with commercial organizations.

As professionals, we should be aware of the importance of each service provided in the library. While we may not feel comfortable or qualified performing in specialized areas of librarianship outside of our own, all areas of the profession are vital to sustaining a thriving information community. As such, it is important to understand and promote transparency in all areas of librarianship. This will demonstrate to management, staff, and our community the need for a variety of service areas within the library, and how each service depends on or complements another.

The purpose and intent of this chapter is to encourage relationships between frontline and backroom public services. As such, it is important to realistically acknowledge the silos within your organization, including the biases and the reasons behind divisions between services. After identifying these factors, you can begin to build new relationships and strengthen existing ones. However, if you view certain services as inferior, believe they are poorly managed, or lack the understanding of what their function is, you cannot expect your collaborative efforts to succeed.

BLURRING THE LINES BETWEEN PHYSICAL AND VIRTUAL SPACE

It is easy to focus on the idea that our profession performs its daily activities in a silo structure. We can point to a variety of reasons why we have not taken advantage of each other's expertise, or why we are so late in realizing the importance of relationship building between frontline and backroom public service. However, rather than focusing on the past and trying to determine the causes of possible divisions between services, it is with an optimistic view and lists of possibilities that we can look to developing rich relationships between backroom and frontline public service staff.

In many respects, we need to thank the Internet and the Web 2.0 movement for the role it has played in revealing just how much potential there is for developing stronger relationships between these two areas of public service. When our libraries went online and developed a virtual and social presence, many of us began to recognize the implications of working—and not working—together. Those libraries with strong bonds between the frontline and backroom services began collaborating in an effort to extend the services from physical library into the online environment. An online environment was often controlled by backroom services. What we began to see were catalog records with additional content reflecting readers' advisory services, links to programming, and the ability to recommend books for purchase—all within the catalog. These types of elements were the result of collection development staff, readers' advisory staff, programming individuals from across departments, and cataloging staff all working together toward a common goal: to extend the services of the physical library into a virtual environment. We now recognize that this is gaining ground as the only space in which we interact with the majority of our customers.

Interestingly, there are libraries that are successfully bridging the dichotomy gap by flattening their hierarchical structures and advocating for staff to participate in all areas of the library profession: from doing reference work to getting trained as readers' advisors and performing copy cataloging. These arrangements tend to be found in small libraries where librarians and library support staff are expected to wear many hats.

COLLABORATION

A new set of eyes is often all we need to turn a good project into a great one. Building relationships between the frontline line and backroom takes advantage of this new set of eyes, offering new perspectives, solutions, and procedures. In the article "Bringing Public Services Experience to Technical Services: Improvements in Practice," vanDuinkerken (2009) discusses the success that Texas A&M University (TAMU) Libraries had in handing over the reins of the Acquisitions Monographs Unit to a reference librarian. With a mandate to improve their users' experience, this reference librarian was chosen due to her strong user-services background. The rationale for placing a frontline librarian in a backroom position was that the new perspective and strong user-services expertise may offer insight into existing procedures (vanDuinkerken 2009). Charged with adding transparency to the acquisitions process for selectors and evaluating the daily processes and skills necessary to fulfill these tasks, this reference librarian-turned-acquisitions-librarian ventured into the unfamiliar territory of the backroom with great success (vanDuinkerken 2009). Not only did this librarian develop a list of best practices that exceeded the expectations of her management team, but also the Acquisitions Monographs Unit was nominated for the Texas A&M President's Meritorious Service Award. This award is given for outstanding service to the university community (vanDuinkerken 2009).

Although this success story takes place in a university setting, the best practices that were established have direct application to public library practices as well. And, although many of us view the placement of a reference librarian into a collection development role, without training, as a radical notion, we can see the benefits that are gained through fresh perspectives, new outlooks, and wide ranges of expertise. Offering opportunities to job shadow or swap positions within an organization for a set period of time may provide many of us with a new outlook on other services that run concurrently with our own. This also allows us to develop a deeper understanding and transparency of the services. After having walked in someone else's shoes, it is easier to understand existing procedures, influence change, and begin collaborative relationships.

Although collection development is often classed in the hierarchy of a library under technical services, this is a service that relies heavily on subject experts (often frontline librarians) and is, indeed, a public service (Brooks 2012). While traditional structures may continue to house this department in the backroom, it is a service that relies heavily upon its relationships with subject experts (Brooks 2012). In return, subject experts also need to initiate meaningful conversations with the backroom in an effort to understand the inner workings of collection development. Often, these conversations do not go beyond the budget allotment for specific subjects. In other words, the conversation between collection development and frontline staff ends after the subject expert is aware of the areas for which they purchase and the money that has been allotted for each collection. Shouldn't the relationship go beyond this? Steps taken at TAMU to continue this conversation include providing selectors with frequent, informal training sessions and inviting conversations that address selector concerns and questions regarding the processes and procedures that begin at purchase of the book and end with its receipt (vanDuinkerken 2009). Creating an open dialogue not only establishes a transparent window into the functions of acquisitions but also invites selectors to provide feedback for existing practices. Getting to know selectors and starting a dialogue also impacts the acquisitions staff. These new relationships allow staff a greater understanding of their role in the big picture of the library (vanDuinkerken 2009).

In his article "Technical Services-Public Services Partnerships," Brooks also suggests that relationship building between collection development staff and frontline subject librarians not only involves partnerships but also an awareness that frontline partners are also customers of backroom departments (Brooks 2012). Highlighting this idea requires that you consider the position in which that places backroom staff. If "we serve the people who serve the public" as well as partner with them, this gives backroom staff an even greater reason to seek opportunities for collaborative relationships (Brooks 2012). Increasing communication will not only invite a new perspective and outside expertise to view, understand, and comment on current practice models, but it will also provide invaluable feedback into how our users perceive backroom processes.

Readers' advisory service is another area that benefits from a strong relationship between backroom and frontline public services. At the PLA 2012 Conference, Neal Wyatt advocated for the saturation of readers' advisory content within the library catalog. With the knowledge that the majority of all holds placed on library materials happen remotely, as well as understanding the need to meet readers where they are, it is in our best interest to look at mash-ups between services. While staff at the physical library may hold conversations with readers, this is a self-selective group. These are often social readers interested in sharing reading experiences. But for many, reading is personal, as are reading preferences, suggestions, and requests for purchases. Providing readers' content where the reader is—presumably the catalog, as that is where the collection resides—and wherever the reader is physically located, strengthens three services: collection development, cataloging, and readers' advisory services. An argument can also be made that a relationship between staff in those departments extends to staff in adult services, teen services, and children's services.

Providing readers' services in the library catalog emphasizes the strong relationship needed between staff as well as cross-training. Terminology, ease of use, and content are all factors in this decision. Building a partnership between readers' advisory services staff and cataloging staff creates benefits for both services. The relationship creates a conversation between the two departments, which in turn results in knowledge sharing of the latest trends in reading, current buzz words being used to describe genres, and cataloging practices that may allow this content entry into the catalog. Collaboration, education, and a willingness to examine current practice models based on library-wide feedback to meet the needs of today's society are essential.

FUTURE ROLES AND TARGET AREAS FOR BUILDING RELATIONSHIPS

The library, now more than ever, has become a social gathering place for our community. This is never so apparent than when community members, who are not library patrons, book our rooms for events and meetings, or teenagers drop in after school to chat, text their friends, or listen to their iPods. The physical library is a popular gathering place because it is centrally located and convenient. Libraries are easy to access and provide immediate gratification of users' needs—even if it is not what the user expected or wanted. The physical library is and continues to be successful because it provides the same type of elements that the Internet provides—convenience, ease of use, location, social interaction, and information. But, the one thing the physical library cannot do is always be where the people are—in homes, on the bus, at the airport or the grocery store. We will continue to see an increase in the need for extending our services in virtual environments. Rather than performing our services separately, a greater focus on shared resources will be emphasized in the future. Emphasizing shared resources includes cross-training staff between departments as well as expectations that we may be called upon to assist in performing these services. This is also evident in the blurring of responsibilities between paraprofessionals and professionals. As outsourcing and vendor products continue to offer services to libraries that were traditionally performed in-house, we are left with staff with fewer responsibilities. This is an opportunity for us to look at our services and focus on areas for improvement. It provides us with individuals *looking for* increased responsibilities and knowledge.

In the past, backroom services staff were often viewed as performing mundane, daily processes. However, with increasing emphasis on remote, online presences, the tasks and responsibilities of backroom staff are transitioning. And, while we are now accustomed to defining our branches and to some extent our online presence as social spaces, our organizations are still based on the premise that patrons use our library primarily to access our collections. If we still believe that our collections are important, and perhaps the most important part of our library, then we also need to seriously explore the idea of the library catalog as a collaborative and interactive space. With successful collaboration between frontline and backroom public services staff, library catalogs "provide the branch library experience virtually. For example, they can link to recorded author readings or programs, as well as provide pathways to program announcements, special events within the library and, links into the greater community," all within the catalog (Tarulli 2012).

Library patrons who visit the physical library branch belong to the culture and community within that branch or library system. The sense of community they share in this social space has to do with trust, familiar faces, comfortable surroundings, and the knowledge that they are in a safe, communal environment. Our online presence, often controlled by backroom public services staff, can provide an experience, while virtual, that mimics our experience within physical libraries. Drawing from frontline and backroom expertise, we can create a new, virtual frontline that "draws together elements of trust, interaction and contribution, discoverability, personalization and customization, intuitiveness, belonging and immediate access to information. In all, we can create a level of experience that has been, up until now, only been found in the physical library" (Tarulli 2012).

CONCLUSION

This chapter examined reasons why relationship building between frontline and backroom public services should be promoted. While it is important to understand why there may be barriers that prevent relationships, or have prevented relationships in the past, it is more important to understand the many benefits obtained through engaging in cross-training within library specialties and open, transparent service models within departments.

In the 1983 special issue of *The Reference Librarian*, Michael Gorman wrote an article addressing "two kinds of librarianship" in which there are " 'people people' versus 'book people'" (Gorman 1983). With this in mind, he states that there are

two "kinds" of librarianship . . . [one] concerned with esoteric "technical" matters and populated with reclusive adepts, has concerns which are mysterious and methods which are suspect. . . . The second is concerned with "The Public" and populated by bluff men and women (democrats all), deals with real issues, real people, the library user in tooth and claw. (56)

While it is unlikely many of us take such a dark and negative view of an existing or imaginary dichotomy today, we can certainly look at this statement as a situation and belief system to avoid at all costs. Many of us have built strong and successful relationships with our frontline or backroom colleagues: one of the most successful and well-known being Williamsburg Regional Library. For smaller libraries, these relationships have often extended further, by sharing responsibilities and expecting feedback from colleagues in other departments. In fact, in many libraries that have developed strong relationships between frontline and backroom services, there is an expectation that staff will contribute across library silos and add value to workflows. With the amount of user expertise, subject expertise, and technological expertise found within libraries, our libraries are bursting with potential to create increasingly dynamic, interactive social spaces, both virtually and within our physical walls. Understanding every cog in the wheel and how all of the pieces fit together results in a work environment that welcomes creativity, new ideas, and perspectives. These are characteristics in a workplace that both employees and employers admire and hope for. In an effort to strengthen the collaborative environment within libraries, we can focus on the best practices that are found within vanDuinkerken's article. When there is a transparency in workflow, invitations, and opportunities to understand, train, and provide feedback among staff, and a genuine interest in improving processes and service, the natural results are stronger relationships and increased communication between departments.

By extension, this also results in improvements in two areas: the library as a whole and the community we serve. The implications for library management and staff include the potential for an increase in effective workflow, an increase in job satisfaction, and shared institutional knowledge and expertise. Resources, including budgetary resources, may also be affected positively. The customers, or community, will also benefit from the forging of strong and lasting relationships among frontline and backroom staff. By working together, the increase in effective workflows and shared expertise will directly impact the quality of services offered online and within library branches. The flow from one service to another will create seamless offerings and interactions with customers.

Whether working in a culture where shared responsibility and open communication is standard practice, to enjoying a position where the potential for collaborative opportunities is only beginning, we can all look forward to the exciting and rewarding outcomes from building relationships between technical services and public services staff.

REFERENCES

Brooks, Stephen M. 2012. "Technical Services-Public Services Partnerships." *AcqWeb.* Available at: http://www.acqweb.org/node/143. Accessed October 22, 2012.

Gorman, Michael. 1983. "The Ecumenical Library." *The Reference Librarian* 9 (Fall/ Winter): 55–64. Quoted in Henry Wessells. 2010. "Gap between Technical and Public Services Librarians." *Information Science Today.* Available at: http://www.infoscience today.org/type/articles/gap-between-technical-and-public-services-librarians.html. Accessed October 31, 2012.

Tarulli, Laurel. 2012. "Library Catalogues of the Future: A Social Space and Collaborative Tool?" *Library Trends* 61 (1): 107–31.

VanDuinkerken, Wyoma. 2009. "Bringing Public Services Experience to Technical Services: Improvements in Practice." *Library Collections, Acquisitions, & Technical Services* 33: 51–58.

4

Evaluating Subscription Databases

Nadine P. Ellero and Juliet T. Rumble

In light of all that has been written on evaluating databases and the millions of dollars that libraries have invested in these resources, it is quite remarkable to read Bernard Reilly's report from the 2011 Charleston Pre-Conference on evaluating research databases: "There is no single, uniform approach to database evaluations. 'Best guesses' about local user needs and potential user uptake are the norm" (Reilly 2012, 54). Reilly's characterization of the current environment with respect to databases raises a number of questions. Is database evaluation an art that a professional cultivates over time, based more on experience and intuition than on analysis (Johnson 2009, 108)? Do local users' needs resist generalization? Or is it the case that the nature of databases, especially the colossal and continually expanding Web-scale variety, introduces elements that defy attempts to develop a uniform approach to evaluation? How is true value to be determined when user needs differ and resources are in continual evolution?

The current information landscape abounds with general and specialty databases covering traditional and emerging research areas. Journal-based databases now coexist with databases that provide access to primary source collections, raw data, and resources in various media, including sound, image, and video. In the past five years, we have seen the emergence of Web-scale discovery systems that centrally index much of the content contained in these disparate databases, promising one-stop searching from a single search box.

How do we wrap our minds around these varied and evolving databases and research tools? They live on Web platforms, feature an array of different search interfaces, and offer a variety of different user-based functions. The costs associated with database content and services are not trivial and often require ongoing financial commitments. Now more than ever, libraries are challenged to ensure effective return on investment (ROI) and to participate in the current culture of evidence-based practice.

This chapter focuses on current and emerging issues in evaluating subscription databases. Unless otherwise noted, the term database refers to abstracting and indexing (A&I) resources, full-text aggregators, or hybrids of the two. The decision-making processes involved in evaluating databases are examined with particular attention to the users for whom these databases are acquired and the various contexts within which the selection activity operates. The evaluative process is examined from the perspectives of both database content and platform. Considerations for strategic action as well as the authors' thoughts on desired outcomes are discussed.

HUMAN MINDS AND INFORMATION SYSTEMS

Databases, like libraries, are information systems and services. Information systems take many forms, as do the information resources they store, which range from raw data to books and articles to audio and video files to artifacts. What is important to note, as Losee and Worley observe, is the common function of these systems, namely "to acquire, store, organize, and retrieve information" (1993, 2). Databases exist, as do libraries, to enhance the information processing capacities of human beings.

Atkinson, writing on the individual's interaction with the organized collections of libraries and databases, notes that human beings create knowledge through the discovery and invention of relationships:

> Unitary objects of information are useless for purposes of knowledge production. In order for them to be made useful, they must be related to other objects. . . . Such a relationship is not so much something that "is," as it is rather something that the user does. The creation or perception of that relationship is an event, and the production of knowledge is a consequence of such event experiences. Ensuring that such experiences are possible, and that users have the ability to record, apply and communicate the results of those events, must form the abstract foundation . . . for any truly effective information services in the future. (Atkinson 2005a, 23)

As database systems have continued to evolve, so has their capacity to support this kind of activity. The early pioneers of relational databases envisioned a new, casual user group and developed an underlying architecture designed specifically to remove the technical barriers standing in the way of nonprogrammers querying the system. As the central figure in the development of the relational database Edgar "Ted" Codd proclaimed: "Future users of large data banks must be protected from having to know how the data is organized in the machine (the internal representation)" (Gugerli 2012, 293).

The prescience of Codd and other early developers of relational databases helped pave the way for the sophistication, flexibility, and user-centered designs of present-day systems. The shift toward user-driven information systems was further accelerated with the advent of Internet search engines operating in a networked, global environment. The simplicity and elegance of Google's single search box and the power of its search algorithms have become the gold standard by which all information systems are judged.

Libraries and library users now find themselves embedded in a hybrid environment engendered by the World Wide Web. In 2000, Manoff observed that "the boundaries between our libraries and the rest of the world are becoming more porous. . . . The scholar and his work have become nodes on a vast information space that both integrates and confuses commerce and culture. . . . Patrons often cannot distinguish precisely where a library's Web site ends and where resources mounted elsewhere begin" (858). These words are as true today as they were a decade ago.

The richness of this environment together with the individual's unfettered access to it has the potential to be both mind-expanding and overwhelming. "What most of us find on the net is not the fulfillment of a utopian fantasy of free information but rather a vast array of consumer choices in a sea of poorly organized information," notes Manoff (2000, 859). According to Atkinson, access to information is only part of what users require from their information systems (and information professionals): "Utility and access are, of course, inseparable. . . . But access can also be understood as a necessary but insufficient condition for utility. A relevant object of information may be accessible, and yet it may, for a variety of reasons, lack utility. Its relevance may not be evident, either because the user cannot decipher the object or because the user does not perceive the relationship between the object and the task at hand" (Atkinson 2005a, 13–14).

The preoccupation of libraries with providing access to information threatens to overshadow a critical need of users, namely for intellectual structure and context. In 1997, Miller cautioned that librarians and administrators need to ask: "access to what and what kind of access?" "The quality of access," Miller noted, has "momentous consequences for library users" (101). If anything, this issue has grown more pressing in the intervening years. Granted, such powerful search tools as Google enable users to circumvent the intermediaries that have traditionally separated individuals from the information they are seeking. However, mediation services, whether they are provided by libraries, publishers, database vendors (or increasingly, by authors or users), are not barriers to information. Rather, they are a means by which users discover and create relationships. Indeed, in a rapidly expanding information universe, mediation services are vital. As Atkinson notes, they "help people to think" (2005b, 61). The ability of databases to address this fundamental information need of library users is a key feature by which they are, or ought to be, evaluated.

DATABASES IN CONTEXT

Subscription databases emanate from and form a part of the dynamic and complex research ecosystem in which scholarship unfolds. Once selected, they become a part of the library's collection of resources. The composition of these collections, Miller notes, is "an increasingly complex mix of formats and means of access" (2000, 663). As collections and user needs continue to evolve, evaluation methods that are responsive to both must be developed.

"All selection decisions," says Johnson, "begin with consideration of the user community and the long-term mission, goals, and priorities of the library and its parent body" (2009, 108). This remains a fundamental maxim for libraries, but more global issues are also at play. For example, when libraries form consortia and negotiate collectively with vendors, they surrender a measure of control over the selection process. In these contexts, decisions regarding the appropriateness of a resource may reflect the priorities of the cooperative rather than the local institution. In addition, since so many databases and electronic resources are leased rather than purchased, the reputation of the vendor and the terms of the licensing agreement must also be considered along with the merits of the database itself. As Hazen observes, libraries are "actors within a web of interdependent agents, institutions, processes, and agendas" and this "complex matrix both shapes . . . possibilities and establishes . . . limits" (2000, 822).

A significant influence on libraries' decision-making process is the growing emphasis on performance outcomes. Whether in the context of accreditation, student retention, or strategic planning, administrators and other stakeholders are focused on positive, measurable benefits for users. "Although librarians may think of collection analysis as measuring the collection's quality (an amorphous concept, at best)," writes Johnson, "the real objective is to measure the collection's utility—how effective the collection is in satisfying the purpose for which it is intended" (2009, 225). This consideration also comes into play when evaluating databases. Gorman and Miller note that "libraries everywhere are driven by the need to determine the adequacy of their collections . . . in relation to intended service priorities" (2000, 316).

The current climate in higher education highlights the contrast between two activities involved in collection management: evaluation and assessment. Both these activities play a role in database selection. According to Johnson (2009), these activities, while frequently conflated, can be differentiated by intent. "Evaluation seeks to examine or describe collections either in their own terms or in relation to other collections and checking mechanisms" (226). Assessment, in contrast, seeks "to determine how well the collection supports the goals, needs, and mission of the library" (226). Evaluation addresses the question: "Is the item worthy of selection?" (109). Assessment considers: "Is the item appropriate for the collection?" (109).

Today's culture of assessment pushes libraries to articulate more clearly their core values and mission. Without guiding principles, libraries have no standards against which to measure utility or success. In an ideal world, these core values would be easily harmonized and balanced, but, in practice, they often prove to be in tension. Further complicating the decision-making process is a rapidly evolving information environment. Davidson, commenting on crises and opportunities in the future of scholarly publishing, observes, "We are not in an environment where long-range planning makes sense because all of the conditions are in flux at once: market conditions, tax structures, demographics, state spending, technology infrastructure, new methods of evaluating productivity, and so on" (Alonso et al. 2003, 34). Despite these challenges, reflection on the purpose of resources and collections is essential to providing a sound basis for selection choices.

The following sections of this chapter examine databases from both content and platform perspectives. Assessing the content and functionality of databases in relation to user needs is central to a library's selection process. However, as the considerations mentioned earlier suggest, contextual criteria used to judge databases—and the priority assigned to each—will vary according to institutional differences in core values, service priorities, and budget. There is no mechanical formula that can be applied to database selection—no one-size-fits-all approach. Context, above all else, is the decisive factor.

CONTENT-BASED EVALUATION CRITERIA

When selecting or comparing databases, the content of the database(s) and how well that content meets users' needs are key considerations. Jacsó (1997), citing Tenopir, writes: "At the core of all aspects [of databases] is content: the information itself as created by the author, secondary publisher, or database producer. Without quality content, other aspects (powerful and usable search software, acceptable response time, etc.) become unimportant" (233). Evaluation of content takes into account a number of different variables, which have been extensively reviewed in the scholarly literature (see, e.g., Jacsó 1997; Allison, McNeil, and Swanson 2000; Blessinger and Olle 2004; McMullen et al. 2006; Johnson 2009; Gregory 2011). The quality of content—to a certain extent always in the eye of the beholder—can be gauged in various ways. In journal-based databases, quality can be evaluated according to journal-citation impact factor or by the number of peer-reviewed journals in the database. The total number of journal titles indexed and the comprehensiveness of journal coverage are also basic evaluation criteria. Journal coverage entails not only the breadth, or time span, of coverage, but also the depth of coverage (complete vs. selected content) as well as the continuity of coverage (Have journals in the database been subject to cancellation? Are there gaps in coverage?). The scope and composition of the content is also a consideration: Is the database a general, multidisciplinary database or a discipline-specific or niche database? If the former, are certain subject areas emphasized over others? Are the titles that are included in the database appropriate to its scope, or is there evidence of title padding? Today's researchers place a high premium on both the currency of content and the availability of full text. Librarians need to consider the frequency with which journal content is updated and any embargo periods on full-text content. Finally, the number of unique titles also plays a role in selection; overlap or duplication of content is a key factor. So, too, is the increasing amount of content that may be freely available from other sources on the Web, including government publications, news sites, digital collections, open access journals, or institutional repositories (Reilly 2012, 55).

While many of these evaluative criteria have their counterparts in print collection analysis, the realm of digital resources is a much more challenging environment in which to collect this kind of data. Jacsó refers to the "daunting" and "very time-consuming tasks of learning the true profile of databases, the pros and cons of their real versus purported assets" (2010, 806–7). To some extent, database vendors themselves are responsible for these challenges. The product data they provide to libraries is sometimes incomplete, erroneous, or even misleading. A lack of standardization in defining and reporting data elements is another issue. (To cite just one example, database providers have no standard, agreed-upon definition of peer-reviewed content.) To address the thorny issue of journal coverage and content overlap, various assessment tools, both nonprofit and commercial, have been developed. These include Serial Solutions' Overlap Analysis, the United Kingdom's Joint Information Systems Committee's (JISC) Academic Database Assessment Tool (ADAT), the CUFTS service from Simon Fraser University, the Colorado Alliance of Research Libraries' (CARL) Gold Rush Reports, and Ulrich's Serials Analysis System (USAS) (Jacsó 2010; Stranack 2006; Oberg 2003; Jacsó 2012). Another important assessment tool is *The Charleston Advisor* (TCA). This publication provides critical reviews of databases and other Web-based electronic resources. It provides a freely available review scoreboard (http://charlestonco.com/index.php?do=Scoreboard) that rates products based on content, and also searchability, price, and contract options or features (http://www.charlestonco.com/index.php?do=About+TCA&pg=ScoringGuide).

While the most common type of research database remains the journal-based variety, these increasingly share space with databases based on primary source material or large data sets that are available in a variety of formats, including text, image, video, and audio. While some of these resources have counterparts in print or other formats, and in theory could be compared with these, Horava notes that researchers often use and interact with these types of databases in different ways (2011). Uncoupled from scholarly journals and the assessment tools associated with them, non-journal-based databases can be difficult to evaluate. For this reason, knowledge of how researchers use these resources in actual practice, and the contexts in which they are used, is essential.

In addition to evaluating the intrinsic merits of database content, assessing how database content supports curricular programs, addresses the research interests of faculty, and advances the mission of the research institution is integral to the decision-making process. As we have seen, this is an increasingly complex and multifaceted process. Horava observes that, in previous times, "mapping resources to an institution's collective needs was challenging but not impossible. The universe of available formats and publications was finite; with professional experience, one could connect the dots . . . in relation to a specific collection's desired parameters." "While these core activities remain integral to our work," writes Horava, "their scope has altered significantly" (2010, 142). In part, this has to do with the sheer volume and variety of potential acquisitions. In addition, as Machovec notes, rapidly changing technologies are mirrored by changing expectations, standards, and values: "What was great a few years ago may be unacceptable today" (2011). One of the greatest challenges facing selectors, institutions, and consortia is to weigh and balance diverse, and occasionally competing interests, and to discern potential issues with the interoperability of multiple systems. Selectors now wrestle with questions such as these: Can large indexing tools or aggregator databases replace specialty, discipline-specific indexes? In an era of tight budgets, can full-text databases stand in for traditional A&I databases? How do emerging Web-based discovery tools factor into this mix? Are they poised to edge out A&I databases?

PLATFORM-BASED EVALUATION CRITERIA

Database evaluation needs to consider not only the quality of content but also how well the database supports the individual's use of that content. The users of databases are diverse—from the undergraduate looking for sources for a paper due the next day to the serious researcher conducting an extensive literature review. The questions to which users seek answers are varied also, as are the practices and contexts—scholarly, professional, and personal—from which these information needs arise. What cuts across user types, however, is the thoroughgoing way in which information-seeking practices have been impacted by advances in information technology.

An evaluation of the quality of a user's interactions with a database necessarily focuses on the database's structural or platform aspects. For the purposes of this chapter, features of databases that can be said to be platform-based include the search interface, core search and retrieval functions, indexing and thesauri, and database workbench features. As databases have matured, there has been increasing standardization of certain of these platform-based elements. Most databases, for example, have both basic and advanced search options. At the same time, new database workbench tools are appearing that are designed to more effectively integrate databases into users' "workflow," "learnflow," and "researchflow" (Dempsey 2008, 111). This is an area ripe for innovation as developers harness the potential of networked technologies. Likewise, subject and niche databases continue to introduce features and functions that are specific to their disciplines and research methodologies. Non-journal-based databases are also rolling out platform features formulated to work with the entities they index (e.g., data sets, multimedia).

When evaluating a database's search interface, librarians can refer to widely accepted best practices for interface design. Today's users expect the same ease of use and navigation when searching databases as they do when interacting with commercial Web interfaces. McMullen et al. (2006, 73), Hariri and Norouzi (2011, 702, 715), and others reference Jakob Nielsen's classic 10 usability heuristics for user interface design (Nielsen 1994) as a standard for evaluating digital libraries and databases. These heuristics are (1) visibility of system status (or "Where am I and where can I go next?" [McMullen et al. 2006, 73]); (2) match between system and the real world (i.e., the system should speak the user's language and follow real-world conventions); (3) user control and freedom (including clearly marked "emergency exits" for unwanted outcomes); (4) consistency and adherence to standards; (5) error prevention; (6) recognition rather than recall (i.e., the system should be intuitive and minimize the user's memory load); (7) flexibility and efficiency of use (e.g., adaptable to the needs of both novice and seasoned researchers); (8) aesthetic and minimalist design; (9) help for users to recognize, diagnose, and recover from errors; and (10) general help and documentation (ideally, context-sensitive). As the gateway to a database's content and tool functions and the means by which the user interacts and communicates with the system, the database interface significantly impacts the user's search experience.

Search and retrieval functions are at the heart of database operations, and, for journal-based databases, there is a growing standardization of features. Allison et al. (2000) and McMullen et al. (2006) offer helpful checklists of important features. In addition to basic and advanced search options, support for natural language and Boolean logic searching increases the user's flexibility and efficiency. Field-specific searching (e.g., author, title, subject terms) increases precision and is another sought-after feature. Depending upon the information need, users may want to browse or execute direct, targeted searches; both types of searches should be enabled. In addition to browsing, features that assist with lateral searching (e.g., hot-linked subject headings, author names, publication titles) help to facilitate serendipitous discovery (Allison et al. 2000, 60). The options that a database provides for working with search results are especially important. Many databases allow users to sort results by relevance as well as chronologically. Options for expanding, narrowing, and refining searches, as needed, should ideally be available from the results screen, obviating the need to re-execute a search. Some databases employ search facets to accomplish this. A growing number of databases provide what Allison et al. refer to as "system-assisted searching" (60), which, in addition to natural language searching and relevancy ranking, includes "find articles like this" suggested search queries and spell-check features. Users also need reliable "saved search" and "saved results" functions and expect printing, downloading, emailing, and, increasingly, bibliographic management features to be standard.

The quality of the indexing provided by a database also has a significant impact on search and retrieval. Atkinson has written extensively on the importance of metadata and the intellectual infrastructure it provides to the researcher. "The purpose of metadata," writes Atkinson, "is to facilitate the creation of [information] object contexts" (2005b, 65). Metadata enhances discovery by exposing the relationships between information objects and enables various kinds of deep linking. It is "data about data" (Atkinson 2005b, 64). Databases employing thesauri (indexes based upon central concepts linked to narrower, broader, and related terms) allow researchers to refine searches by either broadening or narrowing the search terms used. Thesauri may also afford less coding complexity in search algorithms. Not all metadata is created equal, however.[1] Miller recommends that libraries take a close look at a database's controlled vocabulary: "Is there a controlled vocabulary based on the literary warrant of the actual collection of items in the database, or has a database aggregator simply adapted a one-size-fits-all vocabulary specific to nothing and of little true value in bringing users all of the available items on a topic?" (2008, 53). Miller also advises libraries to determine whether indexing is performed in-house by trained, qualified staff or outsourced to "who-knows?" (53). Facilitating hierarchical and relational searching, exposing more relevant search results, and creating deeper discovery experiences are key mediation services of databases and are some of the primary ways they add value for researchers.

In addition to search and retrieval functions, a number of databases are developing scholarly workbench functions. Increasingly, the value of research databases will be judged according to how seamlessly they can be integrated into scholars' workflows and how well they support the wide array of activities that constitute scholarly research. Horava argues that research content and users' interactions with it "cannot be separated into discrete compartments for attention. . . . Being a creator, publisher, and consumer of information are facets of the same continuum of activity" (2010, 143). In our emerging culture of participatory engagement, users expect to be able to contribute content and/or metadata to a database. Databases specifically designed to operate in this environment represent an advance over those in which tool functions have been developed in a more ad hoc manner. As Horava notes, "We need to focus on the ways our patrons communicate, search, share, and repurpose information" (2010, 148).

In recent years, a number of studies have documented scholarly research practices in order to identify ways that library services and information systems can better support these activities. These studies, together with database trials and usability studies, provide rich data that can be used to inform the database selection process. A 2006 University of Minnesota Libraries project report identifies four basic functions in which scholars across disciplines were "regularly and consistently engaged" (38). These functions were "discover," "gather," "create," and "share" (38). The report notes that, while a great deal of progress has been made in enhancing retrieval of content, there has been less attention paid to assisting scholars with other aspects of the research processes (56). In addition to difficulties associated with content discovery and retrieval, scholars face significant challenges with organizing, managing, and gaining intellectual control over content. Scholars seek support with analyzing and synthesizing content, sharing data, and working collaboratively. These are all areas in which database workbench tools have an increasingly important role to play.

In a recent two-part study, Fagan (2011, 2012) attempts to match the features of four online search engines to a select set of scholarly information activities detailed in an OCLC report authored by Palmer, Teffeau, and Pirmann (2009). Fagan examines features of Google Scholar, Microsoft Academic Search, Scopus, and the EBSCO Discovery Service in order to determine how well each supports (1) direct searching, (2) chaining (e.g., hyperlinked bibliographies or cited reference search features), (3) browsing or "open ended exploration," (4) probing (i.e., "exploring relevant information outside one's usual discipline"), (5) accessing or "unfettered direct access to materials," (6) gathering and organizing (i.e., "managing a personal collection of content"), (7) assessing (i.e., "quickly determining documents' relevance and utility: differentiating, comparing, and sifting"), (8) monitoring or "regularly reviewing new relevant information," and (9) translating or "navigating the research and publications of another discipline" (328). While Fagan found that no single system combined all desired features, a number of these workbench features were being addressed in innovative ways by one or more of the systems reviewed.

Other studies of users' information-seeking behaviors have focused on the specific scholarly practices of researchers in the sciences, humanities, and social sciences, and in individual disciplines.[2] These studies reveal differences in scholarly practices driven by discipline-based research needs and methodologies. Given these differences, it seems unlikely that large, broad-based search engines such as those studied by Fagan will ever completely replace individual subject databases. There will always be a need for PsycINFO's thesaurus or the MLA International Bibliography's subject headings, predicts Fagan. That said, Fagan acknowledges the "separate appeal" of large, general databases and suggests that their presence in the information ecosystem could mean that "subject-specific databases will be relieved from the pressure to become more mainstream, and instead [can] focus on becoming even better tools for the disciplines they serve" (2012, 75).

TRANSFORMATIVE DISCOVERY

Databases, in concert with their service platforms, are doorways leading to rich discovery. By means of these tools, researchers elicit meaning or understanding, acquire intellectual mastery over fields of study, formulate effective decisions, and create new knowledge. By means of these tools, insights are born. Databases and related discovery services are transformative when they inspire understanding within the mind of the seeker.

Today's researchers face a host of challenges. They must manage large retrieval sets to effectively make comparisons, detect trends, formulate theories, and construct models. Frequently, they must cross disciplinary lines as they pursue their inquiries. The systems they search contain data created, collected, and curated with varying degrees of standardization. To address these challenges, databases need to operate in more integrated ways to harmonize with other products and services in the digital realm. In order to accomplish this, they must continue their structural and functional evolution from individual silos to networks of linked data. A mature Semantic Web in which data and scholarly works are increasingly linked or embedded in meaningful ways through the utilization of standardized metadata, systems, and practices appears to be the way of the future. While databases and the next generation of discovery tools have the capacity to transform users' engagement with data and information, there are, at present, persistent sociopolitical, legal, commercial, and practice-based barriers that prevent true system interoperability and the emergence of tools capable of exposing deep levels of relationship between information objects.[3] These are concerns that Clifford Lynch and the Coalition for Networked Information have been addressing for several decades.

One critical barrier for transformative discovery is the lack of consistently applied standards. For library and database systems, the creation and assimilation of inconsistent and incomplete metadata frustrates computational functions such as de-duping and gathering like terms. Giles describes the purpose of quality metadata as one designed "to maintain the continuing usefulness of information so that it can be understood, exploited, reused and repurposed" (2011, 29). Metadata that is standardized and consistent (i.e., accurate and complete in accordance with agreed upon sets of rules or practices) enables computerized systems to make meaningful connections between data. When metadata can be referenced by unique numerical codes, computational activities such as matching, comparing, grouping, or inferring can be done with precision and speed.[4] This increases efficiency in mining text, data, images, and other information objects.

Global and national efforts have been established by such groups as the International Standards Organization (ISO), American National Standards Institute (ANSI), and NISO to encourage consistent practice and to build increasingly complex (or deeply linked) system interoperability. All library systems, with varying levels of compliance, adhere to these standards. Among others, these standards include ANSI/NISO Z39.50 for information retrieval (http://www.loc.gov/z3950/agency/), ANSI/NISO Z39.88 OpenURL Framework for Context-Sensitive Services for resource linking (http://www.niso.org/apps/group_public/project/details.php?project_id=82), and ISO 26324

Digital Object Identifier for identifying specific digital objects (http://www.doi.org/). Another significant initiative for creating and applying standard metadata is the Open Researcher and Contributor ID (ORCID). ORCID is a unique identifier, which is assigned to an individual researcher. The aim of assigning a unique number to a researcher name is to disambiguate equivalent or similar names by computational means and to achieve a level of author normalization.[5] The ORCID registry can be integrated within the digital information ecosystem to achieve accuracy for name searching and discovery within and among databases.[6]

With the exponential growth of data and research networks, system integration and interoperability will become a more prominent criterion for evaluating and assessing subscription databases. Every library will want the databases it selects to function in a deeply integrated (cross-platform) environment. A grand-scale, yet-to-be-developed infrastructure may someday seamlessly integrate most databases (Schreur 2012, 237). Because human language is a living phenomenon subject to continual change, there are challenges associated with maintaining database thesauri and, by extension, machine interoperability. Despite these issues, thesauri transmit valuable intellectual enrichment. Hider notes that "controlled vocabularies provide context not only for computers, but also for people" (2012, 195). At this time, no single universal and comprehensive ontology (i.e., structure of known knowledge) or super thesaurus has been systematically deployed. However, fields such as medicine have been working on these types of structures. One such example is the National Library of Medicine's Unified Medical Language System (UMLS).[7]

As part of their strategic planning, libraries will need to assess subscription databases for their functional value as discovery services in the library's overarching discovery plan (Okerson 2011). Is the acquisition of specialty subscription databases effective for the library's overall discovery picture? What of the monolithic Web-scale discovery services that index much of the content in these subscription databases?

Web-scale discovery services offer libraries the ability to reveal all of their licensed, locally created, and free resources through one discovery interface. Each library implementing these Web-scale services maintains individual local instances of the discovery system, including an integrated knowledge base of resources. In addition, these libraries must engage in periodic exporting of their local catalog and digital repositories for re-harvesting by the discovery service in order to insure their local instance is up to date. While these systems have been growing in popularity for one-stop searching and locally centralizing resources, they duplicate, to some extent, the indexing done by subscription databases. They also create systemic duplications by locally maintaining indexes of largely nonunique resources.

This raises a compelling question: Should libraries continue to locally centralize all subscribed resources? As scholarly communication and practices become more open, do closed or hybrid systems unnecessarily complicate or disenfranchise linked data systems and specific user groups? An alternative strategy to current discovery services might feature less local centralization and more external centralization or cloud-based connectivity. The result would be an economy of less system or service duplication and fewer mechanical intermediary systems. More direct connections via knowledge base registries and link resolvers would reduce errors of omission multiplied or perpetuated through machine mismatching or mistranslation. What is more, the library's dwindling purchasing power could be directed toward content procurement.

As Dorner observes, "being a collection manager in the digital environment . . . involves a blurring of boundaries which requires a holistic perception of information services and what constitutes a collection" (2000, 41). Today's collections, in effect, connect endless combinations of collections and data located throughout the digital information ecosystem. One day, databases and discovery tools may become part of a system in which "a library may want to synchronize data with union catalogs, Google Scholar, and other network level disclosure services" (Dempsey 2008, 117; see also Dempsey 2012). As library collections and scholarly practices continue to evolve, can discovery become more open?

Lewis, writing on collecting in academic libraries, sees open practices as a "central driver" for change in libraries and scholarly communication (2013, 161). Lewis references Burton's view of open scholarship (2009), which includes open review, open dialog, open process, open formats, and open data (2013, 166). To Burton's list could be added open access, open standards, open software—and the next logical step—open discovery. Lewis gestures in this direction, noting that studies by Herrera (2011) and Howland et al. (2009) suggest that "Google Scholar will be a, if not the, major discovery tool for the scholarly journal literature in the near future" (165).

Indeed, transformations in the information discovery space are beginning to appear. In February 2013, OCLC and ProQuest announced an agreement to exchange metadata within their discovery services (ProQuest 2013). Project Muse lists among its "discovery and linking partners" both proprietary systems like EBSCO and public systems like Google (http://muse.jhu.edu/about/linking_partners.html). As the authors were finalizing this chapter (October 2013), they received an email from a Thomson Reuters account manager, stating that an announcement would be made at the November 2013 Charleston Conference describing a new Web of Science and Google Scholar collaboration. Another email from Elsevier brought news that the publishing company is partnering with Google to share libraries' ScienceDirect holdings information and make these accessible via searches on Google. Open principles are also in evidence in JSTOR's initiative, Register & Read, "a new, experimental program to offer free, read-online access to individual scholars and researchers" (JSTOR 2012). If content can be open in limited ways, could not open discovery (i.e., search functionalities) be open in fuller, more robust ways?[8]

If the discovery of scholarly resources were open, libraries would be able to apply limited funds toward content procurement via a blend of free- and fee-based systems. In return, libraries could test database and discovery tool utility and provide critical feedback for various discovery implementations via evidence-based practices. In this way, libraries and the commercial sector could engage in collaborative partnerships to promote open discovery while harvesting return on investment for both parties.

CONCLUSION

This chapter has surveyed best practices and emerging considerations for evaluating and assessing subscription databases through the examination of key content- and platform-centered functions vital for transformative discovery. Rapidly expanding global networks and exponential growth of data urge a questioning of recent library and corporate strategies with respect to databases and the systems by which they are connected. These decisions center around the suite of research tools offered to library users. Data and information resources need to reside in an intelligent ecosystem that incorporates standardized metadata and effective platforms to enable users to meaningfully mine information and manage retrieval sets (Dempsey 2012; Lewis 2013). Scholars and students should be able to easily navigate and master this complex environment. The task facing libraries today is to identify the information systems and services that are best designed to facilitate transformative discovery.

Financially sustainable solutions also need to be part of the decision-making process. Tensions surrounding libraries' abilities to seek effective, economically sustainable information systems have not lessened. Balancing budgets and crafting collections to meet user needs in a 24/7 information-now economy require deeper, more collaborative partnerships between libraries and the commercial sector. More standardization, less duplicative system intermediation, and more open discovery systems and databases have the potential to create deeper, transformative discovery for all.

Writing more than two decades ago, George Machovec urged libraries to "be aggressive in embracing technological alternatives for access to information." Today these words remain a challenging call for change. As Machovec foresaw, the challenges and opportunities outlined in this chapter call for a rethinking of "traditional thinking, traditional organizational structures and traditional funding patterns" (1991, 2).

NOTES

1. The National Information Standards Organization (NISO) has created a standard for the construction of thesauri. For more information see ANSI/NISO Z39.19–2005 (R2010) Guidelines for the Construction, Format, and Management of Monolingual Controlled Vocabularies (http://www.niso.org/apps/group_public/project/details.php?project_id=46)

and Project ISO 25964 Thesauri and Interoperability with Other Vocabularies (http://www
.niso.org/schemas/iso25964/).

2. For further reading on transformations in scholarly communications and researcher
workflows, see Rutner and Schonfeld (2012); Swan (2012); Palmer, Teffeau, and Pirmann
(2009); University of Minnesota Libraries (2006); Meho and Tibbo (2003); and Brockman
et al. (2001).

3. For a discussion of barriers to interoperability, see Uhlir (2012) and Hepfer and
McElroy (2004).

4. Tim Berners-Lee (2010) sees linked data referencing and relating specific information via functional uniform resource identifiers (URIs) as the next logical steps in fostering
intelligent design on the Web.

5. The issue of disambiguation of names is discussed by Fagan (2012, 72–74).

6. For additional information on ORCID, consult the ORCID Web site (http://about
.orcid.org/about). ORCID follows the ISO 27729 International Standard Name Identifier
(http://www.isni.org/) conventions. This registry is similar in function to the Library of
Congress Name Authority File (LCNAF) in fostering the standardization of names of persons (http://authorities.loc.gov/help/name-auth.htm).

7. For additional information on the UMLS, consult the UMLS Web site (http://www
.nlm.nih.gov/research/umls/).

8. There are other encouraging signs of movement in this direction, including, for example, open searching in Science Direct; open topic collections in SPIE Digital Library
(http://spiedigitallibrary.org/collections.aspx); and Oxford Reference Online's Index Un-
derbar (http://www.oxfordreference.com/page/OI_underbar), described as a "free search
and discovery service, which shows links to related content from all Oxford University
Press online content."

REFERENCES

Allison, Dee Ann, Beth McNeil, and Signe Swanson. 2000. "Database Selection: One Size
Does Not Fit All." *College & Research Libraries* 61 (1): 56–63.

Alonso, Carlos J., Cathy N. Davidson, John M. Unsworth, and Lynne Withey. 2003. *Crises
and Opportunities: The Futures of Scholarly Publishing.* American Council of Learned
Societies Occasional Paper, No. 57. New York: American Council of Learned Societies.
Available at: http://www.acls.org/uploadedfiles/publications/op/57_crises_and_oppor
tunites.pdf. Accessed October 29, 2013.

Atkinson, Ross. 2005a. "Toward a Rationale for Future Event-Based Information Services."
In *Community, Collaboration, and Collections: The Writings of Ross Atkinson*, ed. Robert Alan and Bonnie MacEwan, 13–25. Chicago: Association for Library Collections &
Technical Services. Originally published in Patricia Hodges and Wendy Pradt Lougee,
eds., *Digital Libraries: A Vision for the 21st Century* (Ann Arbor: University of Michigan Library Scholarly Publishing Office, 2003).

Atkinson, Ross. 2005b. "Toward a Redefinition of Library Services." In *Community, Col-
laboration, and Collections: The Writings of Ross Atkinson*, ed. Robert Alan and Bonnie
MacEwan, 57–70. Chicago: Association for Library Collections & Technical Services.
Originally published in Peggy Johnson and Bonnie MacEwan, eds., *Virtually Yours:
Models for Managing Electronic Resources and Services* (Chicago: American Library
Association, 1999).

Berners-Lee, Tim. 2010. "Long Live the Web." *Scientific American* 303 (6): 80–85.

Blessinger, Kelly, and Maureen Olle. 2004. "Content Analysis of the Leading General Academic Databases." *Library Collections, Acquisitions, & Technical Services* 28 (3): 335–46.

Brockman, William S., Laura Neumann, Carole L Palmer, and Tonyia J. Tidline. 2001. *Scholarly Work in the Humanities and the Evolving Information Environment*. Washington, DC: Digital Library Federation, Council on Library and Information Resources. Available at: http://www.clir.org/pubs/reports/pub104/reports/pub104/pub104.pdf. Accessed October 29, 2013.

Burton, Gideon. 2009. "Scholarly Communications Must Be Open." *Academic Evolution* (blog). Available at: http://www.academicevolution.com/2009/08/scholarly-communi cations-must-transform-2.html. Accessed October 29, 2013.

Dempsey, Lorcan. 2008. "Reconfiguring the Library Systems Environment." *Portal: Libraries & The Academy* 8 (2): 111–20.

Dempsey, Lorcan. 2012. "Thirteen Ways of Looking at Libraries, Discovery, and the Catalog: Scale, Workflow, Attention." *EDUCAUSE Review Online* (Monday, December 10). Available at: http://www.educause.edu/ero/article/thirteen-ways-looking-li braries-discovery-and-catalog-scale-workflow-attention. Accessed October 29, 2013.

Dorner, D.G. 2000. "The Blurring of Boundaries: Digital Information and Its Impact on Collection Management." In *The International Yearbook of Library and Information Management, 2000–2001: Collection Management*, ed. G.E. Gorman, 15–44. London: Library Association Publishing.

Fagan, Jody Condit. 2011. "Search Engines for Tomorrow's Scholars." *Journal of Web Librarianship* 5 (4): 327–33.

Fagan, Jody Condit. 2012. "Search Engines for Tomorrow's Scholars, Part Two." *Journal of Web Librarianship* 6 (1): 69–76.

Giles, Jeremy R. A. 2011. "Geoscience Metadata—No Pain, No Gain." In *Societal Challenges and Geoinformatics*, ed. A. Krishna Sinha, David Arctur, Ian Jackson, and Linda C. Gundersen, 29–33. Boulder, CO: The Geological Society of America.

Gorman, G.E., and Ruth H. Miller. 2000. "Changing Collections, Changing Evaluations." In *The International Yearbook of Library and Information Management, 2000–2001: Collection Management*, ed. G.E. Gorman, 309–38. London: Library Association Publishing.

Gregory, Vicki L. 2011. *Collection Development and Management for 21st Century Library Collections: An Introduction*. New York: Neal-Schuman Publishers, Inc.

Gugerli, David. 2012. "The World as Database: On the Relation of Software Development, Query Methods, and Interpretative Independence." *Information & Culture* 47 (3): 288–311.

Hariri, Nadjla, and Yaghoub Norouzi. 2011. "Determining Evaluation Criteria for Digital Libraries' User Interface: A Review." *Electronic Library* 29 (5): 698–722.

Hazen, Dan. 2000. "Twilight of the Gods? Bibliographers in the Electronic Age." *Library Trends* 48 (4): 821–41.

Hepfer, Cindy, and Emily McElroy. 2004. "Serial Conversations: A Man for All Reasons: An Interview with Clifford Lynch." *Serials Review* 30 (4): 343–53.

Herrera, Gail. 2011. "Google Scholar Users and User Behaviors: An Exploratory Study." *College & Research Libraries* 72 (4): 316–330.

Hider, Philip. 2012. *Information Resource Description: Creating and Managing Metadata*. Chicago: American Library Association.

Horava, Tony. 2010. "Challenges and Possibilities for Collection Management in a Digital Age." *Library Resources & Technical Services* 54 (3): 142–52.

Horava, Tony. 2011. "Evaluating Major Research Databases." Presentation at the Center for Research Libraries Preconference Weighing the Evidence: Evaluating Major Research Databases, Charleston, SC, November 2–5. Available at: http://www.crl.edu/sites/default/files/follow_up_material/Weighing%20the%20Evidence%20-%20Evaluating%20Major%20Research%20Databases%20%28Tony%20Horova%29.pdf Accessed October 29, 2013.

Howland, Jared L., Thomas C. Wright, Rebecca A. Boughan, and Brian C. Roberts. 2009. "How Scholarly Is Google Scholar? A Comparison to Library Databases." *College & Research Libraries* 70 (3): 227–34.

Jacsó, Péter. 1997. "Content Evaluation of Databases." *Annual Review of Information Science and Technology* 32: 231–67.

Jacsó, Peter. 2010. "The JISC Academic Database Assessment Tool—Virtues and Vices." *Online Information Review* 34 (5): 806–14.

Jacsó, Péter. 2012. "Analysis of the Ulrich's Serials Analysis System from the Perspective of Journal Coverage by Academic Databases." *Online Information Review* 36 (2): 307–19.

Johnson, Peggy. 2009. *Fundamentals of Collection Development and Management*. 2nd ed. Chicago: American Library Association.

JSTOR. 2012. "Register & Read." JSTOR. Available at: http://about.jstor.org/rr. Accessed October 29, 2013.

Lewis, David W. 2013. "From Stacks to the Web: The Transformation of Academic Library Collecting." *College & Research Libraries* 74 (2): 159–76.

Losee, Robert M., and Karen A. Worley. 1993. *Research and Evaluation for Information Professionals*. San Diego: Academic Press.

Machovec, George S. 1991. "Recession, Electronic Media, Networking and Libraries." *Online Libraries and Microcomputers* 9 (3): 1–3.

Machovec, George S. 2011. "Assessment Tools." Presentation at the Center for Research Libraries Preconference Weighing the Evidence: Evaluating Major Research Databases, Charleston, SC, November 2–5. Available at: http://www.crl.edu/sites/default/files/follow_up_material/Weighing%20the%20Evidence%20-%20Assessment%20Tools%20%28George%20Machovec%29.pdf. Accessed October 29, 2013.

Manoff, Marlene. 2000. "Hybridity, Mutability, Multiplicity: Theorizing Electronic Library Collections." *Library Trends* 48 (4): 857–76.

McMullen, Susan, Patricia B. M. Brennan, Joanna M. Burkhardt, and Marla Wallace. 2006. "Collection Development Strategies for Online Aggregated Databases." In *Handbook of Electronic and Digital Acquisitions*, ed. Thomas W. Leonhardt, 61–90. New York: The Haworth Press.

Meho, Lokman I., and Helen R. Tibbo. 2003. "Modeling the Information-Seeking Behavior of Social Scientists: Ellis's Study Revisited." *Journal of the American Society for Information Science and Technology* 54 (6): 570–87.

Miller, Heather S. 1997. "The Little Locksmith: A Cautionary Tale for the Electronic Age." *Journal of Academic Librarianship* 23 (2): 100–7.

Miller, Ron. 2008. "Twelve Point Plan for Quantitative and Qualitative Evaluation of Databases." *Computers in Libraries* 28 (7): S2–S3.

Miller, Ruth. 2000. "Electronic Resources and Academic Libraries, 1980–2000: A Historical Perspective." *Library Trends* 48 (4): 645–70.

Nielsen, Jakob. 1994. "Enhancing the Explanatory Power of Usability Heuristics Tools for Design." In *Proceedings of the ACM CHI'94 Conference on Human Factors in Computing Systems*, vol. 1, 152–58. New York: ACM Press.

Oberg, Steve. 2003. "Gold Rush: An Electronic Journal Management and Linking Project." *Serials Review* 29 (3): 230–32.

Okerson, Ann. 2011. "How Librarians Buy Databases." Presentation at the Center for Research Libraries Preconference Weighing the Evidence: Evaluating Major Research Databases, Charleston, SC, November 2–5. Available at: http://www.crl.edu/sites/default/files/follow_up_material/How%20Libraries%20Buy%20Databases%20%28Ann%20Okerson%29.pdf. Accessed October 29, 2013.

Palmer, Carole L., Lauren C. Teffeau, and Carrie M. Pirmann. 2009. "Scholarly Information Practices in the Online Environment: Themes from the Literature and Implications for Library Service Development." Report Commissioned by OCLC Research, Dublin, OH. Available at: http://www.oclc.org/resources/research/publications/library/2009/2009-02.pdf. Accessed October 29, 2013.

ProQuest. 2013. "OCLC and ProQuest Collaborate to Enhance Library Discovery." ProQuest news release. Available at: http://www.proquest.com/en-US/aboutus/pressroom/13/20130228.shtml. Accessed October 29, 2013.

Reilly, Bernard F. 2012. "A Report on the Charleston Pre-Conference Weighing the Evidence: Evaluating Major Research Databases." *The Charleston Advisor* 13 (3): 54–55.

Rutner, Jennifer, and Roger C. Schonfeld. 2012. *Supporting the Changing Research Practices of Historians*. New York: Ithaka S+R. Available at: http://www.sr.ithaka.org/sites/default/files/reports/supporting-the-changing-research-practices-of-historians.pdf. Accessed October 29, 2013.

Schreur, Philip E. 2012. "The Academy Unbound: Linked Data as Revolution." *Library Resources & Technical Services* 56 (4): 227–37.

Stranack, Kevin. 2006. "CUFTS: An Open Source Alternative for Serials Management." *Serials Librarian* 51 (2): 29–39

Swan, Alma. 2012. "Transforming Opportunities in Scholarly Discourse: Workshop Report." Birmingham, UK: JISC/CNI. Available at: http://www.jisc.ac.uk/publications/reports/2012/transforming-opportunities.aspx. Accessed October 29, 2013.

Tenopir, Carol. 1995. "Priorities of Quality." In *Electronic Information Delivery: Ensuring Quality and Value*, ed. Reva Basch, 119–39. Brookfield, VT: Gower Publishing Limited.

Uhlir, Paul F. 2012. *The Future of Scientific Knowledge Discovery in Open Networked Environments: Summary of a Workshop*. Washington, DC: National Academies Press.

University of Minnesota Libraries. 2006. "A Multi-Dimensional Framework for Academic Support: A Final Report," Minneapolis, MN. Available at: http://purl.umn.edu/5540. Accessed October 29, 2013.

5

PERSPECTIVES ON WEEDING IN ACADEMIC LIBRARY COLLECTIONS

David A. Tyckoson

Print collections in academic libraries are an interesting phenomenon. Traditionally, they have contained the books, journals, media, maps, and reports that support the teaching and research in the various disciplines of the college or university—providing faculty and students with information to guide and support their intellectual efforts. For generations—and in some cases, for centuries—academic library collections have been painstakingly built to accumulate the knowledge needed within the disciplines served by the parent institution. Academic libraries have continuously purchased, organized, and made available the resources required of and requested by the academic community that the library served. Over time, collections grew larger and larger, building an accumulated knowledge base for everyone working, studying, and learning at the institution. When information existed entirely in print formats, people came to the library because that is where the scholarly information was located. Over time collections grew as new materials were added, often reaching into the millions—and in some cases, tens of millions—of volumes. Growth was good and rarely was anything removed from academic library collections.

Libraries began to be evaluated and rated by the sizes of their collections. The more volumes a library had, the better it must be. Volumes were easy to count and more was always better. Bigger collections by their very definition contained more information than smaller collections. Growth was viewed as the objective and weeding was rarely done. Collection development was associated with collection building, constantly accumulating and never deleting.

Starting in the early 1990s, the nature of academic library collections changed forever. The introduction of networked electronic resources provided academic libraries—and more importantly, academic library users—with access to information at an unprecedented level. The astronomical growth of the Internet provided students and researchers with instant access to information wherever they were located and whenever it was needed, not just from print resources in the library when it was open. When the World Wide Web was created, one of its primary objectives was to allow scholars to share information across borders regardless of geographic location. In fact, some of the first documents added to the Web were preprints and documents in physics. The idea of constructing a web of scholarly information was part of the impetus for building the Internet as an open platform rather than as a proprietary network. Clearly, this model was a success.

Although commercial and personal interests quickly discovered the Internet and its power for marketing and communications—resulting in most of the information on the Internet being far from scholarly—there is in fact a tremendous amount of valuable research information. Any search of Google Scholar brings up a huge amount of material on just about any subject area. Today, researchers turn to the Internet as their source of first resort for most of their research needs. Library collections are consulted only when desired information is not readily available online.

As subscription databases and electronic journals became the preferred format for scholarly information, use of the equivalent print resources declined dramatically. Yes, a few patrons—primarily older faculty members—would still come into the library and consult the print volumes, but most usage of these resources moved online. Circulation figures in academic libraries declined while database statistics skyrocketed. In the 20 years since the World Wide Web was introduced, we have seen a true revolution in the way that scholars access information. As a result of this revolution, print collections have become less relevant—and it has become time to reduce the size. Yes, it is time to weed academic library print collections.

TERMINOLOGY

Although the weeding of academic library collections sounds like a simple concept, there can be many misconceptions about the process due to varying understandings of the nature of higher education and of libraries. For the sake of this chapter, the following definitions apply.

Academic Institutions

Academic institutions are schools, colleges, and universities that grant degrees above the secondary level. These include community colleges, four-year liberal arts colleges, universities with graduate programs at the master's and doctoral levels, trade schools, and some specialized educational institutions. Academic institutions may be public or private, nonprofit or for-profit.

Library Collections

Academic libraries are the libraries that serve students, faculty, and researchers in specific academic institutions. Library collections are the accumulated information resources selected and organized by library staff, which are made publicly available to all users of the library. Collections contain materials, including books, journals, databases, sound recordings, video recordings, microforms, and archival materials, in a wide range of formats. They do not include materials on the open Web or information that is restricted to only a few users, such as teaching materials developed by faculty for specific courses or student research papers. Most materials in a library collection may have been purchased or licensed specifically for that purpose. Others may be deposited by government agencies, gifts from users, or freely available electronic resources.

Most academic library collections contain a variety of subcollections that contain specialized resources. These materials may be of interest to a particular campus community (departmental library), serve a specific purpose (course reserves), or play a role in preservation (archives). Some subcollections are housed in different physical locations, such as departmental libraries based on subject area (law library, medical library, or business library) or educational level (undergraduate library or graduate library). Other subcollections may be groupings of types of materials within a library (reference collection, periodicals collection, or music collection). The term library collection refers to the contents of the entire library, including all subcollections regardless of their physical location.

Print Collections

Print collections are the analog collections traditionally found in libraries. Print collections include printed books and journals, as well as maps, government documents, music, videos, and microforms. The term print is used because it represents the largest component of analog library collections, but in the context of this chapter it is intended to represent all physical formats included in the library collection.

Weeding

Weeding is the process of permanently removing materials from print library collections. Other terms often used for weeding include deaccession, deselection, deacquisition, and discarding. When materials are weeded, they no longer remain in any part of the library collection. The transfer of materials between subcollections is not weeding because the material remains a part of the overall library collection. Similarly, materials that are discarded because they are damaged or lost by users are not part of the weeding process. Weeding is the intentional decision that specific items will no longer be included in any part of the library collection.

TYPES OF ACADEMIC LIBRARY COLLECTIONS

While academic libraries obviously have much in common, each one is unique and no two academic library collections are identical. Each collection has been built and maintained, usually over a period of many years, to match the needs of the college or university that the library serves. Variations in subject disciplines, degree programs, preferred formats for materials, historical retention rates, languages used, and other factors make each academic collection unique. Weeding must always take into account the local needs of the institution.

However, while each collection is unique, there are also many similarities among the various types of academic libraries. Most academic libraries fall into one of the following categories.

Comprehensive Collections

Comprehensive collections are those that attempt to obtain and preserve as much information on as many subjects as possible. Typically containing millions of volumes, these libraries have become vast intellectual warehouses of published scholarly information. They tend to serve large, comprehensive universities that offer undergraduate and graduate degrees in a vast array of disciplines. Comprehensive collections range in size from truly massive collections at institutions such as Harvard, Yale, Illinois, and the University of Toronto to those that are somewhat smaller (yet equally impressive) at institutions such as Georgia Tech, Colorado State, SUNY-Albany, and the University of Guelph. Comprehensive collections tend to be international in scope, collecting all of the research in the subject areas of interest regardless of the nation of origin.

Comprehensive collections have long been viewed as the pinnacles of academic library collections. Throughout the 20th century, the building of such collections was the primary goal of many academic libraries. At a time when print collections were the primary means of distribution and preservation of scholarly information, such collections were considered to be the measure of a university's commitment to scholarship. Comprehensive collections contain not only the primary books and journals on the disciplines that they collect, but also the more obscure resources used by scholars in those areas. The larger the collection, the greater the chance that the collection would contain information needed by researchers at the university. From a purely mathematical perspective, large is always better—it is twice as likely that a collection of 10 million volumes will have what any researcher wants as one of five million volumes. In that sense, comprehensive collections have long been the poster children for academic libraries. In comprehensive libraries, weeding has traditionally not been a common practice or priority. Since weeding reduces the number of volumes available, it is done very sparingly in comprehensive collections.

Libraries with comprehensive collections are also the laboratories for much of the research in the field of librarianship. Academic librarians frequently look to their peers at institutions with comprehensive collections for direction. Comprehensive collection libraries not only have more materials, but they usually have more staff and more funding than other academic libraries. They also are part of institutions with a deep research culture that encourages the assessment of collections, practices, and service. In addition, the faculty and students that comprehensive collections serve are often the leading researchers in their fields, publishing at a higher rate and bringing in more grant funding than faculty and students at other institutions. The ARL, whose membership includes most such libraries, was created to serve as an organization to discuss and to research the issues affecting libraries with comprehensive collections.

Although comprehensive collection status may have long been the aspirational goal within academic librarianship, it has rarely been achieved. While there is no firm definition for such libraries and any line of demarcation between comprehensive and other types of collections will be decidedly gray, there simply are not many academic libraries that have reached comprehensive collection status. Of the over 4,000 academic libraries in the United States and Canada, fewer than 150 would be considered comprehensive if the figure of 2 million volumes is used as the threshold collection size for this type of library. Furthermore, of these 150 libraries less than one-third contain over 5 million volumes and only about a dozen have collections of over 10 million volumes. Although these libraries are a tremendous resource for the scholarly community, they represent only a very small percentage of the total number of academic libraries.

Research Collections

Based on size, the next largest level of academic library collection is the research collection. Defining research collections as containing between approximately 500,000 and 2 million volumes, most academic libraries at colleges and universities that grant graduate degrees fall into this category. An estimated 1,000 academic libraries would be considered research collections, which represent approximately 25 percent of all academic libraries in the United States and Canada. Libraries at campuses such as James Madison, Bowling Green, Northern Illinois, and San Jose State are typical of research-level library collections.

Research collections usually provide a strong breadth of coverage of the disciplines taught at the college or university, but do not have the depth of comprehensive library collections. Research collections were built to meet the

research needs of most faculty and students, but they also rely on other libraries for more esoteric materials. Research collections may be comprehensive
in a few selected subject fields, but not in all areas taught at the university.
Research collections are more selective than their comprehensive cousins,
containing the primary books and the most significant journals in each discipline but not the more esoteric publications found in comprehensive collections. Research collections tend to be geographically focused, collecting
primarily North American publications and have fewer European, Asian, and
third-world materials.

As a result of their more limited scope, weeding is more common in libraries with research collections than those with comprehensive collections. Since
librarians who build research collections are not attempting to provide everything in the subject fields that they collect, they are more likely to discard
out-of-date or little-used materials. Research collections will grow in size over
time, but not as rapidly as comprehensive collections.

Teaching Collections

The third level on the scale of academic library collections—and the level that
includes the most total institutions—is the teaching collection. Teaching collections support colleges and universities whose primary focus is the instruction
of students rather than research by faculty. Many four-year colleges and almost
all community colleges fall into this segment of the academic library universe.
Teaching collections are typically fewer than 500,000 volumes in size.

Teaching collections contain only the most important books and primary
scholarly journals in the subject areas taught at the college or university. They
rarely contain the secondary journals or more esoteric materials found in
research and comprehensive collections. Budgets and staffing are typically
much smaller than those of research and comprehensive collections.

Since the goal in teaching collections is to support the needs of students,
weeding is much more common in teaching collections than in research or
comprehensive collections. Teaching collections focus on current materials—
those that are out of date are frequently discarded. Weeding is very much a
part of collection development in teaching collections.

Specialized Academic Collections

Some academic institutions focus on only one subject field. These are not
comprehensive colleges teaching students in a wide range of disciplines, but
are independent educational institutions teaching a single discipline. These
academic institutions are not colleges or institutes that are part of a larger
university, but are independent educational institutions. Libraries supporting these institutions might collect at the research or even the comprehensive

level, but their collections only contain materials in a single discipline. Institutions that fall into this category include independent law and medical schools, seminaries, art institutes, music conservatories, and some trade schools. Depending on the research interests of the institution and its faculty, the library may or may not support research-level collections. Weeding needs of these academic libraries will vary tremendously, but all will most likely be involved in weeding at some level.

Virtual Academic Libraries

Over the past two decades, a new type of academic institution has evolved—the online virtual college or university. These institutions have very quickly taken a prominent place in North American education. They teach hundreds of thousands of students and grant thousands of degrees, many of which are accredited by the same accrediting agencies that serve more traditional residential institutions. The success of National University, the University of Phoenix, Kaplan College, and a host of other for-profit educational institutions is forcing academia to revise how education is delivered to students—and how libraries support those students.

Libraries at these institutions are almost entirely virtual, existing almost exclusively in the electronic world. Students in these programs primarily use electronic resources provided by the host institution. While some of these virtual colleges do have libraries with print collections, those collections tend to be housed far from the students that the institution teaches. Material is delivered to the students on demand—or those students go to academic or public libraries in the area where they live. Since libraries at these virtual institutions have very limited print collections, weeding of those collections is almost irrelevant. While this chapter is aimed at libraries with print collections, the fast rise and increasing market share of this new type of academic institution is forcing academic librarians in more traditional settings to rethink the role of print collections—and is a symptom of the diminished need for such collections in all types of academic libraries. In that sense, these new online institutions will have a strong influence on weeding in academic library collections.

RESOURCE SHARING—THE EXTENDED COLLECTION

Most academic libraries are members of one or more resource sharing systems that allow users to borrow materials directly from other member libraries. OhioLINK, I-Share (Illinois), and Link+ (California and Nevada) are all examples of this type of resource sharing network. Each system allows users to search, find, and request materials directly from other libraries—effectively expanding the local collection to include the materials in the collections of all other system members. Collectively, the network raises the collection level of each of its members—often up to the size and scope of a comprehensive collection. The rapid availability of materials from other libraries reduces the pressure of each member to purchase—and especially to retain—materials of marginal local value. In other words, it frees each member to weed the local collection because it knows that copies will be available through the resource sharing network. The network becomes an insurance policy that allows access to these materials—even when they are no longer available in the local collection.

In addition to resource sharing programs, other cooperative collection arrangements make materials available to academic libraries. The Center for Research Libraries (CRL) in Chicago is one of the oldest cooperative collections and it serves as a global repository for low-use academic research materials. Members—most of whom are institutions with comprehensive or research-level collections—are able to deposit collections and to freely borrow any materials in the collection. Much of what is held at CRL is unique research material that is not readily available from other sources. Even nonmember libraries may borrow materials on a fee-based basis.

On a more regional or local basis, several library networks have created shared storage facilities for their members. The University of California, the Five Colleges Consortium (Massachusetts), PASCAL (Colorado), and the Tri-Universities Group (Ontario) are all examples of shared storage facilities that provide materials freely to their members. Members may submit items to the facility and researchers may request materials from the facility, regardless of which institutions contributed it. The collection of the consortium provides expanded access for each of its members, effectively expanding the collection size of all participating libraries.

MOTIVATIONS FOR WEEDING

Ideally, weeding is done on an ongoing basis to keep academic library collections fresh and relevant for the community that the library serves. However, in practice, weeding is usually a low-priority activity in most academic libraries. Staff shortages, multiple assignments, and time-critical activities in other areas of the library (e.g., instruction sessions, reference duties, committee meetings, and administrative activities) leave weeding as a low-priority project for most academic libraries. While weeding is viewed by most academic librarians as a common good, it is usually a process that is relegated to a secondary or tertiary priority in actual practice. However, three common scenarios where weeding becomes a higher priority in academic libraries arise.

Policy Decisions

Academic libraries do weed collections on an ongoing basis, and most frequently it is due to retention policy decisions. Retention policies are predetermined lengths of time that a library will keep a specific item or type of item.

Some journals and serials have a short lifetime in which they are useful, in which case libraries will decide to keep only a designated timeframe, such as only the current year or only the most recent three years. As new issues arrive, the older ones are replaced. Similarly, some reference works are often weeded based on retention policy. With some types of reference works, including almanacs and directories, libraries retain only the most recent volume. While comprehensive collections may wish to keep back volumes for historical purposes, most research and teaching libraries weed those volumes as a matter of course. Weeding due to policy decisions is a standard practice in teaching collections, is common in research collections, and is used selectively in comprehensive collections.

Space

In practice, the motivating factor most responsible for weeding in an academic library collection is the space in which the collection is stored. Nothing motivates academic librarians to weed their collections more than the need to shift or move thousands of physical volumes. The larger the collection, the more important this aspect becomes in the decision-making process. Libraries that are under renovation, building an addition, changing locations, integrating other collections, moving into an entirely new space, or simply running out of room in existing shelf space are suddenly forced into emergency weeding projects. Almost every academic library that is moving into new or renovated space weeds the collection before the move is done. Unfortunately, many do not continue to weed the collection until the next shift is needed. This motivator applies to any kind of academic library collection.

Obsolescence

Academic library collections contain multiple formats of materials, not just print on paper. And while print remains a viable format for library materials, not all formats that were used in the past are worth retaining. Academic libraries contain many older formats in their collections, including VHS tapes, floppy disks, vinyl records, and a variety of microforms. As those formats get superseded by newer and better equivalents, libraries must decide to keep, weed, or transfer the information that they contain. Comprehensive collections may try to transfer or retain the content, but research and teaching collections are likely to weed those materials from the collection. As formats become obsolete, materials in those formats should be weeded.

USAGE DATA FOR DECISION MAKING

Deciding whether to retain or discard any individual volume or title is often the result of an educated guess by the librarian—a guess that is based on that librarian's knowledge of the contents of the collection, research habits of its users, and overall knowledge of the discipline. However, rather than relying entirely on that knowledge, librarians have specific usage data available to help make weeding decisions scientifically. Circulation systems all retain checkout data for individual items, allowing librarians to see what has been checked out and what has not. For circulating collections, this information is invaluable in determining whether library users value the item in question. The more that an item is used, the less likely it will be weeded. By consulting usage data for any item being considered for weeding, the librarian is able to verify that it is—or is not—something that is likely to be requested by future users.

Unfortunately, not all items in an academic library circulate. Reference sources, journals, music, and microfilm are all components of most academic library collections—and do not circulate in most libraries. Fortunately, several methods are available for collecting usage data for these collections. Most circulation systems also have a separate means for capturing in-house library use. These systems allow the staff to scan items before they are re-shelved, tallying the number of times that they have been off the shelf. Collecting this data over a period of time will provide the librarian with a snapshot of collection use. While there is staff time required on a daily basis to scan materials before they are returned to the shelf, the data gathered allows the librarian to understand what aspects of the collection are being used.

While using the circulation system is the most effective way to gather use data, several other methods are also available. Perhaps the most time-honored method is to simply mark the books that get used. This can be done by placing a flag in the book, pasting a dot on the spine, or making a physical mark on the volume. The flags, marks, or dots provide a visual clue that the volume has been used. Some libraries that use this method mark each book only once, whereas others add multiple marks to show frequency of use. Since flags or stickers can disappear, this method is less accurate than counting use by the circulation system. However, it provides the staff with an indication of which materials are being used.

Another simple method for collecting use data is to simply write down or copy the call number of materials being used. This works best for collections with low use, but it can be used in many different situations. Entering that data into a spreadsheet or word-processing file allows the librarian to manipulate the data as desired. Comparing the data on the materials used to the entire collection allows the librarian to determine what should be weeded. No matter what method is used to collect data, it is important to use all available data when weeding. By checking the usage data, librarians are less likely to discard something that a faculty member or researcher will want in the future.

THE PROCESS OF WEEDING

Since weeding involves the permanent removal of materials from the library collection, it must be taken very seriously. Once an item is weeded and removed from the collection, it can be very difficult to replace if that weeding decision needs to be reversed. Ideally, libraries develop a process for weeding that includes checks and balances to ensure that only items that are no longer necessary are removed. An ideal weeding process looks something like those described in the following.

Shelf Review

A librarian or staff member goes to the collection area being weeded and reviews the materials on the shelf, one at a time. That individual searches for out-of-date, superseded, or superfluous materials and selects items for review. Those materials are either pulled from the shelves or flagged for identification later. Shelf review is the first critical step in the weeding process because it allows the staff to see all materials in an area in the context of the collection as a whole.

Usage Review

Next, the usage data for each potentially weeded item is determined. While most potentially weeded items will show low usage (which is very often why they are being considered for weeding), a few will demonstrate high or moderate levels of use. Staff then determine if those materials that are being or have been used should remain in consideration for weeding. In some cases, materials that demonstrate use will be retained in the collection—in others they will still be weeded.

Alternate Availability Review

It is usually a good idea to check to see if materials being weeded are readily available online or from any resource sharing partners. The insurance policy provided by resource sharing allows libraries a safety blanket when removing materials from their own collections. If an item can easily be obtained from other libraries, it can be safely weeded. If it is not available—or not available easily—from other sources, the library might decide to retain it even though it has low use.

Replacement Review

In most cases, weeded materials will not be replaced. However, in some cases items will show high use because there are not newer or more appropriate materials available in the collection. In this case, staff may look for newer or better sources to replace the items being weeded. In this sense, weeding not only eliminates old and inappropriate materials from the library collection but also contributes to the selection of up-to-date and appropriate materials to replace them.

Final Review

Ideally, a staff person other than the one making the initial decision should look at all of the items selected for weeding before they are discarded. This second-level review serves as a balance to ensure that items that might be of future use are not discarded. Since materials that are weeded are usually gone forever, it is good to have more than one person involved in deciding which materials will actually be weeded.

The process of weeding is definitely an art and not a science. Although weeding should be approached scientifically, taking into account a variety of factors related to each item, the ultimate decision whether to retain or weed any given item from the collection can be a very difficult one to make. Retention is always the easier choice, but weeding requires that staff make the tough decision to eliminate materials from the collection. Knowing what else is available in the collection, what is available through resource sharing, and what library users may wish to consult in the future helps make that decision easier.

WHAT TO WEED

Weeding academic library collections is really very simple. The librarian just has to get rid of the materials that no one wants, and keep those that someone does want—or that they will want in the future. However, failing in the skill to read the minds of the thousands of students and faculty members who use the library—and lacking the ability to travel forward in time to see what future users will be interested in—the librarian must weed based on educated guesswork. This can paralyze some librarians and is one reason that weeding often is not conducted in academic libraries. Barring space considerations or other incentives to weed the collection, it is often easier to just leave materials on the shelf than to try and figure out what should be weeded. This is how many research and most comprehensive collections are built—with the addition of new materials and very little withdrawal of older volumes. However, even in the most weeding-averse situations, there are certain categories of materials that should definitely be considered for weeding, which include the following.

Bound Journals

Back volumes of journals comprise a large segment of just about every academic library collection. Once considered the best way to preserve paper journals, bound volumes have created large back files of journals in most academic libraries. When print was the primary format for the distribution of journals, these volumes received a lot of usage. However, now that virtually all academic journals exist almost exclusively online, people do not use bound volumes as much—if at all. Whenever a journal is available online, students and faculty go there instead of coming to the library to find the print equivalent. Library users have voted with their feet and have demonstrated that online is the preferred format for almost every single journal title. As a result, academic libraries contain large collections of bound volumes that receive very little use. These volumes are prime targets for weeding.

When e-journals first appeared, there was much concern about whether this format would survive in the long run. Not only have they survived, but they have almost completely supplanted paper. By buying collections from publishers and aggregators, most academic libraries now provide their users with access to more journals today than at any time in their history. Not only are current issues available online, but most vendors also provide a significant and sometimes complete back file. JSTOR, Project Muse, professional organizations (including the American Chemical Society, IEEE, and American Institute of Physics), and many major publishers provide stable platforms for journals. As a result, most such volumes are no longer needed in print in the library. Weeding those volumes will free up space with no loss of access to the information that they contain.

Microforms

If it is rare for users to touch print journals, it is almost unheard of for them to consult microfilm. Microfilm has always been a preservation format and not a user format. Despite advances in technologies for reading and copying from microfilm, this is the format of last resort for users and librarians. If a journal is available in any other format—and especially if it is online—weed the microfilm version.

Duplicates

As the use of print collections has decreased, so has the need for multiple copies of any given title or volume. Whereas at one time academic libraries used to purchase multiple copies of a given title, such as supporting collections in different locations on campus or to support multiple users for course reserves, today it is very rare to purchase multiple copies. And for anything available in electronic format, one copy serves all students and faculty on campus. Even for materials available only in print, demand has dropped to the point that one copy may usually be shared by all interested users. Many academic libraries—especially comprehensive and research libraries—have retained multiple copies of materials purchased decades ago. By keeping one copy and discarding all of the duplicates, the collection will lose no access to information while still freeing space for future growth.

Old Editions

Many academic libraries—especially comprehensive and research collections—retain older editions of works when a new edition is purchased. The idea behind this practice is to allow researchers to see the changes in the title over time. In practice, students and most faculty prefer the current edition of any title and very few consult the older versions. Usage data can verify this fact at any given library, but most would build better collections by weeding older editions of current titles.

Outdated Resources

Many libraries keep older books on every subject field that they cover in order to provide a historical perspective for that discipline. While this works well in the arts and humanities, it may actually be a dangerous practice in some other subject fields. Old books on medicine, law, science, or business may mislead any library users who expect the collection to provide accurate and current information. Unless a library is interested in the history of a discipline, old materials in that discipline should be weeded. Each library should identify the subject areas that it wants to keep current—and not only buy new materials in those subjects, but also make sure that older volumes are weeded.

WHAT NOT TO WEED

Even more important than knowing what to weed is knowing what *not* to weed. Every academic library contains unique materials that are not available elsewhere and that need to be retained in the collection. These materials include those that are related to the history of the institution, such as course catalogs, yearbooks, and campus newspapers; those that document the operations of the institution, such as committee meeting minutes, departmental and college newsletters, sports programs, and reports on new initiatives and degree programs; and those that represent the intellectual and creative output of the institution, such as faculty research papers, books written by campus researchers, data sets generated by faculty research projects, images of student art exhibits, and recordings of music performances or theater productions. These materials are unique to each academic institution and would not be available anywhere if they were removed from the library collection.

In the past, libraries were measured by the range and depth of the collection, usually by covering as many subject disciplines as possible. The result was that these collections often duplicated those at other libraries collecting at the same level. The same journals and books on English literature, psychology, or chemistry could be found in any college or university library that supported a teaching, research, or comprehensive collection in those fields. In the future, academic library collections will be measured by how they preserve—and promote—the unique materials generated by the college or university. How well we collect and digitize those resources will determine how well academic libraries will serve their campuses in the future.

THE POLITICS OF WEEDING

While the process of weeding may be difficult, it is the politics of weeding that can sometimes make it unbearable. Weeding can bring out very strong emotions from library staff and from campus constituents, especially faculty. It may not matter that no one has looked at a given book for over 30 years. When faculty see that weeding is in process and that books have been selected for removal, cries will go out across campus: *OMG—the library is throwing out the books!*

That reaction is common in academia—and shows how deeply faculty and researchers care about the library and its role as a source of scholarly information. Library administrators must be ready to explain and defend the process of weeding and what it means for faculty, students, and the collection. Outcry over weeding is really a public relations problem and not a weeding problem, but if managed poorly it can stop the weeding process entirely. Some solutions that will minimize the political fallout from weeding the collection include the following.

Get Library Staff on Board

Before news of weeding reaches the rest of the campus, make sure that everyone in the library understands the weeding program and its implications. In most cases frontline library staff are the people doing the weeding and they need to know the reasons behind and scope of the project. They will also be the first to encounter faculty from outside the library who have questions about the process. If all library staff can explain the rationale for and the process of weeding, they will be able to defuse much political fallout before it rises to critical levels. At a minimum, make sure that the staff know who to refer those questions to in collection development or library administration so that an accurate and consistent message is provided to all who ask.

Tell the Campus What Is Going On

Be proactive in getting the message out to the campus by publicizing any large weeding project. Identify a message that explains why you are removing materials from the collection and use campus communication channels to let people know about it. If appropriate, use campus newsletters, the college newspaper, email listservs, and other communication media that are commonly used to notify campus constituencies. Most political fallout comes from people who are surprised by weeding—and that surprise leads to suspicion that the library is conducting nefarious activities. Telling the campus in advance minimizes this problem.

Advise Campus Administration

Make sure that the administrative unit that the library reports to knows about the weeding project and its objectives. It is very likely that an upset faculty member will communicate directly with the president or provost of the university—and they are the last people that the library administration will want to upset. Keeping the higher administration in the loop will minimize political damage at that level.

CONCLUSION

The past two decades have seen a dramatic shift in how academic library collections are used. Academic journals—which in many ways are the quintessential scholarly publications, containing peer-reviewed articles presenting the results of original research—have shifted almost completely from print to electronic formats. Scholarly books are still published in print, but more and more are also available as eBooks. Government documents and many technical reports are available freely online. Music and video is being streamed and maps are created globally by Google as well as personally on GPS devices. The materials that have traditionally been major components of academic library collections—in some cases for centuries—are all moving away from physical formats and becoming electronic.

Students, faculty, and researchers are following the lead of those materials and are looking first to online resources, and only when not readily available online are they turning to traditional library collections. Our physical materials are seeing decreased use and possibly decreased relevance. More and more often we are using shared collection facilities and resource sharing networks to obtain physical materials for our users. Because of the shift to electronic and shared resources, academic libraries no longer need to worry about retaining physical copies in their local collections.

Academic libraries are caught in this squeeze of shifting resources and traditional expectations. At the same time that more information is available to more researchers than at any time in history, the relevance of physical library collections is declining. Yet most libraries continue to build strong physical collections. While it will be years before physical collections are irrelevant—if that ever happens—those physical collections are clearly less critical to today's educational environment. Ranking libraries by the size of their collection has no meaning when most of the information that students, faculty, and researchers are looking for is available online.

As the importance of print collections goes down, the need for weeding goes up. There is less of a need to retain print materials in library collections when that same information can be obtained online or through a resource sharing program. Over the next several decades print library collections will get smaller, not larger. Comprehensive collections may continue to collect print materials and grow, but teaching and research-level collections will probably become smaller. Size will no longer matter and new measures of collection effectiveness will be developed. And weeding will play a large part in ensuring that libraries provide the best possible collections for the institutions that they serve.

SUGGESTED READING

Bravender, Patricia, and Valeria Long. 2011. "Weeding an Outdated Collection in an Automated Retrieval System." *Collection Management* 36: 237–45.

Burgett, Shelley Wood. 2006. "A Comprehensive Weeding Project for a Community College Library Collection or Bye Bye Books." *Kentucky Libraries* 70: 17–21.

Carey, Ronadin, Lindsay Simonsen, and Bryan S. Vogh. 2009. "Low-Cost Method of Removing Periodical Duplicates Using a Collection Growth Formula at a Medium-Sized Academic Library." *Library Collections, Acquisitions, & Technical Services* 33: 119–22.

Crosetto, Alice, Laura Kinner, and Lucy Duhon. 2008. "Assessment in a Tight Time Frame: Using Readily Available Data to Evaluate Your Collection." *Collection Management* 33: 29–50.

Dubicki, Eleonora. 2008. "Weeding: Facing the Fears." *Collection Building* 27: 132–35.

Farber, Evan Ira. 1997. "Books Not for College Libraries." *Library Journal* 122: 44.

Gore, Daniel, et al. 1975. "Zero Growth: When Is NOT-Enough Enough? A Symposium." *Journal of Academic Librarianship* 1: 5–11.

Handis, Michael W. 2007. "Practical Advice for Weeding in Small Academic Libraries." *Collection Building* 26: 84–87.

Herzog, Susan. 2004. "Collection Development Challenges for the 21st Century Academic Librarian." *Acquisitions Librarian* 16: 149–162.

Lawrence, G. S. 1981. "Cost Model for Storage and Weeding Programs." *College & Research Libraries* 42: 139–47.

Lucker, J. K., and S. J. Owens. 1986. "Weeding Collections in an Academic Library System: MIT (Massachusetts Institute of Technology)." *Science & Technology Libraries* 6: 11–24.

Lugg, Rick, and Ruth Fischer. 2008. "Future Tense—The Disapproval Plan: Rules-Based Weeding & Storage Decisions." *Against the Grain* 20: 74–76.

Maskell, Cathy, Jennifer Soutter, and Kristina Oldenburg. 2010. "Collaborative Print Repositories: A Case Study of Library Directors' Views." *Journal of Academic Librarianship* 36: 242–49.

McGowan, Beth. 2011. "Weed, Yes! Discard, No! There May Be a Collection in That Trash!." *Community & Junior College Libraries* 17: 87–90.

Metz, Paul, and Caryl Gray. 2005. "Public Relations and Library Weeding." *Journal of Academic Librarianship* 31: 273–79.

Phillips, R. 1990. "Weeding the Books at Taylor University." *Christian Librarian* 34: 4–6.

Reed, L. L. 1993. "Weeding: A Quantitative and Qualitative Approach." *Library Acquisitions* 17: 175–82.

Slote, Stanley J. 1997. *Weeding Library Collections: Library Weeding Methods.* Englewood, CO: Libraries Unlimited.

Soma, Amy K., and Lisa M. Sjoberg. 2011. "More Than Just Low-Hanging Fruit: A Collaborative Approach to Weeding in Academic Libraries." *Collection Management* 36: 17–28.

Thomas, William Joseph, and Daniel L. Shouse. 2012. "Rules of Thumb for Deselecting, Relocating, and Retaining Bound Journals." *Collection Building* 31: 92–97.

Tillman, H. N. 1988. "The Politics of Weeding." *Education Libraries* 13: 16–19.

William, Mick. 2007. "Weeding the Circulating Collection." *Christian Librarian* 50: 59–60.

6

WEEDING THE COLLECTION: PERSPECTIVES FROM THREE PUBLIC LIBRARIANS

Merle Jacob, Sue O'Brien, and Bonnie Reid

In building and maintaining library collections, the evaluation of the materials already owned is as important as the selection of new materials. By periodically reviewing what should be retained, discarded, or repurchased, the librarian keeps the collection responsive to patrons' needs, ensures its vitality and usefulness to the community, and makes room for newer materials. Although materials are selected on the basis of reviews, examination, and subject need, the value of these materials changes over time. Knowledge is not static. Materials become dated because of a change in the facts, conditions, format, or viewpoint reflected in them. The physical condition of books and audiovisual materials also deteriorates over time and with use, thus making them unusable. The collection should also change when the community that uses it is no longer interested in certain subjects, authors, or audiovisual formats. Librarians must recognize that public libraries are not archives.

Weeding becomes even more essential as more physical space in libraries is devoted to meeting rooms, public computers, and technology labs. As parts of the collection such as magazines, reference books, and even best sellers become digital, the print collections may need to be weeded extensively. By weeding these materials, a collection remains fresh and relevant to user needs, or as Ezra Pound (1934) in the *ABC of Reading* said, "The weeder is supremely needed if the Garden of the Muses is to persist as a garden" (17).

REASONS TO WEED

Studies of weeding practices in all types of libraries by Kathleen Joswick and John Stierman (1993), F. W. Lancaster (1993), Stanley Slote (1997), and others show the many benefits of weeding. Some of the most important benefits include the following:

- Relevance—The collection better reflects the community's needs and interests.
- Reliability—Removing out-of-date and unreliable information ensures patrons get accurate information.
- Currency—Information is up to date.
- Value of materials—Collections must reflect changing communities and tastes.
- Appeal—Removing worn and unattractive materials makes the collection physically appealing to patrons.
- Circulation or turnover rate—Circulation increases because patrons can more easily browse less-crowded shelves and turnover rates goes up.
- Accessibility—Library staff can locate materials faster and reshelf more quickly.
- Space—Weeding unattractive, underused, and out-of-date materials makes room for new materials and gives the librarian the room to promote materials.
- Awareness—Staff who weed understand what is used, what is missing, what is needed, and what gaps are in the collection.
- Balance—Without weeding, new materials can be overwhelmed by older titles, and important older relevant works are often lost in the collection.
- Feedback—Weeding and evaluation of the collection lets librarians give continuous feedback to superiors who can budget for the long-range needs of the collection (Jacob 2001).

OBSTACLES TO WEEDING

Despite the benefits of weeding, many librarians find weeding or deselection difficult to do. Librarians look at books as the transmitters of knowledge and are upset by the idea of removing a carefully chosen book. There is also fear of being called a book burner or destroyer of knowledge by patrons or colleagues. Other librarians fear they will make a mistake and weed a book someone may want. Librarians also resist weeding as they equate quantity with quality because official emphasis in the library world is often based on the collection size. Finally, given all the other pressures of work, there never seems to be the time to weed. When collections have not been weeded in many years, the task of weeding can seem daunting. Because weeding may not be discussed in library school, many librarians do not know where or how to begin the task.

GETTING STARTED

Before starting to weed, be sure you understand your library's mission and goals and the community being served. By looking at the library's mission statement and collection development plan, you can see how the collection should be developed and set appropriate guidelines. By using reports, statistics, and observation, you will understand who lives in the community, who is and is not using the library, and how the community has changed or is changing. Knowing the community allows you to develop collection goals and make weeding decisions that enhance the collection. Next, using reports from your integrated library system (ILS) and special weeding programs will help determine what should be weeded, kept, or replaced. Looking at reports on usage statistics, turnover rates of subject areas, dusty book reports, lost book lists, interlibrary requests, and publication dates of subjects will help determine what to weed. Then walk the shelves to see the condition of the materials and what areas need weeding the most. Examine placement of the materials and signage to understand if materials are not circulating due to one or more of the following factors: They are not visible to patrons; they are difficult to reach or remove from overcrowded shelves; or they are in poor physical condition. Finally, be aware of the schools, book groups, and community organizations that the library serves and understand the types of materials and subjects these constituencies need, as the library may need to shift resources from print materials to eBooks, databases, and audiovisual formats and from one subject area to others to better serve them.

After you gather all of this information about the collection, you will want to enlist the support of the administration, and make staff aware of the information you have gathered so that they too understand and support the weeding project. It is also important to talk to the technical services department staff to understand how many books they can process for deselection each week, and how quickly they can reorder needed replacements, so the staff are not overwhelmed. Have the technical services staff set up clear guidelines on what books can and should be repaired as it often costs more to repair a book than to buy a replacement. With all of this knowledge, you can then start to set the guidelines for weeding since no single weeding standard can be used for each subject and format in the library.

CRITERIA FOR WEEDING

Items may be weeded for condition, use, or content. To weed by condition, check the physical condition of the book. Weed books that have yellow, brittle, torn, marked, stained, or missing pages. Damaged books or books with broken bindings and paperbacks with tattered covers should also be removed from the collection. Unattractive extra copies of books that are no longer in high demand should be weeded. Damaged books that no longer have current information or are earlier editions of titles should also be removed. If a book still circulates, and is in good condition except for a broken spine, it may be sent to the bindery. Fiction books still relevant to the collection but in poor condition should be replaced with new copies, in paperback if the hardcover is no longer in print. For nonfiction books, replace the book with a new copy or with a similar book on the same topic.

Books may also be weeded for lack of use. Studies have shown that the way a book has circulated in the past may indicate the way it will circulate in the future. To help determine use, computer systems can generate reports, including the last date a book circulated and the number of times it circulated. Pick a date, such as within the past five years, and get a report of those titles that have not circulated in that time period. The drawback to only using circulation records is they cannot tell you whether the book was used in-house. Patrons may copy material from a book or read it in the library. Stanley Slote (1997) recommends setting up a system to mark books found on tables before they are re-shelved, so in-house use will also be recognized. This system also helps determine whether to keep reference books. However, the amount of dust on the tops of the books is a big tip-off for showing lack of use.

Determine the appropriate cutoff date. Has the book circulated in the past two years, three years, or five years? Choose the cutoff based on the type of material and the goals for the collection. There may be items that have not circulated that you decide to keep—books on local history, books by local authors, classics, or holiday music. Remember, weeding is a professional judgment; standards should be adjusted to fit the needs of each library and its patrons. Items that still circulate should also be reviewed. Even though a medical book circulates, if it contains out-of-date information, it should be weeded.

Weeding by content resurfaces all the factors that were initially considered in selecting the material. Look at the other books on a subject and decide whether the item still belongs in the collection, whether there are newer, more current titles in the collection, whether there is a newer edition of the book, or more current books available to purchase. Standard lists and bibliographies such as *Public Library Core Collection: Nonfiction* and *Fiction Core Collection* (two H. W. Wilson databases available via EBSCO) are available to help in making weeding decisions. Lists of award-winning books are also helpful. Collection development articles in *Library Journal* include the best books in a given subject area. It is also important to include titles that represent a balance of viewpoints on subjects such as religion or the social sciences.

It is important to weed out-of-date titles, especially in areas such as medicine, science, law, and finance. Weed superseded editions, outdated textbooks, titles with out-of-date language, photographs, or illustrations, and ephemera such as celebrity biographies, as well as duplicate copies of older best sellers, both fiction and nonfiction, and out-of-date study and test guides, and travel books.

Keep books of local history and books by local authors. Retain older editions in areas such as auto repair and appliance repair. Keep classic authors and titles, both fiction and nonfiction. Nonfiction classics include travelogues, history, and science books such as Rachel Carson's *Silent Spring*. Replace worn copies of classics with fresh copies.

SUGGESTED WEEDING PROCEDURES

- Run ILS reports on books that have not circulated, missing books, most circulated titles, and last checkout date, to help in setting up weeding guidelines.
- Set up clear guidelines on the condition of books to be weeded, the dates of inactivity to consider, and what can be mended.
- If necessary, consult subject specialists such as the American Medical Association (AMA) to help decide on what to weed.
- Work with your director to determine how you will explain the weeding project to the public and other staff members.
- Schedule a regular time for staff to do weeding each week. Weed in two-hour periods. Set up a yearly schedule so that the entire collection is weeded once every two to three years.
- Break the collection down into manageable portions. First weed those areas that need immediate attention because they are overcrowded or outdated.
- Have the shelves dusted and put in order before each section is weeded.
- Gather the equipment you will need: a book truck, Post-it notes for labeling books for disposal or repair, notepad and pen, bibliographies you are using as guidelines for what to keep or weed.
- Study the shelves one book at a time and look at the books for the following conditions:

  ○ Is the information dated, misleading, or inaccurate?
  ○ Is the book worn, tattered, yellow with age, or marked up? Is the spine damaged?
  ○ Is this edition superseded by a newer edition or by a much better book on the subject?
  ○ Is this book on a trivial subject that is no longer popular or requested?
  ○ Is this a book that has no place in your collection because of lack of community interest, subject matter, or reading level?

- For each book you weed, decide whether it should be discarded or put in a book sale. Destroy books with outdated information such as medical, science, financial, tax, and test books. The AMA recommends that all outdated medical books be destroyed.
- Keep a list of subjects, authors, or specific titles that have been discarded and need to be replaced.

- Create displays for high-quality books that have not circulated well, to determine whether exposure will generate use.
- After weeding, shift the books so that each shelf has some empty space at the end. Use this space to market books by placing them front side out.
- Discuss with your director what should be done with weeded materials since every municipality has different rules about public property disposal. If books can be sold, have annual sales or ongoing sale shelves in the library. Other books can be donated to organizations that can use them. Independent book sellers may be willing to purchase weeded titles, depending on the content and condition. Look for recyclers in your area who will take books that need to be destroyed. Do not put discarded books in your dumpsters as patrons may see this and become concerned about the disposition of the books.
- Remember, all mistakes can be corrected; keep repeating to yourself, "I can't keep it all. I'm not the Library of Congress."

FICTION WEEDING GUIDELINES

Theoretically, fiction books may be read and enjoyed years after they were written, and some still are. However, in reality, many fiction books, especially former best sellers, become dated. When an author dies and new titles are no longer being published, his or her books languish on the shelves. Trends also change in fiction. For example, the gentle romantic suspense titles of the past have been replaced by sexier, harder-edged stories, leaving many of the older titles sitting on the shelves. Classic and local authors should be kept. However, remember that a classic in one library may not be a classic in another library. As communities change over time, the collection should change to reflect the current population. Finally, in most libraries there is only so much space, so the fiction collection needs to be weeded to make room for new titles. Plus, weeding makes it easier for patrons to browse the shelves.

First of all, decide on a cutoff date based on the goals set for weeding the collection. Next, run a report from your ILS and pull the books that haven't circulated after that date. Check to see if the item is part of a series or a trilogy. KDL (Kent District Library) *What's Next* (ww2.kdl.org/libcat/whatsnext .asp) is a great source to determine whether a title is part of a series, trilogy, and so forth. Keep all parts of a series or trilogy; if most of the series doesn't circulate, remove the entire series or all volumes of a trilogy.

Check *Fiction Core Collection* or similar resources to see if a title is included and consider keeping it unless the book hasn't circulated for a number of years, in which case it should be withdrawn.

Check to see if the library owns other copies of the title. If so, keep the nicer-looking copy. If the library owns two copies of an item, check to see if both circulated at the same time. If not, withdraw one of the copies. Also withdraw any missing copies at this time to clean up the database.

While weeding, use the opportunity to replace any unattractive-looking copies of classics as well as genre and literary titles that are still popular with patrons. Also purchase new copies of books that librarians like to include in displays or are favorites likely to be suggested to patrons in readers' advisory interactions.

Weed mass-market fiction and nonfiction paperbacks rigorously since these are ephemeral titles meant for browsing. Paperback originals in genres such as romance, science fiction, mystery, or fantasy should be weeded using the criteria defined for fiction.

NONFICTION WEEDING GUIDELINES

When weeding the nonfiction collection in the public library, the librarian will most often look at the age of the item, the currency of the information, and interest in the topic by the community. What follows is a summary of weeding recommendations in specific nonfiction areas: they should be changed to reflect your collection and community needs.

000

Encyclopedias and directories—Withdraw encyclopedias five or more years in age. Weed superseded directories.

Computers—Weed computer titles after three years, although you may want to keep a few older titles for patrons with older computers and programs.

100

Philosophy and psychology—Weed self-help and pop psychology titles after the fad is over. Weed psychology books that have outdated ideas on topics such as homosexuality.

200

Religion—Make sure major trends and issues as well as basic material on most religions are retained.

300

Sociology—Keep collection balanced with books that present a diversity of lifestyles and a diversity of thought on controversial issues. Keep classic titles if possible. Weed titles that don't reflect current understanding and treatment of social problems.

Political science—Keep titles on current political topics for five years. Keep citizenship books and test guides current.

Economics, jobs, and careers—Investment, personal finance, job search, and resume-writing titles age rapidly; weed after five years. Titles on taxes can be discarded after three years.

Law—Keep only newest edition of legal titles.

Military—Keep histories of the military, wars, and equipment as condition and use dictate.

Education—Keep only the latest edition of test preparation books, directories of colleges, and guides to financial aid. As tests such as the GED and the SAT are totally revised, withdraw all previous editions.

Customs and etiquette—Weed etiquette titles after five years. Keep titles on the history of individual holidays as needed.

400

Language—Keep English and foreign language dictionaries up to date; weed after 10 years.

500

Science—Since information in all areas of science (except mathematics) changes rapidly, weed titles 5–10 years old. Be aware of major changes in knowledge and weed aggressively in that instance. Keep math titles with older teaching methods as well as newer methods. Keep classics such as Darwin's *The Origin of Species*.

600

Medicine—Since information in medicine changes rapidly, weed often and rigorously. Groups such as the AMA and American Dental Association recommend keeping titles on health, medicine, nutrition, and diet for three years. Fad diet books can be weeded as interest declines. Alternative medicine titles should also be kept up to date. Destroy all other medical, diet, and nutrition books rather than selling or giving away.

Technology—This area rapidly changes; most materials are outdated in 5–10 years. Keep histories of and repair manuals for cars, as well as titles on TVs and appliances, depending on use and condition.

Gardening—Weed books that are more than 10 years old.

Pets—Weed on condition and use. Keep a variety of breed books.

Cookbooks—Discard older titles as newer ones on the same subject are published. Keep older titles by well-known authors (Julia Child, etc.). Cookbooks on special diets can be weeded after three years.

Home repair—Weed titles 5–10 years old as techniques, products, and taste in design change.

Fashion and grooming—Weed grooming and fashion books older than five years as styles change rapidly.

Business—Weed business titles after five years. Keep classic business authors and titles on management theory.

700

Art, architecture, and drawing—Weed older titles without color illustrations. Keep representative titles on major artists and movements and titles on local architecture. Keep drawing technique books up to date.

Crafts and interior decoration—Keep basic histories of furniture, antiques, and collectibles. Withdraw superseded editions of price guides. Weed interior decoration titles after 5–10 years as tastes and illustrations change. Patrons may still want older titles on crafts such as knitting, quilting, and crocheting; keep as usage dictates.

Photography—Techniques and equipment change rapidly, so weed most titles after 5–10 years. A few older titles may be kept for patrons having older equipment.

Music—Basic histories, biographies, and songbooks of music date slowly, so weed on condition and use of the title. Titles on popular music date rapidly; weed after popularity fades.

Sports—Weed out-of-date books on sports techniques and coaching, especially look at the equipment used to see if it is current or outdated. Keep books on local and regional sports teams and personalities.

800

Literature and drama—Many titles continue to be relevant regardless of age so weed judiciously. Depending on the depth of your library collection, anthologies of poetry, plays, speeches, and quotations can be retained unless condition and usage dictate weeding.

900

Travel and geography—Weed travel guides that are more than three years old. Weed atlases after three years or when names of countries or major boundary changes occur. Consider keeping historical atlases as newer editions may eliminate older maps. Weed outdated and biased views of peoples of the world. Keep classic travel titles if usage warrants.

Genealogy—Retain titles that include current methods and sources for genealogical searching. Directories of sources and organizations should be kept current. Keep family and area histories as long as space allows.

History—Titles may remain useful regardless of age. Weed books with dated views and inaccurate facts. Weed books about countries that are more than 5–10 years old. Weed superseded editions of textbooks and historical works. Maintaining a collection with a variety of interpretations on a period or event is important.

Biography—Weed titles on individuals as they fade from interest.

FOREIGN LANGUAGE GUIDELINES

Weed foreign language titles using the guidelines for English language books.

MAGAZINES AND NEWSPAPERS GUIDELINES

Weed after two to five years unless you are archiving. Use, space needs, and availability online should be considered and may dictate weeding decisions.

REFERENCE GUIDELINES

Use, currency, and timeliness are key criteria to consider when weeding. With the availability of online titles, it may not be necessary to maintain a large print reference collection. Weed print copies when available online or reclassify to circulating collection if better used by patrons out of the library.

AUDIOVISUAL WEEDING

Audiovisual material should also be weeded for condition, use, and content. When weeding audiobooks, keep unabridged copies over abridged copies. Otherwise use the same criteria as weeding fiction or nonfiction books.

Weed extra copies of music CDs if both copies do not circulate simultaneously. A title may not appear on a weeding report since both items may have circulated within the stipulated time period, but one may safely be withdrawn if their circulations do not overlap. Look at all the music CDs owned by a particular group. Some will be more popular than others; weed the less popular ones. Greatest hits CDs are very popular and should be kept.

Take seasonality into account. Christmas music may not have circulated since the last holiday; Martin Luther King, Jr.'s speeches may not have circulated since Martin Luther King Day.

There may be very little to weed in the movie or TV show DVD collection since often virtually everything circulates well, and every TV show is someone's favorite. Nonfiction DVDs are also very popular. Consider weeding titles that haven't circulated in a year. Weed nonfiction DVDs using the nonfiction subject guidelines. In some cases, use timeliness and accuracy rather than circulation figures since DVDs will often still circulate even though they may be out of date.

When is it time to weed an entire format, such as VHS tapes or audiotapes? You should weed an entire format when circulation drops off, when you are not able to buy the format anymore, or when you need the space for more popular collections.

DIGITAL COLLECTIONS

Most libraries' digital collections are relatively new. Staff should use the fiction and nonfiction guidelines when weeding digital collections. Since the library is not devoting physical space to online titles, fiction and popular nonfiction can be retained as long as usage continues. Online reference titles, including databases, should be evaluated for usage and currency and weeded accordingly. Vendors such as Overdrive and Gale can mask titles that are no longer being used or databases that are out of date from your circulation system so that patrons cannot see them, but the library still retains ownership of the items and can reinstate at any time. Removing unused items from the online circulating system makes it easier for patrons to find newer items in the digital collections.

CONCLUSION

Remember these are just guidelines. They have helped us decide what to pitch and what to keep, but you need to adapt them to your situation. Your goal is to have a good, well-rounded collection that your community will use. Give your books a chance by keeping them in good condition and marketing them to your public. The better your marketing, the more books will circulate and the less you will have to weed. Do remember that you will make mistakes—a week or two months after you've pitched a title, someone will come in and ask for it. You can always get a book though interlibrary loan for patrons or go into the out-of-print market where a book in good condition with a dust jacket can often be purchased very reasonably. Don't berate yourself; we all make mistakes, and we can't predict when someone will ask for a title. Using the knowledge you have of your community and where to go to find an answer will help you know what to weed. Finally, keep repeating this mantra "I can't keep it all. I'm not the Library of Congress."

REFERENCES

Jacob, Merle. 2001. "Weeding the Fiction Collection: Or Should I Dump Peyton Place?" *Reference & User Services Quarterly* 40 (3): 234–39.

Joswick, Kathleen E., and John P. Stierman. 1993. "Systematic Reference Weeding: A Workable Model." *Collection Management* 18 (1/2): 103–15.

Lancaster, F. Wilfred. 1993. *If You Want to Evaluate Your Library.* 2nd ed. Champaign, IL: University of Illinois, Graduate School of Library and Information Science.

Pound, Ezra. 1934. *ABC of Reading.* New York: New Directions, 1960 (orig. pub. 1934).

Slote, Stanley J. 1997. *Weeding Library Collections.* 4th ed. Englewood, CO: Libraries Unlimited.

SUGGESTED READING

Crawford, Scott. 2012. "At the Corner of Baker & Taylor: Librarians Embracing New Collection Software." *Booklist Online* (February 15, 2012).

Dilevko, Juris, and Lisa Gottlieb. 2003. "Weed to Achieve: a Fundamental Part of the Public Library Mission?" *Library Collections, Acquisitions & Technical Services* 27 (1): 73–96.

Gregory, Vicki L. 2011. *Collection Development and Management for 21st Century Library Collections: An Introduction.* New York: Neal-Schuman.

Greiner, Tony. 2007. *Analyzing Library Collection Use with Excel.* Chicago: American Library Association.

Gwinnett County Public Library. 2002. *Weeding Manual.* Chicago: Public Library Association.

Hibner, Holly, and Mary Kelly. 2010. *Making a Collection Count: A Holistic Approach to Library Collection Management.* Oxford, UK: Chandos Publishing.

Hoffmann, Frank, and Richard J. Wood. 2005. *Library Collection Development Policies: Academic, Public and Special Libraries.* Lanham, MD: Scarecrow Press.

"Innovation Goes POW: Paperless Online Weeding." 2011. *Library Journal* 136 (12): 19–20.

Jacob, Merle. 2001. "Weeding the Fiction Collection: or Should I Dump Peyton Place?" *Reference & User Services Quarterly* 40 (3): 234–39.

Larson, Jeannette, and Belinda Boon. 2008. *CREW: A Weeding Manual for Modern Libraries.* Austin, TX: Texas State Library and Archives Commission.

Moroni, Alene E. 2012. "Weeding in a Digital Age." *Library Journal* 137 (15): 26–28.

Penniman, Sarah, and Lisa McColl. 2008. "Green Weeding: Promoting Ecofriendly Options for Library Discards." *Library Journal* 133 (15): 32–33.

Slote, Stanley J. 1997. *Weeding Library Collections.* 4th ed. Englewood, CO: Libraries Unlimited.

Vnuk, Rebecca. "Weeding Tips." *Booklist Online* (Ongoing series, bimonthly: April 20, 2012, June 15, 2012, August 22, 2012).

Wilson, A. Paula. 2004. "Weeding the E-Book Collection." *Public Libraries* 43 (3): 158–59.

7

EDUCATION FOR COLLECTION DEVELOPMENT AND MANAGEMENT

John M. Budd

INTRODUCTION

Is collection development an unnecessary function in libraries at this time? Are the practicalities of building physical collections handled in ways that no longer require judgment on the parts of professional librarians? If the answers to these questions are yes, is there any need to require a course in collection development or collection management in educational programs? The asking of the questions in this way presume something: the actions of the profession of librarianship influence (if they do not determine) curricular decisions in graduate programs. A different presumption is possible: educational programs decide on curricular matters independently, at least to a considerable extent, from professional practice. The examination here will not address that last issue, save to say that the ideal of all education for professional action should be symbiotic. That is, close attention by professionals to present and future needs of practice and forecasts of thoughtful educators should be essential components of a dialogue. The fruits of that dialogue could inform both practice and programs' content. In fact, the resolution of educational issues should probably follow Jürgen Habermas's discourse ethics. Curricular decision making is an area that appears to be readymade for Habermas's program. For one thing, the deliberations of a faculty must avoid a pitfall observed by Habermas (1993): "our way of using language can no longer serve as an unbiased witness, since it is already informed by an outlook that limits the rational to the sphere of purposive action" (20). It is easy to fall into a trap of accepting the language we use as logical, rational, and objective. It may well be the case, though, that considerations of things such as curricular matters are influenced by deeply ingrained (so ingrained that may no longer be conscious) bias or ideology.

An open discussion of the serious matters of curriculum should stand upon some ground rules, including a commitment to open discourse, to fair access by everyone not only to what is said but also to the underlying rationale, and to opportunities to question premises and assumptions. These conditions may sound easy to meet, but the entrenchment of opinion and belief can be so deep as to conceal that which lies below the surface of stances that are advocated by some. Habermas (1993) provides a strategy that can be employed in the course of deliberation on matters of importance: "Every justified truth claim advocated by someone must be capable of being defended with reasons against the objections of possible opponents and must ultimately be able to command the rationally motivated agreement of the community of interpreters as a whole. Here *an appeal to some particular community of interpreters will not suffice*" [emphasis added] (53). For Habermas, discourse ethics is not possible unless all parties who could have an interest in the outcome have a place at the table. Moreover, discussion must be open, in the sense that no person or group can silence any others. Perhaps the most important element of his idea is that reason must be the governing mechanism. Every stance, every position, every argument requires rational claims that can be evaluated by means of logical analysis that is empty of attack or vituperation.

DISCOURSE ETHICS IN ACTION

This strategy begs for some elaboration. As a hypothetical exercise, assume that the faculty of an American Library Association (ALA)–accredited master's program is revisiting the makeup of required, or core, courses. They may state at the outset that the core courses should be comprised of the common body of knowledge, skills, and values that every graduate of their program should possess. Some faculty argue that books and print serials are diminishing in number and importance in libraries and to user communities, so a course on collection development and management does not comprise a component of the common core. The faculty's discussion is limited to an in-house conversation, so no representatives from graduates of the program or employers of graduates are at the table. The rationale may be based primarily on polemical pieces in the professional literature that state books and libraries are no longer relevant in society.

As part of this hypothetical, let us assume that the discussion does not include topics such as the pricing and licensing of electronic access to information, the complexity of libraries opening their collection management to eBooks, audiobooks, and emerging technologies as a means of meeting user needs. The discussion also omits the thorny matter of evaluation of collection use, access, information services that depend on the formal provision of mechanisms to which users can avail themselves. In short, there are discursive communities that have not been included. What, for example, would employers tell the faculty? If their message would run counter to the assumptions made by the faculty, the ultimate decisions might end up quite differently. It must be emphasized here that the foregoing is a hypothetical; a different set of assumptions, plus the inclusion of other discursive communities, could have very different results.

The how of curricular decision making is largely opaque to anyone outside a given university's educational program, and that is usually intentional. The University of Alabama's School of Library and Information Studies states that its mission includes developing "leaders for the information world through a supportive teaching and learning environment, collaborative research, and community engagement" (http://slis.ua.edu/vision-and-mission/). Curricular priorities are to be aligned with the vision, mission, and directions. External entities, including representatives from the profession, are not mentioned. On the other hand, Florida State University's Mission, Vision, Values, and Goals statement includes as a goal, "To foster commitment through active growth and ongoing engagement in professional associations and the literature of the field" (http://slis.fsu.edu/about/mission/). The University of Oklahoma also states that one of its goals is to "encourage participation in professional activities and organizations at the School, university, state, national, and international levels" (http://slis.ou.edu/vmgo). While the latter two institutions make some claims about involvement in professional activities, it is not readily evident how these ideals translate into specific curricular manifestations. Many, if not most, programs have some sort of advisory group, and those groups usually include practicing professionals (and frequently include employers). It is quite likely that curricular considerations are reviewed by members of these groups. In short, educational programs are probably making curricular decisions with the advice of some professionals (although it is impossible to ensure such participation). Some philosophers dismiss Habermas's discourse ethics as ideal, and not pragmatic. The critics misunderstand just what American pragmatism (which Habermas draws from) is, and how it can be applied to affect meaningful decisions about such things as curricula. The requirement of reason and openness is fundamental to decision making that has the best opportunity for acceptance and for effective implementation.

WHERE CURRICULA STAND

There are still few, if any, overt indications about the details of faculty deliberations. Also, there are always going to be competing considerations when decisions are to be made. No program wants to have too many required courses; students would not be able to create specializations by means of taking elective courses. That said, programs and their faculty do have to make decisions about requirements—courses, course content, student learning experiences, and so forth. The state of the requirement of collection development and management as a discrete course can be assessed. As of the fall of 2012, only 11 (of 56 programs whose curricula could be examined) listed a course on collection development and management as a requirement. Two additional programs included this kind of course as components of groups of requirements (i.e., as possible choices that could fulfill requirements). For the most part, this status quo has defined curricula for the past several years. Investigation using the Internet Archive (the "Wayback Machine," http://archive .org/web/web.php) reveals that three programs did recently require a collection development and management course (two in 2006 and one in 2004). Granted, the coverage available via this source is sketchy, so some additional programs may have offered the course as a requirement.

While the course is, in general, not required, the vast majority of programs do offer a course (or even additional related courses) as electives. Some syllabi are available for examination, and they provide indications about the content of courses and the topics to which students are introduced. The courses with some variation of the title, collection development, and management state that the coverage is intended to be introductory and not to delve deeply into specialized subject matter. While the indications are that the elective courses are introductory, there are prerequisites in several programs. Fifteen list a variety of prerequisites, most of which include the entirety of the program's core courses. Where not all core courses are prerequisite, the most common courses are an introduction to library and information science and/ or organization of information. There are no explicit rationales offered for the prerequisites; one can only presume that there is a perceived need for students to obtain some foundational knowledge prior to taking electives.

A few of the syllabi provide a bit more data related to content of courses, although few are accessible online. For example, some indicate whether there is a required textbook and, if so, which one is required. Five require Vicky L. Gregory's *Collection Development and Management for the 21st Century: An Introduction* (Neal-Schuman, 2011). Three require Peggy Johnson's *Fundamentals of Collection Development and Management*, second edition (ALA Editions, 2009). All of the available syllabi also list additional readings, almost all journal articles related to the specific course topics. The greatest amount of variability occurs within the actual content of courses. The content can be evaluated in two fundamental ways—course objectives and course topics.

The one point that must be emphasized regarding Tables 7.1 and 7.2 is that what is presented is descriptive; it is in no way prescriptive of what *ought* to be included in collection development and management courses. There will, though, be certain bodies of knowledge and skills that faculty members believe should be common to every student's experience. There are, one would suspect, some items in Tables 7.1 and 7.2 that many professional practitioners would expect, even hope, to find in courses. One indicator of expectations may

Table 7.1 Most Frequently Identified Course Objectives

Course Objectives	Frequency
Agency attributes	1
Acquisition of materials	1
Environments (libraries)	1
EResource management	1
Evaluation (collection and use)	3
Intellectual freedom	2
Issues in collection development and management	1
Policies (collection development and management)	3
Printed materials	1
Selection of materials	4
Web (scholarly)	1

Table 7.2 Most Frequently Stated Course Topics

Course Topics	Frequency
Academic libraries	1
Acquisition of materials	3
Allocation formulas	1
Budgets and budgeting	5
Collection-based assessment	3
Cooperation	3
Definition of collection	2
Digital collections	1
EResource management	4
Ethics	1
Intellectual freedom or censorship	4
Journals or serials	2
Multimedia materials	2
Open access	1
Outsourcing	1
Policy	4
Public libraries	1
Publishers or publishing	2
Scholarly communication	1
Use-based assessment	4
Vendors or jobbers	3

be found in "ALA's Core Competences of Librarianship," the final version of which was approved by ALA Council on January 27, 2009. The second competence, "Information Resources," addresses collection-based concerns directly:

2A. Concepts and issues related to the lifecycle of recorded knowledge and information, from creation through various stages of use to disposition.

2B. Concepts, issues, and methods related to the acquisition and disposition of resources, including evaluation, selecting, purchasing, processing, storing, and deselection.

2C. Concepts, issues, and methods related to the management of various collections.

2D. Concepts, issues, and methods related to the maintenance of collections, including preservation and conservation (http://www.ala.org/educationcareers/sites/ala.org.educationcareers/files/content/careers/corecomp/corecompetences/finalcorecompstat09.pdf).

The Core Competences are not intended to be exhaustive, but they represent fundamental knowledge, skills, and values that graduates of programs should possess. One observation that must be made is that, if the competences mentioned earlier are indeed considered by the ALA to be *core*, is there a reason why a small minority of accredited programs requires a course in collection development and management?

WHAT PROFESSIONALS SAY

Much of the literature on library collections and access to information focuses on academic libraries. Speculation may suggest that academic librarians have motivation (publishing requirements, tenure, rewards structures) to inquire into problems and to communicate their findings formally. There are some similarities between the challenges faced by academic libraries and public libraries. The course topics listed earlier indicate common concerns, such as the need for a collection development policy, selection and acquisition of materials, budgeting, intellectual freedom, and other things. Some courses also include digital and electronic resources; it is worth noting that not all syllabi mention these topics, though. There is no doubt that all libraries are facing decisions relating to electronic resources of several types, with emerging technologies to be considered as well.

The issues of concern are far-reaching and transcend the traditional topics that collection development and management has included. A curious phenomenon that becomes evident when the course documents are examined is the absence of challenges that have been present for years. Only two syllabi speak of journals or serials being covered in the courses. Journal price inflation has been afflicting libraries for decades, and one outcome of the rising prices has been the diminution of funds available for the purchase of books and other media. It would require minutely detailed information about the precise contents of the courses, but matters like the selection of materials being affected by financial shifts are not new issues. In particular, the fiscal issues have a large impact on decision making. For example, the state of allocation formulas in many libraries has altered over the past several years. The libraries are no longer able to assume that they will have a stable and substantive amount of money to devote to the automatic selection of materials. In other words, the old methods of selection and expenditure of funds no longer pertain: a different set of dynamics (and dynamics must be emphasized, since the structures are not what one would call stable) apply. A course concentrating on collection development and management, to prepare graduates to succeed in professional positions, must educate for flexible and nimble decision making.

Matt Goldner, of OCLC, spoke at the MidSouth eResource Symposium in 2011 and offered advice to the audience. Much of what he had to say applies beyond the academic environment; librarians everywhere should attend to his message. Ning Han (2012), in reporting on Goldner's presentation, stated,

> Goldner used the term "shell game" to imply how complex another aspect of e-resources collections is. This issue is all about who has what title this week. Librarians are aware of the fact that electronic titles are transferrable among different publishers. But sometimes the change in ownership happens too frequently for librarians to catch up. For example, a week ago, a particular title was a ProQuest title and this week, suddenly it becomes a Gale title—and notification of the change is non-existent or obscure. (164)

It may be likely that courses in accredited programs—required or electives—cover the licensing of databases and aggregators of information resources. It may even be that the financial element of the licenses is covered, but the extent to which the courses include the dynamics of which titles are included in which databases (or aggregators) is an open question. Again, if the genuine purpose of the courses in a program is to prepare graduates for success in the profession, the uncertainty should be a key component of education; presumptions among students of instability are unlikely.

Goldner presented another observation that librarians and educators should heed. While he spoke about academic libraries, the point applies equally to public libraries. As is indicated earlier, some courses include use-based assessment of collections. That could be as simple and straightforward as measuring circulation data and, perhaps, in-house use of materials. It may even include some evaluation of what is *not* used according to the traditional measures. Goldner, though, urged that librarians enter what he called the "user's workflow" to comprehend more completely the ways users learn, seek to become informed and entertained. The key point of the message is that waiting for potential users to come to the library (or purposely use resources) is

inadequate insofar as these potential users can benefit from enhanced awareness of the materials, access, and services provided by the library. The upshot
is that librarians should reach out to communities, both to inform potential
users of what is possible and to learn from potential users what they wish
were possible.

Goldner's latter point was illustrated in an organizational revision in a single library. Sarah C. Michalak (2012) couched the revision in terms of the
"outward facing library," a metaphor for embracing the community and its
needs in the totality of library operations. As she said,

> To change the way the [University of North Carolina] library builds collec-
> tions, reference and collection development merged, eliminating a formerly
> rigid organizational line between the two. This wasn't simply a merger on
> the organizational chart, but a fundamental change in the jobs of over thirty
> librarians. The library no longer has bibliographers; all Research and In-
> structional Services librarians now have selection responsibilities. In addi-
> tion, acquisitions budget lines were streamlined and pooled into five fund
> groups representing broad disciplinary areas such as social sciences, hu-
> manities and so on. A team of librarians representing multiple subjects now
> manages each fund. (415)

The example here is presented as illustrative; it may well be that libraries of
various sizes and types have adopted a similar organizational and managerial
tactic. In any event, the structural alteration represents a service shift and, indeed, an epistemological change regarding the libraries role in the lives of the
members of its user community.

Much more could be said about education for collection development and
management, especially regarding it in relation to practice, but, to conclude,
two features will be mentioned. One is the phenomenon of patron-driven acquisitions (PDA). In a very real sense, PDA is a kind of back-to-the-future
mode of operations. Decades ago the professional literature included discussions of just-in-case versus just-in-time provision of information resources
and services. At the present time libraries are developing technological responses to user desires that were not possible in, say, 1990. Kizer Walker
(2012) provided a succinct definition of PDA as "a service in which the selection of content for the library collection is placed directly in the hands
of library users" (126). It may be that the essential word in his definition is
content. Emphasis is not necessarily on a single medium or product; rather,
the content that works well for the user is a component of the activity. PDA
relies on some assumptions that need to be contemplated by professionals,
and that need to be presented in the courses of programs. Is it a panacea to
obtain budgetary challenges faced by libraries? Perhaps not. Technological
applications usually do not save money, but they may enhance services, thus
being more cost-effective. That cost-effectiveness measure is something that

must be included in both use-based and collection-based assessment. Since the service breaks with tradition, there may be unique variables associated with the evaluation of the service. As Michael Levine-Clark (2010) asks, will there be a substantive impact on the future of scholarly communication? PDA is not explicitly addressed in the course syllabi.

The second issue to conclude with is that of eBooks. Lest one think this medium is brand new, versions of it have been around since the concept of memex (Bush 1945). In the late 1990s NuvoMedia released the Rocket eBook. It is no longer manufactured; one might say it was ahead of the market for eReaders. For a tool like an eReader to succeed there must be content ready to be read. If the content had preceded the device, eReaders of more than a decade ago might have captured markets. As it was, purchasers of early eReaders had relatively few content options. At this time there are, of course, a number of devices that can be purchased and an enormous amount of content that can be downloaded. With the explosion of the market, libraries must be sensitive to demands that members of their communities will make. Observations such as those made by Pauline Dewan (2012) have indicated that, for the time being, print remains an effective and necessary medium, but eBooks are becoming both more ubiquitous and more popular with readers. Challenges facing the profession (and which should be introduced to students so that they are prepared to face them) include prohibitions placed on libraries by publishers: "In late February [2011], HarperCollins announced that its ebooks could be checked out by library patrons 26 times, after which a library would need to re-purchase the eBook in order to lend it out again to its patrons (again, for a maximum of 26 times). That 26-checkout limit begins today [March 7, 2011]" (Kellogg 2011). Another matter of concern associated with digitization and, ultimately, eResources available to readers is copyright. In 2011 the Authors Guild filed suit against the HathiTrust Digital Library initiative and several university libraries, claiming infringement of copyright. On October 10, 2012, a U.S. District Court Judge dismissed the lawsuit. This is yet another issue that is seeing rapid and profound developments of which students should become aware.

CONCLUSION

A final conclusion regarding education for collection development and management cannot be reached, given the absence of complete information about what is taught. Some tentative claims can be made, though. Since few programs require such a course, and given that the content is strongly recommended as core to educational programs by ALA, there are shortcomings. Perhaps the faculty of accredited master's programs do not believe this content is vital to students' education; again, access to discussions would be needed to render judgment. Of greater concern is that the demonstrable content of courses tends to adhere to traditions of practice that may not hold in a time of dynamic change. This conclusion is of particular concern given statements by practicing professionals that librarians are situated to effect changes in spheres that include technology, organizational restructuring, innovation of services, and advocacy for content accessibility for their communities. Insofar as these issues are covered in courses, master's programs are serving their students well. To the extent that they fall short, the entire profession should be concerned about present and future preparation of professionals in all environments.

REFERENCES

Bush, Vennevar. 1945. "As We May Think." *Atlantic* 176 (1): 101–108. Available at: http://www.theatlantic.com/magazine/archive/1945/07/as-we-may-think/303881/. Accessed January 8, 2013.

Dewan, Pauline. 2012. "Are Books Becoming Extinct in Academic Libraries? *New Library World*, 113 (1/2): 27–37.

Habermas, Jürgen. 1993. *Justification and Application: Remarks on Discourse Ethics*, trans. Ciaran P. Cronin. Cambridge, MA: MIT Press.

Han, Ning. 2012. "Managing a 21st-Century Library Collection." *Serials Librarian* 63 (2): 158–69.

Kellogg, Carolyn. 2011. "HarperCollins' 26-Checkout Limit on Libraries' Ebooks Starts Today." *Los Angeles Times*, March 7, 2011. Available at: http://latimesblogs.latimes.com/jacketcopy/2011/03/harpercollins-library-ebook-checkout-limit.html. Accessed January 8, 2013.

Levine-Clark, Michael. 2010. "Developing a Multiformat Demand-Driven Acquisitions Model." *Collection Management* 35: 201–7.

Michalak, Sarah C. 2012. "This Changes Everything: Transforming the Academic Library." *Journal of Library Administration* 52 (5): 411–23.

Walker, Kizer. 2012. "Patron-Driven Acquisition in U.S. Academic Research Libraries: At the Tipping Point in 2011?" *Bibliotek Forschung und Praxis* 36 (1): 125–29.

PART II

ACQUISITIONS

8

DEMAND-DRIVEN ACQUISITIONS: JUST IN TIME

Robert Alan

INTRODUCTION

Academic libraries have traditionally purchased books to support current and future research and curricular needs at their institutions. While user input has always been encouraged, libraries have often collected in excess to ensure that books were available to users just in case they were needed. Collecting in excess can also be attributed to concerns that trade and university press publications will go out of print sooner rather than later and be unavailable for purchase if needed in the future. Anderson (2011) believes that "the problem is that the current publishing marketplace evolved in an environment in which library customers had no choice but to buy lots of books and articles that they didn't need, because that was the only way to guarantee access to books and articles they did need."

Budgetary constraints combined with a growing culture of assessment have libraries more closely evaluating acquisition levels and collection use. Considering use as a primary measure of the value of a collection, studies have shown that just-in-case collection development models can result in low or no circulation for a significant percentage of print books over time. The landmark University of Pittsburgh study showed that 25 percent of monographs would not be used in 10 years and 50 percent of monographs would circulate once or not at all in a 10-year period (Kent 1979). The University of Arizona's reported use over a 10-year period has been approximately 60 percent for English-language materials (firm orders and approvals) and approximately 50 percent for approval books (Levine-Clark et al. 2009). An assessment of large approval plans at Penn State and the University of Illinois, Urbana-Champaign (UIUC) compared circulation rates for books received in fiscal year 2004/2005 over a five-year period following receipt (Alan et al. 2010). The results were comparable to the University of Arizona as the study found that 31 percent of Penn State's approval plan receipts did not circulate during the five-year study period at a cost of $217,382.70. Forty percent of UIUC receipts did not circulate at a cost of $164,339.50. Sinha (2011) suggests that low circulation of books can be linked to a collection-building philosophy "equating large collections with prestige and better economic times."

Traditional publication and acquisition models have publishers publishing new books and making them available to libraries and other prospective customers to either purchase directly from publishers or purchase more commonly from book vendors. Print and eBooks are purchased on a title-by-title basis, via approval plans, or in the case of eBooks in publisher and aggregator packages. One of the advantages of eBooks over print is that eBooks offer perpetual access, ensuring that titles will not go out of print and will be available for the long term.

The transition from print to eBooks combined with new technologies has allowed libraries, publishers, and vendors to reconsider traditional business models and develop new methods for acquiring and delivering eBook content to libraries and end users. One such model is patron driven acquisition (PDA) that directly involves end users in eBook purchase decisions at the point of use. The remaining chapter discusses Penn State University Libraries' implementation of a PDA just-in-time model.

PDA/DEMAND-DRIVEN ACQUISITION

Patron driven acquisition (PDA) and demand driven acquisition (DDA) have been considered to be one and the same. However, the NISO recently offered the following distinction as it currently works toward developing standard practices for PDAs (Levine-Clark 2012, 11).

- PDA: acquisition of library materials based on direct or indirect patron input, including faculty requests and analysis of collection usage.
- DDA: acquisition of library materials based on patron selection at the point of use.

For purposes of this chapter, DDA, as opposed to PDA, will be used to discuss patron-initiated eBook purchasing at the point of use.

Under the traditional upfront purchase model for books, the acquisition process essentially ends after books are received (or activated in the case of eBooks), paid for, and processed by the library. DDA is based on the deployment of new methods of providing eBook content to users and enabling purchases to be made based on a predetermined level of use by patrons using the library catalog. DDA allows libraries to present more eBook titles to users for potential use and purchase than is feasible under the traditional book purchase model. The cost to the library is incurred only when a book is used and ultimately purchased for the library. DDA challenges traditional monograph acquisition models by allowing libraries to allocate collection funds to pay for books acquired at the point of use rather than prior to use resulting in higher use for DDA titles at the time of purchase. Esposito (2012a) states:

> One way of viewing PDA [DDA] is that it is an attempt to manage the level of "waste" downward. If some books circulate rarely, circulate only years after they have been purchased, or don't circulate at all, how can a library acquire books that circulate with greater frequency, circulate as soon after they are acquired as is reasonably possible, and do in fact circulate in the first place?

In support of the DDA just-in-time purchase model studies have shown that user-selected titles can circulate at higher rates than librarian-selected titles. One study found that of 8,665 user-generated order requests, 78 percent circulated during a three-year study period (Reynolds et al. 2010). Price and McDonald (2009) found that user-selected titles were used twice as often (8.6 times per year vs. 4.3 times per year) than subject-selector-selected titles.

DDA does offer libraries an opportunity to better measure users' information needs and supplement, not necessarily replace, more traditional methods of selecting and acquiring eBooks. At this time DDA is being carefully evaluated by libraries, publishers, and vendors to determine its value and sustainability.

PENN STATE CONTEXT

The Penn State University system includes 23 campuses located across the Commonwealth of Pennsylvania. Penn State is organized as a single university, geographically dispersed, and therefore, all campus libraries are part of the University Libraries system. Campuses range in size from fewer than 700 students to more than 43,000 students at the University Park campus (administrative hub for the university system). Penn State's total enrollment in 2012 totaled approximately 84,000 students (both full time and part time) supported by over 6,000 faculty members. The university's rapidly growing virtual campus (called the World Campus) now supports an additional 11,000 students from around the world. Each of the 23 campuses maintains a library and collection to support campus research and curricular needs. Technical service operations for all campuses (with the exception of the law and medical schools) are centralized at the University Park campus.

eBooks fit nicely into the university libraries' strategic goal of increasing system-wide access to more digital resources as soon as possible. Penn State had acquired a significant number of NetLibrary eBooks (now EBSCO eBooks) through the Access Pennsylvania project since 2004, although the NetLibrary model was not well received by librarians or end users. The library also loaded large record sets for scholarly resources such as Early English Books Online (EEBO), eBook packages (e.g., Springer and Elsevier), as well as added catalog records for individual titles purchased from publishers and aggregators. In fiscal year 2008/2009 the availability and demand for eBooks increased and the eBook selection and acquisition process was integrated in the YBP (Yankee Book Peddler) Gobi3 workflow. Penn State has also relied heavily upon approval plans to acquire monographs since the 1990s, which subject selectors supplement with firm orders for print and eBooks. The YBP approval plan, managed at the University Park campus, is the largest of seven plans, and has supplied between 12,000 and 14,000 print books to the library over the past several years.

Duplication of print books across the multicampus system had been a costly issue at Penn State for many years. In fiscal year 2008/2009 the cost of duplication of print books was $307,566.51 (7,755 duplicates representing two or more copies). While some level of duplication can be justified due to user demand, a significant percentage of the titles had low or no circulation bringing the rationale for duplicate acquisitions into question. It was expected that a strategy of acquiring more eBooks and fewer print titles available would provide system-wide access to more resources and reduce the need to duplicate in print across campus locations.

DDA AT PENN STATE

Customer service has always been a significant driver in planning and decision making at Penn State. In 2009 Penn State Libraries convened an eBook task force to review current eBook publishing and distribution models and recommend library-wide policies and best practices. The task force investigated patron-driven initiatives in relation to the libraries' strategic goal of effectively supporting scholarship and research worldwide. One of the task force recommendations was to establish a patron-driven pilot project using EBL (Ebook Library).

Questions the task force addressed included the following:

- What range of books would appear in the library catalog? Initially, DDA titles would be selected based on a broad subject- and publisher-based profile with EBL. However, the development of an EBL/YBP DDA process based on the Penn State approval plan was thought to be a better approach for DDA title selection, as records for titles would be provided based upon preferred subject and content levels.
- How many (if any) short-term loans would be allowed prior to an eBook purchase? The task force recommended two short-term loans with the third use triggering the purchase. This suggestion was based on use and cost information gathered from comparable academic libraries that had already implemented DDA.

- What level of funding was needed to sustain the DDA pilot for one to two years? Funding DDA for the first year was problematic given our inability to predict the volume of rentals and purchases. Fortunately, end of year collection funds allowed the library to commit $350,000 to the project.

PENN STATE EBL/YBP DDA PILOT

Penn State was the beta test site for the EBL/YBP DDA pilot. The pilot began the last week of February 2011, and was scheduled to continue for at least one year, contingent on the rate of expenditure for short-term loans and purchases. There was an expectation that the pilot would need to continue for two years to gain sufficient data and user feedback to make informed decisions on the future of DDA at Penn State.

The initial record load included 9,500 titles with imprints from 2008 to 2010. The EBL-supplied records were brief catalog records lacking call numbers and subject headings. Unfortunately, the EBL titles were not de-duped against print and eBook titles already purchased through YBP, resulting in some duplication. EBL DDA records were manually removed from the catalog on a case-by-case basis (as duplicate titles were found). The EBL record load was followed by weekly loads of YBP DDA records that were primarily full-level records cloned from catalog records for the print equivalents and included call numbers and subject headings. As the program moved forward, the weekly YBP DDA loads averaged between 200 and 300 records.

DDA title selection was linked to an approval plan that consolidated the University Park subprofiles and campus slips plan to increase the number of DDA titles that would be of interest to both University Park (more scholarly content) and other campus locations (more general academic content). YBP sent title lists of DDA candidates, based on Penn State's approval profile and publisher information, to EBL on a weekly basis to determine if these titles would be available from EBL as DDA records. YBP also updated the records for these titles in Gobi3 with the note Probable DDA, meaning the titles fit the profile and had been sent to EBL to determine if an e-version would become available. Initially this was confusing to acquisitions staff and selectors, who were unsure whether to firm order the title. For some it was an initial lack of confidence in the DDA process and concern that titles needed in the collection would not be received, resulting in gaps in holdings. However, as the DDA implementation moved forward, concerns about Probable DDA diminished as most of those titles appeared as DDA records in the catalog within one to two weeks. Once the record was sent by YBP for loading into the catalog, a note and subaccount information was added to Gobi3—"EBL auto DDA record sent (9/2/2012)."

An important outcome of the DDA pilot was the need to carefully review titles that would have been received on approval but had either moved to DDA or a slip plan. There was an expectation that if a title that fit the approval profile had not been released as an eBook within a reasonable period of time following release of the print equivalent, the print would be sent to the library. Books were not always sent, however, resulting in approximately 600 books that were not received in print or included in the DDA plan. The library worked with YBP to identify the gap and retrospectively add the print books through the approval plan. As a result of this gap, the approval plan in several subject areas was changed to e-preferred for eBooks directly available from Oxford, Cambridge, Gale, and Wiley. This change will result in fewer DDA records being added to the catalog.

Feedback received from users indicated some level of dissatisfaction with the EBL platform and DRM (digital rights management) restrictions. These concerns carried over to other aggregators and publisher platforms as well—they were not unique to EBL. It appeared to be less a problem with the DDA model than how aggregators and publishers made the content available to end users. When DRM issues made the e-version of a title less useful, subject selectors could request removal of a DDA record from the catalog and firm order the print version or, if available, order the eBook directly from the publisher.

OUTCOMES

Initial concerns that users would purchase EBL DDA eBooks in excess and thus expend earmarked funds at a rapid rate did not materialize. From March 1, 2011, to October 1, 2012, a total of 27,429 DDA records were loaded into the catalog. Of the total records available to users, 841 titles (3.1%) were purchased at a cost of $87,280.13, averaging $103.78 per title. There were 3,349 short-term loans, costing $69,634.97 and averaging $20.81 per loan. The total expenditure on DDA purchases and short-term loans was $156,915.10 for the first 19 months of pilot, which was less than 45 percent of the initial $350,000 allocation. This allowed the DDA program to be adequately funded for at least a second year.

Concerns that titles purchased would primarily fall out of the scope of Penn State's collection also did not materialize. Titles purchased by users covered all subject areas with an emphasis on science and technology, which is a research strength at Penn State, with 323 titles purchased (38.4%). Approximately 60 percent of the content purchased by users was scholarly, 20 percent general academic, and 15 percent professional, with only 5 percent considered popular and basic. These results are also a reflection of the DDA titles supplied based on the approval profile that is weighted toward scholarly content.

CONCLUSION

At the same time that eBooks and DDA are becoming more widely accepted, academic library service models are changing. Questions we are addressing include what is the role of academic libraries in the 21st century? what are the roles of collections and collecting? and how shall we determine the value of collections (Dahl 2012)? The strategy of acquiring more digital resources and less print over time has allowed libraries to reconfigure space to support new services for students, faculty, and researchers. DDA can also be viewed as a new service that supports users' just-in-time needs, guarantees use of purchased content, and does not require storage space.

Sinha (2011) argues that selection may be an inefficient use of library resources given reduced collection budgets and the low use of book collections. There are concerns that DDA may make the subject selector in academic libraries unnecessary, since the user becomes responsible for selecting titles they need. However, that will not be the case at least for the foreseeable future. "The content available through patron-driven access programs, although valuable in fulfilling immediate need, is a small subset of what is published. An academic research library requires more content than current eBook aggregators can provide, just as it requires more content than a single domestic approval plan can provide" (Hodges, Preston, and Hamilton 2010, 219). Librarians will continue to be needed to serve as subject liaisons to their constituents and shape library collections and services. Henri (2012) argues that if we do away entirely with subject expert collection development, might that mean that users would only ask the library to purchase titles they know about, thus limiting their exposure to alternative ideas? As new courses and programs are offered, the library could be put in a position of not being able to respond just in time and need quickly to fill gaps in the collection at some expense to the library. Esposito (2012b) points out that while DDA plans may be implemented in many more academic libraries in the coming years, DDA cannot be implemented in a comprehensive fashion. Funds budgeted for DDA will likely continue to be a relatively small percentage of overall library collections budgets. At Penn State the DDA budget will average approximately 1 percent of the overall collections budget for fiscal years 2011–2013.

The just-in-time DDA model is still in its infancy and there is little data available to assess the pros and cons of the model. At Penn State, DDA assessment will eventually be part of an overall collection assessment program that is currently being developed. What future role, if any, will DDA at Penn State and other academic libraries play in helping to shape collections has yet to be determined. Stay tuned!

REFERENCES

Alan, Robert, Tina Chrzastowski, Lisa German, and Lynn Wiley. 2010. "Approval Plan Profile Assessment in Two Large ARL Libraries: University Illinois at Urbana-Champaign and Pennsylvania State University." *Library Resources & Technical Services* 54 (2): 64–76.

Anderson, Rick. 2011. "Is Selection Dead? The Rise of Collection Management and the Twilight of Selection." *Against the Grain* 23 (2). Available at: http://www.against-the-grain.com/2011/05/v-23-2-is-selection-dead-the-rise-of-collection-management-and-the-twilight-of-selection/. Accessed November 19, 2012.

Dahl, Candice. 2012. "Primed for Patron-Driven Acquisition: A Look at the Big Picture." *Journal of Electronic Resources Librarianship* 24 (2): 119–26.

Esposito, Joseph. 2012a, September 26. *PDA and the University Press*. Available at: http://scholarlykitchen.files.wordpress.com/2012/10/pda-and-the-university-press-5-2-final.pdf. Accessed November 19, 2012.

Esposito, Joseph. 2012b, May 8. "Sizing the Market for Patron-Driven Acquisitions (PDA)." *The Scholarly Kitchen*. Available at: http://scholarlykitchen.sspnet.org/2012/05/08/sizing-the-market-for-patron-driven-acquisitions-pda/. Accessed November 19, 2012.

Henri, Janine. 2012. *Crossing the Line into Patron-Driven Acquisitions in the Arts?* [Power Point slides]. Presented at the 40th Annual ARLIS/NA Conference: Colouring Outside the Lines, Toronto, Canada. Available at: http://www.arlisna.org/news/conferences/2012/ses_hot-henri-ppt.pdf. Accessed November 19, 2012.

Hodges, Dracine, Cyndi Preston, and Marsha Hamilton. 2010. "Patron-Initiated Collection Development: Progress of Paradigm Shift." *Collection Management* 35 (3–4): 208–21.

Kent, Allen. 1979. *Use of Library Materials: The University of Pittsburgh Study*. New York: Marcel Dekker.

Levine-Clark, Michael. 2012. *A Proposed NISO Work Item: Recommended Best Practices for Demand-Driven Acquisitions (DDA) of Monographs*. Proposal for Consideration by the NISO Voting Membership Approval Ballot Period: May 21–June 19, 2012. Available at: http://www.niso.org/apps/group_public/download.php/8559/DDA%20Work%20Item%20for%20Voting%20Member%20Approval.pdf. Accessed November 19, 2012.

Levine-Clark, Michael, Stephen Bosch, Kim Anderson, and Matt Nauman. 2009, November 4–7. *Rethinking Monographic Acquisition: Developing a Demand-Driven Purchase Model for Academic Books*. [PowerPoint slides]. Presented at the 2009 Charleston Conference: Necessity is the Mother of Invention, Charleston, SC. Available at: www.katina.info/conference/2009presentations/Fri2_Rethinking.ppt. Accessed November 19, 2012.

Price, Jason, and John McDonald. 2009. *Beguiled by Bananas: A Retrospective Study of the Usage & Breadth of Patron vs. Library Acquired eBook Collections*. Available at: http://ccdl.libraries.claremont.edu/cdm/singleitem/collection/lea/id/177. Accessed November 19, 2012.

Reynolds, Leslie, Carmelita Pickett, Wyona vanDuinkerken, Jane Smith, Jeanne Harrell, and Sandra Tucker. 2010. "User-Driven Acquisition: Allowing Patron Request to Drive Collection Development in an Academic Library." *Collection Management* 35 (3–4): 244–54.

Sinha, Reeta. 2011. "Is Selection Dead? The Rise of Collection Management and the Twilight of Selection." *Against the Grain* 23 (2). Available at: http://www.against-the-grain.com/2011/05/v-23-2-is-selection-dead-the-rise-of-collection-management-and-the-twilight-of-selection/. Accessed November 19, 2012.

9

HAM: A HYBRID ACQUISITIONS MODEL FOR PUBLIC LIBRARIES

Sian Brannon

DEFINING ACQUISITIONS

Acquisitions can mean so many things, and there are various ways to do it. Public libraries range in size and budget; therefore their concepts of acquisitions vary as well. When asked what it means to them, a librarian from a one-branch public library serving a small town of fewer than 20,000 people said, "when it comes to public libraries I think of [acquisitions] more as a collaborative process than an individual person. The receipt and processing of the material are handled by a mixture of professional and paraprofessional folk." A director of a four-branch system defines it as "the process of selecting, purchasing, and processing various materials and content to make available to the public." Finally, the head of technical services at a 22-branch system says that to her, acquisitions is "the complex, behind-the-scenes, migration of library material that begins as a thought in a public librarian's head through the placement of an order, to the eventual delivery of that material to the shelf."

There are also many formal definitions of acquisitions. In 1942, Tomlinson described an acquisitions department as "the part of a library which selects, orders, and accessions a book," with "accessioning" being "the act of recording a book in the accession book and of assigning the accession number to the book" (Tomlinson 1942, 7). A more modern, yet nebulous, definition is "the processes of obtaining books and other items for a library, documentation center or archive" (Prytherch 2000, 7). For some, though, acquisitions encompasses more. The *Online Dictionary for Library and Information Science* defines it as "the process of selecting, ordering, and receiving materials for library or archival collection by purchase, exchange, or gift, which may include budgeting and negotiating with outside agencies, such as publishers,

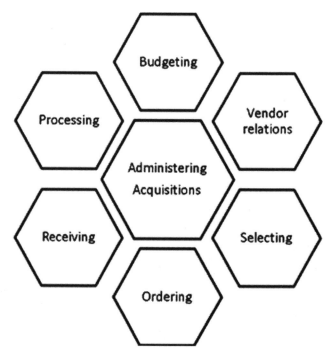

Figure 9.1 Acquisitions Components

dealers, and vendors, to obtain resources to meet the needs of the institution's clientele in the most economical and expeditious manner" (Reitz 2013).

For the purposes of this chapter, we will operationalize this last definition of acquisitions to include selection of materials, and exclude collection analysis for deselection. In discussion of various models of acquisitions, the process will encompass budgeting, working with vendors, selection, ordering, receiving, processing, and overall administration of the process. This is represented in Figure 9.1.

ACQUISITIONS MODELS

In order to provide current, relevant, and desired items (whether in print or electronic versions) to our constituencies, public libraries need to have an acquisitions system in place. Multiple models of acquisitions systems are available to public libraries. Depending on the size, staffing, and budget of the library, one model may work better than another. The four models are centralized, decentralized, outsourcing, and hybrid.

Centralized acquisitions can exist in all types of libraries, but is often seen as the method used in small public libraries with just one physical location and limited staff. In centralized acquisitions, all decisions and actions in the acquisitions cycle are made in one location, sometimes by just one or two people. The same person or department that selects materials also places the orders, handles the budget, and processes the accessioned items.

Decentralized, or local, acquisitions exists in two or more connected public libraries that are members of the same system, consortia, or county system comprising multiple, disparate locations. Decentralized acquisitions can also exist in a large public library with multiple departments, such as business, genealogy, and reference departments in a multilevel central library. When a library uses a decentralized acquisitions model, each component of the process is handled completely separately from each of the other branches, libraries, or departments within the system. In a decentralized model, there is no collaborative purchasing, consolidated budgeting, or unified processing.

Outsourcing for libraries means enlisting for-profit entities outside the physical library to do library-related functions rather than having in-house staff complete them. Common outsourced activities for libraries include janitorial work, security, and foreign-language cataloging, but for acquisitions most aspects of the process can be outsourced. Outsourcing acquisitions means having a vendor, or multiple vendors, take responsibility for the duties involved in the process. Essentially, you are centralizing your acquisitions but in a business outside of your public library. We can use vendors to create approval plans for selection, consolidate orders, choose opening-day collections for new branches, and process items to make them shelf-ready. It is possible that very small libraries could ostensibly have all of their selection, purchasing, and processing done by vendors. Just tell the vendor your budget, clientele, and processing needs and then let them take care of the process.

According to Wilkinson and Lewis (2003), outsourcing became more popular for libraries in the late 20th century, and the most popular outsourced acquisitions tasks are selection and processing. Outsourcing allows libraries to determine what could be done by an outside party, and thus refocus staff efforts on other core library operations. Its benefits may be outweighed, however, by negative implications on staff morale, and has been cited in the literature as a "sort of punishment when the management and the library staff encounter on-going friction in their personal relationships" (Alvin 1999, 263).

HYBRID ACQUISITIONS MODELS

An arrangement that works for many public libraries is to have a *hybrid* acquisitions model (HAM). In this case, the library system incorporates aspects of centralized, decentralized, and outsourcing models to fulfill its acquisitions needs efficiently and economically. Certain parts of the process are done centrally, some are handled by individual locations, and parts may be outsourced. Table 9.1 shows which functions in a hybrid acquisitions process are centralized, decentralized, outsourced, or integrated into some combination therein.

Table 9.1 Components of a Hybrid Acquisitions Model

Aspect of Acquisitions	Centralized	Decentralized	Outsourced
Budgeting	X	X	
Vendor relations	X	X	X
Selection	X	X	X
Ordering	X		X
Receiving	X		
Processing	X	X	X

Budgeting is done both centrally and locally. A designated department or person in a main location or administrative unit would have the responsibility of setting an overall materials budget, allocating money to various branches, locations, departments in a central library and other specialized collections funds. Even with a central materials budget, however, each designated location receiving funding would have some control over their designated monies in order to decide how much to spend on specialized materials. Designing budgets for materials selection is usually done by librarians and not outside vendors.

Vendor relations integrate how libraries locate, negotiate, communicate, and handle technical issues with the various companies and individuals who provide information resources and services to public libraries. In a HAM, most of this would be handled centrally. Again, a designated department or person in a main location or administrative unit would be the main contact for all vendors. This streamlines the communication channel for evaluation of the vendor's resources, ensuring correct description of technology requirements, and discussion of billing issues. On occasion, a public library in a consortia or county system may have the need for an individual relation with a vendor in order to procure a specialized resource or service. Also, in some periodicals systems, such as EBSCO Subscription Services or WT Cox Information Services, a public library can outsource those vendor relations, and have that vendor talk to multiple periodicals providers on the library's behalf.

Selection of materials would be handled centrally, locally, by outsourcing, or an amalgamation of the three. Centralized selection involves a few designated staff making group purchasing decisions for books, periodicals, and electronic resources on behalf of all branches or departments. Assuming most public libraries would want to have certain materials, such as best sellers, a general research database, or an updated World Book Encyclopedia, a central acquisitions department can identify these materials for ordering and do it in one place for multiple locations in a singular instance. On a local level, individual libraries or departments would need to order the items unique to their constituencies, such as foreign-language materials, a preponderance of children's or young adult materials, or genealogical resources. Selection can be outsourced by giving vendors a profile of what the library generally would like for their collections, and letting the vendors choose new materials without further library input.

In a HAM, the ordering of materials is either done by a centralized acquisitions staff or done by the vendors through approval plans and standing orders. Centrally, staff would receive all unique orders from various library locations and place them in addition to the general common selections mentioned in the previous paragraph. By placing all orders through a centralized model, larger orders can be processed at one time, thus giving the possibility of larger discounts, and increased efficiency in the tracking of orders and handling of issues. Outsourcing orders to vendors, in periodicals for example, frees up library staff to concentrate on other orders or functions such as reference or programming.

Receiving of materials involves the physical receipt of deliveries or the virtual receipt of electronic materials. Packages need to be opened, items need to be checked against invoices, and materials need to be checked against original orders. Receiving in a hybrid model would occur centrally, and involve the same benefits mentioned earlier—increased efficiency and handling of issues. Inputting materials data into an integrated library system in bulk is more efficient than having multiple locations do it, and reduces the potential for error. If there are errors in an order, such as missing items, damaged materials, or incorrect coverage in a database, vendors would prefer to hear from one location, rather than field the same issues from multiple staff. For a good list of receiving errors, see Chapman (2004).

The last part of the acquisitions cycle is getting materials ready for the public, or processing. After items have been received, they will be put through a series of steps to become ready for public library shelves. Processing varies according to library preference, and could therefore be done centrally, locally, or by vendors in a HAM. Initially, vendors can provide general processing tasks, such as affixing a barcode to each item, or putting a property stamp in a prescribed location. Centrally, the public library can expand on these general vendor-provided services to apply protective covers or applicable security devices. At each specific public library location, a special location sticker might be necessary, such as a designation for a new book shelf, or the library might wish to remove supplemental materials like CD-ROMs or workbooks for placement in a secured area. All of these functions are dependent on the decisions of the staff of the individual libraries.

CONSIDERATIONS FOR A HYBRID MODEL

Beyond the general overall facets of the acquisitions process, there are more things for public libraries to consider in a hybrid acquisitions model. There are aspects of selection, administration, reporting, assessment, procedure, and more that were discussed earlier.

Selection Considerations

In selecting materials, public libraries that work together in acquisitions, whether in the same system or not, need to determine how selection will work and coordinate related activities. Common ground needs to be established and communicated on many issues, such as the following:

- What subject areas overlap?
- Which can be handled by approval plans?
- What selection will be handled by centralized selectors?
- What librarians will have control over selection at their individual locations?
- What expert librarians at individual locations might be recruited to order centrally for certain collections, such as music CDs, foreign-language materials, or children's picture books?
- How will patron requests be handled? Will they be sent to a central ordering location for consideration by other selectors?
- How will interlibrary loan requests be incorporated into the selection process? Are they to be handled the same as general patron requests?

Gifts are another portion of selection for consideration. Individual libraries often received donations of materials from their customers and local entities. HAM libraries will need to decide the following:

- Can these be offered to other libraries for their potential selection? Are there other viable methods of gift disposition?
- If you dispose of gifts through an out-of-print dealer, how will earned funds be allocated?
- Do you want to send gifts to a vendor for processing?
- Does each library offer thank-you notes to donors? If so, do you want to handle these centrally?

Procedural Considerations

Many procedural pieces of the acquisitions process require deliberation, including types of orders, how electronic materials will be considered, and more. Some questions to keep in mind for a HAM include the following:

- Will rush orders of immediately needed materials be handled in a centralized or decentralized fashion?
- What processing needs of each library could be eliminated in order to have a vendor make everything completely shelf-ready?
- Are all involved library branches or departments utilizing the same formats of audiovisual materials? How can consolidation of these varying

formats be leveraged in order to negotiate the best discounts with vendors?

- Which location(s) or staff will be responsible for determining deadlines for order placement and budget encumbrance?
- Who will be responsible for coordination of the technology requirements of each location in order to provide electronic access to information?
- How do you want to handle trials of electronic resources?
- Can a central department manage all standing orders?
- Who has the authority to enter into contracts on behalf of all HAM entities?

Periodicals require special consideration, as multiple publishers and individual issues of each magazine can become burdensome and complex.

- Is there a print periodicals subscription vendor that will meet your multifaceted needs?
- Will all periodicals be delivered to and processed at one location, and then distributed to branches and departments? Or, can a vendor handle multiple destinations?
- Where will periodicals problems, like missed issues, be handled?
- Will you have an electronic preference for your periodicals? How will those be acquired? Centrally or locally?
- How will specialized magazines not available through a subscription vendor be ordered? Locally or centrally?
- Will a subscription vendor's service charge for subscription services be split evenly among branches and/or departments, or split based on number of subscriptions?
- Will selection of open access materials be done by individual departments or branches?
- What renewal cycle do you want?

Administrative Considerations

Two budgeting issues could arise for those adopting a HAM. The first is whether the allocations of funding will be done centrally, locally, or in a combined fashion. A completely centralized budget would be rigid and steadfast, with the central acquisitions staff designating exactly how much can be spent in each branch or department on each type of material. Giving local library departments or branches the authority to decide how to spend some of the funds may provide for a better collection development strategy overall.

The second area of budgeting to consider is who will administer, review, and report on the budget. Municipalities, city councils, mayors, and auditors have strict requirements and regulations surrounding fiscal activities. It may be hard to justify allocating control of funding to an outside vendor, and letting that vendor make purchasing decisions for the library. When materials budgets are decentralized in any form, an audit trail may be more difficult to document, and reconciling encumbered monies against expended monies becomes more difficult. A centralized budget allows for closer scrutiny and ease of monitoring. Finally, budget reporting done by multiple locations can be less efficient than that done by a centralized acquisitions staff.

Another large aspect of administering a HAM is personnel. Who, where, when, how—all involved parties must decide various things about staffing. Acquisitions tasks are done by librarians, paraprofessionals, part-time employees, and others (Evans, Intner, and Weihs 2011), and those employees can sometimes feel threatened by the idea of sharing their job duties with other libraries or vendors (Agee 2007). Public library staff must also be prepared to endure and get behind the changes that come along with implementation of a HAM (German 1999). Considerations for personnel include the following:

- What level of training or education or experience is necessary for each step in the acquisitions process? Can paraprofessionals handle them?
- Who will be assigned to which tasks?
- Who are the backups for these staff?
- Do all portions of the acquisitions process need to be *physically* centralized? Or, can ordering be done at one location, and receiving at another?
- What communication requirements are expected?
- From where will training be coordinated?
- Can volunteers be used for any parts of the acquisitions process? Centrally, locally, or both?

Administration of a HAM could include the use of an interagency agreement or a memorandum of understanding that states what each library branch or department is accountable for, and increase collaboration between them. It will delineate what libraries or staff are involved, exactly what the responsibilities of each are, the time period for the agreements, what payments may be involved, and who has the ultimate authority for relevant tasks.

Assessment Considerations

Public libraries assess all manner of their services. Librarians solicit feedback from their customers about satisfaction with summer reading clubs, customer service, and staff capabilities, and the adequacy of the library's collections. Also worthy of assessment are the internal processes and workflows. There will be a need at some point after the implementation of a hybrid acquisitions model to assess the effectiveness of the system thus far, and gauge the worth of continuing the acquisitions process in this manner. While materials budgets in public libraries are monitored constantly, the overall materials budget should be reviewed annually for appropriate allocation to participating libraries and departments in accordance with whatever protocol the library has in place. Some libraries utilize algorithms involving the average cost of materials and circulation statistics. Others may use enhancement programs to allocate money to special funds on a rotating basis.

Relationships with vendors also require evaluation. In a HAM, interactions with vendors are generally handled centrally in order to streamline the interactions, accurately report issues, and ensure that the correct information is relayed back and forth. HAM users will need to review vendor choices and gauge satisfaction levels of the vendor's customer service. Public libraries generally will be required to initiate a bidding process, or Request for Proposal, on a prescribed basis to update contracts and verify that money is being spent on the best available vendor option. Commonly assessed features of vendor services are delivery time of materials, comparison of discounts, accuracy in invoicing, and reliability in processing.

Selection procedures should be analyzed as collection development policies are reviewed. Selectors in a HAM must ensure they are working in accordance with prescribed policy. New staff with differing collection strengths may be available. A periodic assessment of selection procedures and selectors themselves will ensure that libraries utilizing a HAM are being as efficient as possible.

Ordering, receiving, and processing workflows certainly warrant regular assessment to maintain the efficiencies of each. It may benefit all involved parties to determine whether certain portions of these workflows are still necessary pending new vendor offerings and technological changes, and on the individual needs of each library.

CONCLUSION

There are various positive and negative aspects of each model described earlier. These are represented in Table 9.2. The HAM incorporates the pros and cons of each model, but also presents some of their own.

Acquisitions needs in public libraries have shifted rapidly over the past century (Agee 2007). We have moved from print to microform to audio to electronic content, and from traditional book and periodicals purchases to more complex offerings to our constituencies, such as video games, MP3 players, and storytime kits. As the materials used in public libraries become more diverse, new acquisitions models will emerge. The hybrid model will evolve to encompass multifaceted formats, changing librarian abilities, and vendor options. There may be a more concentrated effort to share collections among groups of libraries, distribute selection, and have special public libraries with extremely focused collections, thus affecting budgeting priorities.

Table 9.2 Pros and Cons of Acquisitions Models

Acquisitions Models	Pros	Cons
Decentralized	Works well for specialized collections or libraries Keeps staff in more direct contact with their specific constituencies	Can be inefficient Harder to handle issues Lose subject area expertise of staff in other public libraries
Centralized	Efficient workflows Reduces need for training of staff at multiple branches Reallocate staff or free up staff time for other duties; reduce staffing costs Keeps budget issues to a minimum and allows payments from one place Easier to work with vendors to resolve issues Consistent application of policy and procedures	Can ignore specific branch needs Might necessitate a transit system for delivery of physical materials
Outsourcing	Utilize vendor-provided automatic ordering profiles Ostensibly more cost-efficient Reallocate staff or free up staff time for other duties; reduce staffing costs Improve turnaround time, increase efficiency Supplement deficiencies in staff, such as foreign language selection	May lose control over selection for specialized collections Vendors can change costs at any time Can reduce staff morale Perceived as belittling professionalism Requires a lot of oversight
Hybrid	All of the above	All of the above

In this vein, vendors will evolve as well. They will modify their offerings to libraries in order to increase outsourcing options. Ordering and receiving may become even more automated as integrated library systems become more intuitive and advanced. It is prudent for those public libraries utilizing a hybrid acquisitions model to keep their eye on acquisitions trends, especially those regarding vendors. Contingency arrangements are necessary for when vendors close or are merged with other vendors. It is essential that HAM libraries be nimble, communicative, and as forward-thinking as possible. Then we can keep acquiring and providing what our customers want as economically and efficiently as possible.

REFERENCES

Agee, Jim. 2007. *Acquisitions Go Global: An Introduction to Library Collection Management in the 21st Century*. Oxford, UK: Chandos Publishing.

Alvin, Glenda. 1999. "Outsourcing Acquisitions: Methods and Models." In *Understanding the Business of Library Acquisitions*, ed. Karen A. Schmidt, 262–84. Chicago: American Library Association.

Chapman, Liz. 2004. *Managing Acquisitions in Library and Information Services*. London: Facet Publishing.

Evans, G. Edward, Sheila Intner, and Jean Weihs. 2011. *Introduction to Technical Services*. Santa Barbara, CA: Libraries Unlimited.

German, Lisa. 1999. "Acquisitions Personnel Management, Organization, and Staffing Issues." In *Understanding the Business of Library Acquisitions*, ed. Karen A. Schmidt, 346–59. Chicago: American Library Association.

Prytherch, Ray. 2000. *Harrod's Librarians' Glossary and Reference Book*. Aldershot, England: Gower Publishing Company Limited.

Reitz, Joan. 2013. Acquisitions, in *Online Dictionary for Library and Information Science*. ABC-CLIO. Available at: http://www.abc-clio.com/ODLIS/odlis_A.aspx. Accessed April 2, 2013.

Tomlinson, Laurence. 1942. *The Library Science Glossary*. Waco, TX: Baylor University Press.

Wilkinson, Frances, and Linda Lewis. 2003. *The Complete Guide to Acquisitions Management*. Westport, CT: Libraries Unlimited.

10

BEYOND REVIEWS: UNDERSTANDING THE SELECTION CYCLE IN PUBLIC LIBRARY COLLECTION DEVELOPMENT

Neal Wyatt

In "What Is the History of Books?" Robert Darnton suggests a life cycle for the production and dissemination of printed books (Darnton 1982). The primary actors within the cycle are producers, agents, readers, and suppliers. Influencing the cycle and exerting pressures upon it are social, cultural, and political forces. Extending Darnton's idea to the work of collection development, it is possible to posit a parallel: the selection cycle. This cycle accounts for the promotion, evaluation, selection, and reevaluation of a given title. It begins with the first notice of a book deal, extends through initial publicity and the major promotion of a title, includes various types and phases of evaluation, encompasses the moment a selector orders a title, and ends when a title falls off the radar for the final time. The cycle includes authors, editors, publicists, reviewers, librarians, and readers. Social, political, technological, and cultural forces, as well as space and budget limitations, exert pressure upon the cycle, as do library policies and library metrics. All of the agents involved consume and create the cycle in various ways. Selectors, for example, track the cycle, make purchase decisions based upon it, influence and change the cycle through demand and response, monitor the cycle's reverberations, and feed the resulting data back into the cycle in a continuous loop.

Viewing the work of collection development as a cycle highlights the multipoint chronology of selection. Rather than understanding selection as a process of steps largely triggered by a traditional review in a traditional trade source, selectors can view their work as occurring at any point along the cycle: at the first notice of a title, at the point of review, as an old title receives new attention, or at any moment between and among these examples. The cycle model also allows selectors the widest conception of their work and expands the possible inputs for selection beyond traditional trade reviews to a broader universe of considerations.

THE SELECTION CYCLE

The selection cycle is both chronological and atemporal. It often begins with early notice and then flows from publicity to reviews to retrospective evaluation. It becomes atemporal when selector scanning and reader requests introduce data into the cycle serendipitously and often out of sync with the temporal flow of publishing. The cycle, while operating as a continuous loop of selection triggers, is also influenced and shaped by collaborating and conflicting forces. These forces, including internal library concerns and the social, cultural, and political conditions of the local and extended community, exert as strong an influence on collection decisions as any other selection trigger.

EARLY NOTICE

Early notice marks the launch of the selection cycle. It involves the announcement of book deals and the nascent publicity surrounding forthcoming titles. As responsive collection development is largely a prospective undertaking, early notice often serves as the initial prompt for title selection.[1] Selectors work as far in advance of the publication calendar as possible and often make purchasing decisions for blockbuster titles long before critical reviews can be written and disseminated. Patrons demand such titles and it is part of almost every public library's mission to supply them in sufficient quantities and in the necessary (and available) range of formats to meet the needs of readers. Early notice also aids selectors in another aspect of collection building, identifying titles that, while not written by proven best-selling authors, are likely to become popular such as was the case with Justin Cronin's *The Passage*, Susanna Clarke's *Jonathan Strange & Mr Norell*, and David Wroblewski's *The Story of Edgar Sawtelle*.

Sources of notice vary widely but their goals are always the same, to inform their audience of forthcoming titles as far in advance as possible. Publishing houses, trade-review publications, various media outlets (social and other forms), authors, and library wholesalers all provide early notice. Perhaps the purest form is the publisher catalog, either in print or, increasingly, electronic and made available through online sites such as Edelweiss. Even given the changeability of publishing catalog data, scanning catalog pages (or keyword searching) for big names, popular subjects, perennial favorites, and indications of marketing attention is a time-tested and simple way of getting ahead of the arc of demand. Browsing catalogs also allows selectors to identify titles that fill and match particular needs, such as books that echo themes, subjects, and trends of past popular titles. Talking to the library marketing staff of various publishing houses at trade shows is also a method of early notice that reinforces what a selector gleans from browsing catalogs. While marketing staff might be most interested in sharing books recently, or soon to be, published, they are also more than willing to talk about what is forthcoming in the following season. They too are a deep well of information on trends and subjects and can identify titles that seem to echo each other, sometimes over decades.

While it might seem that the mechanism of early notice simply reinforces the popularity of the usual suspects, it actually exposes selectors to the widest possible field of title data so that they can begin to see trends and identify books that fulfill an unmet demand. Over time, by tracing early notice, selectors can come to anticipate arcs in publishing rather than merely following trends.

Social media plays a large role in early notice. Librarians, authors, editors, prominent reviewers, and others involved with the publication and review cycle post about books on their Facebook pages, discussing titles as they discover them, sign deals about them, or read very early copies. Similar activity takes place on Twitter. Both of these sources provide a great deal of useful early notice, well before a title is in print.

Trade publications such as *Booklist*, *Library Journal*, and *Publishers Weekly* also supply early notice. In addition to their pages of reviews, which vary in the amount of lead-time supplied, these sources highlight big titles even further in advance, long before the work reappears as a reviewed title. *Booklist* offers such notice through its "High Demand Hot List," *Library Journal* offers "Prepub Alert," and *Publishers Weekly* offers an online "On-Sale Calendar" that runs months in advance. Publishers Marketplace (and the shorter, but free version, Publishers Lunch) also offers advance book information and industry news that can be of use for selectors. Additionally, some consumer publications, such as "Forewords" from *RT Book Reviews* and audiobook "New Releases" in *AudioFile*, provide advance notice of varying degrees.

Library wholesalers also supply a needed form of notice: advance details on titles featured on TV and radio shows. Just as selectors do not need a review of the latest Nora Roberts to know it will be in high demand, they do not need a review of the latest cookbook being highlighted on *Good Morning America* to know that their readers will be searching the library's catalog the moment the book appears on air to see if it can be reserved. While this form of notice is not as timely as collection development librarians really need (it is often only a few days or weeks ahead of the appearance), it provides a quick review of trending titles and supplies selectors with a few extra days to double check their order numbers and supplement their copies if necessary. Baker & Taylor's "Fast Facts" and the "National TV, Radio & Online Publicity" section of Ingram's ipage are two examples of such tools of notice. In addition, selectors can use the search feature of library wholesaler databases to scan for potential orders, looking for titles by various criteria such as print run, subject, and publication date. This is a very effective way of keeping on top of popular subjects and large print-run titles long before they gain widespread notice.

Buying based on notice is not without its risks. Given the state of library budgets and the pressure on selection librarians to ensure every purchase earns its keep through turnover, notice can be a double-edged sword. Recognizing this, some streams of notice offer a small amount of residual review or extended information beyond pure title notice. *Booklist's* "High-Demand Hot List" often explains why a book will take off or gives an indication of print run. Barbara Hoffert of *Library Journal* offers selectors a similar service through "Prepub Alert." Early Word (discussed in more detail later in this chapter) is also a critical site, providing an overview of media coverage and notice of books gaining momentum. This kind of information is especially helpful in conjunction with another aspect of collection development selectors must navigate: the question of how many copies of a given title should be ordered. While it is relatively straightforward to decide the appropriate quantities of the next Michael Chabon, it is very difficult to forecast the numbers for a first novel, a mid-list author who appears to be breaking through, or an established author who is radically changing styles, such as J. K. Rowling's publication of an adult nonfantasy title. Having an indication of print run or a clue of potential demand helps collection development librarians make better educated guesses when they select based on notice.

CURRENT PUBLICITY

Building a collection is a symphony of many parts. While notice provides the earliest possible indication that a title will be in demand, selectors must also track what is popular in the current moment. Doing so requires following the publicity wave surrounding titles as they are released and gain focused attention: those appearing in the media, on the Internet, and that are being featured in outlets beyond those geared to the library market.

As with early notice, there are multiple channels of publicity. Common sources include influential blogs and Twitter feeds, various national and local best-seller lists, IndieBound's "Next List," Amazon.com's "Movers & Shakers" and "Top 100," *Entertainment Weekly, People,* and *USA Today* as well as morning, comedy, and late-night TV shows. Reviews can be sources of buzz as well, especially a string of glowing reviews or a notable reviewer appearing on a well-regarded outlet such as National Public Radio. Other forms of buzz include the newsletters produced by the library marketing offices of various publishers (and their Twitter feeds and Facebook pages) and Web sites such as The Millions, Shelf Awareness, and Book Riot.

Selectors can also access a number of less-obvious sources of buzz. Local newspapers, particularly independent weeklies, are good sources of publicity, providing information about the community that selectors might not know—such as the local music scene, author readings at college and civic programs, and street parties and festivals around various themes and cultures. Paralleling local print sources are Web sites and blogs created by members of particular communities who pay attention to the cultural beat of their locale. Along the same lines, selectors should also be aware of the manifold ways readers in their communities gain access to the publicity machine, be it through specialized magazines or social media, and monitor those sources as well. Doing so can help selectors tap into their local area so that they are as in tune with their particular location as they are with the national scene.

Librarians are not only consumers and users of the publicity machine but active producers of it as well. They create buzz in their awards, programs, blogs, electronic mailing lists, and readers' advisory efforts. Two particular librarian efforts of note are Early Word and the Reader's Advisors Online blog. Each seeks to aggregate publicity (and in some cases also offers forms of notice). Early Word, created by Nora Rawlinson, is a rich source for collection development news. One of its most useful and unique contributions is its tracking of holds around the country. This alerts selectors to titles breaking through in other libraries and which might bear watching in their own. Early World also monitors titles rising on a variety of best-seller lists, aggregating movement and alerting selectors to titles gaining ground.

The Reader's Advisors Online blog, maintained by Libraries Unlimited/ ABC-CLIO and edited by Cindy Orr and Sarah Statz Cords, offers selectors a vital news service as well as a quick weekly review of titles new to the best-seller lists. Of particular use are the blog's collected lists. Numerous publications create lists on various subsets such as seasonal titles, subject groupings, and genre picks. They are exceptionally useful as they cut through the flood of titles and highlight (often repeatedly) those that are getting a great deal of attention. Librarians might find such lists serendipitously or know about a few and deliberately seek them out, but Orr and Cords gather them in one location and thus save selectors a great deal of time.

Depending on the sources of early notice selectors track and the decisions they have made based upon that tracking, a title is likely already part of the collection by the time it hits the publicity stream. In this case selectors need to only monitor hold ratios to ensure that demand is met. This is the ideal situation. Selectors will miss titles; it is an unavoidable part of the job. Titles can be missed because they appear in tools of early notice a selector is not tracking, because the title rose so quickly that the various parties that create notice became aware of it at almost the same time it gained widespread publicity, because of changes in publication date, or because there was no way to predict the buzz trigger before it was announced (e.g., an Oprah book pick). Collection development, for as many tools and methods of measurement that exist, remains a speculative proposition. Selectors can only do the best job they can, knowing their communities, circulation metrics, and budget constraints. By tracking publicity, selectors improve the odds that they will discover a title at the earliest stage of this part of the cycle and buy before everyone else in their community has heard the growing buzz.

The downside of publicity is that it is ephemeral. What is popular today is often tomorrow's old news. Selectors should be constantly aware that many titles highlighted in the buzz machine have a very short lifespan and buy accordingly. They should also look critically at the source of the buzz. Ultimately, the most reliable information comes from sales data, a wide range of reviews, and readers' responses. Using hold ratio reports, print-run data, PR budgets, and considering historical long-term subject and genre demand in their libraries will help ensure that selectors are both responsive and responsible.

REVIEWS

While this chapter largely explores the use of selection sources that do not conform to the standard concept of a review, my intent is not to diminish the importance of traditional reviews, either in print or online. Consumer reviews, such as those in *People*, *Entertainment Weekly*, the *New York Times* Sunday Book Review, *Bookmarks*, *Locus*, and *All about Romance*, and trade reviews, such as those in *Booklist*, *Kirkus*, *Library Journal*, and *Publishers Weekly* provide collection development librarians with an essential body of evaluation and summation. Some trade reviews in particular offer librarians comparisons between titles, pointing out the best translations, the most important biography, or the most exhaustive reference. This invaluable service supports the core work of collection development and helps selectors build strong and useful collections. Readers' advisory librarians likewise would be lost without reviews as they provide clues to appeal, a quick summation of plot, and increasingly, read-alike pairings.

However, for all their usefulness, reviews do have limitations. Review sources must be selective and thus exclude from review thousands of titles each year (Evans and Saponaro 2012). Many only typically review those titles submitted to them by publishers, therefore excluding some small publishing houses as well as entire ranges of titles (e.g., self-published work) from their considerations. Embargoed titles are also completely removed from the timely review process. Additionally, both trade and consumer reviews can frequently suffer from a true lack of critical analysis. When almost every title reviewed is given some form of tepid support or review sources are pressured to give attention to advertisers' titles, the value of reviews decreases. Adding to this flattening of critique, some crowd-sourced reviews are subject to great skepticism by selectors and readers alike who have come to understand the various ways such reviews may be for sale.[2]

Despite such concerns, knowing what experienced, vested, reflective, and critical readers think of titles will always be important. Reviews remain, despite our multichannel world, a central way selectors can easily gain exposure to a wide range and number of titles. They also, depending on the title and topic, can constitute a form both of early notice and publicity for any number of works where the review itself stands as a selector's first introduction to a title. This is often the case with entire classifications of works such as science titles or those on animal care. For these reasons reviews remain a central tool and bedrock method of collection building.

Well-crafted collections have to be both rich and responsive. They must fulfill the needs of readers who expect what they are hearing about to be held by their public libraries and the needs of readers who expect the library will also hold titles that they come across in less obvious ways. Reviews enable selectors to curate collections that are deep and broad, and collections that allow for serendipity and surprise, for browsing and exploration. Without them, collections would tend to become uneven and narrow, reflecting only the small percentage of books that get the lion's share of public attention each year.

SELECTOR SCANNING

Collection development is a constant activity. While the selection cycle is largely fueled by data generated and supplied by trade and consumer publications, in order to build rich and useful collections selectors must pay attention to cycle inputs that extend beyond such sources. They must scan the environment in which their readers are immersed.

The most basic method of scanning is for selectors to pay attention to what they read. In an echo of the advice given to all readers' advisors, collection development librarians should read, watch, and listen as widely as they can, exploring as many formats, genres, subjects, and styles as possible. This way the titles they read about will have contextual meaning. It is far easier to discount a small press steampunk novel if the selector has never experienced the addictive levels of world building and description found in that subgenre of science fiction. Consuming culture in all its forms and as widely as possible keeps selectors in sympathy with fans and allows them to read reviews, advanced galleys, and other selection materials with an eye to what those fans crave. One of the best habits a collection development librarian can cultivate is to be interested and curious.

A related method of environmental scanning is to pay attention to from-the-field insights. A key group able to offer such insight is staff involved with delivering readers' advisory service. Asking what advanced galleys they have enjoyed and plan to suggest to readers or what titles and authors they are particularly interested in for the upcoming season is an excellent way to introduce local field advice into the selection cycle. This method also works with communities created on book-related social media sites. While the input is not as localized, it has the great benefit of being specialized. Knowing what fans and readers' advisory experts in certain genres and subjects areas are excited to read or suggest in the upcoming months is of great use when crafting collections. Field input can be found in other sources as well. For example, if a selector reads *Southern Living* and sees an article that indicates quilting will be the next hip craft, then it is worth his or her time to review the collection and add a few new quilting titles—and to keep an eye out for any repeated mentions of the trend.

Selectors can also use scanning to ensure they create well-rounded collections for particular high-interest areas such as cooking or crafts. Rather than basing selection decisions only upon reviews, selectors can instead explore the entire field of publication monthly or quarterly by searching vendor databases and other resources by topic and publication date, looking for titles worthy of further investigation. Doing so ensures that the collection does not, for example, have a dozen books on kitting socks because those titles drew review attention and, by contrast, holds no new titles on knitting hats.

Another method is to pay attention to what is happening within the community the selector serves. Which titles, in what formats, are being read on planes, the subway, and on the bus? Which book is everyone reading at the beach or talking about on the sidelines of the soccer field? Which local authors are gaining traction? Who is coming to town for author tours or lectures? What is hot on TV, in movie theaters, or trending on the radio or Web? A similar principle holds true for popular community activities. If a selector lives in a city that sponsors a yearly music festival, regularly hosts sports events, or often attracts exhibits by well-known artists, then the collection should be developed to support and augment interests in these activities. Such information keeps selectors in touch with the reading, viewing, and listening culture of their locale and ensures that if these works have not been mentioned in the systems of notice, publicity, and reviews he or she tracks, the selector can still ensure they are purchased.

Selectors can also craft collections by consulting local experts. A selector can ask his or her mechanic to recommend any basic car repair books or ask the local garden center about plant books. If a selector's dentist builds telescopes on the side, then discussing best resources is a fine way to augment the collection. If a selector has a friend in a local band, then asking about the best books on audio software and music groups will enrich the collection. Selectors can also reach out to local support groups and hospitals to see if they have suggested titles on particular conditions and diseases and to various community groups representing special interests (e.g., the local running club) to get input. Just as selectors can build on the wealth of knowledge of other librarians across the country, they can do so within their communities and circles of acquaintances, building not just better collections but community support as well.

The point of such selector scanning is twofold. The first is to craft the collection so that it reflects and supports the interests of the community without the community having to request the titles. The second is to ensure that the collection remains broad. While experienced selectors actively work against the tendency to create collections that support their own interests, paying attention to the environment ensures the instinct to self-curate is muted by many other voices.

RETROSPECTIVE BUYING

As much as collection development is a prospective process, it is also a retrospective one. There are many titles selectors purchase far after their publication dates. Part of this work is collection maintenance, such as ensuring that the library holds a full run of a series, replacing worn copies, and updating classics. The other part of retrospective buying is shaping the collection based on books that have become popular with readers some time after their initial publication.

A book winning an award is a standard reason to circle back and pick up the title. So too is back buying the titles of an author who has suddenly broken through. Classic examples of such authors are Dan Brown and John Grisham whose first books got little, if any, attention but whose subsequent books became blockbusters and created demand for their earlier titles. Another time-honored way to curate a collection retrospectively is the use of subject guides. A generation or more ago librarians would pore over the contents of such revered bibliographies as the *Public Library Catalog*, comparing their collections to the titles within its pages. Today such bibliographic selection has been replaced by more targeted and brief forms of bibliography such as *Booklist's* "Top Ten" lists and "Core Collection" guides, *Library Journal's* ongoing series of collection development pieces that offer in-depth coverage of a number of topics each year, *Publishers Weekly's* buying guide overviews that offer genre, topic, and subject profiles, and *Reference & User Services Quarterly's* "The Alert Collector." Selectors can also make use of the many subject bibliographies offered by trade sources such as *Cooking Light's* series on the 100 best cookbooks and *Outside* magazine's list of essential books for the well-read explorer.

Buying books based on their adaptation into other media is another classic retrospective buying technique. In this case the goal is not simply to ensure that the library has the title but that the library holds the title in the form that will trigger a connection in readers. For example, when movie tie-in editions become available, selectors can augment their collections with copies of the book with the movie stars on the cover. This more easily enables readers to make connections across platforms and carry their interest in the film into the library. Understanding the uses of selection in this layered way helps librarians connect the narratives gripping their communities to the collection.

Still another retrospective collection method is to buy books that enhance an already established title getting a great deal of attention. For example, if a particular book on raising backyard chickens suddenly garners a large readership, then a host of other titles on the same and related subjects (e.g., DIY chicken coops, urban homesteading, and organic gardening) should be evaluated if the selector believes that demand is deep, and long-lasting enough, within the community to justify expanding the collection.

Technology has also shaped retrospective collection development. With the advent of ILS that track circulation data, selectors can monitor precise segments of the collection, generate hold ratios, and see daily snapshots of what is in high demand. The metrics possible with advanced automated systems allow selectors to track their own internal buzz and see what titles, subjects, genres, and authors are in demand and evaluate how well that demand is being met. Hold ratios enable selectors to add copies as needed while a title is at the top of its popularity wave as well as be alerted when a title regains popularity after its initial demand has waned. Through reports that track circulation by classification, selectors can see what areas are in demand and begin to select titles that reflect their communities' interests. Selection is not only an external process, driven by reviews in the *New York Times* or a feature in *Entertainment Weekly*. It is also an internal process, driven by data that empirically illustrates the use of the collection.

Another method of retrospective collection development created by advances in technology is that selectors can now measure their collections against peer libraries and evaluate and augment their collections based on the holdings of others. A decade ago, selectors might have done this by searching the catalogs of libraries known for certain areas of expertise, seeing what books were held in those collections, and building selection lists based on their findings. This is now possible through a number of collection analysis systems such Collection HQ and WorldCat Collection Analysis, as well as through the resources of consortium libraries. These systems allow selectors to compare their collection against others in a variety of ways. Collection HQ, for example, can generate a list of the top circulating titles in a given subject, published in a given date range, and held across all subscribing libraries and transfer those results to an order cart. Selectors filling in collections or who have been given specific funds to develop a collection in a target area can use such systems to identify high circulating titles and evaluate them as part of their research.

COLLABORATING AND CONFLICTING FORCES

Within the selection cycle there are forces pushing against it, binding it together, and interrupting its flow. Obvious forces include the library's philosophy, collection budget, free shelf space, administrative policy, workplace culture, collection development policy, and the community's social, political, and cultural environment. Popular culture and attention also shapes the cycle, even when in conflict with other collaborating and conflicting forces. The cycle is, therefore, subject to a great deal of interference and influence. Selectors themselves shape the cycle by how they respond to the materials other agents produce, their level of confidence and experience, their understanding of the ethical obligations of selection, and the pressures they must navigate in their place of work. While the ways the selection cycle is influenced by the agents that create it and by the exterior forces that bind it are many, I focus my considerations of such forces here to the community that uses the collection. I do so because their input directly affects the work of collection development librarians, and can teach selectors a great deal about the collection the community desires.

THE COMMUNITY

As Helen Haines reminds us, "there is no living world of books apart from the living world of readers" (Haines 1950, 17). Selection librarians curate the collection for their community, not as gatekeepers to the collection but in partnership with the community they serve. In addition to paying attention to the statistical data generated by their ILS, selectors have a direct form of community input: patron suggestions and ILL requests. Both are essential aspects of collection building and should be given serious attention as they directly express the desires of the community. Used well, they transcend sources of selection and become teaching and public relations tools.[3] Patrons have their own streams of early notice and are tuned into their own systems of publicity. They develop interests outside the mainstream channels of popular culture, interests that selectors may not have yet noted, but which might be gaining a popular footing within their district.

Evaluating community requests is not simply another task in the library. Requests tell collection development librarians as directly as possible what their users want. While many requests often reinforce the streams of notice and buzz a selector already monitors, some requests will be for titles not yet mentioned in such outlets. When this occurs, the source of the title expands the selector's data stream, widening the circle of notice and buzz a selector might want to follow. Even when requests reinforce data streams a selector already monitors, such repeated mentions of a title are instructive as they confirm that selectors are monitoring the same resources their community values and that the titles they notice are the same titles their community also notes. Tracking these repeated instances of requests allows selectors to filter notice, publicity, reviews, and environmental scanning through a screen of local interest. Over time, selectors can learn enough about patron requests so that they get a sense of what will be in demand and can begin to craft the collection accordingly. When selectors view requests as teaching tools, they can proactively create the collection with their community in mind. Ideally, such attention will reduce the number of requests submitted and indicate that selectors have become more in tune with their communities' needs.

Additionally, how selectors respond to requests offers the library a new stream of patron dialogue and public relations. When a selector communicates with the requestor, he or she affirms the patron's interest in the library and learns more about that patron's sources. It could be that a local civic club is starting a new project or that a new book club has begun. This type of micro knowledge of how the community finds and uses titles can feed directly back into the selector's work: widening his or her streams of notice and buzz, teaching him or her what is important to the community, and offering him or her a chance to collect proactively rather than to respond retrospectively to requests. As a form of community engagement, there are few things as effective as responding to a request and purchasing materials the community asks for. Encouraging patron input, and then acting upon it, places collection building directly in the hands of the community that uses the library and for whom the collection is designed.

CONCLUSION

The selection cycle is yet another way to consider the project of collection development. It offers selectors a model that places emphasis on crafting collections that fulfill readerly desire prior to its demand spike so that collections are responsive to patrons rather than reactive to their requests. It is a model that, while it does not discount reviews, places emphasis on additional sources of selection data so that collection development is understood as taking place both prior to and following the publication of a review. Finally, it offers a model of collection development that understands selection as a continuous loop rather than a series of end-oriented steps. Building a collection that fulfills the needs of one's community takes every resource possible and a commitment to working ahead of demand. Understanding collection development choices as existing within a selection cycle widens the amount of data from which a selector can draw, and helps create collections that are of use and that delight and surprise their community.

NOTES

1. For more on responsive collection development, see Sharon L. Baker, *The Responsive Public Library: How to Develop and Market a Winning Collection* (Englewood, CO: Libraries Unlimited, 2002). This chapter assumes that selectors are seeking to build the most responsive and useful collections they can within the limitations imposed upon them by budgets, shelf space, and publishing models.

2. For examples of how crowdsourced reviews have come under scrutiny, see Andrew Hough, "RJ Ellory: Detected, Crime Writer Who Faked His Own Glowing Reviews," *The Telegraph*, September 2, 2012. http://www.telegraph.co.uk/culture/books/booknews/

9515593/RJ-Ellory-detected-crime-writer-who-faked-his-own-glowing-reviews.html (accessed October 1, 2012) and David Streitfeld, "The Best Book Reviews Money Can Buy," *The New York Times*, August 25, 2012, http://www.nytimes.com/2012/08/26/busi ness/book-reviewers-for-hire-meet-a-demand-for-online-raves.html?pagewanted=all&_ r=0 (accessed October 1, 2012).

3. My thanks to Corinne M. Hill, executive director of the Chattanooga Public Library, Tennessee, for sharing her library's use of patron and ILL requests. Her philosophy and approach informed much of this segment. She also shared her approach to buying cross-platform titles such as movie edition reprints. I also want to thank Wendy Bartlett, collection development manager, Cuyahoga County Public Library, Ohio; Stephanie Chase, Library Strategies, BiblioCommons; Brian Kenney, director of the White Plains Public Library, New York; Megan McArdle, Manager for Collection Development and Adult Services, Berkeley Public Library, California; Cindy Orr, library consultant; Nora Rawlinson, cofounder and editor of *Early Word*; and Barry Trott, digital services director, Williamsburg Regional Library, Virginia, for sharing their sources of notice, buzz, and collection development methods. This chapter is richer for their input.

REFERENCES

Darnton, Robert. 1982. "What Is the History of Books?" *Daedalus* 111 (3): 65–83.

Evans, G. Edward, and Margaret Zarnosky Saponaro. 2012. *Collection Management Basics*, Sixth Edition. Santa Barbara, CA: Libraries Unlimited.

Haines, Helen E. 1950. *Living with Books: The Art of Book Selection*. New York: Columbia University Press.

11

THE BIG DEAL AND THE FUTURE OF JOURNAL LICENSING IN ACADEMIC LIBRARIES

Jeffrey D. Carroll

What do we mean when we talk about a Big Deal journal package? When did such a thing begin? And although it may be a Big Deal, is it a good deal, and what do we make of its future?

The Big Deal dates back to at least 1996. In that year Academic Press made what may have been the first of its kind—a package deal of e-journal content containing most, if not all, of the press's publications (Poynder 2011a). The term Big Deal itself, however, was not popularized until 2001 when Kenneth Frazier published his article, "The Librarian's Dilemma: Contemplating the Costs of the 'Big Deal'" in *D-Lib Magazine*. In a nutshell, the Big Deal is any deal in which a publisher bundles a large number of its titles and offers the bundle to libraries for subscription at a substantial discount to what it would cost the library if it were to subscribe to the same titles on an individual basis. One of the most compelling factors of the Big Deal is that it usually offers libraries access to a far greater number of titles for the same price the library had been paying for fewer print titles in an a la carte model. Additional benefits of the Big Deal can include limits, or caps, on annual price increases, and the ability to swap titles in and out of the package from year to year. Sometimes a Big Deal will include a cancellation allowance if the annual level of spending for the bundle is above a certain dollar value.

Most deals of one kind or another, however, include a catch, and the Big Deal is no exception. Big Deal journal packages often require a commitment from the library to maintain the same level of spending, or higher, over multiple years—usually three to five. Large academic libraries are likely to have multiple Big Deals in place simultaneously with different publishers. Since, by nature the Big Deals are offered by big publishers, and because big publishers tend to get bigger, libraries may find over time that a growing percentage of their budgets are earmarked for these Big Deals with less and less money to spend on material not covered by these agreements. This can be especially problematic in times of budget cuts, when libraries are forced to reduce expenditures, but find that many of their low-use journal titles are protected by cancellation restrictions inherent in their Big Deal agreements.

Anyone who has looked at the cost of a subscription to an academic journal, particularly a journal in the areas of science, technology, or medicine (STM), will understand that the numbers can be significant. It is not uncommon for an institutional subscription to a journal in chemistry, physics, or neuroscience to be priced in the thousands of dollars. A library subscribing to thousands of these STM journals will have an annual commitment in the millions of dollars. Because a handful of large scientific publishers, many of whom offer their content via the Big Deal, control production and distribution of the majority of these journals, a library's outlay with any single publisher might range from the hundreds of thousands to over a million dollars.

Furthermore, when libraries contemplate breaking a Big Deal at the end of their contract period, they might find that it would actually cost more to drop low-use titles than it would to simply renew their Big Deal contracts for another multiyear term (Thornton-Verma 2012). This has led many to criticize Big Deal publishers for providing content that libraries do not need and do not want in order to get the content they require (Anderson 2012).

TWO CRISES

In order to understand the role the Big Deal plays in journal collection development and management, we need to understand the environment that existed in the years leading up to the offering made by Academic Press back in 1996. The Big Deal emerged partly in response to an untenable situation commonly referred to as the serials crisis, which was marked by an escalation in the cost of journal subscriptions in relation to the overall budget of the typical academic library. Kyrillidou and Bland (2009) discuss the rapid increase in serials expenditures at ARL libraries between 1986 and 2007. The serials price increases far exceed price increases for every other library expenditure and is 273 percentage points higher than the consumer price index (CPI)—a common measure of inflation.

Since it is hard to fully appreciate the impact of these figures without a specific example, let us use a hypothetical one. The libraries of Hypothetical University (HUL) in 1986 had an overall budget of $4 million grouped into three broad categories—salaries, operating expenses, and library materials. Library materials consist of two categories—monographs and serials. To see the full impact of serials price increases in sharp relief, let us further assume that in 1986 HUL's expenditures were equal in all categories. The numbers are laid out in Table 11.1, and are represented graphically in Figure 11.1.

In 1986 expenditures on serials and monographs were equal at $1 million each, whereas by 2007 expenditures on serials were more than two-and-a-half times the expenditure level for monographs. Furthermore, serials expenditures represented 41 percent of the libraries' overall expenditures in 2007 as compared to just 25 percent in 1986. The effect is even more dramatic if we look only at materials expenditures. In 2007 serials represented 71.8 percent of the overall materials budget, compared to an even split at 50 percent in 1986.

Table 11.1

	1986 (in million)	**2007**
Salaries	$1	$2.57
Operating expenses	$1	$2.38
Serials expenditures	$1	$4.74
Monographs expenditures	$1	$1.86
All materials	$2	$6.6
All library	$4	$11.55

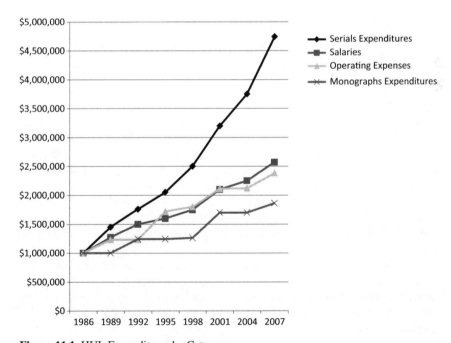

Figure 11.1 HUL Expenditures by Category

Figure 11.1 then shows what our example might look like if we plotted Hypothetical's expenditures by category from 1986 to 2007.

By the 1990s librarians, growing increasingly alarmed, began to refer to the situation as a serials crisis (Iowa State University 2003).

The serials crisis was a component of a larger complication commonly referred to as the crisis in scholarly communications, which can be defined as "the system through which research and other scholarly writings are created, evaluated for quality, disseminated to the scholarly community, and preserved for future use" (Association of College & Research Libraries 2006). The researcher is primarily involved in the first step (creation), the publisher in the second step (evaluation for quality), the publisher and possibly the library in the third step (dissemination), and the library in the fourth step (preservation). But we also know that there is interaction among all parties throughout every step—libraries can assist the researcher in the creative process; publishers can solicit topical contributions from researchers in an effort to affect or stimulate that process; researchers are involved in peer review, part of the evaluation process; researchers can also have a hand in the dissemination process when they recommend or encourage their institutions' libraries to subscribe to the journals in which they publish or on whose editorial boards they serve; and finally, libraries are often partners with publishers and other organizations in addressing preservation issues. These multidimensional interactions make the scholarly communications process a decidedly complicated one, and one increasingly dominated by for-profit publishers.

It was not always that way. Scholarly publishing began centuries ago when societies stepped in to provide the framework for the scholarly communication process described earlier. Prior to the 17th century the results of scientific research were shared, for the most part, in small circles. Feedback was limited, and reviewers of the results were mostly chosen because of their close association with the researcher. Scholarly societies changed this when they began to formally publish the results of scholarly research and to make them available for scrutiny to a broader audience. One of the earliest societies to step into this role was the Royal Society when it published the first issue of *Philosophical Transactions* on March 6, 1665 (Royal Society 2013). Although societies are still represented in this process—*Philosophical Transactions* remains the oldest scientific journal in continuous publication—over time for-profit publishers took on the role of qualitative evaluation (filtering and peer review) and dissemination. This evolved to include the division of content into discreet, topical journals that provided a more convenient way for a scholar to keep up with developments in his or her specific field. The benefits of economies of scale and the expertise in business strategy that for-profit publishers brought to the mix afforded competitive advantages when compared to the staid, tradition-based societies. These competitive advantages allowed the more successful, for-profit publishers to acquire as well as start more journals. Sometimes these advantages also enabled for-profit publishers to acquire titles from societies themselves, either by contractual arrangement or through outright purchase. As a result, by the 1980s and 1990s academic journal publishing was consolidating in the hands of a few large publishers, even though the number of journals and the amount of content continued to expand. Arguably, this has made for a more efficient system of gathering, filtering, evaluating, and disseminating the results of scholarly research.

The second half of the twentieth century, however, saw an explosion in the growth of scholarly output (Mabe and Amin 2001). Libraries tried to keep up, subscribing to an increasing number of journals to support the needs of their researchers, so that they, in turn, could produce even more research that needed dissemination. Budgets increased, and in a still print-based world, physical library space expanded as well to accommodate rapidly growing bound journal collections.

The serials or scholarly communication crisis can be summarized as follows: college and university researchers—who receive salaries, some of which may be derived from state funding—carry out research that is funded by government grants. These researchers are then put under extraordinary pressure to share their findings through publication in refereed journals in order to gain promotion and tenure. To have their work appear in one of these journals, researchers are contractually obligated to cede their article copyright to the journal publisher. The same institutions that are employing these researchers then buy back, via their libraries, these same research results repackaged as journal subscriptions. With the rapid increase in research output and subscription costs, the result was a vicious cycle. One can understand how this cycle would be an enticing model for a publisher—it offers a rapidly expanding market, a captive audience, and seemingly unlimited potential for growth. The situation was summed up by one librarian in an editorial for *The Serials Review* in a thematic issue on this topic:

> The exorbitant costs of journals, and their inability for any one library, or even library consortia, to subscribe to the breadth or depth of the published scholarly literature, seriously jeopardize the resources libraries will be able to offer future generations of students and researchers. (Hepfer 1992)

The entire issue, in fact, is a good read for anyone wishing to gain an idea of the sentiment at this point in the early 1990s, with a particularly good summary by Clifford Lynch (1992).

Anxiety over the immanent transition from print to electronic content further complicated the situation. Among other things, librarians worried that the transition would exacerbate an already emerging digital divide, a concern that continues today. In addition, connection speed, bandwidth, and storage were of great concern at a time when dial-up was the primary means by which individuals connected to the Internet, and the floppy disk, with its 2.0 megabytes of capacity, was their primary unit of data storage. Preservation of electronic content also became an issue. Finally, librarians did not want to be in the position to pay twice, in two different formats, for the same content, particularly as the volume of content increased. These converging factors created the context within which Academic Press offered that first Big Deal.

In 1996 Jan Velterop, a managing director at Academic Press, is credited with describing a vicious cycle, or price spiral, in the subscription costs of academic journals (Poynder 2011a). Every year saw a new round of subscription cancellations because library budgets were not keeping up with the ever-increasing cost of academic serials. This caused publishers to raise their prices even more in an effort to maintain the same revenue from a smaller number of overall subscriptions. Each subsequent year brought another round of cancellations and further price increases to compensate. Applying the argument to a simple example, we might say that a journal that had cost $500 a year when 1,000 subscriptions were sold would eventually cost $250,000 when only two subscriptions were sold, and $500,000 a year for the last remaining library. This prompted Velterop to rethink Academic Press's business model, proposing the first Big Deal package offer to the Higher Education Funding Council of the United Kingdom. The agreement would make the full range of Academic Press's journals available to all institutes of higher education in the United Kingdom. Other publishers eventually adopted a similar model, although these agreements do not tend to be at the national level, but at the consortium level and are paid at the library level. In time this allowed publishers to single out institutions in order to customize deals to specific libraries that, on balance, seemed better than the deals they were getting through their consortiums. The expanding popularity of this pricing model led Ken Frazier, then University Librarian at the University of Wisconsin-Madison, to call it the Big Deal, stating that "simply put, the Big Deal is an online aggregation of journals that publishers offer as a one-price, one size fits all package" (Frazier 2001).

Frazier went on to describe the negotiation process between librarians and publishers, used to establish use and business terms, as the librarian's dilemma. This is an allusion to Albert Tucker's prisoner's dilemma, which is used as an illustration in game theory. Two suspects are arrested and placed in separate cells in the local jail and are forbidden to communicate with each other. The prosecutor feels that there may not be enough evidence to convict the suspects for the crime in which they are implicated, but he can have them each convicted for a lesser crime such as illegal possession of firearms. In an effort to elicit a confession, the prosecutor offers each suspect a deal. He tells Prisoner A that the firearms conviction would carry a two-year prison sentence. However, if Prisoner A confesses, the prosecutor will ensure that

Prisoner A will go free, while Prisoner B will be convicted of the primary offense and receive the maximum three-year sentence. If both prisoners confess, they will each get one-year sentences. He then makes the same offer to Prisoner B. There is a strong incentive for both prisoners to betray the other; if either remains silent, he faces a minimum two-year sentence for the firearms charge and a maximum three-year sentence for the full conviction if the other prisoner betrays him. If either confesses, he faces a maximum one-year sentence but also has the prospect of going free if the other prisoner remains silent. The range of possible decisions is often depicted in a matrix. Figure 11.2 depicts our earlier example.

Frazier (2001) railed against the Big Deal, imploring other library directors to "not sign on to the Big Deal or any comprehensive license agreement with commercial publishers." Applying Tucker's theory to the Big Deal, Frazier argued that librarians may seem at first to be acting rationally, and that the Big Deal is a win-win situation for libraries and publishers alike. But, Frazier went on to argue that in the long term it is win (publisher) lose (library) as libraries get locked in to paying for content they do not need or do not want, unable contractually to drop titles from the package.

Taking Figure 11.2 as a model, I have relabeled Prisoner A and Prisoner B as Library A and Library B, and changed the decisions within the matrix to reflect Frazier's assertions (see Figure 11.3).

Frazier argued that eventually the Big Deal becomes more of a burden to libraries than a benefit; it results in coerced customer loyalty because the libraries are contractually forbidden to cancel titles they may not need or want. It can also result in disintermediation as the publishers of Big Deal content may eventually try to eliminate the middle men (i.e., journal vendors), ultimately resulting in librarians attempting to change publishing rules in order to mitigate the control publishers have over scholarly content.

		Prisoner A	
		Remain silent	Confess (Betray Prisoner B)
Prisoner B	Remain silent	A and B get 2 years for illegal firearms	A goes free; B gets 3 years
	Confess (Betray Prisoner A)	B goes free; A gets 3 years	A and B get 1 year

Figure 11.2 Prisoner's Dilemma

		Library A	
		Cooperates with broader library community	Acts alone and signs Big Deal agreement (Betrays broader library community)
Broader Library Community	Cooperates with Library A (and others like it)	Affects change in academic publishing and in the scholarly communications process	Library A gets a good deal in relation to its peers in the short term. Long term may find deal unsustainable.
	Each library acts alone and signs Big Deal agreement (Betrays Library A and others like it)	Willingness in community to cooperate, but lack of real power or leadership for meaningful negotiations	Each library acts alone and signs Big Deal agreement (mutual betrayal; terms primarily dictated by publisher)

Figure 11.3 Librarian's Dilemma

ANATOMY OF THE BIG DEAL

So, what might a Big Deal look like in practice? What follows is a hypothetical Big Deal between a publisher and an academic library, with the potential for the library to benefit further from membership in a consortium. Let us call the publisher XYZ Publishing Inc. Again, our library is HUL. It is the fall of 1998, and HUL has 775 print subscriptions to 750 titles (including some duplicates for more popular titles) from XYZ Publishing, which offers a total of 1,215 titles overall. The total cost is $620,000, with the average cost per subscription at $800 ($620,000/775).

Now it is time for HUL to renew its titles with XYZ for 1999, and the strategy is to convert some subscriptions from print to online—particularly those titles for which it has maintained multiple print subscriptions. HUL sees this as a logical way to save money and increase access—a single online subscription to a popular journal should provide access to the entire institution and obviate the need to maintain multiple print subscriptions.

This is understandably problematic for XYZ. If institutions across the country, and around the world, begin cancelling duplicate print subscriptions in favor of online access, then XYZ is likely to see substantial drops in revenue even though it is providing expanded access to its content. So XYZ has come up with a proposal for HUL that it touts as a win-win situation for both sides—HUL can convert all of its subscriptions over to online-only, thus expanding access to XYZ's journal content across the institution, if HUL agrees to maintain its 1998 level of spending plus 5 percent to cover access to more

Table 11.2 HUL's Expenditures by Category

Year	Continue with Print Only	Move to E-Only (Three-Year Contract)	Savings
1998	$620,000		
1999	$663,400	$651,000	$12,400
2000	$709,838	$683,550	$26,288
2001	$759,527	$717,728	$41,799
Cumulative savings			$80,487

content. Furthermore, HUL agrees to maintain that level of expenditure plus a 5 percent annual increase per year for the next three years. XYZ argues that the average increase for journals has been and is projected to be around 7 percent, so the deal should save HUL a significant amount of money over the next three years.

HUL does a quick calculation (see Table 11.2) and determines that this offer appears to be a win-win scenario and signs the three-year contract.

SOLUTION TO A CRISIS

Although the Big Deal has its critics, many would argue that it has been an effective solution to the serials crisis. In an interview for *Information Today*, Derk Haank, CEO of Science & Business Media at Springer, argues that journal subscription rates must increase to keep pace with the increasing output of scholarly information (Poynder 2011b). Haank notes that it is in the best interests of both publishers and librarians to keep the Big Deal going, because it enables libraries provide access to those titles they were forced to cancel under the old print models. Ideally, the research community would have access to the entire scholarly record, and the Big Deal is the only model that makes that even remotely possible. In short, for some, the Big Deal was the solution to the serials crisis. Additionally, the Big Deal could be seen as an effective means of "increasing the exposure and the survival of journals in small or emerging fields" (Van Orsdel and Born 2003). But is the Big Deal truly a long-term solution, or did it merely buy us time?

FUTURE SOLUTIONS TO A RETURNING CRISIS

As we have seen, the Big Deal was presented as a possible solution to the serials crisis and the larger crisis in scholarly communication. It seemed to have worked in the short term; however, its limitations began to appear as a result of the first economic downturn in the Big Deal era. Beginning in 2000, with the dot-com meltdown and subsequent recession, academic libraries saw their materials budgets reduced drastically. The Big Deal may have provided a way through the transition from print to electronic, but it was only a matter of time before the continuing growth of scholarly output began to stress the system again. It was, essentially, another version of kicking the can down the road. The Big Deal restored the ability of librarians to make available the scholarly content needed to support the teaching and research missions of their institutions. Over time, however, the caps on annual increases built into the Big Deal outpaced inflation as well as budget increases. What, then, are viable alternatives to the Big Deal?

It all begins, of course, with breaking up the Big Deal itself. This is no easy task, and one to which the publishers are understandably resistant. A number of options are available, but first content in the Big Deal should be analyzed in order to determine relative value. While there are perhaps many ways of going about this, any such effort should include the following basic factors:

- Analysis of usage statistics to determine the most heavily used titles
- Cost analysis and cost-per-use
- Consultation with faculty

After conducting this review, and determining what savings, if any, they need to generate, librarians may choose to cancel the Big Deal outright and use alternative methods to provide access. One solution would be to license access to individual titles directly with the publisher. This alternative will, in some cases, highlight one of the benefits of the Big Deal—the inflation cap. If a Big Deal has been in place for a number of years, the cost of an individual title has been suppressed. The list price of the same title could be quite a bit more. It is the latter price that will be charged when licensing individual title access, so the library will be paying more money for fewer titles. Another option could be to offer pay-per-use directly with the publisher. Some publishers, such as Wiley, offer both librarian-mediated and unmediated pay-per-use, which the library funds through the purchase of tokens. This might be an option if the cost-per-use of the journals in the Big Deal is higher than the price of an individual token. One drawback, however, is that this cost, if unmediated, is also not predictable.

Other options to provide access to journal content are also available. A less appealing alternative for some might be to rely on journal aggregator products for full-text access. ProQuest Research Library and Ebsco's Academic Search Complete, for example, both offer a wide variety of full-text journal content. Two major drawbacks make this solution unsatisfactory to many. First, publishers have the option to pull content from aggregators, making access unreliable. And, if the library opts to cancel a subscription to an aggregator, all access to this content disappears. Another alternative to the Big Deal might be to rely on ILL, although it should be understood that this solution is not free. ILL is a staff-intensive process, with a cost per request calculated to be around $17.50 (Jackson 2004). Finally, if access to the most current issues of some scientific journal content is not necessary, an option might be to rely on open access. Mandated public dissemination of publications emanating from government-funded research is becoming more common, although there is almost always an embargo on new content.

CONCLUSION: THE FUTURE OF JOURNAL LICENSING IN ACADEMIC LIBRARIES

If we think about the long term, the lack of sufficient budgetary resources is not necessarily the core issue. It is unlikely, given current trends in academic publishing and library funding, that libraries will ever be able to purchase all of the content they need, let alone the entire universe of academic output. Alternative models for managing the scholarly communications process will be necessary. Breaking up the Big Deal and pay-per-view are two options discussed earlier, although some institutions have encountered fiscal barriers in breaking up their Big Deal packages. The cost-per-use of articles in the Big Deal may be less expensive than either ILL or pay-per-view. Or, the price per journal title is higher for those journals that are retained after the dissolution of the Big Deal, and any journal subsequently subscribed to will be added at list, rather than a discounted price. Thus, libraries can ultimately end up with significantly less content for the same outlay of money. Nor does a break-up of a Big Deal package do anything to address the observation made earlier that scholarly output is expanding exponentially. The Big Deal may be unsustainable, but so is its breakup.

Given these challenges, we run the real risk of seeing an ever-widening gap in what libraries need and what they can afford. One interesting and promising idea mentioned earlier that has gained some traction is open access. While the concept itself is not new—Frazier (2001) advocated for it in his Librarian's Dilemma article—it has recently captured the attention of the very publishers offering Big Deal packages for which open access is seen as an alternative. As recently as 2011, Derk Haank asserted that open access would never be anything more than a niche model (Poynder 2011b). Yet Haank's own company, Springer, acquired open access publisher BioMed Central in 2008 as a hedge, perhaps, in case open access ever becomes more than just a niche.

It is important to remember that open access is not free, per se. There are still costs associated with the upkeep and maintenance of electronic storage and Web delivery systems. Resources also need to be committed to copy editing, peer review, dissemination, and preservation. However, since the basic tenet is to make the content available without the price barriers defined by subscriptions, we now have the promise of making a large range of scholarly output available to anyone who wants it regardless of his or her ability to pay. Stuart Shieber (2009) argued that "in a world where the first-copy cost of publishing an article is essentially the entire cost, a business model for publishing that charges per article for article-processing services . . . makes a lot of sense." Various business models have arisen to cover the costs mentioned earlier, and new ones are being proposed each year. Public Library of Science and BioMed Central are two success stories, among several, indicating that open access publishing can be a viable alternative to traditional subscription-based models.

What does this mean for the future of journal licensing in academic libraries? We have seen how the Big Deal emerged as a means to enable the transition from traditional print-based subscriptions to electronic access defined by license agreements. And we have seen how the Big Deal has been, arguably, an effective short-term solution during this transition for libraries and publishers alike. In the longer term, however, we have seen that the Big Deal may prove untenable as the cost of maintaining it outpaces both the rate of inflation and library budget increases. And we have discussed briefly some possible alternatives to the Big Deal. In the near to medium term, journal licensing in academic libraries will likely become more varied and complex as libraries and publishers experiment with multiple models for access. In the long term, it is anyone's guess.

REFERENCES

Anderson, Rick. 2012. "The Big Deal, the Medium Deal and the Tiny Deal." *Scholarly Kitchen* May 30, 2012. Available at: http://scholarlykitchen.sspnet.org/2012/05/30/the-big-deal-the-medium-deal-and-the-tiny-deal/. Accessed October 7, 2012.

Association of College & Research Libraries. 2006. *Principles and Strategies for the Reform of Scholarly Communication.* September 1, 2006. Available at: http://www.ala.org/acrl/publications/whitepapers/principlesstrategies. Accessed January 5, 2013.

Frazier, Kenneth. 2001. "The Librarian's Dilemma: Contemplating the Cost of the 'Big Deal.'" *D-Lib Magazine* 7 (3). Available at: http://www.dlib.org/dlib/march01/frazier/03frazier.html. Accessed October 7, 2012.

Hepfer, Cindy. 1992. Editorial. *Serials Review* 18 (1/2): 9.

Iowa State University. 2003. *The Crisis in Scholarly Communication.* Available at: http://www.lib.iastate.edu/libinfo/reptempl/origins.html. Accessed October 29, 2012.

Jackson, Mary E. 2004. *Assessing ILL/DD Services: New Cost-Effective Alternatives.* Washington, DC: Association of Research Libraries. Available at: http://archive.org/stream/assessingillddse00jackrich/assessingillddse00jackrich_djvu.txt. Accessed May 1, 2013.

Kyrillidou, Martha, and L. Bland, Comps. and Eds. 2009. *ARL Statistics 2007–2008.* Available at: http://www.arl.org/stats/annualsurveys/arlstats/arlstats08.shtml. Accessed October 29, 2012.

Lynch, Clifford. 1992. "Reaction, Response, Realization: From the Crisis in Scholarly Communication to the Age of Networked Information." *Serials Review* 18 (1/2): 107–12.

Mabe, Michael, and Mayur Amin. 2001. "Growth Dynamics of Scholarly and Scientific Journals." *Scientometrics* 51 (1): 147–62. Available at: http://link.springer.com.ezproxy .cul.columbia.edu/content/pdf/10.1023%2FA%3A1010520913124. Accessed October 29, 2012.

Poynder, Richard. 2011a. "The Big Deal: Not Price but Cost." *Information Today* 28 (8): 1, 32–33.

Poynder, Richard. 2011b. "Not Looking for Sympathy." *Information Today* 28 (1): 14–15.

Royal Society. History. Available at: http://royalsociety.org/about-us/history/. Accessed January 6, 2013.

Shieber, Stuart M. 2009. "Equity for Open-Access Journal Publishing." *PLoS Biology* 7 (8): e1000165. doi:10.1371/journal.pbio.1000165.

Thornton-Verma, Henrietta. 2012. "Plan B: Life after the Big Deal." *Library Journal Reviews*, April 10, 2012. Available at: http://reviews.libraryjournal.com/2012/04/reference/plan-b-life-after-the-big-deal/. Accessed October 7, 2012.

Van Orsdel, Lee, and Kathleen Born. 2003. "Big Chill on the Big Deal." *Library Journal* 128 (7): 51–56.

12

COLLECTION DEVELOPMENT BETWEEN TEACHING MISSION AND RESOURCE MANAGEMENT: THE CASE OF CARLETON COLLEGE

Kathy Tezla and Victoria Morse

Collection development at Carleton College is the joint responsibility of faculty and library staff in the service of the teaching mission of the college. This collaboration is not unusual in itself, but it seems to be unusually deep and unusually central at Carleton. In this chapter we would like to explore from our different departmental perspectives the exact nature of this collaboration and the opportunities as well as the challenges that arise from it. Instead of undertaking a systematic survey, this chapter pairs a study of the historical development of collaboration between librarians and faculty members at Carleton with one current faculty member's view of selecting library content.

Carleton College is a highly selective private residential liberal arts college located in Northfield, Minnesota. With a small student body (under 2,000 students) and a 9:1 student/faculty ratio, the emphasis is on close collaboration between students and faculty. In this context, student research is an essential and growing part of the teaching mix, underscoring the centrality of the library collection and the library staff in delivering high-quality resources and instruction that support vigorous student learning. Working together with the faculty, the library provides students with a rich collection, shaped to fit closely with the contours of the curriculum, of 477,067 monographs (general collection, reference, and special collections), 809 print periodical subscriptions, 36,509 e-journal direct subscriptions, 1,945 reference books (sources, indexing and A&I services, databases, data, and Web sites), access to 42,424 journal titles in databases and in packages, and access to 473,652 eBooks.

EARLY HISTORY OF THE COLLECTION

In 1868, two years after the school was founded, the Carleton College library had an opening collection of 375 volumes. Starting with this small book collection, the development of information services, which includes collection development and institutional support, continues to be an integral part of the library's mission. The data for the following discussion of the history of faculty involvement in collection development has been collected from Carleton librarians' annual reports and from meeting minutes of the Committee of the Faculty for the Library, all held in the Carleton College Archives.

During the library's first 15 years (1868–1883), various faculty members and students loosely guided the development of and access to the collection. In 1883 Charles H. Cooper, who was the sole instructor in the Department of History and Political Science, became the first librarian. He was the first librarian to retain this position for more than two years, serving in this capacity until 1899 when Rev. George Huntington, professor of logic and rhetoric, became the second librarian, a position he held for the next eight years.

The first mention of allocating book funds directly to teaching faculty is found in the librarian's 1903–1904 annual report, which Sabra Nason, the assistant librarian to George Huntington, wrote on his behalf. She reported that the practice of equally appropriating library funds to academic departments that Huntington had introduced two years prior was used again for the 12 departments of the college. In addition to the funds allocated to the academic departments, funds—that the librarian expended—were given to the library for the purchase of books necessary for general use. In the same report the appointment of a special advisory faculty committee to the library by Huntington is mentioned, as well as his intention to make this committee a standing committee of the college (College Librarian Annual Reports).

Until 1902 the college librarian was selected from the faculty. Between 1902 and 1907, Carleton graduates Sabra L. Nason and Eleanor J. Gladstone were hired in the newly created positions of assistant librarians. Both were credited for laying the groundwork for a well-organized and serviceable library at Carleton, with most of the credit given to Eleanor Gladstone, who served as the third librarian from 1907 to 1920. With Gladstone's appointment the library became more structured, which is reflected in the librarian's reports. Her annual writings focused on the growth of the collection, including books not being returned either by students or by faculty, specific donations of collections to the library, reference and cataloging services, staffing, and the cost of books and periodicals. Gladstone's annual reports served as a template for future annual reports, and only changed in structure as issues confronting the library evolved.

Walter M. Patton, the fourth college librarian (1917–1928) did not mention working with a faculty committee in his 1923–1924 report, but he did name specific departments of the college and used the phrase "cooperated in the enrichment" of the library's resources by "wise selection" of recent books for their respective disciplines. He also commented that the library's budget continued to be appropriated to departments according to need. When departmental library budgets were not fully expended, funds were transferred to those departments that had expended their funds (College Librarian Annual Reports).

The next mention of an advisory faculty committee appears in the college librarian's report for the year ending May 31, 1928. Carleton's fifth librarian, Bessie G. Frost, devoted a paragraph to the issue of working more closely with a committee, to review not only book allocations to departments but also periodical subscriptions. In that same year, the library committee became a college standing committee, which Charles N. Smiley, a professor of Latin and chairman of the department, chaired. For the next five years (1934–1938) the committee was led by Thomas Ernest Rankin, chair of the English department. After Professor Rankin's term, the college librarian took over sole chairmanship of the advisory committee when Robert W. McEwen was appointed the sixth librarian. With the appointment of McEwen, a professional degree in librarianship became a requirement for this leadership position. During his period, the collection contained 125,000 volumes and 550 periodical titles. In his first annual report for the year ending June 30, 1940, he says, "The quality of the collection is a reflection of the ability of the faculty, the quantity, the long-continued support and interest of the administration" (College Librarian Annual Reports).

Between 1939 and 1945 McEwen worked closely with the faculty to help them develop a more systematic method for building the library's periodical collection. In 1940 he instituted the practice of having the faculty committee review individual issues of new titles being considered. He stated that such a policy could eventually prevent the acquisition of often-donated short runs, or incomplete journal titles, which he felt were not appropriate to have in a permanent periodical collection.

For many years prior to 1940 the major responsibility for faculty book selection rested with the chairs of the departments. This resulted in highly focused collections reflecting the interests of a select few faculty members. In his 1940–1941 annual report, McEwen recommended a procedure to diversify collection content. According to McEwen, the ultimate purpose of this proposed procedure was to "strengthen faculty responsibility in this important area" (College Librarian Annual Reports). The specifics of the procedure are worth repeating because they serve as a template, providing the academic departments guidance on how they could fold book selection into their roles as teaching faculty:

1. At meetings of the department held about the middle of each semester, the several members of the department would present requests for books for consideration by the department. These book requests would then be rated in the order of their importance to the work of the department and the growth of the book collection in that field, and cards recommending the purchase of books requested would be forwarded to the librarian with order of importance indicated.
2. Members of the faculty, and especially department heads, would keep in mind two types of books to be added to the collection:
    a. New publications in the subject field
    b. Classics in the field, which have not yet been added for our holdings.

    The division of funds between these two types of purchases would vary considerably with the departments. Special consideration to the second type should be the concern of a department in ordering content for a new course, or for any course not offered for some years.
3. A small percentage of funds available, perhaps 20 percent, would be reserved at the time of the departmental meeting, and held uncommitted for immediate needs as they arise, or for the purchase of real bargains from sales catalogs.
4. The departments, through such meetings, would compile lists of desiderata for the guidance of the librarian in encouraging gifts for the collection, or for special purchases from general funds in his or her hands.

By the time McEwen's successor, Marian F. Adams, became the seventh college librarian in 1945, the collection consisted of 140,000 volumes and 500 periodicals. She continued the practice introduced under McEwen of having all librarians provide expert bibliographical counsel to the librarian as she expended the special funds allocated directly to her. Succeeding college librarians' annual reports discussed results of librarian-led, discipline-based projects, such as comparing the library's collections with special lists, evaluating the library's holdings in relation to the curriculum and comparing holdings to those of peer institutions.

The college librarian annual reports throughout Adam's term through the hiring of John Metz as the 11th college librarian in 1978–1979 continued to document the various levels of faculty involvement in the development and management of the book and periodical collections. These reports also discuss issues related to the operations of a residential liberal arts college library, which, between 1949 and 1979, had grown from 1,120 to 1,725 students and had 158 faculty who were based in 26 departments and taught approximately 660 courses.

LIBRARIAN AS FACILITATOR OF COLLECTION DEVELOPMENT

In 1969–1970 Robert K. Bruce became the ninth college librarian. Bruce hired Ann Niles as the acquisitions librarian at a time when the faculty had begun to raise great concern over the quality of the periodical collection and the reliance on microfilm for accessing periodical back files. In the 1960s Carleton had joined the Associated College of the Midwest (ACM) and participated in a cooperative interlibrary lending venture among these 10 Midwestern colleges called the AMC Periodicals Bank. Participating members would send print periodical back files to the bank and would receive microfilm subscriptions in exchange. Though it was a common theory held by others in the library profession that converting periodical back files to microfilm would save binding costs, Niles did not agree. After evaluating the situation, she agreed with the Carleton faculty and stopped microfilm acquisitions and reinstated the binding program. Niles held the firm belief that the most important role of a college library was to hold as complete a periodical collection as possible. She spent the next 30 years trying to fill in as many of the back files as she could (Niles 2002).

As the college librarian's administrative attention focused on budgets and space needs, Niles was given complete responsibility for overseeing all book selection—both by faculty and by librarians. The faculty would talk to Niles about gaps in the collection and about large purchases that their departmental allocations could not cover. Over time, the head of acquisitions became the contact for issues related to the ongoing development of the library's collections.

Since its beginnings the library's collections existed to support the curriculum. Niles believed the faculty were in the best position to know what was needed for their teaching. She and the other librarians partnered with the faculty, but with the understanding that librarians were responsible for acquiring a balanced collection of library materials in many formats, selecting reference, general, and interdisciplinary materials, and filling in gaps in the collection. Between 1976 and 1979 Phillip C. Wei, the 10th college librarian, facilitated dramatic changes in the library, including the switch from the Dewey Classification System to the Library of Congress and the consolidation of separate title and subject card catalogs into one. This was a tumultuous period for all concerned, but it was also a time during which both the library and the faculty worked together to adjust to the necessary changes to ensure that the collections met the needs of the library users.

During the 1980s' renovation of Gould Library, which was built in 1956, Niles and the faculty continued to work together developing the collections. As mentioned previously, the academic departments and the library used several collection development methods to respond to the typically changing curricular and teaching needs of a liberal arts college. Under Niles the library modified its budget formula for annual departmental allocations to include: average cost of books, enrollment by department, number of books published in a field, circulation of books by classification, previous year's allocation, and actual expenditure.

In 1989, to systematize book selection and save faculty time, Niles worked with the representative from Blackwell's North America and the Carleton faculty to set up an approval plan. The faculty defined the profile, emphasizing support for the curriculum. Books fitting this profile were sent weekly for the nine months school was in session. Only notification slips were sent during the summer months. Faculty members were expected to review titles that were received as part of the approval plan to determine which were appropriate to add to the collection. Niles reviewed the remaining titles and retained those suitable. Unfortunately, faculty did not consistently review titles, and so after three years the plan was discontinued and title-by-title selection resumed (Niles 1991).

In 1997 the library began to warn the college community that in order for it to continue to support the undergraduate liberal arts college curriculum, users would need to have access to information both in traditional formats (print, video, audio) and in digital formats. Niles noted on the first page in that year's winter issue of the library newsletter, *Bookmark*, "the future of the Gould Library lies in preparing for and coping with the 'both/and' world of paper and electronic resources, not an 'either/or' environment of excluding one for the sake of the other" (*Bookmark* 1997).

REORGANIZATION FOR DEVELOPING AND MANAGING A HYBRID COLLECTION

In 1999 Samuel Demas was hired as the 12th college librarian and began to tackle the various challenges the library faced in facilitating the shift from print to digital collections. To do so, a new department named Collection Development was created, which brought together ongoing management of the library's material budget and collections, preservation, and special collections. The rationale for creating this department was to guide collection development, acknowledging the need for print materials while facilitating the integration of electronic resources into the collection. The department was and continues to be responsible for: developing policies and selection strategies; defining funding requirements; managing expenditures; selecting materials in all formats; and representing and interpreting the collection to the faculty. In 2001 a printed brochure titled "Faculty Participation in Collection Development" was sent to all faculty, outlining guidelines designed to ensure that the materials acquired met the changing needs of the curriculum.[1] As new strategies are developed to accommodate the technological advancements in the delivery of scholarly information, the electronic version of this document is regularly updated. Included in this brochure are the criteria in place for selecting electronic reference titles and e-journals. The library also works with its book providers, first Blackwell's North America and now YPB, setting up accounts for each member of the Carleton faculty so they receive electronic notifications of newly published books delivered to their desktop.

The library continues to work closely with the faculty in the management of the materials budget for books and journals. And this collaboration now extends to St. Olaf College, which is also in Northfield. With the assistance of three Mellon grants received between 2003 and 2005, the libraries at Carleton and St. Olaf combined their library catalogs and formally became a consortium of two libraries. With the two collections combined into one access point, the goal became building complementary collections to expand resources available to faculty and students at both colleges.

TEACHING THE COLLECTION, BUILDING A TEACHING COLLECTION: A FACULTY MEMBER'S EXPERIENCE OF COLLECTION DEVELOPMENT

For new faculty members at Carleton, there is exhilaration as well as anxiety in realizing that we can and should actively shape the library's collection in our fields. It takes time to learn what the library has, which courses you will teach and at what level, and what kinds of resources are needed for what kinds of project. As these questions resolve themselves, other questions arise: which titles will best support my courses and which will provide students doing independent research with adequate on-site resources to excite their interest and give them research momentum? Learning how students engage with the library in pursuing their intellectual interests and developing a keener sense of what kinds of acquisitions are most likely to be used and to inspire takes time and attention, which are often in short supply at Carleton. An important feature of faculty collection development, therefore, is that there is a real learning curve in which both departmental and program colleagues play a part and the library staff are crucial.

I came to Carleton as a medieval historian with research interests in 14th-century Italy. Because I have local colleagues who collect in Byzantine and early medieval history, ancient history, and early modern Europe starting with the Reformation, I have been able to focus on the period between approximately 1100 and 1600. Carleton has had a long tradition of teaching medieval history and so the collection, broadly speaking, was strong when I arrived. At the same time, there were idiosyncrasies of emphasis reflecting the interests of former faculty—we were strong on the history of peasants and women and Benedictine monasteries, but weak on the crusades, exploration, heresy, and the Mendicant religious orders. I also have interests in urban history, the history of cartography, and the Mediterranean world, which were not well supported. As I developed courses and directed comprehensive projects (required of all Carleton seniors), I found myself amazed at what we did have and surprised by what we did not. Even with a stable curriculum, it remains difficult to know what students will choose to work on for their senior projects and how best to build the collection to support and encourage exploration and serendipity. It is a complex process of information gathering and decision making and I will describe it as I do it now, 12 years on in my career at Carleton.

Two preliminary notes on the culture and structure of teaching at Carleton will provide some context. First, courses tend to be small and unique in their coverage and approach. Few classes rely primarily on a single textbook or reader. Instead, most course materials are highly personalized mixes of primary sources, secondary articles, books, and selections from longer works. To create this menu of resources for their courses, faculty draw heavily on the breadth and depth of the library's collection and, of course, its reserve services. Crucially in my department we have woven information literacy into our curriculum through collaboration with our reference and instruction (R&I) librarian, a relationship that continually shapes my use and development of the collection. Second, Carleton operates on a 10-week academic term—timely access to materials is therefore essential for courses and for student research projects.

While collaboration with our R&I librarian has convinced me that students must develop the ability to draw on a pool of materials extending far beyond Carleton through Web-based resources and ILL, it remains true that all the materials that students will need for projects assigned and due within one to two weeks have to be available on campus.

As I review possible acquisitions, I select heavily for the courses that I teach regularly. I know that I need to assign readings for the course as a whole, assign or point toward readings for student presentations and research projects, and have materials available for my own course preparation. I have a mental list of the topics that I currently cover and to what depth, as well as topics that I am interested in adding to my teaching portfolio. One example is peasant life: I do not address this topic frequently and students only occasionally have chosen it for their senior comprehensive project. Nevertheless, it is clearly a central aspect of the medieval world and I make sure that a small but relevant collection of materials is available to me and to students who might want to pursue it as a research project. I choose fundamental works and sources as well as works that can offer gateways to the literature, which I and my students can then use to access other resources. On the other side of the spectrum is the history of cartography. Although it is a small field, I offer a popular seminar largely devoted to the topic, and it is an ongoing area of personal research interest. I have worked with our Head of Special Collections to build a rich collection of early maps in facsimile, and I seek to build a comprehensive collection in this area.

As a faculty member, I become aware of books to consider acquiring through a steady flow of book catalogs. I look at book reviews and *Choice* slips that come from the library. I note useful recent titles in the bibliographies of books and articles, checking to see if the library owns them or can acquire them whether new or used. I will buy books myself when I am traveling or otherwise have an unusual opportunity to acquire something worthwhile. The book vendor's Web site (YBP's GOBI) is also helpful, though ordering systems can vary enormously in their effectiveness and usability.

With a title in view for acquisition, I run through, almost unconsciously, a set of key questions. First, is the book relevant to my teaching in its field, level, and quality? Is it in English? If not, is it in a language that we do offer? Can I imagine students really using it, or can I imagine actively teaching this text? I consider the cost of the book and the opportunity cost that it represents in a rough and ready way. I also consider use by students beyond my own classes. For expensive items, I normally seek support from other departments both to help out financially and to ensure that the materials will be widely used.

My development of Carleton's collection thus has been and continues to be organically connected with my evolving curriculum and the research interests of my students. Although developing the collection with intention takes time and a nuanced and changing process of assessment, I nonetheless consider this time well spent. I am supported by the collection as I grow and change; I can nimbly respond to opportunities and new fields as they emerge; and I stay in touch with the library collection and so can guide students and help them design projects that utilize our materials most effectively. At the same time, members of the collection development team at the library have been vital not only in facilitating my work but also in supplementing the collection in areas that I or my colleagues may miss. They research, test, and implement new databases, eResource packages, and e-journals and offer overall guidance and real support and leadership in helping faculty understand the array of options (and their implications) available to them to provide the content essential to their work and the mission of the college.

COLLECTION DEVELOPMENT IN THE AGE OF ELECTRONIC RESOURCES

As the history of collection development sketched earlier suggests, the massive expansion of electronic databases, e-journals, and other licensed information resources, which are becoming an increasingly large part of the library's collections, its budgetary expenditure, and the faculty's and students' expectations, has brought many challenges and opportunities. The complexity of the issues and the deep and immediate impact of these decisions on the possibilities for teaching and research make the historically effective collaboration between collection development professionals at the library and the faculty at Carleton an even more important asset to maintain and grow. There are challenges, however. The structure of eAcquisitions inherently diminishes the role of the individual faculty member in a single department in selecting. These same factors likewise pose budgetary pressures that cannot be clearly assigned to particular departments or even divisions. How will this affect the system of departmental allocations currently in place for monographic purchases? How will the library and faculty deal with the inequalities in the digital information landscape, where some fields are almost entirely digital and others remain more heavily print-based?

In this new landscape, communication between librarians and faculty members will be essential; indeed, it will have to be enhanced in both directions. A recent initiative to start a conversation about eBooks offers several salutary lessons. The library formed a task force to understand the range of eBook options currently available, and then followed up their research with a public talk, a survey, and focus groups. Although the participation rates in these efforts were lower than desired, this effort represents an important step in reshaping a collaborative culture in this new digital age. The digital information landscape has great potential to further the mission of the college. To realize this potential at Carleton, collection development staff and faculty need to continue to be fellow laborers in the work of collection development and also to recognize that new media require a rethinking of how their respective expertise and resources can be best harmonized. The nature of collaboration and consultation may be changing, but the need for a robust culture of collaboration remains essential as we work together to create a library collection in service of the curriculum.

CONCLUSION

Over the years Carleton College has developed a deep-seeded institutional culture of collaboration between the faculty and the library. This culture has allowed for an unusually high level of faculty investment in the library. The result has been a collection that reflects and supports the liberal arts curriculum directly and organically, and will continue to do so despite new challenges the electronic landscape presents. Time will tell how faculty-library collaboration will evolve, but we are certain it will remain the center of our collection development model moving forward.

NOTE

1. The electronic version of this brochure is available at https://apps.carleton.edu/campus/library/for_faculty/working/collection_development/.

REFERENCES

Bookmark. 1997. College Archives. Laurence McKinley Gould Library, Carleton College.

College Librarian Annual Reports. College Archives. Laurence McKinley Gould Library, Carleton College.

Niles, Ann. 1991. "An Approval Plan Combined with Faculty Selection." In *Collection Development in College Libraries*, ed. Joanne Schneider Hill, William E. Hannaford Jr., and Ronald H. Epp, 163–69. Chicago: American Library Association.

Niles, Ann. 2002. "Interview by Jennifer Edwins." Carleton College Oral History Program. College Archives. Laurence McKinley Gould Library, Carleton College.

13

LEASE PLANS IN ACADEMIC LIBRARIES

Anne Behler

INTRODUCTION

Libraries and books are nearly synonymous in the minds of many people. Even in the age of pervasive technology and space-related library services, library book collections—particularly those that include best-selling fiction and nonfiction titles—are a major draw for library users.

Historically, colleges and universities prioritized reading as a vital student skill and activity; the university library was often at the heart of this value. In the early 20th century in particular, this was evident in the amount of effort college and university libraries put into both assessing and promoting student leisure reading habits (Behler 2011).

While the academic library collection of today is typically composed of titles that directly support the university curriculum, many college and university librarians are finding compelling reasons to add small browsing collections of recent best sellers to their libraries. In fact, in a 2007 survey of academic librarians, over 70 percent of those surveyed noted that their library had a book browsing area (Elliott 2007). Among those reasons are the nationwide trends toward user-focused libraries, the emphasis on "library as place," and the drive to promote literacy and lifelong reading (Dewan 2010).

When considering the addition of a popular reading collection to an academic library, the librarian is faced with several options for acquisition methods. The first is to firm order, or purchase outright, the desired titles. This can be done by tweaking a library's approval plan—often easier said than done since approval plans are geared toward research collections—or by making title-by-title selections from services such as Brodart or Amazon. The outcome in this case is a collection of permanently owned books.

Some libraries have elected to go an extremely low-stakes route when it comes to offering a browsing collection. Elliot's study notes the Archbishop Alter Library at the College of Mount St. Joseph. This library implemented a free book-exchange program, which was populated with donations from library staff and publishers to get it off the ground (Elliott 2007).

Some librarians might consider electronic browsing collections, through services such as OverDrive. However, the primary clientele of leisure eBook services is public libraries, and the purchasing model and logistics involved warrant their own separate book chapter!

The final option is to lease popular book titles from a book-leasing company. This is a common practice among public libraries, but is not as often found in an academic library setting.

WHAT IS BOOK LEASING?

Book leasing is a vendor-provided subscription service that enables libraries to lease, or rent, books rather than buying them. The service is especially geared toward collections of popular materials, and allows libraries to keep several copies of the most sought-after titles on hand while the demand is high. As demand for one title wanes and that for another increases, those volumes can be sent back to the vendor in exchange for new selections.

WHY LEASE?

The 21st century has brought resurgence in literacy and reading promotion among academic librarians. Many campuses are offering One Book programs, and many librarians recognize that an effective way to encourage reading for pleasure among their students is to offer high-profile, face-out displays of best-selling fiction and nonfiction. Unfortunately, tradition can serve as a powerful barrier to browsing collections, as they do not fit the mold of the academy. They call for separate locations, processing procedures, and routine maintenance that do not typically correspond well with the support in place for traditional research collections.

However, designed to be flexible and low-maintenance, lease plans offer shelf-ready volumes (with glossy covers intact) and downloadable cataloging records. They also offer a solution for libraries with limited space to dedicate to a leisure reading collection, as selectors can choose from a variety of plan sizes, from as few as 10 books per month to hundreds. Online selection lists allow for quick ordering, and the constant turnover of the collection's inventory creates the possibility for a portion of the library's offerings that is always fresh and responsive to readers' preferences.

THE PLANS

There are two players in the world of book leasing: the McNaughton Plan, through Brodart, and the Baker & Taylor Book Leasing Plan. Each offers a slight variation on the book leasing model, one primary difference being that the McNaughton Plan starts libraries off with a core collection of titles with which to seed the collection. Baker & Taylor does not offer that feature; however, the library's quota can be used at whatever pace the selector sees fit. Table 13.1 offers a comparison of the two services (Brodart Books & Library Services 2012; Baker & Taylor 2012).

Table 13.1 Lease Plan Comparison

	McNaughton	**Baker & Taylor**
Featured content	Nonfiction; fiction; mystery; romance; Western; fantasy; science fiction; graphic novels; debut novels; Spanish novels; large type; special topics; bestsellers; teen	Adventure and suspense; biography; historical novels; horror; large print; mystery; seasonal; Spanish language; romance; science fiction; Western Add-on plans available: popular children's and teen; computer book leasing; spirit book leasing (religious titles)
Ordering	Offers standing order option for best sellers, as well as selection lists and online ordering for desired titles	Quick Call or Quick Click online ordering lists for quick shipment of extremely popular titles; no profile or standing-order option
Processing or shipping	Shelf-ready processing and optional supplied MARC record (included in subscription cost) Shipping is free	Shelf-ready processing and MARC record supplied (included in subscription cost) Shipping is free
Pricing	Annual subscription pricing; 2 percent discount for annual payment Free replacement of lost or damaged books within first six months of possession	Annual subscription pricing; 2 percent discount for annual payment Twenty percent of titles can be retained at no additional cost; additional titles available for purchase at 75 percent discount Twenty percent cushion can also be used to account for lost or missing or damaged volumes Note: if plan is ever discontinued, cost of returns of materials is 100 percent borne by the library

CASES

The Pennsylvania State University Libraries, University Park Campus

Penn State's University Park Campus, known to many as "main campus," is home to over 39,000 undergraduate students and approximately 6,000 graduate students (Penn State University Budget Office 2012). Many of these students are residents either on-campus or in the immediate community, although there is a growing number of both continuing education and online (World Campus) students who reside nearby. The University Park Campus is also home to the university's and libraries' central administration, which oversee 23 other campuses and their libraries in addition to those at main campus. Of these 24 Penn State campuses, 8 offer leased leisure reading collections of various sizes. The largest of these collections resides at University Park.

The Penn State University Libraries at the University Park campus have been leasing popular literature from the Baker & Taylor book leasing plan since 2007, when their leisure reading collection was begun. A response to ongoing student feedback requesting an easily browsable book collection, the leisure reading collection represents the first step the Penn State Libraries took in developing a Knowledge Commons at University Park. As of 2013, the collection holds approximately 5,000 volumes, and is supported by a lease plan subscription for 1,800 volumes per year, or 150 per month. In addition to the leased titles, the selector for the plan has a small amount budgeted each year for firm orders.

Vendor Selection and Processing

The Baker & Taylor Lease Plan was chosen for a number of reasons. Early on, the decision was made to allow leased books at University Park to circulate beyond that campus—via loan to other Penn State locations, as well as ILL to outside institutions. Because the Penn State University Libraries operate under such a large system with a shared catalog, it was important to the selector to be able to make title selections locally rather than through an automatic order system like the one through McNaughton. While the various campuses with leisure reading collections do not collaborate on selection, ordering locally allows the selector to gain the big picture of what is needed within the University Park collection, and helps to avoid duplication between locations when it makes sense to do so. Sometimes a title that would be considered interesting, but might not be a headliner, is already held at one or more campuses, accessible through the catalog, and therefore does not warrant the duplication. In most cases, however, duplication is not considered an important factor in ordering popular titles—holding one or more copies locally means fewer wait lines for users and less cost to the library associated with frequently moving books from one location to another. Because of the visual nature of the browsing leisure reading collection, a majority of its use is driven by local foot traffic rather than catalog discovery. This translates to a selection process that emphasizes the local needs and wants rather than a system-wide collection.

Baker & Taylor's plan structure also allows for ordering that is directly responsive to user reading habits. Orders can be placed at any time, so if special needs arise that are outside the typical month's norm, the selector can place an immediate order to fulfill that need. For example, the leisure reading collection has supported a student-run business book club, and the selector was able to order several copies of the book whenever the club needed it. In addition to the selector-driven acquisition process, Baker & Taylor's plan allows for retention of 20 percent of the annual quota. This was highly appealing, as it allowed the collection to develop a core that represented the reading preferences of the Penn State users.

All books that are leased through Baker & Taylor arrive shelf-ready; however, cataloging, which is typically copy cataloging, is done locally. The decision to create records locally was influenced heavily by the desire to maintain consistency in online catalog records among books that are firm ordered and those that are leased into the collection, particularly in a multiple volume, multiple campus scenario, in which the preference is to have one record to represent all volumes rather than many.

Keeping a leased collection fresh and within the quota does require a significant amount of routine collection maintenance. Staff who work with the collection run monthly use reports and withdraw anything that has not circulated within the past six months of its presence in the collection (titles that are new to the collection are excluded). In addition, any titles that have demonstrated consistent popularity are identified as keepers, books that will remain with the collection as a part of the 20 percent of all books returned that the library is allowed to keep. The transition from a leased to owned title does involve some minor remarking and a change to the notation in the catalog record, a process that is carried out by the library's catalog marking team.

This process enables the collection to remain relevant to users' preferences. It also helps the selector keep the size of the collection relatively stable. The goal for the collection at Penn State is to maintain a collection size of around 5,000 volumes, with 3,600 or fewer (200% of the annual quota) having come from the lease plan.[1]

University of North Carolina at Greensboro

The University of North Carolina at Greensboro (UNCG) is home to an on-campus student body of over 17,000 (The University of North Carolina at Greensboro 2012). Setting UNCG apart from many other universities is its student body diversity. "UNCG is the most diverse institution in the UNC System, with more than 40 percent of the undergraduates identifying as a racial or ethnic minority. For the 2012–2013 academic year, 28 percent of the undergraduate student body identified as African American" (Goins 2012).

Traditionally a research-focused collection, in 2007, the UNCG Jackson Library opened a leisure reading collection in response to consistent formal (LibQual) and informal user feedback requesting "books to read" (Fischer 2012). Previously a small, informal collection of current literature—titles selectors ordered for the research collection but may peak broad interest—the UNCG leisure reading collection grew to a collection of approximately 1,000 titles, leased from McNaughton (Brodart). Located in a high-traffic area of the library, sharing space with DVD and audiobook collections, as well as group study spaces and public computing, the collection is highly visible and is heavily used.

Vendor Selection and Processing Decisions

The McNaughton Plan was chosen because of its easy-to-use preselection service. The acquisitions department was able to set up a profile, and McNaughton's staff sent titles based on those preferences. In addition, the librarians at UNCG favored the ability to purchase a title outright at a significant discount (typically around $2 per volume). Therefore, if a faculty member were to submit a request for a book that was part of the lease plan, the library could simply buy it outright for a fraction of the typical cost. With such a customizable plan, the librarians at UNCG have found that they do very little work in terms of processing. All books arrive shelf-ready, aside from security targets, and the MARC records are sent to the library via ftp download. In the case that the library might already have a copy of the book, the leased copy would be added to the existing record, but this is not a typical occurrence.

The UNCG librarians work to maintain a collection size that is close to their current annual quota of 600 books. In order to do so, they deselect titles two to three times per year, taking the number of volumes to slightly under that quota amount. This is not at the mandate of the vendor, but rather as a result of the librarians' desire to maintain a manageable size for the collection.

Budget Woes

The leisure reading collection at UNCG is funded through a line item in the regular acquisitions budget; however in 2009, in the face of state budget uncertainty, that line had to be discontinued for a period of six months. It was at the end of a subscription year for the lease plan, so the plan was discontinued entirely during that time. Acquisitions librarian, Christine Fischer, related that the McNaughton staff were extremely easy to work with when the plan was discontinued. UNCG librarians made the decision to purchase 50 percent of the books they had on hand outright, for around $2 per volume, and the remaining volumes were packaged and shipped back to the vendor. McNaughton even arranged for a freight company to do the packing and shipping back to their vendor facility at no expense to the library. According to Fischer, this made the decision to re-subscribe with McNaughton an easy one when funding (at a lower level) returned for the collection in November 2009 (Fischer 2012).

CONCLUSION

While book leasing does not come without its challenges—for example, unique maintenance and subscription models, space, and budget—in the cases of the two libraries presented here, it has proven to be an efficient, low-maintenance way to provide a leisure reading collection. At both institutions, user feedback and collection use have demonstrated that the leased collections provide eye-catching, enticing reading options that set those collections apart from the rest of the research library. While funding continues to be a challenge in many libraries, book leasing can offer a low-cost, low-square-foot method of offering titles that both draw students into the library and encourage reading.

NOTE

1. The standard B & T contract calls for a library not to exceed the annual quota; however, Penn State negotiated for a larger collection size that has no cap. The danger here is that the more volumes a library holds, the more it has to deal with should it discontinue its plan (everything has to be returned to the company).

REFERENCES

Baker & Taylor. 2012. "Book Leasing from Baker & Taylor." Available at: http://www.btol .com/pdfs/Book_Leasing.pdf. Accessed 31, 2012.

Behler, Anne. 2011. "Leisure Reading Collections in College and University Libraries: Have Academic Librarians Rediscovered Readers' Advisory?" In *Reference Reborn: Breathing New Life into Public Services Librarianship*, ed. Diane Zabel, 133–42. Santa Barbara, CA: Libraries Unlimited.

Brodart Books & Library Services. 2012. "McNaughton Adult." Available at: http://www .brodartbooks.com/mcnaughton-library-subscription-services/adult/page.aspx?id=270. Accessed October 31, 2012.

Dewan, Pauline. 2010. "Why Your Academic Library Needs a Popular Reading Collection Now More Than Ever." *College & Undergraduate Libraries* 17 (1): 44–64.

Elliott, Julie. 2007. "Academic Libraries and Extracurricular Reading Promotion." *Reference & User Services Quarterly* 46 (3): 34.

Fischer, Christine. 2012. "Interview: Christine Fischer, UNC Greensboro."

Goins, Lanita Withers. 2012. "UNCG Remains Leader in Shrinking Black-white Graduation Gap | University News." *University News*. Available at: http://ure.uncg.edu/prod/ news/chancellor/uncg-remains-a-leader-in-shrinking-black-white-graduation-gap/. Accessed October 18, 2012.

Penn State University Budget Office. 2012. "5 Year Historical Enrollment by Location."
Penn State Fact Book. Available at: http://www.budget.psu.edu/factbook/StudentDyna
mic/HistoricalEnrolbyLocationSummary5year.aspx?ReportCode=Summary&YearCod
e=2012&FBPlusIndc=N. Accessed October 23, 2012.

The University of North Carolina at Greensboro. 2012. "UNCG at a Glance, The University of North Carolina at Greensboro—UNCG at a Glance." Available at: http://www
.uncg.edu/inside-uncg/inside-glance.htm. Accessed October 23, 2012.

14

LEASE SERVICES AS A COLLECTION DEVELOPMENT STRATEGY

Kathleen Sullivan

INTRODUCTION

For many libraries, even those for which the primary purpose is not to collect popular fiction, supplying print best sellers and other current high-demand items is an important service for customers (Odess-Harnish 2002). Large urban public libraries have hundreds, if not thousands, of holds on titles such as the Harry Potter books. While libraries may purchase multiple copies of a title in an attempt to fulfill customer demand, often they cannot supply a high-enough ratio of materials to meet demand and to avoid large holds lists or long waiting periods. Neither the materials budget nor the long-term value of the work demands that all copies purchased will be retained by the system. Furthermore, libraries may need to supply specialized materials for which they have constant demand (e.g., books written by the political candidates prior to a major election), but do not have a long-term need to retain the materials. In selecting needed materials, some libraries may lack staff expertise to search through large vendor catalogs to select high-demand or potential best sellers. Spanish-language books, large print materials, teen fiction, or audiovisual needs may fall into these categories. Over the past 60 years, when confronted with these challenges, some libraries have subscribed to lease services (Berry 1989).

Many types of libraries currently subscribe to leasing services. Public libraries need to have, as a basic service component, multiple copies of best sellers as near to publication date as possible. Some academic libraries have enough demand from faculty and students to dedicate some part of their budget, or endowments, to popular reading collections that may or may not become a permanent part of their collection (Odess-Harnish 2002). Small special libraries, such as hospital libraries, choose to have a collection of current high-demand titles available to staff or patients (PUBLIB Archives 2005–2009). Joint-use facilities choose to make popular adult or teen materials available. Military organizations need popular materials on base or deployed with troops (Anderson 2012). Small libraries find that some collections, once they have fulfilled the need of the intended audience, are no longer needed. All types of libraries are challenged when discarding materials and particularly multiple copies of books that have served high demand over a short period of time.

Therefore, when considering whether to lease, librarians will consider factors beyond the materials' price, to choose the strategy that provides the best service at the best price for customers. Among these factors are costs related to the following:

- Local fiscal rules, regulations, and budgeting
- Selection and ordering
- Estimated delivery date for materials (time sensitivity)
- Cataloging and processing
- Ongoing shelving and maintenance
- Deselection and disposal of materials

This chapter examines the reasons why leasing plans may provide an alternative to purchase. It also offers guidance on what questions one should ask when considering this alternative.

HOW LEASING WORKS

Currently two library vendors are the chief suppliers of leased print and audiovisual materials. Brodart's McNaughton Plan has been offering lease services to public libraries since the 1950s, and Baker & Taylor, Inc., has been offering subscription plans since the 1980s.

Although the programs offer similar services, differences need to be investigated by anyone considering leasing. For instance, these vendors, since they also supply purchasing plans, may offer combined strategies of leasing, lease/purchasing or purchasing that best serves customer needs. Indeed, one may choose to purchase materials from any large vendor, including Ingram, YBP (a division of Baker & Taylor specializing in academic titles) and also choose to lease materials to fulfill other needs. As with purchasing plans, libraries may ask to negotiate some elements of the lease service plans (Harvey 2012).

In general, leasing is based on a service plan for a specific facility or branch. After choosing the optimum size for the collection, a prepaid cost for the annual service plan is designed. The negotiated price includes a basic cataloging and processing package and free shipping. Leased materials include a plastic jacket that easily distinguishes them from items owned by the library. Since most of the materials are to be returned to the vendor who may resell them, libraries are asked not to place ownership stamps on the book or its paper jacket. Spine labels, ownership labels, and barcodes are usually affixed to the plastic jacket that provides the visual clue that the book is leased rather than part of the library's permanent collection.

The prepaid leasing price translates into points or allowances. In the simplest of terms, if a book's retail cost is equal to or less than the price negotiated for one point it will be selected at the one-point rate; if the retail cost is more than the negotiated price per point, another point, or more, will be charged for the item. Thus, determining the best price point is important to the success of the program. Vendors, once they understand the purpose of the collection, can advise the best solution. Libraries beginning with leased plans should determine if they may add points to the plan if needed; staff should also determine what happens if all points or allowances are not used within a year. It is usual in the first year for a rollover to be negotiated.

A new subscriber may choose to have either a starter collection or 13-month allowance for the first year. Whichever is chosen, over time the collection will grow into its optimum size (usually within a 12-month period). Libraries need not return any product to the vendor until the optimum size is reached.

On a monthly basis, the library selection staff is advised that the current selection list is available through the vendor's Web site. These lists will usually include prepublication best sellers as well as current and anticipated high-demand titles. Usually items are shipped free to the library on or near to publication date and require little processing. For many customers this means that the items may arrive ready or near ready for shelving.

Monthly online reports are produced by the vendor indicating the current size of the collection and how many points remain to lease desired items. Vendor staff specialists are available to answer staff questions. Vendors will also alert the selector if it looks like the annual points will be used before the end of the contracted year.

While libraries are not required to return leased items until they have reached their maximum operational size, some may choose to do so. Once they have reached their negotiated collection size, libraries are alerted to how many leased items they must return. Librarians can choose what items they return. They may choose to return slower moving, more recently published materials, while retaining older materials that are still circulating.

Both vendor programs accept that some materials will be lost or damaged by customers; a percentage of the designated materials are not expected to be returned. For example, for every 100 items in the program, the library may be expected to return only 90 items. Also, if the library chooses, they may retain copies of some materials, paying a nominal fee to complete the purchase of items. Once the books are identified for return, the library requests a shipping tag from the vendor, which is received electronically, and the materials are sent back to the vendor with prepaid shipping.

Within these general guidelines, individual differences may exist between the vendor plans or may be negotiated between the library and the vendor. However, even in a noncustomized lease plan the potential benefits, beyond cost, can be identified.

LOCAL FISCAL RULES AND REGULATIONS AND THE BUDGET

Some libraries prefer lease service plans because funding for these materials can be maintained even though other materials' budgets may be reduced. Leasing services may come from a separate contract line in the operating budget. Support organizations or endowments may supply the funds for the lease program. Rental collections with a reasonable fee may provide the funds to support the program (Odess-Harnish 2002; PUBLIB Archives 1995–2009).

While some jurisdictions allow for prepayment for materials not yet received, many do not. However, the same jurisdictions may allow for the purchase of a service that provides, temporarily, high-demand titles.

Furthermore, in terms of daily operations, a prepaid lease service will not only reduce the number of invoices received but also allow for a quick, one-time reduction in a budget line. A further benefit is that if there is a mid-year reduction in the materials' budget, the prepaid plan can ensure that customers will still have access to best-selling materials.

In considering the relative costs of the lease plan and purchasing, libraries should consider that the subscription provides materials that are preprocessed and nearly shelf-ready. Cataloging records are part of the service (both as short on-order records and as complete MARC records). Free shipping is included in the plan. Libraries should compare these advantages with the cost of purchased materials.

The number and level of staff needed to administer and deal with purchased items and leasing plans also should be compared. When considering that leased books must be returned to the vendor, the comparison to the level of staff needed to weed purchased materials may be an important comparison.

SELECTION AND ORDERING MATERIALS

While most library customers highly value being able to read best sellers, the selection and ordering of them usually comprises only a small part of the selector's many duties. Therefore, vendor selection specialists and the lists they create are major assets to library staff, allowing them to quickly identify not only best sellers but also potential high-demand titles. Other benefits related to selection and ordering including the following:

- Vendors track when midlist authors are poised for best-seller status.
- Lists offer books that may have a short but intense use period and for which the library needs few or none in their permanent collection (books written by or about presidential candidates).

- Sleepers, media tie-ins, and other suddenly popular titles are offered.
- Selectors are exposed to a national list of high-demand items and may choose to experiment with authors without needing to maintain the materials in a permanent collection if the experiment fails.

Finally, as many multiple branch systems have moved away from decentralized to centralized selection, many former branch selectors welcome the chance, if offered, to build a collection of popular items that respond to their customers' unique needs.

For other libraries that have critical vacancies in selection staff, a lease service may offer to set up automatic ordering for certain authors at a predetermined number as profiled by the library and ensure that critically needed materials are received on time.

ESTIMATED DELIVERY TIME

If ordered as soon as they appear on the plan Web site, leased prepublication materials usually arrive on or near the publication date. For some libraries this provides a valuable benefit. With most purchase programs, vendors have a first-order received or first-order shipped rule. Thus, only those libraries with a dedicated staff that aggressively order best sellers long before publication can ensure receipt of best sellers on or near street date.

Vendors with lease service plans have a separate operation to supply multiple copies of high-demand items to their customers. The lease service plan groups order for their special operations with a knowledge of how materials have been ordered in the past, and can anticipate need.

It is important when looking at leasing plans that libraries get a clear idea of how near to street date they will obtain best-selling materials. There are relatively few materials that publishers will guarantee to ship to vendors prior to street date. Knowing what these materials are and what library staff's responsibilities are in the process is critical to the success of the program.

CATALOGING AND PROCESSING

Investigating how on-order and full MARC records are received and downloaded to the library's ILS is part of the setup of a lease plan. Since lease service plans are available online, many libraries will find the easy access to on-order and, eventually, full MARC records a major benefit.

Lease materials may not require as much processing as purchased library materials. Because they are not meant usually as candidates for the library's permanent collection, libraries need to train staff to not mark the book with ownership stamps. This is mitigated by the collection's distinctive jackets or packaging, which can signal staff that the item is leased. Some libraries may not require classification spine labels or other markings (although such specifications are part of the package offered by vendors). If a library decides to purchase and keep the item for the permanent collection, removal of the dust jacket is often all that is required to make it fit for library-specific processing.

Since many libraries have small processing groups, obtaining high-demand materials in a nearly complete shelf-ready status is a major benefit.

ONGOING SHELVING AND MAINTENANCE

If leased items are not meant to be maintained for long in the collection, the need to repair them over time is reduced or eliminated. If a book is badly damaged by a customer, the quota of materials that are expected to not be returned due to customer use can cover it. It is important to note that vendors will replace items that are damaged in shipping or have a publication flaw as long as these issues are reported within a specific period of time.

In determining that an item may have value to the permanent collection, and therefore taking advantage of the purchase option in a lease plan, librarians can base the decision on actual use and may choose the least-worn materials to keep.

In general, most leased items will be removed from the collection within a 12- to 24-month period. While ILS reports may be used to determine what should be removed, decisions can often be based on a simple visual scan: if more than x numbers of copies of an item are on the shelf, remove those with the most wear to return to the vendor.

Finally, regular weeding of these materials, as mandated by the program, ensures that these items do not negatively impact valuable shelving real estate. For many facilities this is a critical consideration.

DESELECTION AND DISPOSAL

Determining when a leased item can be removed and shipped back to the vendor can be a clerical function based on rules set up by the local professional. Librarians may concentrate on the selection of materials and on the analysis of reports to determine how customer use is changing over time.

Leasing may address concerns about what to do with items removed from the collection. While many libraries have agreements that allow them (or support groups) to sell items, for other entities this solution is not available. Some libraries may not have a large enough customer base to sell multiple copies of former best sellers. Fiscal rules may preclude discarding and selling materials. Rather than putting discards in a landfill, libraries may choose to send them back to vendors for further use or recycling.

For very large multibranch systems, returning the items to the vendor may avoid political issues of needing to dispose of or sell hundreds of discards. Other libraries may choose to take the purchase option and recycle, sell, or use extra copies for special programs (book club boxes, literacy programs, etc.).

CONCLUSION

As a possible strategy to obtain high-demand materials for customers, many types of libraries have found that a lease subscription plan provides a viable solution. When considering such a plan, librarians should compare the benefits and challenges of such a program. Vendor programs have subtle but important differences. Each library must determine for itself whether this strategy is one that it can or wants to utilize.

REFERENCES

Anderson, Kris. 2012. "Interview: Kris Anderson, Brodart."

Berry, John. 1989. "Fifty Years with Libraries: An Interview with Brodart's Art Brody." *Library Journal* 114 (December): 83–86.

Harvey, Fred. 2012. "Interview with Fred Harvey, Baker & Taylor."

Odess-Harnish, Kerri A. 2002. "Making Sense of Leased Popular Literature Collections." Available at: http://cupola.gettysburg.edu/librarypubs/9/. Accessed December 26, 2012.

PUBLIB Archives. 1995–2009. Available at: http://listserv.oclc.org/archives/publib.html. Accessed December 26, 2012. [Reviewed postings from October 27, 1995 to August 18, 2009, concerning leased materials.]

APPENDIX

Questions for librarians to answer as they consider using a lease subscription plan:

1. What customer need am I fulfilling through the use of a lease service plan? What do I want to accomplish?
2. Will current local, state, or jurisdictional rules and regulations allow for a prepaid lease service?
3. What funds will I use: operational (contract, purchase, etc.), endowment, gift funds, or other?
4. What are the costs covered in the lease plan (cataloging, processing, and shipping). How does this compare with current purchasing costs?
   a. What added cataloging and processing needs to be done by library staff prior to making the item shelf-ready?
   b. Are RFID tags and RFID tags included in processing?
   c. Does this program create or save work for library catalogers and processors?
5. How many library employees at what level are needed to administer the plan(s), and what are the estimated costs when compared to purchasing costs for the following:
   a. selection and ordering;
   b. receiving materials;

    c. library processing and cataloging; and

    d. monitor, maintain, and return leased materials to vendor (this should be compared to costs to deselect and weed purchased materials if selected at the same level as the leased materials)?

6. Does the plan allow me to set up a preorder plan that automatically orders some authors as soon as they become available for order? Will this guarantee receipt of materials on or near street date?

7. How often should the library select materials (if not on an automatic plan or combining with an automatic plan)?

8. May items not on the vendor's lists be added? How? What limitations are there on the type of material that may be added?

9. Does the plan promise to deliver best sellers on or before street date?

    a. If not, how soon will best sellers arrive?

    b. What must library staff do to make sure that materials arrive on, before, or near to street date?

10. How does your plan work with your library's ILS system?

    a. What is included in an on-order record?

    b. What is included in the full MARC record?

    c. Will this record be acceptable and complete for the library or will staff have to customize to meet local needs?

11. How can I obtain ongoing information on the size of the lease collection, points or allowance balance, and so forth?

12. Who will I contact if I have questions or need help? How soon will they respond?

13. What happens if I overestimate or underestimate the points needed for the program?

14. What happens if I decide to change from a lease-only plan to a lease or purchase plan; or from a lease or purchase plan to a lease-only subscription?

15. How often am I required to return materials to the vendor?

16. What happens if I decide to keep a book rather than return it?

17. What are the benefits or challenges of leasing or purchasing in terms of the following?

    a. Shelf space over time

    b. Disposing of no longer needed materials

    c. Revenue (sales of books no longer needed in the collection)

    d. Political considerations

    e. Other considerations

15

SELF-PUBLISHING: DOES IT BELONG IN THE COLLECTION?

James LaRue

PURPOSE OF THE PUBLIC LIBRARY

My premise is simple: "The purpose of the public library is to gather, organize, and present to the public the intellectual content of our culture" (LaRue 2012). We collect stories, ideas, movies, music, and even each other (through showcasing community perspectives and resources). We mine all of these voices for meaning. The library is less like a warehouse than like a big family's holiday dinner.

But the family of our culture's content is growing. And right now, just a dozen years into the 21st century, some of those voices have yet to be invited to the table. Yet they may be among the most vital new voices we have.

THE MAINSTREAM AND THE FRINGE

At this writing, the decades-long market consolidation of a few big publishers has resulted in just five mega-corporations: HarperCollins, Random House/Penguin, Hachette, Macmillan, and Simon & Schuster. Together, at least for the Douglas County Libraries, they source a little more than half of our purchases.

But the legacy publishers are not the only game in town. There are many other highly capable, high-quality publishers. They range from midlist publishers of medium size to hundreds of small and independent publishers whose output and sales are increasing. Kelly Gallagher (2013) of the Independent Publishers Association wrote, "you can convincingly conclude that we constitute the industry's healthiest and fastest-growing segment."

But the focus of this chapter is on yet another player: the self-published author.

According to a 2012 analysis of data from Bowker Books in Print and Bowker Identifier Services (Bowker 2012), "The number of self-published books produced annually in the U.S. has nearly tripled, growing 287 percent since 2006, and now tallies more than 235,000 print and 'e' titles."

This sudden burst of new writing has few parallels in human history. Not since Gutenberg have we seen such a fundamental shift in the proliferation of new voices.

Right now, however, few of these titles wind up in libraries. There are many reasons for that. The key reason is this: the existing systems of review and distribution make it difficult for publishers with fewer than 10 new titles a year to get noticed by either reviewers or distributors. For many public libraries, if it does not get reviewed in a handful of library magazines, and is not carried by our two or three distributors, we do not know about it, and could not easily buy it if we wanted to. Our workflows and purchasing processes evolved to deal with the mainstream. We do not know how to deal with the fringe—even if, now, the fringe outnumbers the mainstream two to one. This moment in library history is a clear example of creative destruction—the replacement of one economic order with another. This new order has the potential to be far more inclusive.

WHY SELF-PUBLISHING?

Why do authors decide to self-publish in the first place? Among the reasons are the following:

- They are unable to gain the attention of an agent or a publisher. The publishing ecosystem up to 2010 has been one of gatekeeping. It is hard to break in.
- Fringe works—as in cross-genre novels that do not fit neatly into predefined reader categories—tend to be marketed poorly. Some authors would argue that none of today's works are really marketed with enthusiasm.
- Authors do not like pressures to change either the content (to meet an editor's belief about what would sell) or the package (the cover, the title). Authors want to have more control.
- Authors typically sacrifice copyright—ownership of their own property—to a corporation.

The longstanding model of the publishing contract has been heavily tilted in favor of the publisher. First-time authors get between 8 and 10 percent of the revenue. Even very well-established authors seldom get as much as 20 percent from legacy publishers. But self-published authors can get from 70 percent (at Amazon's CreateSpace), to 85 percent through Smashwords.

That last point may be the most predictive. It is hard for any author to make a living writing, unless they write a best seller. But it is easier when most of the revenue comes back to the creator. While publishers certainly can and do add value—writing well takes many rounds of good editing, and marketing takes money and a different kind of expertise—is it really nine times more valuable than the creative work itself?

It might be argued, too, that publishers are most important for new writers. Established writers could easily hire out professionals for editing, copy editing, book design, and marketing tasks while still retaining control over those processes and copyright. One does not have to be a seer to predict that writers who have already learned how to write a good book, and who have already found loyal fans, will jump the legacy publishing ship, and thrive as a result.

In 2012, 16 of the *New York Times'* best sellers were self-published. This is not a flash in the pan. For many authors, and thus for many libraries, it is the future of writing.

QUALITY, DEMAND, AND PRICE

Just as there are two issues in cataloging (relevance and retrieval), there are three in collection development:

- the quality of the work (both in terms of literary merit and format);
- the demand for the work (usually measured by advance requests, reserves, and use); and
- the availability of the work.

The relationship among these factors is complex. Unusually fine writing is no guarantee of public interest. Significant demand for an item may be completely unrelated to its quality. Finally, quality and interest often have nothing at all to do with the ease of obtaining a work.

How then is a library to decide how best to respond to the trend of self-publishing? Let's take those points one at a time.

QUALITY

Typically, libraries discover good works through reviews. For self-published works, like Christian fiction before them, library professional journals came to the game late. But once it was clear that library patrons wanted Christian fiction, journal editors took notice. We have already begun to see reviews of self-published authors appearing in *Publishers Weekly* and *Library Journal*, and we can expect that trend to continue.

There are some new players. BlueInk Review and Foreword are just two of the new agencies springing up to identify promising new talent. But as I have learned from personal discussions with the editors of BlueInk, the slush pile problem is real. That is, although many fine writers are considering self-publishing, not all those who consider self-publishing are fine writers. Most of the people who try to write a book (or write a poem, create a song, or paint a picture) are amateurs. It takes disciplined practice, research, and informed feedback to achieve mastery at anything. Few walk that path.

So self-published authors cannot just send a copy of their books to *Library Journal* or any other professional magazine and expect a free, prompt, and glowing review. Journals would be overwhelmed by poorly conceived, poorly executed digital manuscripts. Indeed, they already are.

BlueInk Review, then, charges the author for a review (approximately $500), and pays the reviewer for his or her time. The reviews are professionally done, and anonymous. Once the review is complete, the authors can choose not to have Blue Ink Review post it on its Web site. But they pay either way.

This cost barrier turns away the casual amateur. Nonetheless, after a couple of years of operation, BlueInk staff report that most of what is submitted is not very good. (This is true for legacy publishers, too.) There are a few glorious exceptions. And when BlueInk finds them, they post their recommendations.

We can expect that we will see more of such services springing up. One response might be to simply set up a standing order for anything they recommend. Right now, that is not a flood of titles. But it may become one.

Beyond the existing reviewers and the new breed, what else can libraries do?

While many of these works appear in author blogs, or may even garner good reviews in Amazon (often, alas, by other self-published authors trading favors), the sheer number of such Internet-based resources makes it difficult to keep track of everything.

The obvious truth is this: our systems of review, of librarians vetting the content in advance of acquisition, have broken down. We simply cannot keep up with 300,000 new commercial titles, almost that number of independent press offerings, and yet another 300,000 self-published titles.

No large-scale solution seems to be at hand, then. As always, some titles will be brought to local attention by local readers. Most libraries are willing to try to buy something that comes with a guaranteed reader (or from an author whose previous works have circulated well). That moves us into the area of demand.

DEMAND

Demand for the Big Six titles is a direct result of promotional dollars, either through direct ads, publisher catalogs, or sponsored author tours and interviews. Sometimes instead the legacy publishers capitalize on the celebrity of people who achieve fame outside the publishing machinery.

Few self-published titles will have that initial demand—although I do think this will change as more established authors strike out on their own.

Also, not all authors are natural speakers or self-promoters. So absent a marketing department, self-published authors, right now, face the primary problem of simply getting noticed.

At the end of 2012, as part of the establishment of our Digital Branch, in which we sought to own and manage our own content, Douglas County Libraries purchased and received roughly 10,000 self-published titles from Smashwords. Our intent was to establish an opening-day collection that not only featured the digital version of our print best sellers, but also sampled the worlds of independent and self-published content. We were curious to see what our patrons might think of them.

Smashwords is one of the more successful of the ePublishing startups. For no cost, it allows authors to upload their works to the Smashwords server, then control their sale and price to Amazon, Barnes and Noble, and now, to libraries. For each sale, Smashwords takes 15 percent, and the author gets 85 percent.

Mark Coker, the founder of the company, has long sold to bookstores. More recently, he expressed some interest in selling to libraries. We discussed the deal together at the 2012 ALA Annual Conference in Anaheim. Finally, we decided to choose a package of titles on the basis, first, of sales. Best selling is a relative term, but we indicated our interest in the most popular of his titles. We then amended it to include titles that were part of popular series, even if those particular titles did not hit the sales threshold. Most of the titles were genre fiction, where, we reasoned, the public did not care so much who published it, provided only that the book was well written.

But then we got to the next issue: some of the most popular books in the Smashwords catalog were erotica—about 25 percent. That's probably not surprising, post-"Fifty Shades of Grey." But given that the Smashwords titles would make up about a third of our opening-day collection of our materials, we were inclined not to surprise too many of our patrons with a shift in our holdings. While we do have many popular erotic titles, acquiring more of them was not a collection development goal for us, and erotica has many exotic subgenres we tended to steer clear of.

This is collection development in reverse. Instead of buying only what has been requested or well reviewed, we were requesting a large sample from a new distributor, then deselecting what we did not want.

Once we acquired the titles, and worked through the various issues of matching up the files, cover art, and metadata, we added the items to our collection. At this writing, we only have a few months of use data. But Smashwords titles have already proven to be our most popular single source of library-owned content.

There are several reasons.

First, some of these popular books were not new. Rather, they were titles whose copyright had recently returned to the author, and were finding a second life in the digital world. For instance, I was pleased to see that some science-fiction classics, probably weeded from our collection years ago, were returning. The quality was high. I realized that for those of us who do read and enjoy genre fiction, rediscovering these titles would be a pleasure. It just might be that in the virtual library, we might never have to weed again, although we might still divide the presentation of our content into current and archival.

Second, we have built a recommendation engine into our catalog. If patrons read mysteries, or romances, or science fiction, and if they have an eBook reader, they simply want a steady stream of content. "If you liked this, you might like this" is often a great convenience to our patrons. It does lead to increased circulation. A subset of the recommendation is the importance of user reviews. Trusted reviews (as Goodreads demonstrated for a time) do encourage people to find and try things they would not know about otherwise.

There are at least four other strategies to capture the interest of readers:

- Author visits and events: When we find a personable and articulate author, it makes sense to build a program around him or her, whether in person, as a podcast, or on local cable TV. We use author panels, or lecture and question sessions, and such programs can be very popular. In the past, such programs have put authors' older works back on the local best-seller list both in the library and at our local independent bookstores (who are, incidentally, wonderful partners for such events).
- Displays: Some 60 percent of our adult circulation is driven by displays. We have just begun to try to figure out how to display eBooks. Our attempts to use large touch-screen displays have thus far failed, mostly for technical reasons. But the idea is a good one, and we will keep trying.
- Mobile apps: We have created a couple of phone applications that run on iOS, Android, and Windows. In the past year, more people have downloaded these apps than have attended our physical programs. Again, with our recommendation engine, this makes it much easier to just grab the highest rated or most popular of our titles. Given the growth of smartphones and tablets, it may be that our reach of these customized displays is more powerful in people's palms than in our buildings.
- Handselling: But we continue to have far more visitors than we do mobile app downloads. Ultimately, the most successful strategy to help our patrons find this rich new source of content is to get our staff reading and talking about it. Here is one tactic that worked: we announced at a continuing education day that the library would provide a $50 posttax contribution to their purchase of one of five approved eReaders. A third of our staff took us up on it, and then proceeded to train themselves. That approach wound up not only being cheaper than paying for training, it also proved stickier—our staff became intimately familiar with a range of devices, and could quickly refer patrons to qualified and confident help. These staff also took a much keener interest in our collection.

AVAILABILITY

I want to underscore something vital to the understanding of this new market. The Big Six had set the library price for eBooks, across the board, as anywhere from 20 to 600 percent higher than the consumer price. The reasons varied. They alleged that libraries stole sales from authors, or that we sought free distribution of content. In fact, research by Bowker and *Library Journal* suggests that we boost sales. Libraries are, and always have been, staunch supporters of copyright.

But when confronted with publishers who either will not sell to us, or insist on onerous pricing or licenses, one naturally turns to other channels.

Coker (the Smashwords CEO) surveyed his authors to ask them several questions. First, were they willing to sell to libraries? Unanimously, they were.

Second, if they had to set a price, would they charge more than the consumer price, the same, or less? To his surprise and mine, 20 percent of the 250 authors he surveyed said they would *give* at least one copy of their books to a local library.

At any rate, Coker allowed the authors to determine whether or not they would sell their books to libraries, and at what price.

So after we put together the list of titles we wanted to buy, we found that the average cost of them was $4 apiece. It appears that there was a significant disconnect between what the publishers set as market value for libraries, and what the creators of that content believed was fair.

A second vital factor is that the Douglas County Libraries has its own content management system. Most libraries do not. And as noted earlier, most distributors do not carry self-published authors, even the ones that make it to the best-seller lists. In order for libraries to carry such authors, they either need to invest in their own servers and infrastructure (either individually or consortially), or find vendors who will host and integrate the content for them. The former path is still new; the latter is immature. Both constitute barriers to be overcome.

A NEW ROLE FOR PUBLIC LIBRARIES

Once Douglas County Libraries established its content server infrastructure, we realized that perhaps we could join the publishing revolution ourselves. Why not, we wondered, focus not only on buying the successful self-published authors, but on incubating authors in our own backyard?

Again, the sheer volume of local writing makes it difficult to track across the nation. But libraries might well be able to stay on top of creative efforts by dedicated individuals within the library service area.

One approach might look something like the following:

- The library has a Web site appealing to local authors.
- The Web site includes a roadmap to achieving excellence, a list of resources (current collection, local author support groups, copy editors, book-cover designers, formatting assistance, etc.), and a list of upcoming

programs and events. For instance, there might be author university classes, or local author panels and signings.

- The library advertises for, interviews, and intelligently manages a group of local volunteers. These volunteers would be trained as collection development advisors and reviewers, enabling the community to move from mere consumption of intellectual content to its conscious creation.
- A program of awards, in which the best local writing is annually recognized and rewarded by the library.
- A direct sales component. If libraries help readers find the works of local authors, it might also help sell them. And the library might request a percentage of the sale. In my experience with local writer focus groups, most authors would be more than eager to partner with us.

Helping writers produce better books, then helping them market them, seems a worthwhile goal.

TECHNICAL CONCERNS

There are various technical concerns.

First, we have focused on the ePub format for our titles. At present, that means that we cannot serve them to pre-Fire Kindle users. But the dedicated eReader seems to be giving way fast to the tablet (at this writing, fewer than half of our eReader patrons use pre-Fire Kindles), and our apps will eventually solve the problem on newer platforms.

But even the ePub, an open standard, can be a challenge to some authors. Over time, more software tools will be developed to solve this. Right now, authors may need the help of services or even one-on-one consulting. Can libraries fulfill this role?

Second, discoverability of a title requires it to have good metadata. That is usually not a problem for works that are also in print. But it is clear that we may need to provide everything from ISBN to subject headings—or work closely with such outfits as Smashwords to set a standard.

Third, we have eschewed complicated licensing agreements. See our Colorado State Library-sponsored Web site (evoke.cvlsites.org) to find our Statement of Common Understanding. In brief, we propose to acquire and own a copy of the eBook file. We seek a discount from the consumer price (and will ask local authors for one donated copy). We will help market the piece, and buy additional copies based on demand (typically, one copy for every four holds). We will attach Digital Rights Management (through our Adobe Content Server) by default—although we can also accommodate Creative Commons licenses, at author request. Again by default, we will restrict use to one patron at a time. Finally, we will provide a link to purchase the title, and will ask for a percentage of the sale (not to exceed 10 percent).

CONCLUSION

There are fads, and there are trends. I believe that self-publishing is the latter, a true moment of creative destruction. The old, legacy systems of corporate control are fracturing. It has long been the challenge of the public library to connect writers with readers. That challenge has just gotten a lot tougher. But the times also offer us the opportunity to become far more significant not just in the distribution of content, but in its creation too. Who knows what magnificent new literature is about to be born?

It is time for us to move from gatekeeper to gardener.

REFERENCES

Bowker. 2012. "Self-Publishing Sees Triple Digit Growth in Just Five Years, Says Bowker." Available at: http://www.bowker.com/en-US/aboutus/press_room/2012/pr_10242012.shtml. Accessed May 21, 2013.

Gallagher, Kelly. 2013. "Independent Publisher Power." Available at: https://www.ibpa-online.org/article/independent-publisher-power/#.UZuVOaUrfdk. Accessed May 21, 2013.

LaRue, James. 2012. "The Last One Standing." Available at: http://publiclibrariesonline.org/2013/04/the-last-one-standing/. Accessed June 26, 2013.

16

eBooks in Academic Libraries

Michael Levine-Clark

INTRODUCTION

In 1999 the University of Denver acquired its first eBooks from the newly formed Boulder, Colorado, company netLibrary. Questia had recently been formed and ebrary was founded that year as well (ebrary 2012c; Questia 2012). It seemed that academic libraries were going to move quickly toward building eBook collections; the transition to e-journals, which was largely complete, would be replicated for eBooks. Over a decade later, we are still waiting for eBooks to take off.

Though the Kindle, the Nook, and the iPad have thrust popular eBooks into the mainstream, making them the first choice for many readers and an acceptable choice for many others, academic libraries have lagged behind. Reading the laments of academic librarians over the past decade is a bit disheartening, because many of the problems identified early on are still there. An eBook task force, formed in August 2000 by the California Digital Library, noted "that all the elements that would make the eBook market viable are not quite in place. The partnerships in the market, development of standards, software and hardware features, and business models are still regularly changing" (Snowhill 2001). Lynn Silipigni Connaway and Heather L. Wicht (2007) identified similar problems with eBooks six years later:

> Several themes consistently appear in the literature on the barriers to the adoption and integration of eBooks into library collections, services, and systems. These include the lack of eBook and hardware standards; incompatible rights and operability; unrealistic price, purchase, and access models; and limited discovery and delivery options.

Robert Slater, writing in 2010, wondered "Why Aren't EBooks Gaining More Ground in Academic Libraries?" and concluded that discovery, Digital

Rights Management (DRM), and purchase models were all obstacles (Slater 2010). Slater's concluding sentence is worth quoting: "Ideally, the choice to acquire a print or electronic copy of a book should be as simple as a single choice (print, electronic, or both) integrated into the same acquisition systems libraries already use for print books" (Slater 2010, 328). eBook acquisition is incredibly difficult and incredibly confusing, and we seem to be nowhere near the point that Slater envisions.

Academic libraries have been slow to adopt eBooks for two basic reasons: (1) difficulties in determining when or if a monograph is available in electronic format and (2) concerns librarians and users hold about DRM and difficulty of use. Both of these issues are still with us, well over a decade after the introduction of eBooks into academic libraries.

It is a relatively straightforward process for an academic library to order a print book. Someone needs to determine the correct edition and whether it is available. After that almost any book that is in print can be ordered from one of the library's preferred vendors. Many books that are out of print can be ordered via a wide range of services that aggregate content from used-book dealers. In some cases, such as Amazon, both new and used books can be found and purchased on the same Web site. With eBooks, several extra steps need to be taken: the librarian placing the order needs to determine if an electronic version is available at all and he or she needs to then figure out if that electronic version is for sale to libraries or just to end users. If libraries are able to purchase the eBook, then the librarian needs to decide which eBook platform or vendor to use, and, if the option exists, whether to buy a single- or multiuser version.

Scholarly publishers, fearing that availability of eBooks to an entire campus might decrease overall sales, have been understandably reluctant to make it easy for academic libraries to purchase eBooks. Many publishers release eBooks well after the publication date of the print version, probably in hopes that the print copy will sell to both the library and to individual faculty members, and then the e-copy will be acquired as well. YBP Library Services, one of the two major academic book vendors in North America, estimates that only 42 percent of monographs that it covers come out within two months of each other in print and electronic formats (Matt Nauman, Academic Digital Content Manager, YBP Library Services, email message to author, October 31, 2012). And publishers that expect heavy course adoption of a title may not make it available as an eBook to libraries at all.

Another barrier to widespread acceptance of eBooks in academic libraries has been the implementation of restrictive digital rights management technologies by publishers and aggregators. DRM restrictions vary, but in general they limit access and use in some way. Examples of DRM implementation include restrictions on the number of pages that can be printed or downloaded, on the number of simultaneous users, and on uses commonly made with the print counterpart (ILL, course reserves). Generally speaking, publishers have less restrictive DRM for eBooks on their own platforms. Springer (2012), for instance, has no DRM at all. Aggregators, or third-party eBook platform providers, tend to have more restrictive DRM. They need to have a single implementation that works for all publishers; therefore they tend to match the needs of the most restrictive publishers.

With the difficulties inherent in eBook acquisition in mind, this chapter attempts to provide some guidance for librarians. There is no right way to acquire eBooks. Different selection and access models will work for different academic libraries, depending on collection size, budget, and local philosophy. Some libraries will be best served with a traditional title-by-title selection model that closely mirrors print acquisition. Others will want a bulk subscription model. Still others may be interested in DDA. In reality, most libraries will pick and choose from all of these models.

SELECTION MODELS

Traditionally, academic library book collections have been built on a title-by-title basis. Whether done by a librarian reading reviews or responding to faculty requests, or by an approval vendor selecting books based on librarian-supplied criteria, most books came into the library because that specific title had been selected for inclusion. Though some books came in as part of a standing order—for a series or publisher—also because of librarian input, those titles represented a rather small portion of the books added to the collection. With eBooks there are similarly two broad ways of selecting content—title-by-title and as a package—but so far there has been a much larger emphasis on acquisition of preselected packages than there ever was (or could be) for print books.

As with selection of physical volumes, title-by-title selection of eBooks gives libraries the most flexibility to build collections that meet local curricular and research needs. Acquiring only those titles that have a clear rationale for being in the collection takes more time than acquiring a large package, but is generally cheaper and is one method for ensuring a high level of quality in the collection. The tradeoffs for this level of specificity in collecting are a higher cost per book than other methods, and a greater time commitment. In general, publishers charge full price or more for individual eBooks. In cases where there are both hardbound and paperbound options for the physical book, the eBook is almost always priced at the hardbound level. When a print book is purchased through a book jobber such as YBP, a set discount level is applied. Not only is this discount not applied to eBook purchases, sometimes an additional charge above list price is also included. Librarians who opt to build collections using this model should compare costs of individual title selection, both in real dollars and staff time, to the generally lower costs per title associated with acquiring a package of titles.

Acquisition of eBook packages removes some flexibility for librarians, but frees up time. And often this model provides significant savings at the item level over title-by-title selection. There are multiple flavors of eBook packages—complete publisher collections, publisher subject collections, multipublisher subject collections, complete aggregator collections, pre-selected collections, librarian-selected collections, frontlist collections, and backlist collections—often overlapping with each other. In general, the larger the collection, the deeper the discount from list price, but also the greater the chance of unwanted and unneeded material being included. Librarian-selected collections will meet local needs more closely than will preselected collections, but they will also likely be more expensive since they are essentially a bulk title-by-title purchase. In most cases backlist collections will be cheaper than frontlist collections, but can make sense for subjects in which currency of information is less important. Package acquisition may be the best model for those who collect at a particularly high level in a given subject area, those who would normally acquire a high percentage of books in any particular category through title-by-title selection, or those who aim to introduce users to a critical mass of eBooks.

ACCESS MODELS

Regardless of the method used to select eBooks, there are two basic access models—subscription and perpetual access—each with multiple variations. Some vendors allow only one of these options, while others provide both. Each of these models has benefits—for particular types of books or for particular budget situations.

Subscription packages, which are available from a range of aggregators, allow a library to build a large collection of eBooks for a relatively inexpensive annual cost. In some cases, subscription packages cost just pennies per title for the year. Good examples of this sort of package are ebrary's *Academic Complete* and *College Complete*, both of which provide tens of thousands of titles from hundreds of publishers (ebrary 2012a), and EBSCO's *eBook Academic Subscription Collection*, with more than 100,000 titles (EBSCO 2013). These packages primarily consist of backlist titles with relatively few frontlist titles, but the cost per title is very low, making these good solutions for libraries, particularly those with relatively small collections budgets that wish to introduce large collections of eBooks at once. As with journal aggregator packages, there is no guarantee that any one title or publisher will remain available in these packages, so librarians should purchase direct access to specific titles if there is a need for perpetual access.

Another good reason for a library to consider subscribing to packages of eBooks is to manage rapid obsolescence. Rather than paying for perpetual access to content that will go out of date quickly, many libraries choose to subscribe to packages of computer and technical manuals, business books, and medical materials. New books are added to these packages but are available only for a few years. As new content gets added, older content is removed.

Knovel, Safari, and Books 24 × 7 are examples of vendors that offer this sort of subscription package (Knovel 2012; Safari 2012; Skillsoft 2012).

Some providers—whether publishers or aggregators—make eBooks available through a perpetual access model only. Others (e.g., ebrary and EBSCO) give a choice of models. Perpetual access gives the library licensed access to the content, which theoretically will be available forever to the library's users, but this comes at a cost, as libraries pay a higher price upfront for perpetual access. There are many payment models associated with perpetual access— individual title purchase, package purchase, single or multiple-user access, and many variations of each. If there is a strong likelihood that an eBook will be used sometime in the future or if a title is particularly important for the library's collections, then perpetual access is the preferable model. Unlike with subscription packages, titles licensed for perpetual access cannot disappear from the library collection without warning, so there is greater content stability.

In some cases, perpetual access models can act like subscriptions from a budgeting perspective, though not from an access or licensing viewpoint. When a library opts to pay annually for a package—such as all of the books a publisher produces in a calendar year then that commitment mimics a subscription if this content is purchased year after year. But, unlike the subscription packages described earlier, this content is purchased, not leased, and so will be available to the library's users well into the future, even if the library stops purchasing the annual packages.

Within perpetual access licensing models, there are multiple options for payment based on level of access, typically some variation of a single versus multiple simultaneous users. It is worth exploring this distinction using two of the major eBook vendors as examples. For ebrary, there are two purchase possibilities—Single User Purchase Option (SUPO) and Multiple User Purchase Option (MUPO)—with the not-so-neatly abbreviated Numerous Single User Purchase Option (NUPO) thrown in (ebrary 2012b). SUPO titles—as their name implies—can be used by only one person at a time. If a second user tries to access the document, she will be turned away. This is the cheapest option, and for most eBooks in most libraries, it is the only option needed. MUPO titles are more expensive, but multiple users can access them at the same time. For a title assigned in a course and put on electronic reserves, or for anything else with expected high use, this is the better option, as it reduces potential user frustration, but it is more expensive. And then there's NUPO, which is an option to purchase multiple SUPO copies of the same title when MUPO is not an option. ebrary has just introduced an extended access model that triggers an automatic upgrade of a SUPO title to MUPO if a second user accesses that eBook while someone else is already using it. This model allows for some free discovery before that upgrade is purchased, and gives libraries a way to invest initially in the lower cost SUPO version while allowing for unlimited use (Neil Sorensen, ebrary Specialist, email message to author, October 25, 2012).

Ebook Library (EBL) approaches the single-versus-multiple user issue differently. Instead of providing eBooks for just one user at a time, EBL uses a "Non-Linear Lending" model, which allows for unlimited concurrent users of an eBook up to a set number of uses per year (Ebook Library 2012). Up until that point (325 uses for most publishers, 200 for others), the book is effectively a multiple-user title. When the maximum use threshold is reached, access is shut off until the new year begins—or the library can purchase a second instance of the eBook. At the University of Denver, where we have almost 90,000 EBL titles available, we have never had a title go beyond that use threshold in about two-and-a-half years. Some publishers also allow EBL to offer their titles—for a higher cost per title—using the unlimited access model, but it is unnecessary for us to pay the additional cost.

DEMAND-DRIVEN ACQUISITION

Academic libraries have been moving in recent years to a DDA model in which eBooks are acquired only at the point of use. Though this model was originally used as early as 1999, when the Colorado Alliance of Research Libraries began a six-year project with netLibrary to purchase eBooks based on use (Machovec 2003; Polanka and Delquié 2011, 119–20), it is only in the last three years or so that DDA has been widely embraced as an important model for building eBook collections. Though it is somewhat surprising that it took so long for this to happen, it is easy to see why so many libraries have recently begun DDA programs. By moving the point of purchase to the point of use, DDA allows libraries to pay for only what gets used, and even allows payment for varying levels of use, making it possible to provide access to a much larger number of titles than would be possible under a traditional purchase model.

Though there are multiple models of DDA available, at the broadest level it again boils down to title-by-title acquisition and package acquisition. In 2004 EBL developed the model that has since been embraced in some way or another by ebrary and EBSCO eBooks (formerly netLibrary) (Paulson 2011). Under this model, librarians preselect a pool of titles to make available for potential users. The eBook aggregator provides discovery records for the library to load into its discovery service or online catalog, and the library pays the aggregator based on various types of use. With EBL's model, the first five minutes examining an eBook constitute a free browsing period. Equivalent to pulling a paper book off the shelf and examining it briefly, this period gives the user a chance to determine if the eBook is the right book, and is key to ensuring that libraries pay only for intentional use. Once a user spends more than five minutes examining an eBook, a financial transaction is triggered. Librarians can specify whether that transaction will be a short-term loan (STL) or an auto purchase, and can also specify how many STLs will happen before the library pays for an auto purchase. An STL is a brief (one day or one week) rental of the eBook for which the library pays a percentage of the list price.

Most libraries configure their DDA plans with EBL so that an auto purchase happens after a set number of STLs. When the auto purchase is triggered, the library pays for perpetual access (Ebook Library 2012).

Another DDA model—the one pioneered with the Colorado Alliance of Research Libraries by netLibrary (Machovec 2003; Polanka and Delquié 2011)—utilizes as a purchase trigger a set number of uses of the book. Under this model, the library and vendor negotiate the trigger number. For example, on the third visit by anyone to a particular book for any length of time, the library will purchase that title. ebrary experimented briefly with this model (Fischer et al. 2012; Gibbs 2010) and MyiLibrary still offers it (Moore 2011; email from Ingram Content Group Marketing, October 26, 2012), but with the important distinction that access to the table of contents is always free, giving users some guidance about whether the eBook will meet their particular needs (Ingram 2012). The drawback to this model, especially when there is no option for examining at least the front and back matter of the book, is that it does not always allow enough time to determine if a book is right for a particular use. In the Colorado Alliance project with netLibrary, in which the University of Denver participated, we often ended up purchasing books that matched on keywords but clearly did not match a researcher's need.

Another model that some publishers have adopted is what Elsevier terms "Evidence Based Selection" (Elsevier 2012). Under this model, a publisher that does not have the technical infrastructure in place to manage real-time DDA can still provide use-based access to its eBooks. The library sets up a deposit account and the publisher makes a collection of its eBooks available. At the end of the year, the library uses the funds in the deposit account to purchase titles from this collection, likely basing these decisions on use. In theory this is a good model with all of the benefits of DDA, but libraries risk purchasing low-use material if the amount of money they initially allocated to the deposit account is too high. And, unless the process continues into future years, it will only meet the demands of current users.

THE PROVIDERS

When an acquisitions librarian wants to order a paper book, he or she has many sources available. He or she can order the book from an approval vendor, another preferred vendor, Amazon, a used bookseller, a local bookstore, or anyone else who sells books. The edition will be the same and most booksellers offer some level of discount. The choice of where to order comes down to price and convenience, and consolidating purchase with a limited number of booksellers creates efficiencies. Not so with eBooks. Some publishers make their eBooks available through as many sources as possible, while others limit them to just a few, and a very few insist on working directly with libraries only. There are four broad categories of eBook providers (major aggregators, university press aggregators, specialized aggregators, and publishers), and most libraries will find that they need to work with one or more from each category. In many cases, but not all, eBook acquisition from these sources can be managed through the library's preferred approval vendor.

There are four major aggregators—vendors that aggregate content from all types of publishers for academic libraries. Most libraries acquiring eBooks will find themselves working with at least one of these, and in many cases with more than one. EBL, ebrary, EBSCO, and MyiLibrary are similar to each other in many ways and a library's choice of which to work with will come down to platform preference and the degree to which the company integrates with the library's preferred approval vendor. ProQuest, already the parent company of ebrary, has recently announced its acquisition of EBL and plans to merge the two aggregators (ProQuest 2013). All four current aggregators provide books from both trade and academic publishers. All four have DDA models. All four have perpetual access options. All but EBL have subscription options (Ebook Library 2012, ebrary 2012a, EBSCO 2012, MyiLibrary 2012). The benefits of working with one or more of these aggregators include simplified workflow and a common user interface. The strong benefit of streamlined workflow in allowing a library to manage ordering and payment as well as loading MARC records through a single source cannot be overstated. The drawback is less flexibility in using the content: aggregators tend to have stricter DRM controls than do publishers or university press aggregators. Aggregator DRM often means limitations on downloading and printing which many users find frustrating. In fact, a recent survey of librarians about eBooks indicates that "the most significant factor that hinders users in their use of ebook [*sic*] content is digital rights management (DRM)" (Newman and Bui 2009, 27).

There are currently four university press eBook aggregators in various stages of development. University Press Scholarship Online (UPSO), which is managed by Oxford University Press, offers eBooks from 10 university presses (University Press Scholarship Online 2012). University Press Content Consortium (UPCC) on Project Muse offers eBooks from over 65 scholarly and university presses (Project Muse 2012). Books at JSTOR has eBooks from 21 scholarly and university presses (JSTOR 2012). Cambridge University Press runs University Publishing Online, a platform with eBooks from eight scholarly and university presses (University Publishing Online 2012). All are fairly new and are still developing their access models. One benefit of licensing with university press aggregators is that they have little or no DRM in place; users will find it easier to print, download, and share content. In some cases purchasing from these aggregators is similar to acquiring content directly from the publisher.

There are quite a few specialized aggregators that focus on a particular subject area or type of book—often content with a short shelf life. Libraries may want to consider providing access to computer and technical manuals through vendors such as Books 24 × 7 or Safari. Both of these provide large subscription packages of recently published eBooks. Safari makes available books published only in the last three years, with older content dropping out of the package. Books 24 × 7 also has only recent content available. Since most users prefer the latest version of a manual, and seldom have a need for an older version, it makes sense for a library to subscribe to a package for this sort of material. Books 24 × 7 also offers similar packages in other subjects such as business, finance, and engineering (Collections—Skillsoft 2012). Even libraries that are generally committed to perpetual access models will benefit from these sorts of subscriptions.

Quite a few publishers provide access to eBooks on their own platforms. With some larger publishers, such as Oxford, Cambridge, Springer, Elsevier, and Wiley, this may be a desirable option since these platforms allow easy cross searching with other publisher content, including journals. The other benefit of ordering eBooks directly from the publisher is that generally there is little or no DRM included. Libraries will need to weigh that benefit against the potential confusion for users of dozens of different eBook platforms and the less streamlined workflow for librarians who will need to manage eBook acquisition and discovery through many sources.

APPROVAL VENDORS: BRINGING IT ALL TOGETHER

Academic libraries have more sources for eBooks than they can possibly deal with, and they will continue to collect print books as well. Most libraries are not equipped to manage the complex processes of ordering eBooks from multiple sources, managing duplication across those sources and with print books, and managing the provision of discovery records to allow access to all that content. Approval vendors, which have long been in the business of supplying print books to academic libraries and have expanded into the eBook market, have stepped in to help fill this role. It would be wonderful if all eBooks could be ordered from a single source, but even with approval vendors brokering these deals, libraries will find that they continue to work with multiple eBook providers directly.

There are two major North American approval vendors for academic libraries, and both are able to manage eBook acquisition for their customers. YBP Library Services works with three of the four major eBook aggregators. The one eBook platform company not represented in YBP is MyiLibrary. Ingram Content Group owns MyiLibrary as well as Coutts Information Services, the other major North American approval vendor. YBP also offers the option to purchase eBooks directly from publishers, when the publisher permits. Libraries that work with YBP can integrate eBook acquisition into the approval process by setting up an e-preferred profile, which automatically delivers an e-version of a book to the library when one is available within eight weeks of the publication date of the print (Barbara Kawecki, senior digital content sales manager, YBP Library Services, email message to author, October 30, 2012).

YBP also manages DDA for libraries, allowing them to build the process into the approval plan, work with multiple eBook aggregators (at this point, EBL, ebrary, and EBSCO), and control duplication with print acquisition (YBP Library Services 2012).

Coutts Information Services offers similar services to those available through YBP. The basic difference is that they work exclusively with MyiLibrary and not EBL, ebrary, or EBSCO (Ingram 2012). Libraries that have approval plans in place for print will naturally want to work with their preferred vendor. YBP customers who have an interest in purchasing MyiLibrary titles and Coutts customers interested in the other three major aggregators will need to step outside their main monographic acquisitions workflow in order to get these titles, and manage the challenges that decision entails, including a greater likelihood of duplication with print or other eBooks, additional invoicing, and additional discovery record loads.

CONCLUSION

Academic library eBooks acquisition remains a tremendously confusing process. Publishers do not make eBooks available in a consistent way. Some publishers make their titles available only on their own platform. Others prefer to use aggregators. But they are not consistent in how they do this. It is not unusual to find some eBooks from a publisher on one aggregator's platform but other titles on a different platform. Even when a title is available on multiple platforms, it can be difficult to determine what purchase models are available. And there is no consistency in how long it may take for a print title to be available as an eBook.

Because of this confusion, it has been very difficult for librarians to figure out how to build eBook collections. At this point, there are two basic options, neither ideal. One, working only with a subset of aggregators and publishers—whether managed through the approval plan or not—allows for easier workflow, but means that some titles will inevitably be unavailable. The other option, working with as many aggregators and publishers as possible, means that many more titles will be available, but this strategy results in a much more difficult workflow. Approval vendors can help ease some of that strain, but neither of them works with all aggregators.

Academic librarians need to be aware of the multiple options for acquiring eBooks and the benefits and drawbacks of each option. By taking a mix and match approach across providers and models, they can build as comprehensive an eBook collection as is now possible (recognizing, of course, that the majority of books still come out only in print). Librarians also need to advocate with publishers for better models—eBooks that are available on all platforms, under multiple access models, and with predictable publication cycles. It should be easier to order an eBook than a print book, not the other way around.

REFERENCES

Collections—Skillsoft. 2012. "Collections—Skillsoft." Available at: http://www.skillsoft .com/books24x7/product_information/collections/. Accessed October 27, 2012.

Connaway, Lynn Silipigni, and Heather L. Wicht. 2007. "What Happened to the EBook Revolution?: The Gradual Integration of EBooks into Academic Libraries." *The Journal of Electronic Publishing* 10 (3). Available at: http://dx.doi.org/10.3998/3336451.0010.302. Accessed October 29, 2012.

Ebook Library. 2012. "Ebook Library." Available at: http://www.eblib.com/. Accessed October 9, 2012.

ebrary. 2012a. "Ebrary for Academic Libraries." Available at: http://www.ebrary.com/corp/ academic.jsp. Accessed October 9, 2012.

ebrary. 2012b. "Glossary of ebrary terms." Available at: http://support.ebrary.com/kb/glos sary/. Accessed October 9, 2012.

ebrary. 2012c. "Company." Available at: http://www.ebrary.com/corp/company.jsp. Accessed October 27, 2012.

EBSCO. 2012. "Electronic Book Collections." Available at: http://www2.ebsco.com/ en-us/ProductsServices/ebooks/Pages/index.aspx. Accessed October 12, 2012.

EBSCO. 2013. "Academic eBook Collections." Available at: http://www.ebscohost.com/ ebooks/academic/subscriptions/academic-ebook-subscriptions. Accessed February 2, 2013.

Elsevier. 2012. "Evidence-Based Selection." Available at: http://www.info.sciverse.com/ sciencedirect/subscriptions/evidence-based-selection. Accessed October 24, 2012.

Fischer, Karen S., Michael Wright, Kathleen Clatanoff, Hope Barton, and Edward Shreeves. 2012. "Give 'Em What They Want: A One-Year Study of Unmediated Patron-Driven Acquisition of eBooks." *College & Research Libraries* 73 (September): 469–92.

Gibbs, Nancy J. 2010. "Jumping into the Ebook Waters: A Patron Driven Acquisitions Pilot with ebrary." Available at: http://www.slideshare.net/EResourcesLibraries/patron-driven-selection-of-ebook-gibbs. Accessed October 26, 2012.

Ingram. 2012. "Academic Professional Collection Development." http://www.ingramcon tent.com/pages/academic-professional-collection-development.aspx. Accessed November 3, 2013.

JSTOR. 2012. "About Books." Available at: http://about.jstor.org/content/about-books. Accessed October 12, 2012.

Knovel. 2012. "Technical Engineering Reference Information." http://why.knovel.com/. Accessed October 9, 2012.

Machovec, George. 2003. "netLibrary Revisited." *The Charleston Advisor* April: 21–26.

Moore, Patrick. 2011. "Colorado Alliance eBook Conference: MyiLibrary." Available at: http://www.coalliance.org/sites/default/files/myilibrary[1].pdf. Accessed October 26, 2012.

MyiLibrary. 2012. "MyiLibrary." Available at: http://www.myilibrary.com/. Accessed October 12, 2012.

Newman, Michael, and Anh Bui. 2009. *HighWire Press 2009 Librarian eBook Survey.* Available at: http://highwire.stanford.edu/PR/HighWireEBookSurvey2010.pdf. Accessed October 26, 2012.

Paulson, Kari. 2011. "The Story of Patron-Driven Acquisition." In *Patron-Driven Acquisitions: History and Best Practices,* ed. David A. Swords, 63–78. Berlin: De Gruyter Saur.

Polanka, Sue, and Emilie Delquié. 2011. "Patron-Driven Business Models: History, Today's Landscape, and Opportunities." In *Patron-Driven Acquisitions: History and Best Practices*, ed. David A. Swords, 119–35. Berlin: De Gruyter Saur.

Project Muse. 2012. "UPCC Books on Project Muse." Available at: http://muse.jhu.edu/about/UPCC.html. Accessed October 12, 2012.

ProQuest. 2013. "ProQuest Signs Definitive Agreement to Acquire EBL." Available at: http://www.proquest.com/en-US/aboutus/pressroom/13/20130122.shtml. Accessed February 2, 2013.

Questia 2012. "About Questia." http://www.questia.com/about-questia. Accessed October 29, 2012.

Safari. 2012. "Safari Books Online." Available at: http://www.safaribooksonline.com/. Accessed October 9, 2012.

Skillsoft. 2012. "Skillsoft Books 24x7." Available at: http://www.books24x7.com/books24x7.asp. Accessed October 9, 2012.

Slater, Robert. 2010. "Why Aren't EBooks Gaining More Ground in Academic Libraries? EBook Use and Perceptions: A Review of Published Literature and Research." *Journal of Web Librarianship* 4: 305–31.

Snowhill, Lucia. 2001. "EBooks and Their Future in Academic Libraries: An Overview." *D-Lib Magazine* 7 (7/8). doi: 10.1045/july2001-snowhill. Accessed October 9, 2012.

Springer 2012. "Springer eBooks: Critical Content." Available at: http://www.springer.com/librarians/e-content/ebooks?SGWID=0-40791-0-0-0. Accessed October 30, 2012.

University Press Scholarship Online. 2012. "University Press Scholarship Online." Available at: http://www.universitypressscholarship.com/. Accessed October 12, 2012.

University Publishing Online. 2012. "University Publishing Online." Available at: http://universitypublishingonline.org/. Accessed October 12, 2012.

YBP Library Services. 2012. "Demand-Driven Acquisitions.". Accessed November 3, 2013.

17

eBook Collection Development in Public Libraries

Christopher Baker

I hate those eBooks. They cannot be the future. They may well be.
—Maurice Sendak

One thing is clear about the role of eBooks in public libraries. That is, not much is clear. There are major players, applicable best practices, booming statistics, growing support resources, and increasingly savvy users, yes. But the core model for library service: buy book, lend book remains fraught with new and changing ifs, ands or buts when applied to eBook collections. Not only on the front lines of collection development, but for library support staff, newly acquainted users, and those not-yet-cardholders public libraries are always reaching for. Public libraries and librarians have approached these challenges head on. We have faced and continue to face the reality that eBooks, while a major boon to the business of public libraries, have spurned some of our professions most controversial, insightful, and innovative decisions and discussions and they are definitely not going anywhere.

EBOOKS IN THE WILD

eBooks are steadily converting consumer markets as librarians struggle to provide content and advocate for access. While librarians have long championed eBooks and eReading, the growth in eReading has remained largely in the consumer market, outside of library walls. Library users purchase devices and quickly find content to fill those devices. In most cases they end up buying eBooks from major retailers instead of borrowing them from a library. A recent Pew study found that a majority of library cardholders are not even aware that eBook lending is a service provided by their local library

(Zickuhr et al. 2012a). This is a startling revelation for librarians who have worked to build, market, support, and advocate for eBook collections. Users are finding eBooks, however. The Association of American Publishers *Book-Stats 2012* report found that in 2011, eBooks ranked highest in format selection for adult fiction (Sporkin 2012). And in early 2011, Amazon reported that Kindle book sales had marginally outpaced paperbacks but were outselling hardcovers by three times (Carnoy 2011). Coupled with the rapid adoption of tablets, smartphones, and eReaders, with both tablet and eReader ownership in American adults nearly doubling, from 10 to 19 percent, between December 2011 and January 2012 (Rainie et al. 2012), it is clear that users are well beyond the tipping point for eBooks and eReading. Public libraries are as well, but have had a very different experience thus far.

Like individual users, public libraries have invested time and energy to build and grow eBook collections, learn the ins and outs of associated devices and technology, and enjoy the benefits of a collection available on demand—anytime, anywhere. But public libraries have been yoked with conditions and limits not placed on individual users: paranoid publishers hindering access to in-demand and popular titles readily accessible in physical formats, a complex, multifaceted, and ever-evolving download process, and the very real limits of collection development budgets in the face of the current eBook pricing and lending models offered to public libraries.

EBOOKS IN CAPTIVITY

That is not to say public library eBook collections are not popular despite these issues. In the final week of December 2010, OverDrive-powered digital library sites were literally crushed by the demand for eBooks from users eager to download to devices received as gifts over the holiday season (Stasiewski 2010). eBook usage at public libraries has grown rapidly since, quadrupling between 2010 and 2011 alone with projections of a 67 percent increase in circulation between 2011 and 2012 ("eBook Usage" 2012). As evident by these numbers, eBooks in public libraries are definitely moving. However, librarians who are responsible for delivering eBooks cannot help but imagine what could be with only a few changes. These changes might include the following:

- access to other major publishers' eBook catalogs;
- a less complicated download experience; and
- a more library-friendly model for eBook acquisition and lending.

eBooks are the public library's greatest catch-22. They are what is next, they are in demand, they place no burden on physical space, and they are available when buildings are closed. But, they can also be difficult to purchase, are difficult for users to access, and require no small amount of ongoing support from library staff.

While some public library systems were early adopters of eBooks, the majority have only recently began collecting and investing heavily in digital collections. However, the addition of eBooks has been rapid within the past two years. According to the 2012 Library Journal and School Library Journal's *eBook Usage in U.S. Public Libraries* report: "Almost nine in ten public libraries currently offer eBooks to their users, and 35% of those that don't are in the process of adding them" ("eBook Usage" 2012, 4). That leaves very few library systems that have yet to jump into the eBook game. Public libraries that have not added eBooks cite the lack of funds to support a collection, reservations over available eBook platforms, or a user base without means to support such a collection as the major reasons they have not added eBooks ("eBook Usage" 2012, 21). While these are reasonable concerns considering the current state of eBooks in libraries, public libraries that are reluctant to add eBooks may soon find themselves with a similarly reluctant user base who believes the library is not responsive to their information needs or requests. As a generation of users raised on screens and on-demand media inches closer and closer toward becoming supportive library users, public libraries must recognize that digital content, such as eBooks, are key in addressing the information needs of today's and, more importantly, tomorrow's user.

THE PUBLIC LIBRARY AS PROTAGONIST

It is evident that users are personally interested and invested in eBooks and eReading and public libraries have made heavy investments to address those interests. It is also evident that while usage and demand for library eBooks continues to grow rapidly, current trends and limits in eBook collection development have brought libraries through a crossroads and onto an unfamiliar path. The traditional model for library lending is not concrete and straightforward for eBooks. This is, unfortunately, predicated on the fact that the traditional idea of ownership is not applicable in current eBook purchasing models. Because, unlike physical books, libraries are unable to own eBooks, instead, libraries license access to eBook content. Libraries are in eBook lending purgatory, incapable of fully reaping the benefits of electronic access and delivery while experiencing growing demand and user interest in digital content. Major publishers have had differing reactions to the idea of eBook lending in libraries, from complete avoidance to limited circulations and increased pricing to justify their sales to libraries. Although libraries have never controlled book publishing or publishers, hard work and legislation have given libraries rights to purchase and lend physical books for as long as items can circulate. Limits currently in place to control eBooks in public libraries go much farther than merely damage done to physical books. While physical copies can be replaced or repaired, the complete refusal of sale by major publishers threatens the public libraries' ability to even provide access to popular and relevant titles and information. For users, the proliferation of different eBook formats and restrictions placed on eBooks limits their ability to connect with the information they want or need using the device they have in hand.

Public libraries are in a precarious position in regard to eBook collections. Because libraries must be responsive to customer demand for access to popular and current titles, the leverage in the eBook debate is heavily skewed toward publishers. This lack of leverage has mitigated the voice of the public library as an influence on library lending of eBooks. But librarians have not given up. The role libraries play in eBook collection development and management is changing, from a simple access point to advocator, creator, and negotiator. This change is evident in the profession's constant calls for increased access, in the creation of home-grown platforms, and in libraries' work to adjust and advocate for new models and sources for library lending. Yet, libraries are still not fully in the eBook spotlight. To play a larger role, libraries must continue to engage publishers, vendors, and users alike to ensure each understand how important they are to the success of the eBook. For publishers, libraries create readers who then become customers. For vendors, libraries advance platforms and products through trial and use. And for users, public libraries tirelessly advocate for free, open, and easy access to information in all formats.

There is no doubting the public libraries' important role in the rise of eReading over the past few years. However, in the face of growing demand and limited access, public libraries must take command of and work to expand that role. To draw a literary allusion, public libraries are poised as the protagonist in conflicts that will influence the future of eBook lending for users. To be clear, these conflicts are not presented in an antagonistic manner, but rather as a way of grouping the issues public libraries struggle with and must overcome to realize the full potential of eBooks and what they mean for users. These conflicts are presented with both internal and external concerns and address a range of issues surrounding eBook collection development, management, and support.

LIBRARY VERSUS NATURE: INTO THE WILD

Publishers, and Vendors, and Platforms! Oh My!

The current climate for eBook collection development is not wholly inhospitable to public libraries but it does not support an expanded role for libraries beyond passive content licensee. There are a number of vendors at the ready to assist public libraries in starting or expanding eBook collections. These vendors act as content aggregators and distributors for publishers, giving libraries access to a single marketplace and platform from which to build and manage eBook collections. With adequate funding and planning, eBook collections can be up and running in public libraries with very little effort beyond basic selection decisions and ensuring user support.

OverDrive was the first, and remains the largest, vendor to offer downloadable eBooks to public libraries. Its original vision for library lending and ongoing response to changes in formats, availability, user habits, and devices continues to set the bar for what public libraries expect in an eBook vendor. Other major eBook vendors include 3M, whose Cloud Library offers synced delivery across users' mobile devices, Freading, a pay-per-use platform for library lending powered by PDA, and Baker & Taylor's Axis 360 digital media library and accompanying Blio reader, which also offers cloud-based delivery of content. Public libraries should examine each vendor's model, in depth, prior to any purchase. A number of factors should be considered carefully, including the availability of suitable publisher content, the compatibility of available formats with users' devices, and the sustainability of costs associated with creating and maintaining successful eBook collections.

There are also deeper factors to consider before investing in an eBook collection or a new eBook platform. The content those vendors are able to provide is heavily controlled by the relationships they have with publishers and current limits major publishers have placed on selling to libraries. Those relationships are a key element in how well libraries are able to serve their reading public once the decision is made to add an eBook collection. Above all, and a focus of great concern over 2012, vendors do not and cannot control major publishers' power in removing, adjusting, or altering the availability, prices, or formats of eBook titles in their marketplace and even in previously purchased digital collections. These factors should be carefully considered before adding new, or supplementing existing, eBook collections.

Of the big six publishers, or five with the impending Penguin and Random House merger (Pfanner and Chozick 2012), two, Simon & Schuster and Macmillan, do not make their eBooks available for library lending through any vendor platform. Public libraries are granted access to other major publishers' title lists through third-party vendors such as those mentioned earlier, but that access has increasingly come with a caveat. In 2010, HarperCollins gave libraries access to the entire catalog of titles but altered its sales model to cap the loan of each new eBook purchased at 26 loans before a new copy could be purchased. Luckily, libraries get a discount on subsequent purchases. Hachette removed frontlist titles from library catalogs in 2011, and more recently increased the price of its backlist titles by just over 100 percent. Penguin had stopped selling eBooks to libraries in February 2012, after a tenuous few months that first saw the publisher suspend the sale of new titles to libraries, and then also request that the Amazon Kindle format's Whispersync delivery be disabled for all Penguin titles in OverDrive-powered collections. However, Penguin has recently returned to the library market through a pilot partnership between 3M's Cloud Library, New York Public Library, and the Brooklyn Public Library. Like HarperCollins, Random House gives libraries access to its entire catalog of eBook titles, but increased the cost of its eBook titles by 300 percent in March 2012.

Publishers have justified these restrictions and changes with a variety of explanations, from the need to make prices reflect the nature of a copy that never degrades to the loss of friction due to the remote nature of the eBook checkout and download transaction. It is not necessary to pick apart the details of each explanation, they point to the same end: major publishers believe that library purchasing and lending of eBooks cannibalize sales and place eBooks in danger of being poached instead of purchased. It is beyond the public libraries' reach to pretend to be able to change the current trends in sales restriction, loan limit, and pricing decisions from major publishers. First and foremost, libraries must serve their users. As Jamie LaRue asserts in a recent *Library Journal* article, when it comes to serving users, "We're still going to buy some of the content our patrons want us to buy. And they're still going to ask for what has been advertised. That's the mainstream" (LaRue 2012a, 33). What public libraries can do is change the way they approach the eBook market, beginning with a look at how collection development can enhance and expand digital collections to better serve users while also pushing public libraries' role in the eBook market forward.

A WAY OUT OF THE WOODS

"Technological innovations changed how music and songs are bought and consumed today" (Sen 2010). This simple statement, from an article exploring changes in music in the digital age, may seem like common knowledge to anyone with a current relationship to music, but it should also strike a chord with librarians who have any stake or interest in the future of eBooks in public libraries. eBook collection development dollars are still being used to support outdated and inapplicable models that do not address the technological innovations eBooks offer. Major publishers' current actions toward controlling the eBook market mirror the actions of major music labels faced with the growth of downloadable music and file-sharing. Just like major music labels, major publishers have scrambled for solutions and continued to adjust toward what they feel are workable models. While they adjust internally, eBook channels outside their control have grown. To keep up with eBook demand and usage in consumer markets, eBook availability from independent publishers has skyrocketed and self-published authors have embraced eBooks to great success. Libraries can play an important role in this sea change. The creators and distributors, devices, and user attitudes surrounding eBook content have shifted in the same way they did for music. This comparison may not have proved as strong to public libraries that were, only a year ago, celebrating higher eBook circulation statistics, greater compatibility through the addition of the Kindle format from OverDrive, and comparatively lower-cost eBooks from a wider selection of major publishers' catalogs. However, factors currently controlling and influencing eBook publication, distribution, and use have lined up in the same way they did for the music industry. To stake a claim in the eBook paradigm of tomorrow, public libraries need to heed these flashing signposts.

As noted in an ALA TechSource post by Patrick Hogan, "traditional publishing and distribution channels now control only about 12 percent of new content" (Hogan 2012). Collection development in public libraries can, and should, evolve to embrace new channels for eBooks. The independent and individual streams of publishing are growing exponentially and public libraries have a rare opportunity to play a major role in the promotion and distribution of this content. Public libraries define themselves as content aggregators, in physical terms and as a profession, and should waste no more time in claiming this role in the eBook market. By doing so, public libraries open new doors for access, engage tomorrow's authors today, and cement their place in actively representing the interests and needs of content creators and users alike. The good news is that a few public libraries are already following this path and are well on the way toward reasserting the power of libraries as content aggregators for all types of information.

SO MUCH CONTENT SO CLOSE TO HOME

Diversifying collection development with eBook content from independent publishers could prove the first step to move public libraries in reclaiming that role. As noted by Douglas County Library Director Jamie LaRue, "this stream of publishing is now roughly equal to commercial output yet significantly underrepresented in [public library] collections" and independents "produce a lot of fine, far more diverse writing of often keen local interest" (LaRue 2012a, 33). Independent publisher have embraced the innovations that eBooks offer in expanding their distribution. Additionally, independent publishers have reaped the benefits of an influx of established writers as major publishers shed the traditional midlist to focus on top-selling authors and blockbusters (Deahl 2010). Above all, independent publishers are excited to work with libraries and recognize the inherent value in the library's creation of readers and customers. While public libraries will always advocate for increased access to eBooks from major publishers, eBooks from independent publishers address the library's immediate need for eBook content and help all libraries meet the ultimate goal of collection development: connecting users with information.

There is also opportunity to expand on that goal. Self-published authors are a subset of the eBook market that has seen exponential growth in the past few years without registering a blip on collection development radars. Granted, self-published holds a certain connotation in collection development. Often bringing to mind works of questionable quality, in whichever way one defines quality, be it grammar, style, subject, or other. These wholly independent authors are taking full advantage of distribution channels offered up by eBooks and are doing so with great success. According to data recently compiled by Bowker, the release of self-published eBooks grew by 129 percent between 2010 and 2011 ("Self-Publishing" 2012). By ignoring this trend, collection development librarians are ignoring a great amount of the digital content being written and released into the eBook content stream. While statistics surrounding self-published eBooks in consumer markets cannot assuage quality concerns or influence changes in collection development policy without a much larger discussion, they can go far in proving to libraries the value users find in creating and consuming self-published works. Retailers such as Amazon, Apple, and Barnes & Noble have already tapped into this stream of content by creating publication and distribution platforms to engage independent authors. Public libraries have an opportunity to play publisher and distributor as well by utilizing open platforms that encourage and engage self-published authors alongside other digital content.

In early 2011, Douglas County Libraries and Red Rocks Community College Library partnered with the Colorado Independent Publishers Association (CIPA) to deliver eBooks through a library-managed platform that promotes accessibility and findability through library catalog integration. It also allows users to purchase titles directly from the publishers (Kelley 2011). Douglas County has since expanded the number of publishers it works with to include other independent publishers and publishing groups, and content from publishers such as Gale, Marshall Cavendish, ABDO, and Lerner Digital, who are already well known to public libraries (Sendze 2012). Another benefit Douglas County realized from working with independent publishers is the library's ability to own the eBooks its purchases. This is no small detail when compared to current library sales models available from major publishers. By creating its own platform, Douglas County has made itself the key component in a mutually beneficial relationship connecting users with publishers. Sendze points out that by establishing agreements with publishers to purchase eBooks and manage the digital rights of those eBooks, public libraries, like Douglas County, can "emphasize our role as protectors of intellectual freedom and major players in the book-buying industry" (Sendze 2012).

Readers can learn more about Douglas County's innovative approach to collection development by reading the chapter that James (Jamie) LaRue has contributed to this book (see "Self-Publishing: Does It Belong in the Collection?"). Public libraries should follow Douglas County's lead and support platforms for eBook lending that expand available channels of collection development and enhance user access to eBooks. By working with independent publishers, public libraries can claim the role of content aggregator in a market with a growing number of middlemen. By reaching out to self-published authors and managing the publication and distribution of user-produced content, public libraries expand that role and place themselves on the crest of a wave of change currently hitting the eBook market.

LIBRARY VERSUS SOCIETY: WHAT DO YOU MEAN IT'S CHECKED OUT?

What We Talk about When We Talk about eBooks

Another important aspect of the call for public libraries to expand eBook collection development channels, and move toward in-house platforms for eBook management and lending, is the need for a standardized eBook format or standardized form of eReading access that can serve library users seamlessly across devices. For retail consumers, the device compatibility of eBook formats is not often of concern as retailers have created a seamless process for delivering and syncing eBooks across devices via proprietary readers, Web apps, and mobile apps. Consumers can purchase an eBook from Amazon, send it to their Kindle, access it from their Web browser, and resume reading later on their Android smartphone. The same is true of the Barnes & Noble's Nook experience, among others. The retail model for eBooks removes the customer from format selection and, in doing so, rids eBooks of all physical connotations, respecting their true nature and pushing eBooks as on-demand content rather than in-demand, checked out, on hold, items.

Unfortunately, the direct comparison of eBooks to physical books continues to weigh down public libraries and eBook vendor models. "One copy, one user" remains a predominant theme in eBook sales models. HarperCollins' cap of 26 loans per eBook purchased was a clear and early example of publisher attempts to apply physical limits to digital content. To be fair, HarperCollins' model may be the best currently available to public libraries precisely because it follows the eBook to book comparison to its natural end: giving libraries the power to forgo replacing under-utilized titles while also offering a discount on subsequent purchasing of expired titles. But as Jamie LaRue points out in a blog posting, when it comes to major publisher models, " 'less bad' isn't 'good'" (LaRue 2012b). The comparison to physical items served as a familiar starting point for both libraries enamored with the idea of eBooks and publishers accustomed to print. It has since been used to justify publishers' restrictions and limits while steadily increasing the burden placed on public libraries in explaining the one copy, one user model to users steeped in an on-demand, immediately accessible media marketplace. The most frustrating and ironic aspect of this comparison is major publishers' refusal to recognize the issues that accompany eBooks purchased on this basis as the very real friction they so often say is needed for digital content. Public libraries accepted this model early on to gain access to innovative and, seemingly, ubiquitous channels of information but are now bearing the brunt of decisions made without a full understanding of what eBooks could and would eventually mean to users.

Public libraries continue to call for increased access to major publisher catalogs and, given the current state of eBooks in public libraries, librarians should make their collective voices heard. However, it may be time for a strategic change in the tone of that call. New models of access should be proposed to major publishers in an effort to bridge growing gaps and return popular and in-demand content to library eBook collections. Public libraries deliver information and content to users in a number of ways and formats. Never have two such dissimilar types, book and eBook, been so strongly linked. Regardless of the name, eBooks are not books. They are born digitally, they are managed digitally, and they are delivered digitally. Yes, eBooks can be purchased, they can be checked out, and they can be returned like physical books. But these characteristics have been placed upon them. At their core, eBooks are similar to another type of content readily found in library collections—eContent accessed through databases and other online resources.

Like eBooks, public libraries purchase access to eContent through vendors and associated platforms. Like eBooks, eContent is accessible beyond the physical and temporal confines of library branches. Unlike eBooks, providers of eContent have fully realized the digital collection's power in delivering information to users on demand. They have also realized the value of that access to public libraries. Subscription models for databases and other online resources allow public libraries to purchase access to the eContent they need for the specific period of time it is needed. Similar models of purchasing could work very well for the popular and best-selling titles offered by major publishers that do not often have the staying power suggested by the investments needed to meet initial demand. Subscription models for eBook collections could first work to shift the conversation with major publishers away from the idea of library ownership and toward one of, more simply, access: access to the eBook content public libraries need, when they need it.

Subscription models could help to alleviate some of the hesitancy felt by major publishers in selling copies that never degrade while also addressing the very real demand for popular and best-selling content felt by public libraries. Penguin is exploring a new sales model in its pilot program with New York Public Library and Brooklyn Public Library through 3M's Cloud Library that, in part, seems inspired by subscription models for other eContent. Unfortunately, it does not go far enough. Penguin's relaunch of eBooks in public libraries allows libraries to purchase a one-year license for each eBook copy purchased, with a six-month purchase embargo for new titles (Hoffelder 2012). Like HarperCollins, Penguin's new model does allow libraries to forgo re-purchasing expired eBooks, helping to weed out-of-date or under-utilized titles and copies. Yet, it also continues to push the idea of the eBook as book. While public libraries welcome the return of access to a major publisher's titles, it is important to consider the long-term effects of continued acceptance of models that do not further the usability of eBooks for library users. Bringing major publishers back into the discussion is a move in the right direction, but public libraries must assert that, like other eContent, the investment they make in eBook collections should pay dividends in access and convenience for their users.

The eBook to book comparison issue reaches beyond libraries and publishers. Most major eBook vendors also base their distribution models and platforms on the idea that in public libraries an eBook is simply another item bound by the lending limits of physical items. However, eBook vendors are making platform advancements in direct response to issues of compatibility and availability realized through library use and trends found in the consumer eBook market. OverDrive is the only vendor currently offering Kindle compatibility and is gearing up to offer a new method for delivering EPUB eBooks in library collections. OverDrive Read, similar in nature to the Kindle Cloud Reader and marketed with the tagline "See Book, Read Book," sees OverDrive capitalizing on advancements in HTML5 to deliver eBooks to any device with a Web browser, including tablets, smartphones, and other Web-enabled mobile devices. Since there is no download, there is no need for authentication beyond a user's library credentials. Mirroring eBook retail strategy, 3M's Cloud Library offers synced content on up to six devices through apps available for both Android and iOS devices. Baker & Taylor's Blio application is marketed as "a full-featured eReader for people who care about what books look like" ("Blio" n.d.), and is available for download to computers, tablets, smartphones, and other mobile devices. These enhanced features are clear indications that eBook vendors closely monitor user interactions with eBook content. Public libraries can be certain that major eBook vendors will continue to be responsive within the models and platforms that they control because they have a direct and vested interest in the success of eBooks in public libraries. As discussed earlier, what they cannot control and what continues to affect users is the publishers' control over the availability and compatibility of eBook titles.

USERS ÜBER ALLES

For libraries and library users, the availability of eBook formats varies across major vendor platforms and remains key in vendor selection. Alongside new vendor efforts in delivering content like those described earlier, vendors also support the download of eBook files direct to device or to desktop for transfer to device. OverDrive offers, when available, EPUB, PDF, and within the last year, the Kindle format for eBook titles purchased, Baker & Taylor relies on an adopted XPS file format to deliver eBooks to its Blio mobile apps, 3M's Cloud Library uses the EPUB format for both cloud delivery and desktop transfer of its titles, and Freading offers EPUB and PDF formats for downloads, transfers, and sideloads to devices. What do all these formats and delivery options mean for public library users? They mean steps, as in step-by-step. They mean that while vendors are working toward solutions that attempt to replicate the user experience of retail eBooks, public libraries are tasked with supporting and defending convoluted processes for access to content born with the capability to be delivered seamlessly and immediately.

To that end, user support is crucial for any library implementing a new or additional eBook platform. The formats, accompanying restrictions and limitations, and eBook delivery methods (i.e., the download experience) that come along with each vendor platform can influence a user's ability to interact with an eBook collection on all levels, from the user's initial selection of a title to the user's selection of device on which to read that title. In a 2001 episode of the BBC radio series the "Hitchhikers Guide to the Future," the late Douglas Adams asserted, in regard to eBooks, that "lovers of print are simply confusing the plate for the food" (Adams 2001). This forward-thinking remark is fitting for today's users' view of public library collections—content is content regardless of format. With that in mind, libraries should not only be working toward increased access to food for their users but also working to ensure access to and compatibility with the different plates that users consume that food on.

Users with dedicated eReading devices, tablets, or smartphones are immersed in a media culture of instant gratification. See app, buy app. Need book, buy book. Want music, buy music. They are not faced with limits on the number of copies available for reading, viewing, or listening. Users bring this experience with them when they approach eBooks in the library. Often, frustration with either the availability of eBooks or the process by which an eBook is obtained stops a user before he or she gets started.

The checkout and download process in public libraries has come a long way in the past few years, and vendors have worked hard to increase the compatibility of library eBooks across a growing number of consumer devices. OverDrive's addition of Kindle compatibility in 2012 is a perfect example of this type of work. The addition of the Kindle format allowed libraries to reach an entirely new audience of readers, those already using the No. 1 eReading device in the United States. Unfortunately, that increase in compatibility also came with a cost: Penguin's removal of eBooks from OverDrive. The Kindle checkout and download process via OverDrive is one of the easiest forms of eBook access currently available to public library users. OverDrive's employ of Amazon's Whispersync technology has made library eBooks, once checked out, instantly accessible on a plethora of devices. While other publishers welcomed an influx of new readers, Penguin responded by citing security concerns as its motive for removing Kindle compatibility for Penguin titles. Public libraries should take note. While publishers have a justifiable interest in protecting their content, they also have an interest in controlling the compatibility and ease of access of that content in an effort to protect sales in consumer markets. Faced with this reality, public libraries can only do so much to match the compatibility needs of users. However, the steps they can take are powerful in ensuring they meet the device needs of current users and expand device compatibility for future users.

THE PROPER CARE AND FEEDING OF DEVICES

Despite the growth in device compatibility from eBook vendors, thanks in great part to proprietary apps for smartphones and tablets, there is still a gap between the devices many eBook vendors support and the popular devices users select. Of the major vendors selling eBooks to public libraries, only OverDrive currently offers eBook compatibility with the Amazon Kindle—the eReading device chosen by 62 percent of eReader owners (Rainie et al. 2012). OverDrive's partnership with Amazon was a boon to public libraries and helped bring library eBooks to a new segment of users. Similar compatibility has yet to come from any other major eBook vendor. Public libraries have responded to issues of availability and compatibility by adding other vendor platforms to enhance and grow eBook collections. While this may serve as a stopgap measure to deliver either more eBook content or compatibility for more eReading devices, it does so at great fiscal expense to those libraries and fails to address compatibility issues head on. Investing in multiple eBook platforms forces libraries to hedge bets on content over user experience, sending users in different directions for eBook content that should easily come to them. Public libraries need to recognize that throwing money at eBook issues has only served to complicate matters thus far. By adding multiple eBook platforms, libraries waste valuable time and money chasing unraveling purchasing models, assorted delivery methods, and unpredictable eBook content down unfamiliar paths.

Such an investment of time and money should instead be made toward creating the best possible eBook experience for current users with an eye on how library eBooks may serve future users. The compatibility of public library eBook collections should, above all, mirror the device demographics of current users. Investments in eBook platforms should never influence a user's selection of eReading device. Instead, public libraries should focus current efforts on building eBook collections on platforms capable of delivering the most content to the largest number of users. Compatibility is key. Regardless of eBook delivery method, be it via app, download and transfer, or online delivery, any investment in a vendor platform that excludes an entire segment of users, based on their choice of eReading device, is a failure of collection development to reflect the needs of the community it represents. To that end, public libraries must consider how the selection of an eBook platform will affect their ability to evolve alongside changes in the eReading habits and device choices of their users.

The devices used for eReading continue to change as users adopt and adapt to new technology. A recent study of young Americans' reading habits by the Pew Internet & American Life Project found that users under the age of 30, who read eBooks, read them on a computer or cell phone rather than on a dedicated eBook reader or tablet (Zickuhr et al. 2012b). This shift in where eReading takes place could prove important to public libraries as they look for an eBook solution that addresses both compatibility issues for users and accessibility issues involving both major publishers and vendors. As eReading shifts toward Web-enabled devices including smartphones, tablets, and computers, library eBooks should shift in that direction as well. The immediate, online delivery of eBooks via HTML5 already takes place in retail markets and is set to debut from at least one major library eBook vendor. The delivery of eBooks via Web browser on a user's device could go far in simplifying the eBook experience for users, removing cumbersome steps found in current methods as well as the need for proprietary apps for access and secondary accounts for authentication. Beyond a less-complicated user experience, browser-based eReading could prove revolutionary for libraries in their call for access to major publisher content simply because it treats eBooks like content, not as files that need to be downloaded and delivered through proprietary apps or third-party relationships but as eContent that can grow and change as users, technology, and devices change. The support and advancement of browser-based reading could rekindle the current conversation between libraries and major publishers by championing access above all else. For publishers, browser-based reading could mean access to new models of eBook sales based solely on the demand for access to that content without the dangers they find in current library lending models. For libraries, browser-based reading could mean new models for access to the eBook content they need, when they need it. And for users, browser-based reading could mean simple and straightforward access to library eBooks.

LIBRARY VERSUS SELF: YOU ARE NOT ALONE OR HOW I LEARNED TO STOP WORRYING AND LOVE THE EBOOK

With all of the challenges eBooks still present for public libraries, they may often sound like more trouble than they are worth. But any public library launching an eBook collection will quickly realize the benefits of an eBook collection. First and foremost, the allure of eBooks draws in new library users, providing library services to a larger portion of a library's community. eBooks allow libraries to deliver information and popular content to users outside of regular hours and far beyond the walls of the library branch. They also give libraries the opportunity to engage users on mobile devices, extending the presence of the public library to the smartphones and tablets users have in hand. Internally, eBooks raise the technical skill set of library staff through user-support, device troubleshooting, and the need to stay abreast of changes in eBook services. And without a doubt, eBooks put an edge on traditional library services, showing users that public libraries are dedicated to delivering convenient access to information in new and innovative ways.

Public libraries need to only look at the current use of and growing demand on eBook collections to realize they have quickly become an important part of library collections. eBooks are not going anywhere and for good reason. Regardless of current challenges, there is no denying that eBooks have a bright future in public libraries. It is up to public libraries to determine just how much of an influence they want to have on that future. Above all, public libraries must take steps to ensure eBook accessibility remains at the forefront of all discussions. A collective voice is needed for public libraries expressing the importance of access above all else. Boiling the conversation down to this simple concept gives public libraries a cornerstone on which to build a new future for library eBooks. Access will always mean the ability to deliver needed and requested content to library users, but in the context of eBooks, access is a malleable concept depending on its application. Looking forward, access could mean owning eBooks and developing in-house platforms for discovery and delivery, but by the same token, access could also mean subscription models from major publishers that allow simultaneous use of their catalog for a set period of time. As Christopher Harris points out, regardless of the comparison to physical books, "libraries don't purchase digital content, we license it" (Harris 2011) and a license grants access. Public libraries must change their approach in eBook collection development, shrug off old models and comparisons, and show flexibility in what access can mean for libraries and library users.

To show true flexibility, librarians must also be adaptable in their approach and response to changes in the eBook marketplace. The backlash seen in 2011 over HarperCollins' limit of 26 loans seems a glaring overreaction when compared to the response to recent, and more extreme, changes from major publishers: the total removal of catalogs or price increases that place a much heavier burden on strained library budgets. These changes point to the same end: the honeymoon period for eBooks and public libraries is over. The real work has begun. To thrive, this relationship will require what all great relationships require, communication and compromise.

Understanding is key in both directions. Libraries, publishers, and vendors will continue to experience growing pains as the creation, distribution, and utilization of eBook content evolves. But what has remained important thus far, and will remain important, is the public library's commitment to its users. By championing user rights, public libraries work to create a clearer future for library eBooks. A future that sees ease of access and ease of use for library users grow through mutually beneficial relationships between libraries, publishers, and vendors. A future built upon one clear, and simple, concept: access.

REFERENCES

Adams, Douglas. 2001. "E-book versus Paper," an episode of the Hitchhikers Guide to the Future BBC radio series. BBC Radio (April 21).

"Blio—Don't Just Read Books. Experience Them." n.d. Available at: http://www.meetblio .com/. Accessed October 25, 2012.

Carnoy, David. 2011. "Amazon: Kindle Books Outselling Paperbacks." Available at: http:// news.cnet.com/8301-17938_105-20029839-1.html. Accessed July 23, 2012.

Deahl, Rachel. 2010. "Smaller Presses, Bigger Authors." *Publishers Weekly* 257 (44): 4–6.

"eBook Usage in U.S. Public Libraries: 2012, Library Journal and School Library Journal." 2012. Available at: http://www.thedigitalshift.com/research/ebook-usage-reports/ public/. Accessed May 24, 2013.

Harris, Christopher. 2011. "Rethinking HarperCollins." *School Library Journal* 57 (4): 15.

Hoffelder, Nate. 2012. "Penguin eBooks Return to Libraries—But Probably Never the Kindle—The Digital Reader." *The Digital Reader* (June). Available at: http://www .the-digital-reader.com/2012/06/21/penguin-ebooks-return-libraries-but-probably- never-kindle/. Accessed July 23, 2012.

Hogan, Patrick. 2012. "Douglas County Libraries' DIY E-Book Hosting." *ALA TechSource* (March). Available at: http://www.alatechsource.org/blog/2012/03/douglas-county-libraries-diy-e-book-hosting.html. Accessed September 9, 2012.

Kelley, Michael. 2011. "Colorado Publishers and Libraries Collaborate on Ebook Lending Model." *Library Journal* (March 17). Available at: http://www.libraryjournal.com/lj/home/889765-264/colorado_publishers_and_libraries_collaborate.html.csp. Accessed September 9, 2012.

LaRue, Jamie. 2012a. "All Hat, No Cattle." *Library Journal* 137 (13): 32–33.

LaRue, Jamie. 2012b. "50 Shades of Red: Losing Our Shirts to Ebooks." Blog posting (July 30). Available at: http://americanlibrariesmagazine.org/e-content/50-shades-red-losing-our-shirts-ebooks. Accessed May 24, 2013.

Pfanner, Eric, and Amy Chozick. 2012, October 29. "Random House and Penguin Merger Creates Global Giant Random House and Penguin Merger Creates Global Giant." *The New York Times*. Available at: http://www.nytimes.com/2012/10/30/business/global/random-house-and-penguin-to-be-combined.html?_r=1&. Accessed October 31, 2012.

Rainie, Lee, Kathryn Zickuhr, Kristin Purcell, Mary Madden, and Joanna Brenner. 2012. "The Rise of e-Reading." *Pew Internet & American Life Project*. Available at: http://libraries.pewinternet.org/2012/04/04/the-rise-of-e-reading/. Accessed July 23, 2012.

"Self-Publishing Sees Triple-Digit Growth since 2007." 2012, October 24. *Publishers Weekly*. Available at: http://www.publishersweekly.com/pw/by-topic/industry-news/publisher-news/article/54482-self-publishing-sees-triple-digit-growth-since-2007.html. Accessed October 31, 2012.

Sen, Abhijit. 2010. "Music in the Digital Age: Musicians and Fans Around the World 'Come Together' on the Net." *Global Media Journal: American Edition* 9 (16): 1.

Sendze, Monique. 2012. "The E-book Experiment." *Public Libraries Online* (January/February) Available at: http://publiclibrariesonline.org/issue/januaryfebruary-2012/. Accessed September 9, 2012.

Sporkin, Andi. 2012. "Bookstats 2012 Highlights." Available at: http://www.frontgatemedia.com/news.php?mod=template&id=1066. Accessed May 28, 2013.

Stasiewski, Dan. 2010, December 28. "UPDATE: Significant activity on 'Virtual Branch' Websites." *OverDrive Blogs*. Available at: http://overdriveblogs.com/library/2010/12/28/significant-activity-on-virtual-branch-websites/. Accessed July 25, 2012.

Zickuhr, Kathryn, Lee Rainie, Kristin Purcell, Mary Madden, and Joanna Brenner. 2012a. "Libraries, Patrons, and e-Books. *Pew Internet & American Life Project*. Available at: http://libraries.pewinternet.org/2012/06/22/libraries-patrons-and-e-books/. Accessed July 23, 2012.

Zickuhr, Kathryn, Lee Rainie, Kristin Purcell, Mary Madden, and Joanna Brenner. 2012b. "Younger Americans' Reading and Library Habits." *Pew Internet & American Life Project*. Available at: http://libraries.pewinternet.org/2012/10/23/younger-americans-reading-and-library-habits/. Accessed October 31, 2012.

18

STREAMING VIDEO

deg farrelly

INTRODUCTION

Libraries are undergoing extraordinary change in a digital world. Digital indexes, journals, and monographs are now routinely incorporated into library collections and have become staples of library service. Other collection formats, such as film and video, have been slower to make the transition to digital, for reasons having to do with both the complexities of the technologies involved and the peculiarities of the video marketplace. This chapter provides an overview of the current state of streamed video collection development and acquisition. It focuses on the acquisition and licensing of new, streamed video titles and the incorporation of these into library collections, rather than digital conversion of existing collections or streaming of live events.

The author's perspectives on streaming video emerge from years of experience with media for higher education curricular support. Acquisition and use of streaming video in public and K–12 libraries will vary to some degree, but the basic concepts covered here should hold true across many types of libraries.

WHAT IS STREAMING VIDEO?

Streaming is a means of delivering video content to computer desktops via an Internet connection. A host (server) delivers the file to the receiving computer (client). Settings at the host's end determine whether access is available to multiple simultaneous users or limited to a single user. Unlike video downloads, which must transfer to the viewer's desktop, streamed video plays almost immediately after the viewer initiates play; some content must buffer before streaming begins. Streaming video also differs from video downloads in that no copy of the file is stored on the end user's computer, so files remain relatively secure (farrelly 2012).

Because of the generally large size of moving image data files, streaming videos usually employ file compression, a programming strategy that greatly reduces the size of the file through frame sampling and other complex means of reducing image redundancy. This compression can negatively affect image quality when compressed videos are played full-screen or projected. Even with compression, effective use of streaming video requires a robust, high-speed Internet connection. Dial-up connections generally are too slow to adequately deliver streaming videos.

WHY STREAM?

Libraries' accelerating evolution from hard copy to digital collections is in its third decade. From indexes to full-text indexes to e-journals and eBooks, libraries have recognized the value that digital formats provide. Digital's ease of use, 24/7 access, ability for simultaneous use, service to multiple locations, and reduction in physical space requirements present multiple benefits to both users and libraries. Libraries have embraced this transition (not without some growing pains) to the point that digital content is a norm within contemporary libraries. These same benefits apply to streaming video. Within the digital content trajectory, moving to streaming video is a logical next step for libraries.

Other motivations for moving to streaming video stem from the nature of video use within the curriculum. The use of video in education is well established. It is rare for an instructor to devote class time to reading a journal article or book chapter. But the physical nature of media before the advent of video necessitated limiting its curricular use to in-class screening. Film (primarily 16 millimeter) as a medium was too fragile and complicated to withstand multiple out-of-class or reserve uses. While video formats alleviated some of this difficulty, both videotape and DVDs deteriorate from repeated use and still present obstacles to multiple viewings within the short time frame curricular use necessitates.

Higher education increasingly occurs online. In 2011 nearly one-third of all higher education students were enrolled in at least one online course (Allen and Seaman 2011). Another study reports that in 2011 overall online enrollment grew by nearly 6 percent (Primary Research Group 2012). According to the *Survey on Academic Streaming Video*, 83 percent of U.S. colleges and universities offer online courses (farrelly and Hutchison 2013). In this context hard-copy video formats are unusable. And while faculty anticipate using video more, often they cannot find quality or appropriate materials. Additionally, they are unable to find the content they need in their library and are instead turning to commercial sites (Kaufman and Mohan 2009).

Streaming video collections help to address many of the issues of durability and access. An instructor can still screen the content in class if desired, but also link to the content in a course management shell for asynchronous use. Additionally, many streaming interfaces permit linking to segments or portions of videos, enabling focus on key topics within the video, either in or out of class.

Arguments for adopting streaming video are not limited to academic libraries. The advent of home video resulted in huge increases in library circulation statistics, and DVD circulation remains strong in many public libraries. In a 2011 study, however, *LJ Reports* noted a shift in user preferences; 17 percent of respondents described using streaming services such as Netflix as their primary source for movies (Enis 2012).

VIDEO IN LIBRARIES

The elements involved in selecting, licensing, acquiring, and hosting streaming video are foreign to most librarians engaged in collection development, already largely unfamiliar in general with media collection development. To understand issues in video collection development—seeking balance, just-in-time versus just-in-case collecting, quality, preservation, and other factors, the key text remains *Video Collection Development in Multi-Type Libraries: A Handbook* (Handman 2002). This title provides a strong foundation upon which to look at the evolution of media in library collections. Schools and some public libraries collected visual media in multiple formats for years. Through the second half of the 20th century the dominant media format was 16-millimeter film. Due to its expense, fragility, and need for frequent inspection and repair following use, the collection of 16-millimeter film was often limited to large public libraries, universities, or shared collections such as public library systems and consolidated school centers. It is important to note that films acquired and shared in these collections were licensed, generally for the life of the print, rather than purchased outright. The advent of home video in the mid-1970s, the release and mass-marketing of back catalog content (primarily Hollywood entertainment), and the concomitant development of rental stores resulted in films becoming available and affordable in video format. Driven by user demand, libraries began to acquire video as readily as monographs. In many ways the move to licensing streaming video is a pendulum swing back to the model of 16-millimeter distribution, with libraries not owning, but licensing content. For a detailed history of media formats in library or media center collections, see Lori Widzinski's article, "Step Away from the Machine: A Look at Our Collective Past" (2010).

Librarians are quite familiar with contemporary monographic acquisition models. Making use of jobbers, approval plans, best-seller lists, review sources, and discounted pricing by monograph vendors, those involved in print collection development find it to be largely routinized. This is not the case with video acquisitions, outside of mass-market entertainment titles. To understand why, we must consider the differences between traditional print publishing and video distribution. In general, monographs come from publishers responsible for producing, marketing, and distributing the content, or from jobbers who distribute titles from many publishers. Generally, jobbers do not have exclusive distribution rights to the monographs they handle.

Content from a given publisher's catalog can be acquired from multiple sources such as Ingram, YBP (Yankee Book Peddler), Ambassador Books, Baker & Taylor, and Amazon. Jobbers offer a variety of value-added services, including approval plans which match elements of available product to an individual library's scope of collecting, cataloging, shelf-ready processing, and frequently, content discounting.

The video marketplace most visible and familiar to librarians and consumers alike is the home video market. A much smaller and more obscure segment of the video marketplace consists of independent film titles distributed by small companies that primarily focus on sales to educational, institutional, or other specialty buyers. These distributors tend to have exclusive distribution rights for their titles. Films that one distributor carries are rarely available from another. Many films are self-distributed—only available directly from the filmmaker. A few library jobbers handle media titles, but these distributors generally handle only mass-market, mainstream entertainment titles, with limited independent, documentary, and educational offerings. These sell-through sources distribute only physical formats and do not have authorization to negotiate streaming rights. There are no profile-based video approval plans. Some companies provide for standing order arrangements, but these too focus on mass-market titles such as television series releases or Academy award nominees.

In their 2009 report, the first to examine changes in the use of video in higher education, Kaufman and Mohan (2009) note: "trends noticeable today . . . are as remarkable as the shift from the scroll to the codex over 2,000 years ago." Certainly this shift is already evident in libraries with electronic indexes, journals, and most recently, eBooks. But many libraries, already resistant to media, have been slow to adopt digital video. This reluctance is partially the result of both marketplace issues (lack of hosted content, resistance of distributors to enter the digital realm, shifting licensing and pricing models) and the practical issues associated with the technology. Libraries must find ways to adapt their collection development processes and policies to meet shifting consumer use, expectation, and demand.

COLLECTION BUILDING, HOSTING, LICENSING, AND PRICING

Libraries have multiple options for providing streaming video. Hosting, licensing, and pricing models are interconnected and differ from distributor to distributor. The models discussed here are not mutually exclusive; distributors may offer more than one or variations of these options.

Collection Models

Generally, libraries build video collections on a title-by-title basis; this is the common approach for streaming video as well. All the leading video distributors offer some form of title-by-title licensing for their titles. This approach provides a library the most control over content in its collection, but is labor intensive, and replicates a monographic selection process largely replaced with approval plans and patron-driven acquisitions programs. As noted previously, approval programs for video are very rare, and in the digital realm nonexistent. Instead, some distributors offer media databases or curated collections. A media database or curated collection provides an array of related titles as a package (e.g., *The BBC Shakespeare Plays, Opera in Video, Filmakers Library, Films on Demand*). These collections frequently offer added value through closed captioning, transcripts, segmenting of the videos into discrete units, semantic searching interfaces, and editing tools that permit users to build custom play lists from the content. With a curated collection the library has access to titles that might not have been selected otherwise, but still meet user needs. There is, however, also the probability that many titles in the curated collection will never be accessed. Distributors that offer curated collections may also license individual titles from the collections.

A third type of collection, less widely used, is the clip collection. Generally, a clip collection consists of short-form videos, often extracted from longer videos, addressing or covering a single concept. Used primarily in education, clip collections usually are a subscription product. Key clip collections include those offered by INTELLECOM and NBCLearn. Gary Handman's 2010 article: "License to Look: Evolving Models for Library Video Acquisition and Access" addresses all of these models in greater detail.

Licensing Models

Despite the source of the videos or the type of collection (single title, curated collection, clips), streaming video licensing falls into four dominant models: term, in-perpetuity, subscription, and pay-per-view. Most distributors offer a combination of options, and most licensing is negotiable. It is not uncommon for a distributor to require purchase of a hard copy before licensing streaming rights, though as the market evolves some distributors have begun to license digital files without requiring purchasing a hard copy.

Term License

A term license provides access for a specific period. Term licensing is essentially the de facto standard for streaming video, although the length of the term varies widely. Length of license and pricing vary according to the terms of the license. Term licensing is perhaps the most flexible of licensing options, permitting the library to provide access for a semester, a year, or even a single use.

In-Perpetuity License

In-perpetuity licensing is the model that many media selectors prefer. It most closely resembles the monographic purchase model in that it does not require repeated relicensing. Many video distributors have been resistant to in-perpetuity licensing, noting that they do not have distribution rights in-perpetuity. Media selectors counter that vendors sell DVDs without requiring return of the hard copy when the vendor's distribution rights expire; thus digital files should be treated in the same manner. As the market evolves, more distributors offer in-perpetuity licensing, now sometimes referred to as life of format licensing. This refers to the life of the codec (a program or device that encodes or decodes a data stream) employed to create and manage the digital master. This approach mirrors the life of film licensing employed years ago with 16-millimeter films. If a new digital standard emerges, replacing the file with a new format will require relicensing of the title.

Subscription License

Subscription licensing, essentially a form of term license, provides access to an entire collection or array of videos from a distributor, usually on an annual basis. With a subscription license the library pays a flat fee for use of the collection (or collection subset) for the licensed period. In a subscription license the distributor serves the content, and new titles are available as they are added to the collection. If the distributor loses the right to offer a title, it is pulled from the subscription and is no longer available. Licensing agreements for subscription collections should include provisions to accommodate purchasing discontinued titles before the distributor loses distribution rights. Only a few distributors offer subscription models, usually those with widely scoped, interdisciplinary, or clip collections. As with licensed abstract and indexing services, nonrenewal of the license results in complete loss of access to the collection. There are no provisions for assuring continued access to a previously subscribed to back file.

Pay-Per-View

Pay-per-view is a licensing model common in the consumer mass media marketplace. Amazon Instant Video and cable television providers employ this model for feature films and other specialty content, with viewers paying varying amounts for instantaneous viewing. With most pay-per-view licenses the content remains available for a short time period. A few educational content distributors offer this model, suggesting that it mirrors textbook purchasing. Some librarians argue that pay-per-view offloads financial commitment to the end user. If the cost were to be absorbed by the library, however, pay-per-view has the potential to be both prohibitively expensive and fiscally unpredictable.

Pay-per-view licensing offers no permanent benefit to the community, as no content is added to the library collection.

Other Licensing Models

Swank DigitalCampus licenses feature films for curricular use, based on course enrollment, number of titles, and length of license. This model supports education but is not applicable to general purpose use of feature films. Criterion has entered the U.S. market with a similar model to support curricular use of feature films. A PDA model implementation in the mid-2000s would not scale (farrelly 2008). But as streaming video matures in the library marketplace, larger streaming collections become available, and libraries gain experience with PDA models, it is possible that such a purchase model could prove workable for video. Two emerging approaches approximate a PDA model. Alexander Street Press offers evidence-based acquisition, with funds from an upfront spend applied to the purchase of accessed titles, with the library determining how those funds are applied. Kanopy's access model results in term licenses for titles used. Similarly, there are no viable bookshelf models for streaming video. (A bookshelf model licenses an established number of titles for a predetermined period, but allows changing out the specific titles at intervals.) As streaming video is a relatively new means of delivering library media content, other licensing models may evolve or merit exploring.

Pricing Models

Licensing and pricing are interdependent. As with licensing there are no industry standards for streaming video pricing. Some companies require purchase of a hard copy as part of the licensing process. Others include a term license for streaming with purchase of the content on DVD. Curated and clip collection vendors may base pricing on FTE (full-time equivalent) and/or Carnegie classification. At least one distributor calculates pricing on a sliding scale determined by the number of minutes licensed and the term of the license. Other distributors have offered package deals to library consortia. With these pricing models, generally the greater the number of titles or minutes of content, the lower the cost per video. Almost all distributors offer a variety of pricing models. Negotiation is critical as distributors and librarians continue to seek approaches that work for both parties.

Hosting and Discoverability

Regardless of the source of the digital files, a key consideration in providing streaming video is hosting. Streaming video is not simply a matter of storing a file on the Internet and providing a link. Distributors expect that access will be authenticated and thus restricted to the library's clientele. They also expect that the content will be protected from downloading, duplication, and other forms of content theft. Users expect to be able to access the content easily—on their desktops, in the classroom, and through their mobile devices. This requires transcoded files that will work with multiple computer operating systems, browsers, and playback utilities such as Flash, Mac IOS, and so forth. These expectations, as well as technology capabilities and financial capacity, impact whether a library's digital media will be vendor-hosted, hosted locally, or outsourced to a third-party service.

Vendor Hosting

Vendor hosting is the simplest and generally most cost-effective approach for libraries, mirroring how libraries provide access to databases and e-journal content. In this mode of content delivery, streaming files are served from the distributor's site, and this distributor assumes responsibility for assuring security and the transcoding of files. As codecs change, the vendor is responsible for upgrading the files and assuring compatibility with users' devices. Because of the resources invested in their platforms and the relationship with the original video producer, streaming video distributors can more easily provide added content and functionality such as transcripts, semantic searching, closed-captioning, and tools to create customized playlists. To fund platform development, some streaming media providers, no matter what licensing or pricing model they employ, may charge a maintenance fee. While the number of distributors providing hosting continues to increase, not all vendors host their content, requiring libraries to find their own hosting solution.

Self-Hosting

With self-hosting the licensing institution (library, technology unit, etc.) is responsible for all the processes and support structure to serve the file, secure the file, and enable playback. While some vendors will provide a digital file for self-hosting, others require the library to digitize and transcode the file from a hard-copy DVD. In such scenarios, closed-captioning, transcripts, and segmentation of the video may be too labor-intensive or expensive to be taken on by the library. As of this writing there are few third-party companies or turn-key solutions to perform these functions, so most self-hosting solutions are home grown. A few open-source products are available, but they require knowledgeable programmers to implement fully. Among these products are Omeka, Kaltura, iTunes University, and Vimeo. As the need for hosting solutions grows, new products are certain to be developed. ShareStream, Video Furnace, Media Hub, and Avalon Media System (in development by Indiana University) are some of the emerging tools that show promise for simplified streaming video hosting.

Third-Party Hosting

Libraries that lack the resources for in-house hosting may turn to third-party providers to perform these functions. One of the largest third-party companies is used by some of the largest video distribution companies. When using a third-party solution, it is important that the license from the original content provider includes language to permit such hosting and the storing of files off-site. Given the expense of building and maintaining a self-hosted solution, it is likely that the need for third-party hosting will increase, and that new companies will emerge to provide this service.

Discoverability

"Findability precedes usability. You cannot use what you cannot find" (Greenfield 2010). Regardless of where or how a library hosts streaming content, it is of no use to users unless they are able to identify, locate, select, and connect to that content. A library's streaming video collection most likely will be housed across multiple locations and interfaces, including distributor platforms and local servers. It is essential to establish tools to identify and access this content without requiring users to search multiple access points or interfaces. In the author's view this is best accomplished through full MARC records in the library's catalog with direct links to the streaming file. Yet nearly a quarter of libraries that stream do not provide title-level catalog records for their streaming videos (farrelly and Hutchison 2013). Some distributors provide some form of bibliographic data for their streaming titles, most commonly larger vendors who offer subscription services or curated collections. The quality of this data varies widely. Some provide detailed and complete MARC records, including Library of Congress subject headings. Others offer little more than general subject assignments or records, which, while adequate for K–12 or public libraries, may be insufficient for a research library. Other distributors may provide only a metadata file from which the library can build catalog records. Some librarians argue that library catalogs should not include records for subscription content that may go away if titles are removed by the vendor or the library's subscription lapses. Yet without catalog records the content in such subscriptions is unlikely to be discovered and used. Since renewal of resources is often based on use data, mechanisms to drive discoverability and resultant use are essential. Vendors may see the provision of catalog records as an expense that does little to increase sales. Librarians need to continue to impress upon distributors the importance of bibliographic data for generating use—use that subsequently drives renewal. Libraries with the requisite cataloging skills will need to examine vendor-provided bibliographic data to determine its suitability for local needs, and arrange for other solutions if it does not.

Some libraries opt to edit the existing catalog record for VHS or DVD video already in the collection to include a link to the digital version. Others may find it satisfactory to modify an existing analog record for the digital file. Libraries planning to generate original cataloging for digital video files will want to refer to *Best Practices for Cataloging Streaming Media* (OLAC 2009).

Of course the catalog is not the only way to discover and access resources. Discovery tools such as *ProQuest Summon*, *EBSCO Discovery Service*, *III Encore*, and *Ex Libris Primo*, now being widely implemented in libraries, also serve to identify content and connect users. Some larger distributors already work with discovery tool vendors to assure that their content is included. Libraries also need to work with discovery tool vendors to impress on them the importance of making video content discoverable and to ensure that their own collections are activated within the tools.

As more libraries acquire streaming videos, the likelihood of usable records for copy cataloging through OCLC and other record providers will increase. As more distributors offer subscription and curated collections, the prospects of subject indexes identifying streaming content and providing access through link resolvers will also certainly increase.

SELECTING VIDEOS TO STREAM

Principles of video collection development are well described in multiple chapters of Gary Handman's *Video Collection Development in Multi-Type Libraries: A Handbook*. Individual chapters address public, school, and academic library video collections, while one chapter directly addresses the need to develop collection development policies to address new technologies (Scholtz 2002). The principles addressed in this text remain relevant to streaming collections. Streaming video collections should continue to mesh with existing collection development policies. The scope and nature of the content collected, balance, fit with curriculum or user population, and myriad other points in a library's collection development policy should still apply to streaming titles collected. For a librarian not already familiar with educational and documentary media publishing and distribution, the process of finding, evaluating, and selecting video content, streaming or not, may be baffling. The ALCTS (Association for Library Collections and Technical Services) *Guide to Video Acquisitions in Libraries: Issues and Best Practices* (Laskowski 2011) addresses the essentials, including appendixes covering review and selection tools, and an annotated list of video vendors. There are some vendors who specialize in the distribution of streaming video. The ALA's *Digital Video Collections Guide* describes numerous quality streaming video collections (Spicer 2012). Although structured with an academic focus, the *Guide* lists collections that are also applicable to public and school libraries. The *Guide* is an open access resource; others are invited to contribute descriptions of other digital video collections with high-quality content.

Feature films and television programs present unique challenges for a streaming collection. Consumer interfaces such as *Netflix* are driving the development of streaming options for personal viewing of mass-market entertainment titles. There are fewer options for libraries, including Swank's *DigitalCampus* and the Criterion platform mentioned earlier. *Hoopla*, a platform developed by Midwest Tape, may prove to be a viable interface for streaming mass entertainment titles for public libraries using a pay-per-view model. Some libraries and faculty have explored using *Netflix* or *Amazon on Demand* for curricular use of feature film. It is arguable, however, whether such use is permissible within the terms of use for these products. And such use generally falls within the limitations of the pay-per-view model already referenced. For feature films and television, general market forces rather than educational need drive the availability of content for institutional acquisitions; thus it is unlikely that many viable options will be available for libraries to stream content of this type in the near future.

There is no single guide, Web site, directory, or jobber for identifying and selecting videos. The National Media Market, a trade show featuring documentary and educational video, however, provides an excellent opportunity to preview and select titles from many of the top distributors. Copies of newly produced and released, as well as popular, titles are available for on-site preview, and distributors often negotiate package deals and discounts with attending selectors. Nearly all distributors participating in the National Media Market offer streaming options. Another outlet for streaming video information is the VideoLib discussion list. A general forum for all matters pertaining to video in libraries, list members frequently recommend titles, identify sources for hard-to-locate titles, and offer other advice pertaining to video collection development and management.

Librarians interested in developing a streaming video collection may wish to start by looking at use data for their existing physical video collection. Providing streaming access to heavily used titles, titles frequently used for course reserves, those needed at more than one location, and titles with broad multidisciplinary appeal are good candidates for a streaming collection. Also, as VHS and DVDs need to be replaced, streaming, if available, should be strongly considered.

If jumping into licensed streaming is not viable, openly available collections of high-quality, freely accessible videos that do not require licensing are a possible option. The *Digital Video Collections Guide* mentioned earlier and the author's Libguide on *Streaming Video* (farrelly 2012) provide descriptions of and links to many such collections.

CHALLENGES AND BENEFITS OF STREAMING VIDEO

Early models for streaming video placed inordinate burdens on libraries. It was not uncommon for distributors to require hard-copy purchase before allowing a streaming license, to charge double the price (or more) of the hard copy for a digital file, to require renewal at the same price at the end of a licensed term, or to require the library to digitize and host the content. Had journal publishers promoted e-journals with similar requirements, it is unlikely that libraries would have adopted e-journals at all.

To some degree many of these requirements still persist in some licensing models, but the market is changing. As late as 2007 less than half a dozen distributors for educational or documentary content provided streaming video options. Now virtually every video distributor offers some form of streaming licensing. Still, licensing presents a hurdle for distributors who are relatively new to the game and for smaller, independent production companies.

Benefits of Streaming

Streaming access offers considerable value to libraries and their clientele. Twenty-four-hour and remote access, simultaneous use of a single file by multiple users, segmentation and user editing tools, and the ability to link or embed video into course pages or learning management systems expand the flexibility and usability of video collections for users. Libraries benefit from a huge decrease in staff time devoted to processing, circulation, and shelf maintenance for videos. Other significant benefits include eliminating the need for multiple copies and the costs and efforts related to replacement of lost, stolen, and damaged videos.

Disadvantages of Streaming

Some of the cost benefits of streaming video are countered by the conversion of staff time from collection maintenance to efforts in licensing and negotiation, tasks ordinarily performed at a higher skill level and pay grade. Significantly, term licenses that require paying repeatedly for the same content move video acquisition into the sphere of serials and other continuations of digital content that now consume an ever-increasing portion of library acquisitions budgets. As the streaming video market matures, more distributors are accommodating licenses in perpetuity, but libraries subscribing to curated collections run the risk of replicating in video the current problems with the Big Deal in e-journals packages.

There are expenses associated with streaming video that other digital content does not present to libraries. The major additional expense is hosting. For content not hosted by the distributor, the library faces the ongoing costs of local hosting. Emerging market forces, however, will minimize this ongoing cost as more distributors provide hosting, turn-key hosting solutions emerge, and third-party vendors provide alternatives to hosting locally.

Unlike other digital content providers some video distributors do not provide the digital file, off-loading to the library the responsibility of generating a digital file from a purchased DVD. These locally generated files most likely will lack closed captioning or chaptering, without additional expense incurred by the library.

There are tradeoffs with streaming versus physical copies. Not insignificant is the reduction in image quality of files compressed for streaming. The streaming approach may be less desirable in a classroom setting where image projection magnifies the issues of compression and the equipment and tech support requirements for classroom use are more complex and expensive than for DVD. But streaming delivery is largely a lean-in activity, meant for personal rather than group screening. With the growth in use of tablets and other mobile devices for personal viewing screens, the issue of enlarged image quality is less important. Additionally, compression quality is improving rapidly. Commercial streaming services already provide HD (high definition) streams at a bit rate comparable to standard DVD. As Internet service providers increase bandwidth capability, streaming image and delivery are certain to improve (Brandon 2011).

Emerging Challenges

As libraries acquire streaming video, other service issues arise, not the least among these is the value of shared collections and ILL. If content is locked behind an authentication firewall, will walk-in users be able to access it? Libraries have long depended on ILL to fill in collection gaps and to meet specialized needs of users. If collection access is limited to authenticated users, libraries will be unable to loan their streaming content. More importantly, however, they will not be able to borrow what is not in the local collection. E-journal licenses already address this issue; eBook communities of practice are beginning to. It remains to be seen how the problem will be addressed for streaming video.

Since the advent of home video, library circulation statistics have benefitted from video loans. As video use migrates from hard-copy circulation to online viewing, libraries will need to reconsider how to report this use and measure success in meeting user needs. Video use data collection is complicated by the plethora of portals through which users access streaming video and by the huge variances in how vendors collect and report use data. Use remains an undefined term. Some hosting services employ COUNTER-compliant (Counting Online Usage of Networked Electronic Resources) reporting, but the majority do not. The need to establish both industry and library standards for measuring use of streaming video collections is an issue still to be addressed.

STREAMING VIDEO PRESERVATION

A historic view of libraries is that they serve a major role as the curators, protectors, and guardians of cultural heritage. Libraries already are addressing issues with the preservation of books and journals. Services and protocols such as JSTOR, Project Muse, Portico, and the Western Regional Storage Trust have been developed and refined to assure preservation of the journal record. Project Gutenberg, the Google Books project, and the Hathi Trust are programs to protect and extend the life of monograph content. No such co-ordinated efforts are in place for preserving the video record. The Internet Archive, the Prelinger Archive, and the Vanderbilt Television News Archive are all efforts to assure description and digital access to some video. A more robust, cooperative effort to provide for long-term accessibility of educational or documentary film or video content is a major development that awaits resolution in the 21st century.

CONCLUSION

Streaming video is a relatively new format for libraries but has already reached the tipping point: 70 percent of academic libraries now provide streaming video (farrelly and Hutchison 2013) up from 33 percent in 2010 (Primary Research Group 2010). But streaming video has considerable distance to go to achieve its full potential, and is not without shortcomings and issues. As with other digital formats in libraries, these issues and shortcomings will be resolved as the delivery models evolve and mature. There can be no doubt, however, that streaming already is a major force in shaping user expectations and library video collection development.

REFERENCES

Allen, I. Elaine, and Jeff Seaman. 2011. *Going the Distance: Online Education in the United States*. Available at: http://www.onlinelearningsurvey.com/reports/goingthedistance.pdf. Accessed March 6, 2013.

Brandon, John. 2011. "Video Format War: Blu-ray vs. Streaming," *PCWorld* (October). Available at: http://www.pcworld.com/article/241215/. Accessed March 6, 2013.

Enis, Matt. 2012. "Patron Preferences Shift toward Streaming," *Library Journal* 137 (14): 18.

farrelly, deg. 2008. "Use-determined Streaming Video Acquisition: The Arizona Model for FMG On Demand," *College & University Media Review* 14 (1): 65–78.

farrelly, deg. 2012. *Streaming Video: Internet Sites*. Available at: http://libguides.asu.edu/StreamingVideo. Accessed March 6, 2013.

farrelly, deg, and Jane Hutchison. 2013. "Streaming Video in Academic Libraries: Preliminary Results from a National Survey" (speech). Presented at the Charleston Conference, Charleston, South Carolina.

Greenfield, Mark A. 2010. "The End of the Web as We Know It and I Feel Fine" (speech). Keynote address presented at the CCUMC Conference, Buffalo, New York. Available at: http://hosted.mediasite.com/mediasite/SilverlightPlayer/Default.aspx?peid=5e6f12a14a264567876f0807ef461a471d. Accessed March 6, 2013.

Handman, Gary, ed. 2002. *Video Collection Development in Multi-Type Libraries: A Handbook*. Westport, CT: Greenwood Press.

Handman, Gary. 2010. "License to Look: Evolving Models for Library Video Acquisition and Access," *Library Trends* 58 (3): 324–34.

Kaufman, Peter B., and Jen Mohan. 2009. *Video Use and Higher Education: Options for the Future*. [New York?]: Intelligent Television. Available at: http://library.nyu.edu/about/Video_Use_in_Higher_Education.pdf. Accessed March 6, 2013.

Laskowski, Mary. S. 2011. *Guide to Video Acquisitions in Libraries: Issues and Best Practices*. Chicago: Association for Library Collections & Technical Services.

OLAC Cataloging Policy Committee & Streaming Media Best Practices Task Force 2009. *Best Practices for Cataloging Streaming Media*. Available at: http://www.olacinc.org/drupal/capc_files/streamingmedia.pdf. Accessed on March 6, 2013.

Primary Research Group. 2010. *Survey of Academic Libraries*. New York: Primary Research Group Inc.

Primary Research Group. 2012. *The Survey of Distance Learning Programs in Higher Education*. New York: Primary Research Group Inc.

Scholtz, James. C. 2002. "Developing Video Collection Policies to Accommodate Existing and New Technologies." In *Video Collection Development in Multi-Type Libraries: A Handbook*, ed. G. Handman, 245–76. Westport, CT: Greenwood Press.

Spicer, Scott. 2012. *Digital Video Collections Guide*. Available at: http://connect.ala.org/node/183711. Accessed March 6, 2013.

Widzinski, Lori. 2010. "Step Away from the Machine: A Look at Our Collective Past." *Library Trends* 58 (3): 358–77.

USEFUL RESOURCES

American Library Association Video Round Table. Available at: www.ala.org/vrt.

National Media Market. Available at: www.nmm.net.

VideoLib Discussion List. calmail.berkeley.edu/manage/list/listinfo/videolib@lists.berke ley.edu

PART III

ACCESS, COOPERATIVE EFFORTS, SHARED COLLECTIONS

19

CATALOGING FOR COLLECTION MANAGEMENT

Linda R. Musser and Christopher H. Walker

Academic library collections are evolving away from browsable shelves of print materials to a mixture of online and traditional media. This poses challenges for the patron's ability to discover the available resources and to choose the most relevant from among them: challenges that require collaborative work between public services librarians, materials selectors, and cataloging staff. Transformative changes in the nature and complexity of the collections and in the nature of the metadata that supports discovery of a collection's strengths require that collection managers learn more about cataloging, and catalogers learn more about how collections are used.

Discoverability is an essential part of what librarians do. While historically cataloging has been perceived as being focused on describing materials, the ultimate aim of cataloging is to help people find relevant works via description and organization, and convergently access them. To that end, it is desirable for librarians, regardless of specialty, to collaborate with their cataloging colleagues to maximize description of materials in their collections to the best extent possible. For example, subject specialists will know best which eBook collections would benefit most from supplemental metadata; reference librarians can provide details on which materials are most difficult for users to locate in the catalog as currently described; and ILL staff can help identify which materials are not being retrieved by linking software and possibly prioritized for addition of linking fields such as ISSNs or ISBNs. Given the size of most collections, it is important to prioritize efforts to maximize benefits to users.

Knowing what kinds of metadata improvements, also known as enhancement, can be undertaken locally requires understanding not only some basic cataloging but also how your catalog software functions—what fields are indexed, searchable, and displayed. As new catalog systems are implemented, librarians need to select which fields in existing records should be indexed and how they should be indexed (e.g., alphabetically for browsing, by keyword, or by numeric identifier). These same decisions come into play when choosing what types of enhancements are worthwhile. If your catalog software does not currently support indexing and searching of ISBNs, then that type of enhancement is probably not worth making a priority. Looking to the future, however, retrieval systems will evolve. For example, while most catalog software currently in use does not take advantage of the hierarchical structures inherent in tools such as the Library of Congress subject headings and related classification scheme, future discovery systems may be able to better capitalize on the usefulness of these structures for retrieval.

WHY GOOD METADATA MATTERS

Good metadata improves discoverability and retrieval; it also reduces the number of questions users bring to our service points, both virtual and physical. Full text, while useful, is not the same as catalog access. Catalogs typically utilize controlled vocabularies that can aid users in narrowing their searching along subject lines. The biggest challenge users face in the evolving information environment is information overload—too many results—and good metadata is one method librarians can employ to aid users in sorting through overwhelming numbers of results. Next-generation discovery tools and databases prompt users to retrieve resources relevant to their needs with faceted results derived from the underlying title-level metadata. All library users benefit from good subject analysis through enhanced discovery points and controlled vocabulary that pulls together materials despite disparate terminology and languages. This latter point is significant to remember because materials in other languages and scripts will not be retrieved through use of keywords without metadata to provide English-language search terms.

Beyond providing a useful hierarchy, common thesauri, and keywords for searching, metadata provides a way for librarians to document the history of interrelationships between entities and works. It is one of the unique and valuable services that librarians provide. Via authority files and linkages among records, library catalogs essentially document the history and development of various works. It is via authority file linkages that users seeking works related to Mark Twain are led to works about Samuel Clemens. It is through the catalog linkages that users know that the title of a journal that began as *Geological News Letter* changed to *GeoTimes*, then became *Earth*. The latest iteration of widely accepted cataloging codes, RDA (Resource Description and Access), continues the long-standing efforts of the cataloging community to adjust the rules and standards of their craft to improve users' success at finding the resources they are seeking. Perhaps the most exciting change brought by RDA is to the authority file, a system that assigns authoritative versions of the names of authors, historical persons, corporate bodies, and musical and literary works. Using the assigned form of name in the catalog ensures that references to the same person or work index together, so that patrons find the resources that can assist with their research. Name records written under the new RDA standard will carry much more information, such as notes on the history of a corporate body, and links out to Web sites in addition to the citations for the sources of information that were already there. The new authority file will also interact with sources such as Wikipedia and the Virtual International Authority File (VIAF), an authority file that merges information from over a dozen national libraries in Europe and across the globe.

A COLLABORATIVE ENTERPRISE

The catalog is a shared resource that all librarians should and can contribute to. Among many librarians there is a sense that the catalog is the sole creation of catalogers and therefore territory into which a noncataloger should hesitate to venture. Yet much as librarians provide feedback to publishers and database vendors on the quality and characteristics of their products, they should be as, if not more willing to provide feedback to their cataloging colleagues who quite likely work for the same institution. After all, if we cannot talk with our cataloging colleagues when they are just down the hall, how much more diffi-cult will it be when or if cataloging is centralized across organizations or con-sortia? Librarians put infinite care in selecting materials for the collections, so it behooves us to partner with cataloging staff to make sure that the resources are discoverable. The pathways to becoming an active participant in creating a superior catalog resource are myriad but must include at a minimum find-ing ways to communicate and work with cataloging staff. Illustrations of how librarians can learn more about cataloging, examples of why this knowledge is useful, and ways to contribute to the catalog are explored later.

As new materials are received, it is useful to not only examine the work to become familiar with the content but to examine the metadata as well. Through this method, you can become familiar with the common subject headings for works in your library as well as their accompanying classifica-tion assignment. This is also the best point at which to identify deficiencies in the record describing the piece, such as a need for additional subject descrip-tions or other access points. Given libraries' reliance on copy cataloging, it should not be assumed that the metadata will reflect all the aspects of the work that your patrons need. For example, you may have purchased a work in re-sponse to a subject of local interest. It is important to examine the metadata to verify that the topic of interest is adequately described in the record so that it will be retrieved in a user's search. If more access points are needed, the solu-tion is simple. Ask your cataloger to enhance the record with additional head-ings or notes that reflect your local strengths. In some cases, the classification assignment may need to be adjusted to better collocate the resource with other materials in your collection. In other cases, the subject specialist and cataloging staff may need to consult about whether the item in hand is better treated as a serial publication or as a monographic one. It is important that you know enough about how the cataloging affects searching and retrieval so that your users benefit from the combined expertise of the library's staff.

Knowledge of the major subject headings and classifications in your subject area is valuable for additional reasons. Approval plan vendors and bulk-content providers frequently organize their selection profiles based upon subject or classification schemas such as the Dewey Decimal or Library of Congress classifications. Selection tools such as the *British National Bibliography* are organized by classification scheme. Familiarity with the classification structure helps you ensure that all aspects of a subject are not only collected, but are also collocated in your library. For example, in the Library of Congress system, the G and Z classification numbers, maps and bibliographies, respectively, have validity across many subject areas. To illustrate, if you are trying to collect all major works related to forestry, it is important to realize that bibliographies on the topic may class in Z rather than in SD; maps and atlases on the topic will class in G. Additionally, it is useful to know of the changes in the classification schema over time. As an example, prior to the creation of the GE classification in the Library of Congress system, environmental science materials were classified in a variety of areas, including QH (biology), GF (human ecology), and others (www.loc.gov/acq/devpol/environ.pdf). Knowledge of how the classification scheme used at your institution works at the subunit level is useful in space planning, given that different aspects of a field grow at different rates. Imagine, for example, the challenges faced by the librarian doing space planning in the gaming section of the collection. How fast does the collection grow in the area for board games versus the section on video or computer games? Finally, data on collection usage is generally reported using call-number ranges so it is helpful to know how those correspond to the subject areas. Data on which parts of the collections are being most and least heavily used can inform not only collections managers but also can be used to guide discussions and priorities with cataloging staff. Potentially, records for materials in underutilized areas of the collections could be examined and targeted for metadata enrichment to aid in increasing usage.

The catalog record is also a place to record item-specific data such as signed or numbered copies, donor information, and other information valuable to current and future users. Other examples of information useful to record include preservation work performed and information related to the artifactual value (e.g., quality of binding) of the piece. The Institute of Museum and Library Services–funded project *Publishers' Bindings Online* (bindings.lib .ua.edu) provides a colorful illustration of why such information is useful. As librarians move to shared archives of historic materials, it is important to retain the most complete, most representational originals. Accurate metadata is essential to facilitate this process. Historically, item-level metadata has received much less attention than bibliographic metadata, yet to adequately facilitate the merging and sharing of collections across institutions, item-level metadata is key. For example, does the work retain all accompanying parts and pieces, such as accompanying maps? Which copy of a film was purchased with public performance rights? Some libraries may have bound issues of a periodical yet not noted that the holdings were incomplete, that covers were removed and discarded, or that less-than-facsimile replacement pages may have been utilized (e.g., black-and-white photocopied replacements when the original, color version was lost). Such information can and should be recorded in the metadata.

Increasingly, libraries are able to not only purchase a work, but also its metadata record simultaneously. Major approval plan vendors such as YBP and Coutts provide MARC records, sometimes enriched with tables of contents and other data elements, at the time of purchase. Publisher-supplied metadata, considered by many publishers to be a freebie and not worth investing a lot of time, is unfortunately often less than ideal in terms of completeness and specificity. For example, while the general heading of "Engineering" may adequately describe a subject category among a publisher's offerings of new imprints, it is less than helpful as a subject heading to be used to retrieve a work on dam building. eBooks (and other eFormats) pose particular challenges in terms of the quality and extent of their metadata. From a user's standpoint, it is useful to know whether the work is in the form of an HTML file, PDF, Kindle edition, or other format as well as indicating any platform or license-driven restrictions (e.g., one or more simultaneous user, no downloading, limited number of uses). This information is typically lacking from the metadata record. Bulk purchases of eBook collections pose particular challenges. In some cases, the purchase is really a lease and records may only be temporary (and thus not worth enhancing), whereas in others, the size of collection is such that creation of metadata records on an item-by-item basis is unrealistic. Metadata records for works in collections can sometimes be purchased, in which case knowledge of the basics of cataloging improves your ability to evaluate these records for adequacy and judge whether they are worth the asking price.

Ultimately, it is essential to understand that the catalog record is not sacrosanct. It is okay to edit catalog records and most catalogers will welcome your input, interest, and expertise. Keep in mind, however, the importance of maintaining a balance between enhancing existing metadata records and other needs, such as retrospective work on uncataloged materials. No library has the resources to enhance every record; therefore a focus on the most important, unique, and hardest-working parts of your collection is required. Public service librarians need to share their knowledge of the collections and the ways they are being used with their cataloging comrades in order to set appropriate and reasonable priorities.

SETTING PRIORITIES

In addition to being able to purchase metadata records, several vendors provide fee-based content enrichment services for recently published material, typically providing tables of contents, summaries, genre terms, cover art, and so forth. Enrichment, however, can be done locally on a case-by-case basis. (The term *enhancement* typically refers to bringing a record up to date or to a minimum standard, whereas *enrichment* refers to adding various optional fields above and beyond the minimum.) Given the size of most libraries' collections, librarians must be selective in choosing which materials are worthy of enrichment. Choices of what to enrich should be specific to your situation and institution, along with the decision of whether to contribute your improvements to the broader library community. Some may choose to enrich records in areas of collection strength; others might choose to enrich records based upon other criteria such as those that further the institution's mission (e.g., works related to diversity). Records for items going to storage (or otherwise restricted from user browsing) are particularly important to examine for quality of the base record as well as enrichment. Does it have the typical hooks used by software for match and retrieval, for example, ISSN, ISBN, LCCN? For multivolume works, is it clear what the content range of each volume is? Consider the example of the collected works of Shakespeare: how easy is it to determine which volume contains the play *Titus Andronicus*? Does the record include information about related works, such as a teacher's guide, or where the work is indexed? Are there accompanying pieces worthy of additional access points or metadata? An example might be an accompanying map or poster that has a unique title or subject focus. Is it useful to indicate that the work exists in a translated form or alternative format, such as online? What about the case where the alternate format does not exactly match the copy of record (which is increasingly the online version)? For some periodicals, the title of the online version differs from that of the print, retaining only the latest title for all volumes rather than documenting the history of title changes over the life of the publication. This presents problems for users and ILL staff when a citation to the former title does not match the metadata. In another variation, the online edition of a journal may lack sections contained in the print, such as book reviews or letters to the editor. The metadata record is an excellent place to record such information for the benefit of current and future users (including librarians).

Sometimes the metadata record simply does not provide information sufficient to help potential users identify the work. If the record is old or minimal, it may utilize obsolete cataloging terms or conventions. Standards and capabilities change over time. As an example, for many years the cataloging cooperative OCLC restricted the maximum size of a catalog record to 50 lines. As materials selectors strive to build collections on the topics of special interest to their faculty and students, the cohesiveness of strong, deep collections may no longer be apparent from the metadata that represents the library's holdings to its local clientele and to the world of scholarship. A tune-up of older metadata may be in order. Perhaps the metadata utilizes outdated vocabulary—the subject heading "Groundwater" was once "Water, Underground"; the heading "African American" was once "Negro." New concepts such as nanotechnology or artificial intelligence appear in the literature; however, controlled vocabulary to describe these new fields typically lags behind until usage coalesces around a new term. Few libraries go back to the records of those early works to update the metadata with the newly established subject headings. Metadata for serials may deserve special attention due to likely changes in the resource over time. The journal's supplements spin off as separate publications, and then are reabsorbed. The scholarly society that publishes the work has changed its name. The title on the covers has varied slightly. These changes will not be reflected in the legacy record that was downloaded to your local catalog long ago. It is particularly important to keep your authority records up to date so that, for example, J.Lo's early works will be found when searching for works by Jennifer Lopez. Perhaps the metadata record simply lacks an ISBN or ISSN, which are now commonly used to link related resources. Knowing the kinds of enhancements possible can greatly improve retrieval and use of materials.

Another consideration when prioritizing local efforts is whether another organization might be taking the lead on providing enhanced access. In many cases, such efforts follow geographic boundaries, for example, an Arkansas library enhancing metadata related to Arkansas works. If a government agency or consortium is in the process of digitizing certain publications, perhaps local enhancement efforts should concentrate on other materials that cannot be as readily found. In the end, the specifics of your local situation will influence what can and cannot be done. Accepting imperfect records for some of the materials in your collections is just going to be a fact of life in the future. It is also worth noting that, if portions of your collections remain completely uncataloged, your organization's time may be better spent on describing those materials rather than on enhancing records already in existence, however imperfectly described. With space at a premium, few libraries can afford to retain and continue to store materials that are invisible to users and therefore receiving little or no use. In the end, catalogers must rely on the experience and subject knowledge of public service librarians to help determine the priorities for improvements in metadata.

FUTURE RELATIONSHIPS

The catalog is a collaborative endeavor continually added to by successive generations of librarians and others. Catalogers need feedback in order to maximize their impact and should partner with their library colleagues in building metadata records that will contribute to global efforts to record the fullest history of human knowledge. We will always need to provide access to the new but attention must also be paid to keeping what you currently have (your existing metadata) up to date, fresh and usable, responding to the new queries that your clientele bring to the collections. As such, noncataloging librarians can help improve the corpus of knowledge by keeping catalogers informed of difficulties users are having in locating particular resources, or of the various ways that users are searching for materials (color, size, geographic coordinates, etc.). It is helpful to alert cataloging staff to areas of emerging interest or research priorities that need special attention. Cataloging librarians should seek out opportunities to interact with public service librarians and cooperatively set goals for not only getting materials cataloged but also identifying resources deserving of enhancement or enrichment.

No one library can afford to do it all, when it comes to either collecting or cataloging. Fortunately, librarians have long recognized this latter reality and have a history of collaboration on shared metadata, as evidenced by World-Cat, which is a combined catalog of works contributed to by a multitude of libraries around the globe. Where most libraries currently share metadata, some are beginning to experiment with giving up their local catalog in favor of utilizing this global resource as their primary access tool. This raises the question: in a world of a single, shared catalog, who will be allowed to edit records? As more libraries move from shared cataloging to shared catalogers, communication among public service librarians and those catalogers privileged with writing and editing access will require ever more deliberate efforts by both parties.

Libraries are undergoing rapid change. Online resources have displaced collections formerly devoted to materials in tangible media (i.e., print, vinyl, etc.). Many academic libraries are moving toward sharing collections in remote storage facilities or jointly bundled in online collections. Reciprocal arrangements to collect in complementary topics and subdisciplines are becoming more common. Legacy collections, backed up online, are being reviewed for withdrawal or relegation to remote storage. ILL services, assisted by digital collections and scanning, can now swiftly fulfill many patron requests, freeing shelf space in the library for other uses. Even smaller libraries that have no current plan for shared collection coordination will be impacted, as their ILL options will change when loan partners and major research centers move more and more toward shared collections. Such increased sharing of collections will only increase the need for accurate, high-quality metadata.

CONCLUSION

Cataloging is an evolving craft. Subject headings change and evolve, as do cataloging standards and formats, but the essential goals of cataloging remain unchanged. We catalog in order to help people find information. We catalog in order to document relationships between works. We catalog to describe the uniqueness of items in our collections. In an increasingly interconnected information environment, we catalog in order to connect the information and resources in our local collections with the world of knowledge and the cultural and scientific heritage of each community and academic discipline. We catalog for the future.

SUGGESTED READING

Dempsey, Lorcan. 2012. "Thirteen Ways of Looking at Libraries, Discovery, and the Catalog: Scale, Workflow, Attention." *EDUCAUSE Review Online* (Monday, December 10). Available at: http://www.educause.edu/ero/article/thirteen-ways-looking-libraries-discovery-and-catalog-scale-workflow-attention. Accessed October 30, 2013.

Smith, A. Arro. 2008. "Cataloging Heresy." In *Radical Cataloging: Essays at the Front*, edited by K. R. Roberto, 291–99. Jefferson, NC: McFarland.

Tosaka, Yuji, and Cathy Weng. 2011. "Reexamining Content-Enriched Access: Its Effect on Usage and Discovery." *College & Research Libraries* 72 (5): 412–27. Available at: http://crl.acrl.org/content/72/5/412.full.pdf+html. Accessed October 30, 2013.

20

DO WE NEED DEWEY?
ANYTHINK LIBRARIES
IN COLORADO

Logan Macdonald

INTRODUCTION

Since its creation in 1876, the Dewey Decimal Classification system has been adopted by more than 200,000 libraries in over 135 countries. It has survived the invention of the airplane, two world wars, the rise of television, and the Information Age, making it a global standard for library classification, which has endured for more than a century. Yet a recent trend has some libraries replacing Dewey in favor of word-based models inspired by the Book Industry Standards and Communications (BISAC) subject headings published by the Book Industry Study Group (BISG).

One reason for this shift may be Dewey Decimal Classification's heavy emphasis on Western, American, and Christian thought, which has become limiting and inadequate in our multicultural society. The topic of religion provides the clearest illustration of Dewey's structural biases. People of all faiths utilize the library, but a vast majority of Dewey's classes on religion focus on Christian topics; some major world religions are not even represented as a distinct class (Weinberger 2004; Olson 1998). Religion is just one of many topics where American or Christian ideas are dominant in Dewey Decimal class structure, leading some libraries to replace Dewey in order to present a more balanced system to their users.

Because of these biases, libraries globally are required to do a great deal of work to adapt the system to local needs. For example, much effort has been made to adapt Dewey to the subject needs of Islamic libraries (Sulistyo-Basuki and Mulyani 2008; Khan 2004). Librarians in some countries, like the Republic of Korea, have even built their own decimal classification to address local classification needs (Dong-Geun 2012). For some libraries, word-based systems offer an alternative to modifying Dewey to reflect the communities they serve.

Others recognize that arranging and accessing items classified using a decimal-based system like Dewey no longer reflects the way people access information in the era of keyword searching. Dewey was developed in a time before digitized materials, and linear arrangement was the key to findability. Dictionaries, encyclopedias, indexes, and card catalogs were organized in alphabetical order from A to Z. With its decimal order from 000 to 999, Dewey maintains that linear approach in the way subjects are arranged and materials organized on library shelves.

Modern keyword searching is often ordered by relevance, allowing the user to select the order in which results are displayed. The flexibility of customer-centered arrangement is not easily reflected in a Dewey-organized collection. In a Dewey collection, a user enters the continuum at one point and must navigate forward or backward to find what he or she needs, requiring the user to pass a number of irrelevant titles before reaching the relevant ones. In a keyword system, the user has multiple entry points and can often determine where those entry points appear. A word-based system offers library users more direct entry points to the collection with closer proximity to the most relevant titles they are looking for.

One library in Colorado decided to move away from Dewey Decimal Classification in part because of a shift in its core philosophies. When the Rangeview Library District in Adams County (Colorado) reinvented itself as Anythink, it created the experience model, where all of their services have been reexamined with the customer's experience in mind. Anythink libraries are places where customers have meaningful, empowering experiences; they are no longer simply warehouses full of books and computers. Part of becoming an experience-based library was moving away from some of the features of a traditional library that Anythink identified as barriers to customer empowerment, inclusion, and interaction. Anythink eliminated overdue fines, built libraries for people instead of materials, changed their job roles, replaced battleship-style service desks with smaller perches—coupled with a roving model and heavy emphasis on hospitality—and switched from using Dewey Decimal Classification to a word-based system.

SHIFTING FROM NUMBERS TO WORDS: THE ANYTHINK STORY

Giving up Dewey was not easy, but Anythink was fortunate to have a model to build from in the work of the Maricopa County Library District in Arizona. Maricopa County's experience moving from Dewey to a BISAC system inspired Anythink in 2008 to create its own classification scheme called WordThink. WordThink uses the BISAC subject headings assigned to books by publishers as a guide for classifying materials into 83 classes and 385 subclasses. Classes are arranged in each library by neighborhoods, or groups of similar subjects, to create an intuitive flow between subject areas. Within each class and subclass, individual items are arranged on the shelf in alphabetical order by title. Work began on this reclassification in March 2009. It took more than 1,000 hours of staff time and almost a year to reclassify all of the items in Anythink's nonfiction collection; the WordThink conversion was completed district-wide in early 2010.

Anythink's intent was to create a system where customers were empowered to intuitively find the materials they were looking for. Rather than educate customers about a classification system that few outside of libraries understand on a deep level, Anythink chose to use a word-based classification scheme that allows its customers to encounter information on their own terms. Customers would no longer feel pressured to understand a secret librarian code in order to find materials.

Some may believe that the classification system used in a library has little impact on customer feelings of empowerment, but an online survey conducted by Barbara Fister in 2009 showed that more than 60 percent of library users who have trouble finding nonfiction materials are "intimidated by a classification system they don't understand very well" and/or "want to go straight to the right shelf without having to look anything up" (Fister 2009, 24). In other words, customers are intimidated by Dewey's secret code complexity, which becomes a barrier for people who want to find information on their own.

Anythink also saw a move away from Dewey as an opportunity to arrange materials in ways that would help create positive experiences for its customers. Breaking up the Dewey subject order allows library staff to build associations between materials, encouraging customers to interact with information in new ways. These associations could be on a grand scale in the way subjects are placed throughout the library's spaces, or on a smaller scale through merchandising and displays. As a customer browses shelving or displays, a related topic or beautiful item might catch his or her eye, spark an interest, and lead to a new experience. Anythink sees its materials as an important tool in building experiences for its customers, and the move away from Dewey was the first step in that process.

THE BENEFITS OF A WORD-BASED SYSTEM

Since instituting WordThink district-wide, Anythink has seen a variety of positive outcomes in its libraries. These outcomes include more flexibility and customization for the nonfiction collection, improvements in findability, reduction in cataloging and processing costs, and the removal or minimization of barriers to customer empowerment and self-service.

A word-based classification system is customizable in ways that a standard code-based system like Dewey is not. Word-based systems accommodate new areas of knowledge simply by adding additional top-level classes and classes or subclasses can be easily created for subjects with high local interest. A customized word-based system also allows a library to create relationships between materials that aren't available in standard Dewey classification. To create its own word-based system called WordThink, Anythink made some adjustments to the existing hierarchy of BISAC subject headings and decided to use words on spine labels that were as close as possible to the words its community was already using to describe subjects.

Not only did Anythink create top-level classes outside BISAC standards, like parenting, it also joined some subject headings together to create subclasses while leaving others to stand on their own. For example, users with interests in outdoor sports, such as hiking, fishing, and camping, were often interested in more than one of those topics, so Anythink combined materials with those BISAC subject headings into one WordThink subclass—"SPORTS OUTDOOR." This is a great example of using a word-based system to reflect Colorado's community interests. Spine label words were also carefully chosen to match terms that customers were already using to describe materials. For example, "FARMING" and "CAR REPAIR" were used as spine label terms rather than the matching BISAC subject terms "agriculture" and "automotive." Anythink also created a Colorado history subclass under history unique to WordThink, another example of responding to community needs. Customizations such as these allow Anythink to tailor its collection and classification scheme to its customers in ways that were not available with Dewey Decimal Classification.

While Dewey allows a library to classify all of its materials under a single subject hierarchy regardless of target audience, word-based systems like WordThink can leverage the separate BISAC subject headings for children's materials to offer a unique classification scheme to different age groups. At Anythink, there is a separate classification scheme for children's materials and adult materials. Some of the subjects are the same in both schemes, but Anythink uses WordThink's flexibility to emphasize certain topics in its children's collection. For example, U.S. presidents get their own subclass of biography in the WordThink classification for children while similar titles are included in the single large biography class in the adult scheme. Spine labels are targeted to younger readers with different words like "BUGS" instead of "INSECTS" or "SCARY" instead of "HORROR." These changes allow Anythink to create unique associations between materials and experiences for younger readers.

WordThink increases the flexibility of Anythink's nonfiction collection in the way materials are arranged in the library's physical spaces. With Dewey, there is a direct relationship between subject classification and shelf order. This relationship isn't always clear to library users or library staff, but it is there nonetheless. Maintaining that order can limit a library's ability to modify placement of materials within its physical space because a long, linear classification scheme fits best on long, linear shelving units. Before WordThink,

Anythink's nonfiction collection was spread over multiple long ranges of shelving with one primary beginning of the collection. Customers and staff looking for a specific item or subject needed to understand where they were in the 000 to 999 continuum before figuring out which way to move to find a specific item. Word-based systems like WordThink break that link between subject classification and shelf order, giving the library greater flexibility to design physical spaces that meet the needs of its customers. Shelving sections can be varied in length depending on the size or subject of the class. Popular subjects like cooking or nature occupy shorter shelves to facilitate easy browsing, while other subjects like philosophy or social science occupy taller shelves.

Anythink uses this flexibility as an opportunity to place certain subject areas where they will see the highest use or where they will help create experiences for customers through their relationships to other library services. For example, books on computers and computing are located near public computers whenever possible. Books in the parenting class, from child rearing to baby names, are located in or near the children's area. Children's books on fairy tales, poetry, and concepts are located close to picture books to group them by age appeal rather than Dewey class or subject. Homework help subjects in the adult collection, such as math, science, language skills and test prep, are located together in areas accessible to library users of all ages. Arrangements can even vary from branch to branch, depending on branch size and community interests. Since WordThink was launched in 2009, Anythink staff have also revisited the arrangement of materials at each branch and adapted the layout of materials to reflect customer interest. At one location, customer feedback led to a shifting of materials in the adult collection that made titles in the "REFERENCE" class more accessible. This kind of responsive shifting was facilitated by the flexibility of WordThink.

Merchandising is also easier under a word-based classification system. Materials are shelved at Anythink in such a way that each class or subclass begins and ends on its own shelf. Because of this, facing out items always results in highlighting similar topics. This also makes it easier for staff to pull materials for larger displays since staff can browse for related titles in once place instead of searching through the entire collection.

WordThink is designed for customers to navigate the collection self-guided if they choose, eliminating the need for staff to translate what they are looking for into a code-based call number. Customers now use natural language to access materials without the intermediate step. A customer looking for materials on diabetes can go directly to the shelf marked MEDICAL DIABETES without having to look up a call number. The time that staff spent cracking the code for customers is now spent on readers' advisory, reference questions, and building meaningful relationships with customers.

The same keywords customers use to search the library's catalog are reflected in the classification system, spine labels, and signage. Using BISAC subject headings and word-based classification also allows Anythink to add natural-language entries to the library's catalog records. Some titles have become easier to find with the addition of BISAC subject headings as searchable keywords, since BISAC uses more common words than Library of Congress in its subject headings. At the same time, adding BISAC subject headings to the catalog groups titles in different ways than other subject headings used by the library. This allows customers to discover materials in another way if they choose to browse the catalog using the BISAC subject hierarchy.

Anythink has economized its cataloging and processing tasks with Word-Think. While library staff do minimal original cataloging, it is much quicker to classify materials based on subject using WordThink than constructing Dewey numbers. Printing and applying spine labels is also easier since most of the nonfiction collection uses standardized call numbers and the same spine label for every item in a class or subclass. Staff can now print sheets of labels in advance instead of individual labels for each item.

MAKING THE CHOICE: DEWEY OR DON'T WE?

Although a word-based classification system has been successful at Anythink, it may not be the best solution for every library's collection. Like any classification system, it comes with its own set of concerns and issues that can affect implementation and usage. Consider the following issues before making the switch.

Collection size plays an important role in the suitability of word-based classification. Some of the findability and flexibility benefits may be lost when the number of items in any one category or subcategory exceeds a certain point. At Anythink, target category and subcategory sizes are set at one shelving range per category and about one shelving section or bay per subcategory. Maintaining a cohesive shelving arrangement becomes difficult when a category or subcategory has so many items that it spans more than one shelving range. When a category has too many items, Anythink considers revising that class to add additional subcategories in order to maintain the same level of browsability. Categories with fewer items are also easier to relocate or shift if necessary due to shelving needs or merchandising plans. This becomes more difficult as the number of items in a category or subcategory increases.

A word-based classification system like WordThink is also more appropriate for collections that require only broad categories for classification, not specific and granular classes. Anythink has made the conscious decision not to break down its collection into too many subcategories, resulting in some categories and subcategories that have a fairly broad range of different topics, such as politics or diseases. For libraries that need more granularity, these broad categories may not suit their needs.

Furthermore, word-based systems do not yet have the detailed, written documentation like Dewey or Library of Congress. WordThink is currently documented through two spreadsheets of fewer than 15 pages each and a related translation key that translates BISAC subject headings into WordThink classification. While classification tasks are easier and quicker than with Dewey, there is the possibility that the scope of similar categories is not defined well enough to enable catalogers to precisely locate titles. For example, the distinctions between "SCIENCE" and "NATURE" or "HEALTH" and "MEDICAL" may be too nuanced for quick classification by someone unfamiliar with the system. Further documentation describing the differences between the main classes and subclasses would help improve the clarity of WordThink.

Word-based systems require different shelving arrangements and a stronger emphasis on way-finding tools like signs and maps. Traditional library shelving models of long linear ranges are not optimal for word-based systems. Instead, a variety of shelving lengths and heights may be the best fit so each category can have its own distinct shelving space. This is definitely something to consider for libraries interested in switching to a word-based system. Is there room for flexibility within the current shelving arrangements? Can the space be redefined to support nonlinear organization?

Signage is extremely important to define areas and place categories in context in a word-based system. At Anythink, each top-level category has its own large sign placed on the top of the shelving unit, and each subcategory has a smaller in-shelf sign where the subcategory begins. Detailed maps identify the shelving units for each category. These solutions have worked well so far, but more work still needs to be done at Anythink to improve customer way finding and make accessing the collection even more self-driven for customers.

Once you break the connection between classification number and shelving location, you introduce some shelf order issues not present in Dewey or Library of Congress. Ordering items by title as Anythink does is more difficult when the title of the work is not clearly distinguishable. Most commonly, this issue arises when subcategories contain many works with similar branded titles from the same publisher like *The Complete Idiot's Guide* or *Fodor's*. This issue could be solved by using a different data point to order materials on the shelf like author name or Cutter number, but the addition of those bits of information to each spine label would likely negate the time savings in processing that a word-based system provides. Anythink has decided to leave author, title, and Cutter number off its spine labels to maintain efficiencies in cataloging, processing, and shelving.

Probably the most far-reaching issue related to the use of word-based classification is the lack of a library standard. Though many libraries using word-based systems use BISAC as the foundation for their schemes, the actual implementation varies from library to library. At this time, not having a standard increases the learning curve for customers and staff who may be used to a different system from another library. Each unique system requires some degree of retraining to help customers and staff memorize the differences. Anythink has also struggled at times to find outside technical services vendors (cataloging, processing, collection analysis, etc.), willing to work with the library's classification needs.

THE FUTURE OF WORD-BASED CLASSIFICATION

Word-based classification systems have gained a foothold in the United States, and libraries continue to explore new ways to organize their collections to improve customer service. Large library cataloging vendors are providing services using word-based schemes, and other businesses working with libraries increasingly see the value of adding support for non-Dewey classification. The development of a robust word-based classification community is well in progress although not yet as mature as the Dewey Decimal Classification community.

As flexible and customizable as word-based classification systems are, one of the biggest challenges to making such systems a more widespread choice for libraries comes from the lack of standards. In the United States, there are several distinct word-based systems currently in use. Some stick closely to the BISAC subject headings, whereas others, like WordThink, use them as a foundation but map those headings to locally defined classes and subclasses. It remains to be seen whether these systems will continue to develop in silos or whether libraries using similar systems will join together and develop a common classification scheme.

On an international level, one aspect of standardization is being addressed. In October 2012, the book industries of 15 countries joined forces on a move to combine several book industry subject categorization standards into one global standard. Thema, this new standard, is intended to facilitate the sharing of subject classifications between book markets currently differentiated by language, country, and culture. The long-term plan for Thema is to replace each market's own standard with a global one, replacing BISAC in the United States and other standards in markets across the globe. Libraries currently using systems inspired by BISAC will need to evolve toward Thema as it is implemented worldwide. Thema may also increase opportunities for word-based classification systems to become more prevalent on an international level as more countries begin using this new global standard. Maybe libraries can look to the book industry for inspiration in developing their own flexible, global standard for word-based classification.

CONCLUSION

No classification system is perfect. Like any system, word-based classification has its own strengths and weaknesses. For Anythink, the strengths of flexibility, customization, efficiency, and empowerment outweigh the benefits Dewey brings as a worldwide standard with a high level of subject specificity. As more libraries develop their own word-based systems, vendor support continues to increase, and standards are adopted nationally and internationally, it will be easier for libraries to transition away from Dewey. Library users will ultimately be the driving force, as collections should be organized with their needs in mind.

REFERENCES

Dong-Geun, Oh. 2012. "Developing and Maintaining a National Classification System, Experience From Korean Decimal Classification." *Knowledge Organization* 39 (2): 72–82.

Fister, Barbara. 2009. "The Dewey Dilemma." *Library Journal* 134 (16): 22–25.

Khan, Sher Nowrooz. 2004. "Expansion of DDC 21st Edition Number 297.63 for the Sirah." *Pakistan Library & Information Science Journal* 35 (4): 16–25.

Olson, Hope A. 1998. "Mapping Beyond Dewey's Boundaries: Constructing Classificatory Space for Marginalized Knowledge Domains." *Library Trends* 47 (2): 233.

Sulistyo-Basuki, L., and Alit Sri Mulyani. 2008. "Indonesian Librarians' Efforts to Adapt and Revise the Dewey Decimal Classification (DDC)'s Notation 297 on Islam." *Malaysian Journal of Library & Information Science* 13 (2): 89–101.

Weinberger, David. 2004. "Free Dewey!" *KMWorld* 13 (9): 18–30.

21

RETHINKING ACCESS TO COLLECTIONS IN THE DISCOVERY AGE

Jody Condit Fagan and Meris A. Mandernach

INTRODUCTION

Librarians have long desired to improve the user experience by offering search tools that are aligned with modern expectations, such as using a single search across multiple data sources. Libraries first met the challenge of searching library resources across vendor platforms by developing or acquiring federated search software, which broadcasts the user's search query to many different search engines and returned results that the software attempted to combine into one results set. User satisfaction with this type of software was mixed, but most libraries and vendors acknowledged its inherent limitations, particularly related to relevance ranking and the use of search syntax and limiters across different systems (Cervone 2005; Jung et al. 2008; Randall 2006; Wrubel and Schmidt 2007). Federated searching did not pose many new collection development issues because each data source was still searched individually.

Discovery tools have provided a new, welcome alternative to federated search. A key strategic advantage of discovery tool software has been the combination of records from a library's catalog into one index with journal article metadata in advance of the user's search, interfiling results into a single interface, with facets available for refining results across the system. These tools tend to search extremely large collections of items; Serials Solutions' Summon discovery tool included 950 million de-duped items as of May 2012 (Nagy 2012). Although the tools seem to be an improvement over federated search (Williams and Foster 2011), they still pose challenges for library collections access, growth, and maintenance. This chapter first discusses the ways in which discovery tool software is changing access to information

JMU Libraries' discovery tool provides front-line access to physical and virtual library collections, including books and articles. Its purpose is to support users' most common information needs, such as:

- Finding a selection of relevant sources about a topic
- Determining whether JMU libraries owns or has access to a specific item
- Getting online full text or items-in-hand.

By offering a tool to search library/subscription resources that is similar to Google, we intend to expand our presence in users' virtual worlds, and raise the library's stature in their research context. Such a tool also offers a first tier of search to complement our learning commons service model.

Figure 21.1 James Madison University Discovery Tool Purpose Statement, Fall 2011

sources. Then, it examines how collections are accessed inside and outside of the discovery tool, and the implications of discovery on collection development policies.

An important consideration underlying all these facets is a given library's conception of how the discovery tool fits within its suite of systems and resources. Every library should identify and articulate a purpose statement for its discovery tool to inform the numerous, inevitable decisions that will follow implementation. The statement will specifically identify the purpose of the discovery tool and how it relates to other means of discovery of library content, and therefore how it will affect overall collection development decisions. In 2011, a cross-departmental team at James Madison University (JMU) drafted a purpose statement and presented it to library management, where it was approved (Figure 21.1). It was recently reviewed by a different cross-departmental group that created purpose statements for all the library's major systems, and has been used to inform numerous discussions. This chapter occasionally suggests that some decisions depend on a library's particular situation; the discovery tool purpose statement clarifies the tool's role in individual libraries' collection development approaches.

ACCESS TO SOURCES

Discovery tools provide access to multiple source types (books, eBooks, journal articles, government documents, theses, etc.) simultaneously after combining different databases into a unified index. This creates a search tool that is more aligned with user expectations, at least on the surface, but this new paradigm also raises questions and challenges. The very act of combining records from multiple databases ensures that discovery tools will face challenges in harmonizing different data structures to support search algorithms. Due to ever-changing publisher agreements and library subscriptions, the discovery tool will be able to search full text for some, but not all items. Also, the differing nature of the information source types searched by discovery tools presents issues related to search strategy and information delivery. Finally, while metadata will continue to be important, discovery tools have the potential to change the role of indexing and abstracting databases in the industry as well as at individual institutions.

METADATA AND DISCOVERY TOOLS

At one time, database searching involved a single record structure. A&I companies or professional organizations such as the American Psychological Association (APA) or Modern Languages Association (MLA) created, edited, and enhanced metadata about relevant content in a disciplinary field, often using discipline-specific subject headings and thesauri. This provided a presentation of the literature in the field using the terminology of its scholars (Benjamin Jr. and Vandenbos 2006, 950); although it is important to note that not every index used descriptors or a controlled vocabulary from its inception (Alexander 2001). Additionally, some indexes and abstracts' development was influenced strongly by public policy (Weiner 2009). Both the record structure and the descriptive vocabulary used created a subject-specific experience. Therefore it was easy for libraries to collect and promote access to these collections, as money was available, because of the subject specificity. In fulfilling their single-search experience, discovery tools have taken these subject-specific resources and combined them into one unified index, without much regard for their unique qualities.

This combination of different databases into one unified index has required librarians to rethink how users search these collections. EBSCO Discovery Service and WorldCat Local combine records from many different databases, striving to de-duplicate by choosing which database's record to display; while Serials Solutions aims to "combines data from multiple sources—such as full text, abstracts, and subject terms—into a single, discoverable record" (Serials Solutions 2012a). These techniques are imperfect, because discovery tools still leave some duplication of items within results sets. For tools that choose one record in cases of duplication, librarians need to stay alert to which database records are chosen and whether all relevant metadata have been merged. For example, when EBSCO first merged H. W. Wilson databases into EBSCO Discovery Service (EDS), OmniFile records were used rather than those from subject-specific databases, such as Art Abstracts. Although EBSCO seems to have rectified the situation by merging the records, the important "Artist &

Work" field of Art Abstracts was originally missing. This error drastically impacted the search results and the ability to limit those results.

Metadata from subject-specific indexes and abstracts are still important and relevant in the age of discovery. Metadata allow greater bibliographic control and search precision. Features such as faceted browsing and "find similar items" use metadata to supplement naïve users' search habits. Also, previous studies have shown that subject headings greatly improve keyword search success (Gross and Taylor 2005). The advent of the semantic Web illustrates that although metadata structures are changing, online information requires descriptive metadata for effective use. Even large, public search engines like Google and Yahoo! are using schema to improve search results (e.g., http://schema.org) rather than relying on full-text indexing. In the age of discovery, records and their metadata are an important representation of a library's collections.

Regardless of vendor, discovery tools search records that have different information structures from one another. With EDS, some databases only have their metadata indexed, while others index some or all of the full text associated with the record. Although Serials Solutions is customized to include records for just the library's full-text holdings, the metadata and full text may be from different sources. As they explain, "In some cases, the Summon index may contain a record with citation metadata from an A&I provider as well as full text from a publisher. In other cases, the Summon index may contain a record and full text for an item included in an A&I database, but not contain the metadata from the database provider" (Serials Solutions 2012a). The situation grows more complex when the vendor imports the library's catalog into the index, choosing how the numerous MAchine-Readable Cataloging (MARC) fields are mapped to discovery tool's facets. For example, Figure 21.2 shows an example specification of how MARC fields are mapped to discovery tool fields, the type of indexing, and where the data in the fields displays in the results set. Depending on the discovery tool vendor, this mapping may be customizable by the individual library.

In addition to the questions of what fields are available in the records and whether the fields have controlled vocabularies, some discovery tool records have included full text in the index. Full-text searching adds an important dimension to discovery, but does not replace metadata. Users looking for articles about "student evaluation of teachers" versus "teacher evaluation of students" will benefit from the Education Resources Information Center (ERIC) subject headings, still present in discovery tools. However, users looking for esoteric information, such as the names of less-famous people, events, or works of art, will be glad if the discovery tool has indexed the full text. While full-text searching increases the number of results that are returned, indexing ensures higher relevance for those returned results. Therefore the user's ability to discover relevant collections depends on the level of indexing.

Discovery Tool Field Name	MARC field	Indexing Type	Displays on Results List	Displays on Full Record
Author	100, subfields a–p	word, phrase	X	X
Corporate author	110	word, phrase		X
Title and subtitle	245 a, b, h	word only	X	X
Additional titles	222, 240, 246	word only		X
Publication type	Leader/06/07	phrase only		X
Document type	Leader/06/07 008 006	phrase only		X
Physical description	300	none	X	X
Form of item	008/006	word only		
Subject person	600	word only		X
Subject company	610	word only		X
Subject geographic	651	word only		X
Subjects (other)	611, 630, 650, 653, 654, 655	word, phrase		X

Figure 21.2 Example of MARC field to Discovery Metadata Field Mapping

A traditional role of indexers and abstracters was to select relevant, high-quality content for a disciplinary field; in a sense, they defined some boundaries for a subject collection. This was often accomplished by marshaling content experts or a professional organization's members to review the quality of sources included (Benjamin Jr. and Vandenbos 2006, 951; ERIC 2012). Today's discovery tools offer no equivalent way to provide this focus. For interdisciplinary topics discovery is a boon, but for those looking for a specific field's perspective on a topic or wishing to limit to the core sources in a discipline, a discovery tool is of little help. Vendors attempt to use journal subject headings or other groupings of journals, such as Columbia's Hierarchical Interface to Library of Congress Classification (HILCC), the Serials Solutions Knowledgebase, and Ulrich's Periodical Directory, to provide discipline-scoped searching (Serials Solutions 2012b).[1] EBSCO released a similar feature in beta. In theory, this will improve the user's ability to search within or across discipline-specific literature with ease. This type of system was actually envisioned by information scholars as early as 1982 (Lancaster and Neway 1982).

Librarians have several roles to play in addressing the collection management challenges created by the conflation of information. First, they need to continue to advocate for preserving accurate, complete description, and indexing in article databases and within the catalog. For example, the table of contents will be increasingly useful in discovery environments, where books are searched alongside articles. Collection managers may need to explore catalog record enrichment services, such as adding tables of contents from older book titles to the catalog, in order to enhance their discoverability. New techniques such as using linked data for metadata and sharing metadata are exciting developments (Coyle 2012). Linked data establishes descriptive relationships among the data, which supports more intelligent connections between systems. Librarians can also support developments that facilitate metadata browsing and hierarchical navigation of subjects (e.g., Bland and Stoffan 2008).

Second, collection managers should continue to encourage discovery tool vendors to leverage discipline-specific metadata and disciplinary journal collections in order to allow different views of the collection within the discovery tool. They will need to compare whether discipline-scoped searches are equivalent to those in a subject-specific index, and they will need to defend decisions related to discovery. Another challenge will be to define what non-subject-specific discovery means at each institution. For example, should libraries include online reference sources in a general discovery search alongside large, multidisciplinary journal databases? If the answer is yes, do the technical capabilities within discovery tools support it? Librarians may also need to weigh the discovery of online reference sources when making purchasing decisions.

Librarians need to test information retrieval of discovery tools for content in different subject areas and of different source types. For example, when JMU catalog records were first loaded into EDS, not all the MARC 740 subfields were included, meaning "Beethoven, Ludwig van, 1770–1827, Sonatas piano no. 23, op. 57, F minor" was reduced to "Beethoven, Ludwig van, 1770–1827, Sonatas." This is a significant issue because access to resources the library purchased decreased due to limitations of the search. Also, initially the field was not hyperlinked, whereas now the composer is linked to perform a phrase-indexed author search and the title is hyperlinked to perform the same search limited by the title. Librarians need to communicate with vendors what the mapping of MARC fields should be, and how hyperlinks should be created. Since identifying source types challenges users, librarians should also test how the source type facet limits include or exclude results. If there is a government documents source type, does it include both online and print government documents? Does it include government documents cataloged by the library, or just the ones the discovery tool vendor has added to its main index? These details will influence the way in which a library's collection is accessed in discovery space.

Finally, librarians should continue to promote discipline-specific search tools, and present the discovery tool as a way to cross-search a subset of the library's collections. It is unlikely that discovery tools will ever provide a good discipline-specific search because they are designed to facilitate interdisciplinary searching. Bibliometric studies show that users construct fundamentally different keyword search strategies depending on the discipline. Yi et al. (2006, 1218) found that users of history databases used nonconceptual multiword search strings describing regions, people, and events, while psychology database users employed conceptual terms indicating disorders, abuse, development, and therapy. While discovery tools could provide convenient pathways into sub-interfaces that reproduce the discipline-specific tools, it is difficult to imagine how the molecular searching of SciFinder Scholar would be incorporated into the same search interface as the time period headings of Historical Abstracts in a way that would support usability principles. In this case, individual subject collection development policies could articulate whether databases should be included or excluded from discovery tools.

Looking farther into the future, it is likely that journal article metadata creation will become more standardized and streamlined. Currently, vendor-provided records for books and eBooks have some problems. One study found that 27 percent of records from Yankee Book Peddler and PromptCat exhibited errors affecting catalog access, and records for 39 percent of titles needed modification (Walker and Kulczak 2007, 61). In response, libraries have developed in-house cleanup solutions (Jay, Simpson, and Smith 2009; Sanchez et al. 2006) and workflows for large batch loads (Martin and Mundle 2010). A question asked by Sanchez et al. is still outstanding:

> with the proliferation of eBook sources that use very basic cataloging or none at all, we will face larger issues of how, or if, we can continue to provide consistent, quality cataloging and authority control for these titles. If some entity does not provide cataloging for the universe of eBooks, will other methods such as basic Internet search engines be sufficient to provide access? (2006, 69)

Martin and Mundle (2010, 235) concluded that libraries, vendors, and eBook record services all have roles to play in ensuring quality metadata for eBooks. It is less clear what will happen with other formats, although history suggests they will continue to defy simple integration with article and book searching. Given these limitations, it seems that libraries will need to continue to provide access and discovery through multiple venues to ensure that the many facets of a library's collection can be seen in virtual space.

SOURCE TYPES AND DISCOVERY TOOLS

Even if the challenges of metadata creation and integration were solved, the way discovery tools combine different information objects together brings its own challenges. In the physical world, it is easy to see the difference between a newspaper and a book; clearly the newspaper article will be brief, while the book offers an in-depth treatment of a topic. Determining the source type from search results lists has long confounded users (Wrubel and Schmidt 2007, 300; Jung et al. 2008, 387; Alling and Naismith 2007, 203–4; Ponsford and vanDuinkerken 2007, 171), but discovery brings this issue to the forefront (Williams and Foster 2011, 187–88; Fagan et al. 2012). Indexes and abstracts were historically dominated by periodical articles, with an odd book or book chapter here or there, while catalogs were largely monographic, with the occasional technical report. Information professionals knew that complex, well-thought-out search syntax was necessary for complete retrieval within an A&I (Younger and Boddy 2009), whereas simple searches to identify subject headings often worked better in a catalog (Drabenstott and Vizine-Goetz 1994, 266–67).

With discovery, all source types may be present or dominant in a particular result set. A simple search may retrieve both books and articles, and it may be difficult for naïve users to understand how refining a search excludes or includes certain information objects simply by their breadth of coverage. For example, when searching a broad topic where books would be more useful for providing background information, such as a search on "chemistry teaching" in JMU's EDS retrieves a 167-page book for the first result, but an academic journal article focused on Jordanian teachers as the second. While librarians will understand that limiting to books will find more items with broad treatment, students may not immediately grasp this relationship. Discovery tools do not yet have affordances to permit easy interpretation of the variety of sources in library collections.

Compounding the difficulty of identifying the material type of individual results are the varying pathways to the full manifestations of the item and the confusion these disparate paths may cause. For some records, the full manifestation is a physical book unavailable in electronic format; for others, it is an online eBook, e-journal article, streaming audio file, or even a Web site. Other records will be for books the library does not own or for eBooks to which the library does not have access. The decision whether to include resources that index materials not available locally is related to whether the priority is to point users to the most relevant resources, even those that require a wait time, or to point users to resources that are available immediately. Additionally, in a discovery tool, a user looking for a specific book may wind up confused because book reviews for the sought title appear higher on the results list than the record for the book itself.

eBooks are also introducing complexity to discovery tools. A library's eBook holdings are often on different platforms with different access restrictions and technical requirements, but are presented to the user in one interface through the discovery tool. Individual libraries may have less direct control over how these eBooks appear in discovery tools than they did within their catalog (Hartman 2012). These problems are not new with discovery, but again, discovery may increase the likelihood of confusion due to the sheer size of results sets.

Reference resources present a larger problem. While the problem of limiting a discovery tool to items from electronic reference collections seems solvable, including print reference, items in results seem more challenging. Reference resources were already challenging to find in library catalogs, leading librarians to create canned search strings (such as encyclopedia or dictionary or handbook or gazetteer) to combine with additional search terms. Even if an effective source type existed to limit to reference materials, they have a few additional problems. With the catalog and online reference databases combined, a single reference source in a results list may actually be a multivolume encyclopedia, while another may be a single encyclopedia entry. This makes it harder for the user to understand what is meant by reference information. Reference materials become more confusing to users when mixed in with journal articles and books, because they fulfill such a different function. Even scholars who understand the use of reference sources in providing background information may find them annoying when sprinkled in results lists. Depending on the mission of the discovery tool, institutions may decide to rout users to reference resources through mechanisms other than the discovery tool.

Audio and video items have similar problems to other formats in discovery tools because of the way their source types are tagged for retrieval. An additional issue with such items is that the label "full text" does not apply to audio or video—this has been a historical challenge in other interfaces, but is amplified in the discovery tool because streaming audio and video are full-text limiter options. Music librarians have been especially proactive in describing their needs for discovery (Music Library Association's Emerging Technologies and Services Committee 2012; Music OCLC Users Group 2012).

Electronic resource (ER) records have always been an enigma to users. ER records describe databases, journal collections, eBook collections, or other aggregate resources, providing details about dates of coverage, scope of collection, descriptions, and terms of use. Most users want to search within a database or read journal articles—they do not care about the container in which the resource is marketed and delivered. Although there are a few users who want to know the dates covered by PsycINFO or the previous title of a given journal, most will only be using ER records to get into the product itself and perform a search. So, the fact that ER records appear in discovery tool results may be more confusing than ever before. However, excluding them from discovery may mean that a scholar just trying to find the institution's access point to a specific database is led to believe the library does not have access. One study of a library's Web site search showed 17 percent of searches were for database names (Fagan 2002, 248).

To overcome the challenges differing information source types raise, librarians and discovery tool vendors will need to work together. First, discovery tool vendors must strive to provide effective, accurate source type limits, including definitions of what these source types include. Of particular value would be the ability to limit results sets to just full text, to available eBooks, and to catalog items with an available status. Users should also be able to include or exclude eBooks. While most vendors offer some of these limits, they could be made more intuitive for users and accurate for libraries. Second, library instructors will need to continue to grapple with explaining the nature of different information sources to users, particularly as these sources evolve. Although once it may have been convenient for librarians and users to equate catalog searching with book-length items, and A&I searching with article-length treatments, no such dichotomy exists within a discovery product. Third, vendors should work with librarians to create clusters of resources that mirror the subject-specific databases discussed earlier, or to lead researchers to appropriate resources based upon search terms. One intriguing idea is the database recommender currently in place in Serials Solutions' Summon (Figure 21.3), which employs the user's search terms to find possible subject-specific databases for searching (http://www.serialssolutions .com/en/news/detail/summon-service-debuts-database-recommender). Another tactic for leading users to disciplinary-focused results could be to offer facets for journal subject classifications or subject-based electronic resource collections.

Finally, integrating reference collections into discovery is sorely needed. Microsoft Live Academic provides one model for how this could be done, by providing a definitions page for popular keywords with author, conferences, and journal facets (e.g., http://academic.research.microsoft.com/Keyword/ 18565/human-computer-interaction). Some libraries have chosen to use a federated search connection to add reference book results to their discovery tool (Paratext 2012). The paradigm of finding a Wikipedia entry at the top of search engine results could be a useful model to follow, by including relevant links to scholarly reference sources in the library's collection at the top of search results.

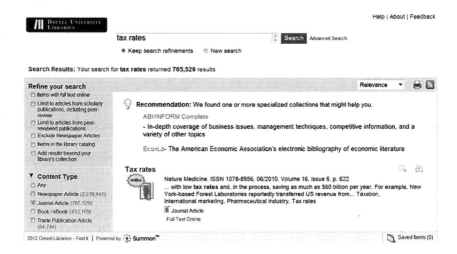

Figure 21.3 Serial Solutions' Summon Database Recommender Tool (June 2013). Courtesy of Drexel University Libraries

THE EFFECTS OF DISCOVERY TOOLS ON COLLECTION DEVELOPMENT AND COLLECTION MANAGEMENT

While the combination of records with different structures creates one cluster of problems in discovery tools, determining what content should be included in the discovery tool is equally challenging. Discovery tools will impact collection development and collection management practices in numerous ways, some philosophical and others practical. At JMU, a checklist has been developed to walk several stakeholder groups through the process of determining whether a given metadata source (e.g., a database) should be enabled in the discovery tool (Figure 21.4).

Some discovery tools have options to activate specific collections. Therefore, the first step in the checklist is determining whether the content of the

1. The Director, Scholarly Content Systems (SCS) will determine if the content is appropriate for EDS. She will consult with other units as necessary (e.g., Collection Management for databases, E-Resources for journal/eBook publisher collections, library liaisons for very subject-specific resources).

2. As designated by the director of SCS, a SCS staff member will check with the serials manager to be sure that we both subscribe to the content, and that our license includes the ability to search that database using a tool like EDS.

3. An SCS staff member enables the new content in the EDS staging area, making sure the databases otherwise match the main EDS profile, and performs the following:

    a. Identifies the number of items indexed in the new resource.

    b. Searches for topics for which records from the new resource should and should not appear, making sure the relevance balance seems appropriate.

    c. Limits results to the source types present in the new collection (book, article, etc.) using the Source Type limiter and the past year using Publication Year limiter, again, making sure results are appropriate.

    d. Looks at the Result List entry for at least five citations from the new resource, noting any ways in which they do not seem similar to citations from other resources (e.g., funny characters in title, strange abstracts (extremely long or short)).

    e. If the resource records link out to Web sites (e.g., ERIC), test at least five links to full text.

    f. Check at least five links to full text using the link resolver. If the new resource contains books and articles, test five books and five articles.

4. Information about the searches and search results (terms searched, number of results, number of results from new resource, and notes about oddities) should be recorded in a spreadsheet.

5. The Director of Scholarly Content Systems will then decide whether to enable the resource in the main EDS profiles.

6. Update the EDS_Data_Providers spreadsheet in ERM, which includes the date tested, date made live, and any notes about why the resource was not enabled (if applicable).

7. Annually, SCS staff will request a report from ILL of cancelled requests that includes which resources the requests originated from, to attempt to determine whether any EDS resource is generating an abnormally large number of ILL requests.

Figure 21.4 Checklist: Enabling New Content in EDS

resource is appropriate given the discovery tool's purpose. The larger philo-sophical question that lingers is whether everything that could be activated within a discovery tool should be. For example, given the issues discussed earlier, should ER records be included? If the native interface for a resource is far superior for limiting and searching, should users also find that content within a discovery tool? Librarians will need to grapple with whether the dis-covery tool will become an all-encompassing index of the library's collections or merely a showcase of select areas that the discovery tool can offer as a first step in the research process. Depending on the purpose of discovery imple-mentation, the choices related to discovery tool setup will differ. If the library decides that the discovery tool is merely a first step in the research process, users should be directed to other library resources that are subject specific to continue with in-depth research. Ultimately, implementation decisions need to be made with the end user in mind. Depending on the library environment, a variety of internal stakeholders may also need to be consulted. In addition to the collection management librarian, subject librarians should look at new content additions in their discipline. For example, if MLA International Bib-liography records are added, the English librarian may best know whether the records are of similar quality and utility to those in the native interface. For some disciplines, it may be very important that the full text be indexed (as mentioned earlier, for art); for other disciplines journal metadata may suffice.

This content question relates to technical capabilities as well. If distinctive fea-tures of a source are not supported by the discovery tool (e.g., chemical structure searching or financial data viewing tools), should the records even be added to the tool? Other issues include the percentage of foreign-language items in the database under consideration and the proportion of records for which library-subscribed full-text is available. Additionally, databases that have records for books (e.g., His-torical Abstracts) may duplicate catalog records and provide no clear path to get the book. These types of content decisions could be made on a case-by-case basis or could be made with an overarching policy. Each library will need to determine whether it is better to load as much content as possible into the discovery tool or whether a more selective approach to source inclusion is appropriate.

Even when the content is appropriate, there may be technical reasons why a certain collection should not be included, which is the reason for the length of step three in the checklist. All database content does not display equally within a discovery tool. As mentioned previously, records may vary based on content, which affects relevance ranking and discoverability. Database vendors other than the discovery tool vendor may place restrictions on how the information displays within the discovery tool. For example, when Alexander Street Press (ASP) initially offered metadata from their databases through discovery tools, libraries could either add all or none of ASP's content, regardless of whether the institution had access to all of the databases (personal communication, EBSCOhost January 23, 2012). Thus, unless a library subscribed to all ASP collections, the end user would not have access to full text for many of the re-cords that would display. If a collection causes problems in the discovery tool at JMU, the vendor is contacted and the records are suppressed or removed until the records meet the requirements. The extent to which a collection supports a discovery tool may become a significant factor in collections decisions.

It is inevitable that some content will never be available through a discovery tool. While a discovery tool has the potential to highlight a library's hidden collections, it also may succeed at hiding valuable resources from the user. Evidence is mixed as to whether users believe the entire library's collections are searched by discovery-type tools (Fagan et al. 2012, 91; OCLC 2011), and their perceptions could change over time. Users' understanding of what is searched by any particular search box is limited (Vaughn and Callicott 2003, 14–15), although not completely naïve. When asked what users thought the discovery tool covered at JMU, seven of eight participants responded that they thought that it covered most resources (Fagan et al. 2012, 91). Because it is unlikely that discovery tools will ever search all library resources, it is important to clarify both what is included and what has been excluded from the discovery tool. For this reason, JMU keeps careful track of which collections are enabled or not (see step six in the checklist) and has also created a public frequently asked question with a bigger-picture view (Figure 21.5).

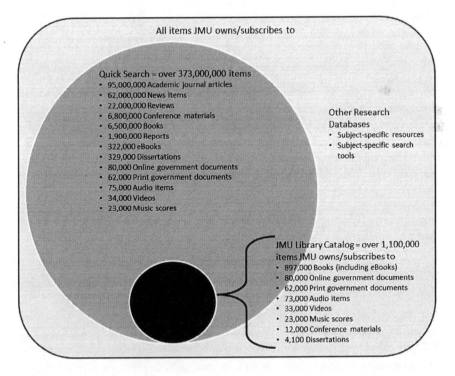

Figure 21.5 Diagram on the Library's Public Web Site Explaining What the Discovery Tool, Quick Search, Contains. See also http://www.lib.jmu.edu/info/faqsitem .aspx?id=2139. Credit: David Gaines

There is also a need to highlight subject databases or niche collections that are either not covered by the discovery tool or that have more robust search limits in their native interface. A library will need to ensure that there are several escape hatches in place within a discovery tool interface that will allow the user to return to the library homepage. While users can and do use the back button to return to the library homepage, clear pathways returning to the library homepage and subject databases should be present. In a recent usability study, users were asked to use a specific database to locate a resource. Although most users were able to complete the task, many started their search by typing the database name into the discovery tool search box, which was unsuccessful (Fagan et al. 2012, 97). Given this tendency, there could be an argument by some libraries for including ER records in discovery tool indexes.

Another area that has not been covered as thoroughly in the literature is how collection policies will need to adjust in the age of discovery. Peggy Johnson indicated that collection policies "serve as plans for building and maintaining a collection, both locally held and accessed remotely" (Johnson 2009, 72–73). While institutional collection policies should cover approaches to collections in broad strokes rather than specifics, it seems that libraries should develop a general philosophy of access to collections, and one means of access is through discovery. Collection policies should indicate the type of content acquired and may include information on shared collection access. Often, they also include information related to ILL—another means of access—but few have indicated specifics related to search or discovery. Policies serve to inform users about what content is included in the collection as well as the scope of collection in order to provide guidance for what is accepted and what is not accepted as part of the collection (Anderson 1996.) While collection policies could remain mute on the discovery issue because policies deal with specific tools rather than content, library collection teams should carefully consider the effects that discovery tools are having on collection decisions. For example, while having a policy stating that collection decisions are made with no consideration of the discovery tool may be a disservice to users, so will having a policy that states that every collection decision is linked to the discovery tool. Clearly delineating the role of the discovery tool in collection building and management will allow institutions to articulate where they land on this decision spectrum. Given the prominent location of discovery tool software on many library homepages, it would behoove libraries to acknowledge its role as a first stop for most users, and therefore the tool should be addressed as a means of access in collection policies.

Library collections are changing in a variety of ways. As more information is available electronically and the amount of information available to users grows exponentially, access to library content in the easiest way possible for end users and should be of the highest importance. With the advent of discovery tools, general indexing and abstracting databases that do not offer full text may no longer be relevant. While specialty and subject-specific databases continue to see high use, general resource use has often decreased following implementation of a discovery tool (Way 2010; Fagan and Mandernach 2011, Figure 11). Therefore, libraries could rely on the discovery tool to provide access to general resources, which would allow more money to be funneled toward acquiring content and providing pathways to niche resources. However, full-text overlap analysis will be necessary to be sure access to important indexing and full text is not lost along with general search engine subscriptions (Fagan and Mandernach 2011, 17).

Finally, discovery tools may make an impact on other collection decisions. These broader decisions may evolve over time. All discovery tool vendors provide other databases on their platforms. An emerging choice for collection managers may be to wrestle with how they provide access to databases on multiple platforms. For example, if a library has a discovery tool with a particular vendor such as EBSCO, should the library favor the EBSCO platform for databases available on multiple platforms (e.g., PsycINFO) due to discovery? Also, given that records can display differently in the native interface than in the discovery tool, the collections committee may come to the conclusion that resources will be acquired only if they are able to meet the core display requirements within the discovery tool. Therefore display requirements on a third-party vendor may impact new resource acquisition decisions. Collection committees will need to wrestle with the role of discovery on acquisition of content. In the past these decisions were primarily made due to economic influences; now, discovery of content may play a more important role in selection.

Usage statistics are often a key factor in collection decisions, particularly as institutions shift from just-in-case to just-in-time collection strategies. Therefore it will be important to consider the impact that discovery tools have on statistics. Discovery tools may report statistics for all databases that are included in the knowledge base for each search performed, thereby increasing search and session reports for all resources. For example, in EDS, when a user searches for the phrase "medical malpractices" within a discovery system, it will be logged as a search both within the discovery tool and in all the databases that were activated within the discovery tool at that time, whether related to the topic or not. While federated search products had a similar, inflationary impact on usage statistics, each database was searched separately and the results were aggregated, therefore reporting individual search statistics for each database made slightly more sense. While COUNTER 4 protocols switch the focus of usage reporting from searches to downloads, discovery tools will continue to elevate usage.

Interlibrary loan (ILL) is also a tool many libraries use for collection development and management purposes, because content that is frequently requested is often acquired for the local collection, and discovery tools can dramatically increase requests for materials from other institutions due to heightened discovery of unowned content. And, when a discovery tool is coupled with a link resolver, requesting content through ILL is made even simpler. At The Ohio State University, when WorldCat Local replaced the library catalog as the default discovery interface on the library homepage, ILL saw an 81 percent increase in the number of requests when compared to the previous fiscal year (Brian Miller, personal communication). Decisions to set limits on undergraduate ILL requests might be one result, in order to relieve an overburdened ILL unit. Or, another solution might be not to activate a particular product or collection in discovery. For example, if a specific resource in discovery generates too many cancelled ILL requests, it might be helpful to exclude this resource from the tool.

CONCLUSION

Discovery tool vendors are aggressively developing discovery software to stay competitive in the information marketplace. In the short term, vendors will work to address specific problems with ingesting and indexing information from the currently available metadata. In the long term, as the semantic Web grows and information publishers and libraries adapt their metadata schema, the information sources to be ingested will themselves change, and vendors will be able to re-think the potential for integration.

Libraries should keep selecting discovery tool software carefully in order to encourage market developments that will serve end users. Usability tests and user studies will be important for understanding these complex tools. Measuring the impact of changes is also important for understanding changes in the usage of content and providing libraries feedback on collection decisions. All librarians will need to keep an open mind as they consider solutions to the inevitable challenges to come.

NOTE

1. As of this writing, this feature is available only through Serials Solutions widgets. A company representative explained that this was purposeful, "so we can allow our customers to work with the functionality in a controlled environment. Discipline faceting is something that we want to incorporate in the UI (user interface) after we gain feedback on how librarians are working with it" (personal communication with Maryellen Sims, Serials Solutions).

REFERENCES

Alexander, Harriet. 2001. "Searching the MLA International Bibliography." *Reference & User Services Quarterly* 40 (3): 228.

Alling, Emily, and Rachael Naismith. 2007. "Protocol Analysis of a Federated Search Tool: Designing for Users." *Internet Reference Services Quarterly* 12 (1/2): 195–201.

Anderson, Joanne S., ed. 1996. *Guide for Written Collection Policy Statements.* 2nd ed. Chicago: American Library Association.

Benjamin Jr., Ludy T., and Gary R. Vandenbos. 2006. "The Window on Psychology's Literature." *American Psychologist* 61 (9): 941–54.

Bland, Robert N., and Mark A. Stoffan. 2008. "Returning Classification to the Catalog." *Information Technology & Libraries* 27 (3): 55–60.

Cervone, Frank. 2005. "What We've Learned from Doing Usability Testing on OpenURL Resolvers and Federated Search Engines." *Computers in Libraries* 25 (9):10–14.

Coyle, Karen. 2012. "Linked Data Tools: Connecting on the Web." *Library Technology Reports* 48 (4).

Drabenstott, Karen Markey, and Diane Vizine-Goetz. 2010. "Choosing among Existing Subject Search Approaches as Responses to User Queries." In *Using Subject Headings for Online Retrieval: Theory, Practice, and Potential,* ed. Diane Vizine-Goetz (Library and Information Science, Volume 94), 266–300. Bingley, UK: Emerald Group Publishing Limited.

ERIC. 2012. Content Experts. Available at: http://eric.ed.gov/ERICWebPortal/resources/html/about/about_eric_experts.html. Accessed June 22, 2012.

Fagan, Jody Condit. 2002. "Use of an Academic Library Web Site Search Engine." *Reference & User Services Quarterly* 41 (3): 244.

Fagan, Jody Condit, and Meris A. Mandernach. 2011. "Discovery by the Numbers: An Examination of the Impact of a Discovery Tool through Usage Statistics." Paper presented at the Charleston Conference, Charleston, SC. Available at: http://www.katina.info/conference/archives/2011/2011_FullProgram_FINAL.pdf. Accessed October 25, 2013.

Fagan, Jody Condit, Meris Mandernach, Carl S. Nelson, Jonathan R. Paulo, and Grover Saunders. 2012. "Usability Test Results for a Discovery Tool in an Academic Library." *Information Technology & Libraries* 31 (1): 83–112.

Gross, Tina, and Arlene G. Taylor. 2005. "What Have We Got to Lose? The Effect of Controlled Vocabulary on Keyword Searching Results." *College and Research Libraries* 66 (3): 212–30.

Hartman, Robin. 2012. "Life in the Cloud: A WorldShare Management Services Case Study." *Journal of Web Librarianship* 6 (3): 186–85.

Jay, Michael, Betsy Simpson, and Doug Smith. 2009. "CatQC and Shelf-Ready Material: Speeding Collections to Users While Preserving Data Quality." *Information Technology & Libraries* 28 (1): 41–48.

Johnson, Peggy. 2009. *Fundamentals of Collection Development and Management.* Chicago: American Library Association: 66–87.

Jung, Seikyung, Jonathan L. Herlocker, Janet Webster, Margaret Mellinger, and Jeremy Frumkin. 2008. "LibraryFind: System Design and Usability Testing of Academic Metasearch System." *Journal of the American Society for Information Science & Technology* 59 (3): 375–89.

Lancaster, F. W., and Julie M. Neway. 1982. "The Future of Indexing and Abstracting Services." *Journal of the American Society for Information Science* 33 (3): 183–89.

Martin, Kristin E., and Kavita Mundle. 2010. "Notes on Operations: Cataloging E-Books and Vendor Records: A Case Study at the University of Illinois at Chicago." *Library Resources & Technical Services* 54 (4): 227–37.

Music Library Association's Emerging Technologies and Services Committee. 2012. "Music Discovery Requirements Draft 2." Last modified February 9, 2012. Available at: http://personal.ecu.edu/newcomern/musicdiscoveryrequirementsfeb92012.pdf. Accessed July 7, 2012.

Music OCLC Users Group. 2012. "Public Services Information and Links." Available at: http://www.musicoclcusers.org/reftools.html. Accessed July 7, 2012,

Nagy, Andrew. 2012. What's New and Upcoming with the Summon Service—May 2012. Available at: http://www.serialssolutions.com/en/webinars/recorded/. Accessed October 25, 2013.

OCLC. 2011. "Some Findings from WorldCat Local Usability Tests Prepared for ALA Annual." Available at: http://www.oclc.org/worldcatlocal/about/213941usf_some_find ings_about_worldcat_local.pdf. Accessed March 11, 2011.

Paratext. 2012. "Discovery Services and the Specialized Reference Collection: College of St. Scholastica Case Study." Available at: http://www.paratext.com/pdf/scholasti caEDS.pdf. Accessed June 22, 2012.

Ponsford, Bennett Claire, and Wyoma vanDuinkerken. 2007. "User Expectations in the Time of Google: Usability Testing of Federated Searching." *Internet Reference Services Quarterly* 12 (1/2): 159–78.

Randall, Sara. 2006. "Federated Searching and Usability Testing: Building the Perfect Beast." *Serials Review* 32 (3): 181–82.

Sanchez, Elaine, Leslie Fatout, Aleene Howser, and Charles Vance. 2006. "Cleanup of NetLibrary Cataloging Records: A Methodical Front-End Process." *Technical Services Quarterly* 23 (4): 51–71.

Serials Solutions. 2012a. "Summon Key Databases and Packages—Full-Text." Available at: http://www.serialssolutions.com/en/resources/detail/summon-key-databases-and-pack ages-full-text. Accessed June 22, 2012.

Serials Solutions. 2012b."Introducing Discipline Scoped Searching and Customizable Search Widgets for the Summon® Service. 19 January 2012." Available at: http://www .serialssolutions.com/en/words/detail/Introducing-Discipline-Scoped-Searching-and-Customizable-Search-Widgets/. Accessed July 7, 2012.

Vaughn, Debbie, and Burton Callicott. 2003. "Broccoli Librarianship and Google-Bred Patrons, or What's Wrong with Usability Testing?" *College & Undergraduate Libraries* 10 (2): 1–18.

Walker, Mary, and Deb Kulczak. 2007. "Shelf-Ready Books Using PromptCat and YBP: Issues to Consider (An Analysis of Errors at the University of Arkansas)." *Library Collections, Acquisitions, & Technical Services* 31 (2): 61–84.

Way, Doug. 2010. "The Impact of Web-Scale Discovery on the Use of a Library Collection." *Serials Review* 36 (4): 214–20.

Weiner, Sharon A. 2009. "Tale of Two Databases: The History of Federally Funded Information Systems for Education and Medicine." *Government Information Quarterly* 26 (3): 450–58.

Williams, Sarah C., and Anita K. Foster. 2011. "Promise Fulfilled? An EBSCO Discovery Service Usability Study." *Journal of Web Librarianship* 5 (3): 179–98.

Wrubel, Laura, and Kari Schmidt. 2007. "Usability Testing of a Metasearch Interface: A Case Study." *College & Research Libraries* 68 (4): 292–311.

Yi, Kwan, Jamshid Beheshti, Charles Cole, John E. Leide, and Andrew Large. 2006. "User Search Behavior of Domain-Specific Information Retrieval Systems: An Analysis of the Query Logs from PsycINFO and ABC-CLIO's Historical Abstracts/America: History and Life." *Journal of the American Society for Information Science & Technology* 57 (9): 1208–20.

Younger, Paula, and Kate Boddy. 2009. "When Is a Search Not a Search? A Comparison of Searching the AMED Complementary Health Database via EBSCOhost, OVID and DIALOG." *Health Information & Libraries Journal* 26 (2): 126–35.

22

CONSORTIA SERVICES IN COLLECTION MANAGEMENT

Kim Armstrong

INTRODUCTION

Without having read them yet, I suspect that many of the projects and programs described in chapters in this book would not be possible if libraries were not consortially or cooperatively minded. Just scanning the table of contents, topics such as floating collections and shared print storage suggest that libraries view consortia as one of the vehicles for accomplishing their collection management goals. Libraries have leveraged participation in consortia as an effective means to save money, save time, mitigate risk, and co-invest to extend resources and services that would be inefficient or impossible for a single library to accomplish alone.

In her article, "Assessing the Value of Academic Library Consortia," Faye Chadwell provides a list of consortial membership benefits gathered by reviewing 48 library consortia Web sites (Chadwell 2011, 649). The benefits are listed as follows:

- shared purchasing of digital content;
- sharing library materials through interlibrary loan or courier services;
- shared catalogs;
- advocacy; and
- expanded access to content not held by a member library.

The list reflects at least a century of collaborative activity as libraries have, by necessity, always needed to be part of some type of resource sharing collective in order to provide researchers and learners with material that was never collected locally. The role of consortia, especially consortia that have a central staff and budget to support member operations and programs, for the most part have adapted successfully to the changing needs of their membership and to embrace the opportunities of collaboration brought about by networking and the digital environment.

The consortia that exist today would likely have no argument with the five benefits listed earlier, whether any individual consortium provides support for all of the listed services. But cooperative collections activities in particular have become much more nuanced and complicated in the digital age. In short, an entire list of consortial benefits around cooperative collections activities currently could include digitization, open access, licensing terms and rights, new business models, digital preservation, print storage, scholarly communication, and so forth. And in many cases, these new and emerging collaborations coexist alongside all of the traditional support services for shared print collections.

In his 2007 article, "The Cooperative Conundrum in the Digital Age," which was in part a result of discussions from the 2005 Janus Conference on Research Library Collections, Dan Hazen reviews the wins and losses from long-held cooperative print collection efforts. He follows it though with an expression of the opportunity presented to collaborate on collections in the digital age. "We have the means to cooperatively create and structure more encompassing digital collections, and our economic constraints reinforce this approach. It's time to act" (Hazen 2007, 109). The rest of this chapter addresses whether indeed we have risen to the challenge from Hazen to act, to bring library partners together not only to meet their collection goals but also to proactively shape their collections futures.

CONSORTIA COME IN MANY FLAVORS

Library consortia have a rich and long history in the United States dating back to the 1890s (Alexander 1999, 2). For the most part, consortia were organized around geographically proximate libraries in order to accomplish common goals; goals that have changed over time from predominantly resource sharing to addressing the advent of automation and the explosion of digital content. Just as the services provided by consortia have changed, so has the landscape of organizations formed by libraries to support their collective goals.

According to the publicly available International Coalition of Library Consortia (ICOLC) Web site, there are currently 63 library consortia in the United States. It would seem libraries can take their pick of collaborative organizations in which to participate and to go to for collection services. And libraries do have multiple allegiances when it comes to participating in consortial collection services. As an example, a library in the Committee on Institutional Cooperation (CIC) consortium will acquire digitized commercial publisher or vendor content through a centralized purchasing program at the CIC; license databases via their statewide consortium; become an affiliate member of a distant consortium in order to take advantage of group licensing discounts;

participate in the Center for Research Libraries Shared Purchase Program; and join national deals offered by large regional consortia such as Lyrasis.

Libraries are free to shop and compare when it comes to electronic licensing deals, since there are consortia who will allow any library to join a deal as long as it pays a service charge to support the operations of the consortium office. Consortial buying clubs are a phenomenon created when libraries that had no other form of collaborative relationship banded together to take advantage of discounts offered by vendors based on a number of participating libraries or aggregating a large spend commitment. Other consortia, like the Triangle Research Libraries Network, Orbis-Cascade Alliance, and California Digital Library (CDL) craft collections services that are specific to their membership and seek to accomplish goals beyond achieving savings on products with a much broader programmatic agenda.

In a 2007 survey of 92 libraries (from 18 states and 9 countries), respondents were asked to denote the determining factor for participating in a consortium. "Access to content" was the highest rated benefit (77%), followed by "lower annual price increases" (58%) and "predictable annual prices" (43%) (Clement 2007, 196). Because consortia are about as alike as snowflakes, educating the vendor community about the goals, strategies, and makeup of any given consortium can be challenging, especially for newcomers into the marketplace that had expected they would market their products direct to libraries. The fact that libraries participate in multiple consortia that may be negotiating for the same products only makes the picture fuzzier. Maintaining robust communication and a level of trust among libraries, consortium staff, and content providers is critical to achieving successful negotiations.

Efforts to determine if there are consortia that are more successful than the rest at keeping prices and inflation low on renewing products have proven inconclusive. In 2009, economist Ted Bergstrom used state open records laws to acquire publisher contracts from 36 institutions. His goal is, "As economists . . . we find that the academic journal industry presents a fascinating case study of such practices as price discrimination, bundled sales, and long-term contracting in an imperfectly competitive industry" (Bergstrom 2010). While Bergstrom reports that his team found a great deal of difference in what libraries of similar size pay to publishers, librarians more familiar with the details of these negotiations know that many factors, not documented, go into determining base pricing and inflation for consortial deals. In short, libraries are the final decision makers when it comes to selecting which consortia return savings and value to them in the electronic licensing arena.

WHAT HAS THE CONSORTIUM DONE FOR MY COLLECTION LATELY?

Coordinated collection activities, some of which were referenced in the previous section of this chapter, are predominantly focused around licensed digital content. There are still very tangible benefits to libraries who work together to license databases, purchase eBooks, and enter into big publisher packages for e-journals. Libraries can demonstrate cost savings, gain access to additional content they would not have acquired individually, and save staff time to negotiate and process licenses. New players have entered the consortial licensing sphere with both the ARL and the CRL hiring staff to develop offerings for their memberships. Clearly, there continues to be demand enough from U.S. libraries to support dozens of consortia acting in this space. As long as each consortium has a clearly defined set of goals and the marketplace sustains the development of multiple and sometimes competing offers, this will continue to be the landscape for libraries seeking content partnerships.

Libraries also have an interest in converting their own paper and microformat collections into digital content. Consortia have successfully come together to get grants to digitize special collections material. As examples, the Greater Western Library Alliance (GWLA) Western Waters Digital Library Project draws on collections from 17 consortial members, and additional non-consortium members, to build and offer a freely available research resource that would not have been possible before. The Lyrasis Mass Digitization Collaborative offers members the opportunity to have materials digitized for a low fee, taking advantage of bulk pricing for digitization services. There are many other examples of grant-funded digitization projects awarded to single institutions or a group of cooperating libraries. Libraries that work within a consortium framework for digitization projects realize lower costs for digitization, have the benefit of consortial staff to coordinate the project, and bring greater visibility to collections through shared platforms and portals for discovery.

Mass digitization projects, in partnership with large for-profit or not-for-profit entities, have also paved the way for libraries to digitize large numbers of materials. These materials, not necessarily drawn from special collections but rather from general collections, still represent a significant preservation challenge because of deteriorating paper quality and the likelihood that they will not draw the attention of traditional library funding partners such as Sloan, Institute of Museum and Library Services (IMLS), and Mellon. The now-defunct Microsoft Book Project, the Google Book Project, and the Internet Archive/Open Content Alliance can be considered forms of meta-consortia that provide investments, equipment, and platforms in which libraries can make their materials available digitally and often freely available to the world.

Print-based collection projects, sometimes referred to as cooperative collection development initiatives, are no longer simply carryovers of long-held agreements within consortia to distribute book-collecting responsibilities. Consortia are coordinating a range of activities that benefit both local libraries and the collective. The idea of the shared collection has taken on increased importance and visibility as libraries grapple with declining budgets for monographs, the high costs of storage in stacks, and low circulation of many materials. With robust resource sharing in place, libraries can reliably look to their partners not only to expand the number of titles available within a group collection, but also to deliver those titles in timely, efficient ways to users.

Consortia like OhioLINK and the Orbis-Cascade Alliance have worked with book jobbers such as YBP to control the number of copies of single titles purchased for a shared collection and to examine gaps of titles that could be added to a collection. The SUNY research center libraries piloted a shared collection of university press titles that included purchases from eight university presses and housed among the four cooperating libraries. Through the services of a shared Japanese bibliographer for three campuses, the CIC libraries were not working from a shared collection model or framework. Rather, the bibliographer was working to build collections for each of the campuses that met the needs of local researchers, though the material would be available through the CIC resource sharing agreement.

In the consortial community currently, much attention is being paid both to DDA and shared print storage. There are entire chapters in this book dedicated to these topics but it would be an oversight not to acknowledge them as another facet of consortial collections activity. As with most cooperative collection projects, these two areas are being addressed in a variety of successful ways in the United States and globally, and the business models will continue to evolve.

BUSINESS MODELS AND OTHER FAVORABLE TERMS BROUGHT TO YOU BY YOUR CONSORTIUM

Even though new products continue to come on the eResources market, weekly it seems, the process for dealing with new offerings, new companies, and the business of acquisitions is quite mature. EResources licensing has its roots in the late 1980s and early 1990s and there are infrastructures in consortial offices to manage and develop membership offers, negotiate license terms, and swap all of the technical information required to provide access to content. But it hardly means that this business is routine. Over the 30-year plus lifetime of eResources, a long list of issues related to licensing terms and business practices continues to be revisited and re-strategized, while new issues emerge as libraries shift their priorities and face fiscal pressures. Consortia can play a key role in bringing issues of importance to libraries to the vendor community. The ability to speak on behalf of a large group of libraries, or a group of libraries that represent a significant revenue stream to a vendor, can give a consortium the muscle to negotiate more aggressively.

The original Big Deal for publisher packages of e-journals is showing its age. Many consortia still hold licenses for these bundles of journal titles and many libraries can still justify the cost of the packages through usage and other metrics of value. A 2008 study of ROI at the University of Illinois reported that $4.38 in grant income is realized for each $1.00 invested by the university in the library (Luther 2008, 12). But for many libraries, the economics of the Big

Deal has either become unsustainable or its simply that year-on-year justifications for inflation are no longer valid since the original terms of these deals were based on historic print spends from the 1990s. In the article, "Is the Big Deal Dying?," 13 representatives from publishing, consortia, and libraries each give their opinion of the future of the big deal and possible alternatives (Boissy et al. 2012, 36). From the responses, it is clear that publishers and consortia alike have spent the past few years trying to reconceptualize a big-deal journals model that meets a new set of criteria. It is not that all libraries want to break apart their deals; rather they need some flexibility to drop titles that perform poorly, are no longer programmatically relevant, and have more options to manage their costs. Libraries and consortia have also become more aggressive about advocating for rights to deposit works by their institutional authors in local repositories. Several large STM publishers are currently running pilots of new big deals, but these have yet to seep more broadly into the rest of the community.

Under the broad umbrella of scholarly communication, consortia are now being asked to introduce language into licenses that allows for author's rights, text mining, and international ILL. Each of these three issues has its own story and development timeline. When negotiating for author's rights, consortia are recognizing the need to act on behalf of authors who sign away their rights to reuse their own created content at the time of publication. By turning over the copyright to publishers, faculty and researchers have also signed away the ability to make educational and scholarly uses of their content without seeking the publisher's permission. The costs to gain permission to reuse this material often fall back to a library.

Text mining is the newcomer to the licensing world, a concept that works only in the world of digital content. While faculty working in the digital humanities have an established history of computational research across digitized textual material, content that is now housed on a publisher's servers requires permissions to access. It is especially important that publishers can distinguish between systematic downloading that often signals piracy and legitimate uses of large blocks of content.

ILL has been at the center of many licensing tugs of war over the year. Early efforts by publishers to control the amount of ILL from e-journals was in an attempt to prevent widespread dissemination of copyrighted material made much easier by electronic distribution. More recently, a group of STM publishers sought to limit the ability of U.S. libraries to provide lending to the international community. Presumably, the confusion on the part of STM publishers was related to the difference between noncommercial lending between libraries and fee-based document delivery services. Regardless of the motivation, the need to reestablish the rights of libraries to make fair uses of material supported by Section 108 of Copyright Law has come back into focus in licensing negotiations.

As libraries continue to evolve in both their fiscal environments and the suite of services that they provide to researchers, faculty, and students, it is imperative that consortia are prepared to represent those interests at the negotiating table. While cost savings is a predominate way that consortia demonstrate value to their members, securing rights and permissions can be equally as important in order to maximize dissemination and use of scholarship.

META-CONSORTIUM INITIATIVES

The digital environment has created the opportunity for consortia to be less geographically based and to allow groups of dispersed but like-minded libraries to come together to accomplish mutual goals. While these organizations are not what might be considered under the traditional definition of consortia, each has a membership, members make investments in the organization, and the libraries involved have come together to accomplish a goal that could not succeed at a standalone institution. Writing on the topic of new forms of library collaboration, Paula Kaufman reinforces the need for thinking beyond traditional relationships to accomplish the new challenges faced by academic libraries, "There are compelling reasons to think that to be effective in the future the ways in which libraries work together must deepen, and the partners with whom they choose to work must broaden" (Kaufman 2012, 54). In many cases, the source of funds for these memberships and pledges of support come from the collections or materials budgets in libraries.

The HathiTrust Digital Library, founded by the CIC and CDL consortia, is housed at the University of Michigan and University of Indiana. Hathi was originally conceived as the storage mechanism for book files being returned from the Google Book scanning project as well as content from the Internet Archive, Microsoft, and locally digitized collections. Currently, the HathiTrust has 66 institutional members, some under the umbrella of a consortial membership. Members have the option of depositing content in Hathi or, if not depositing, "to participate in the long-term curation and management of the repository in return for enhanced services for accessing and using materials in the digital library" (http://www.hathitrust.org/). By investing together in a long-term content repository, the library community has more control over access and usage more in line with fair use rather than contractual language governing vendor agreements.

The open access movement continues to be a beacon of change in the entrenched scholarly communication environment. Although publishers are now trying to wrest and monetize open access options from grassroots movements, organizations such as SCOAP3 (Sponsoring Consortium for Open Access Publishing in Particle Physics) and arXiv are successful examples of consortia that impact collections activities at every level. arXiv is the open access repository for research articles, primarily in physics, math, computer science, and statistics currently housed at Cornell but founded by Los Alamos National Laboratory. arXiv recently restructured its business model to ensure its long-term viability with contributions from the libraries and research laboratories worldwide that represent arXiv's heaviest institutional users. Despite the existence and heavy usage of arXiv, libraries had not typically been substituting freely available arXiv access for journal subscriptions in which the same articles are published. SCOAP3 is now working to facilitate open access publishing in high energy physics. The initiative is led by CERN (European Organization for Nuclear Physics) in Geneva and currently has pledges of support from universities and governments and labs in 30 countries. An outgrowth of arXiv, SCOAP3 is working on sustainable open access models for the peer-reviewed journals whose preprints are often deposited in arXiv.

WHAT'S NEXT?

As a consortium-employed author, it is in my organization's best interest to always be looking for the next big opportunities to enrich and enhance our libraries' collections and to accelerate the adoption of strategies to accomplish this collectively. Cost savings will continue to be an important metric for our success as libraries grapple with budgetary challenges. It will also be important to make strides in efficiencies for selecting, acquiring, and delivering content. Libraries have streamlined staff positions and collective action should reduce the speed of adoption for getting content to the users.

Libraries are facing requests for new kinds of content for which norms for selecting, pricing, and licensing must be established. Datasets, textbooks, and researcher profile systems are examples of new areas to tackle as a result of user demand. In each of these cases, it will require multiple layers of collaboration to manage the integration of these new forms of content into the library space. Datasets will need the support of information technology to ensure usability and long-term curation of the material. Textbooks have typically been in the purview of the bookstore and the individual student, so the transition to libraries for handling the negotiations for price and delivery must take into account preexisting revenue streams. And researcher profile systems will involve discussions among the Offices of Research, provosts, and the libraries. Consortia may also get involved in negotiations for deals that will benefit across institutions.

Libraries have also taken on the role of publisher, many now running operations with their own imprints for books and journals. As a provider of content, libraries are in a position to create business models for more favorable pricing and to give wider dissemination to content through open access. Because most of these presses are not operating at a large scale, consortia and libraries should seek to give support to such efforts. Through these projects and programs there will be a shift, however big or small, in the scholarly communication lifecycle that makes scholarship more accessible and affordable.

Partnerships among libraries, consortia, and commercial information providers should take on new dimensions, whether they are longstanding relationships or first-time meetings. Using the power of the purse, libraries and consortia should provide incentives for publishers to create content for disciplines under-represented in digital form. As large-scale shared print initiatives continue to develop, libraries and publishers should consider how these collections could be converted to digital form without the concomitant price tag that often goes along with format migration for the same content.

CONCLUSION

The long-term and ongoing support for consortial activity in the area of collections indicates that libraries find value in working together to save money, extend access to content, co-invest in digitization, and share in the exploration of new models for creating, managing, and sharing content. The challenge faced by both libraries and consortia is to rightsize the activities and investments made at the local and consortial levels to meet the needs of users in efficient and cost-effective ways.

In a 2005 paper delivered at the Janus Conference, Mark Sandler predicted that "core resources that serve 80 percent or more of users will be selected and served up centrally; with local efforts focused on truly local needs" (Sandler 2006, 241). Whether this should be the goal of cooperative collection activities or is just a natural evolution as a result of the availability of digital content and coordinated effort is yet to play out. Perhaps it is a little of both. Collaboration can be slow and frustrating and requires libraries to yield a certain amount of autonomy and decision making, but the results can and should surpass anything a library would have been able to accomplish on its own.

REFERENCES

Alexander, Adrian W. 1999. "Toward 'The Perfection of Work': Library Consortia in the Digital Age." *Journal of Library Administration* 28 (2): 1–14.

Bergstrom, Ted C. 2010. "Big Deal Contract Project." Available at: http://www.econ.ucsb .edu/~tedb/Journals/BundleContracts.html. Accessed November 1, 2012.

Boissy, Robert W. et al. 2012. "Is the 'Big Deal' Dying?" *Serials Review* 38 (2012): 36–45.

Chadwell, Faye A. 2011. "Assessing the Value of Academic Library Consortia." *Journal of Library Administration* 51 (7–8): 645–61.

Clement, Susanne. 2007. "Skills for Effective Participation in Consortia: Preparing for Collaborating and Collaboration." *Collection Management* 23 (1–2): 191–204.

Hazen, Dan. 2007. "The Cooperative Conundrum in the Digital Age." *Journal of Library Administration* 46 (2) 101–18.

Kaufman, Paula. 2012. "Let's Get Cozy: Evolving Collaborations in the 21st Century." *Journal of Library Administration* 52 (1): 53–69.

Luther, Judy. 2008. "University Investment in the Library: What's the Return?" *Library Connect*. Available at: http://libraryconnectarchive.elsevier.com/whitepapers/0108/lcwp 010801.html. Accessed November 1, 2012.

Sandler, Mark. 2006. "Collection Development in the Age Day of Google." *Library Resources & Technical Services* 50 (4): 239–43.

23

FLOATING COLLECTIONS: PERSPECTIVES FROM AN ACADEMIC LIBRARY

Karen E. Greever

INTRODUCTION

In the *Oxford English Dictionary*, one of the definitions for floating is "having little, or comparatively no attachment." Another meaning is "not fixed or settled in a definite state or place." If one looks up the same word in Thinkmap's *Visual Thesaurus*, one can follow a trajectory through unfixed and free to available and lendable. When librarians decide to implement floating collections, they travel this same path as they make their materials available in new venues for patrons to borrow. What follows is a brief description and discussion about the journey two academic libraries took along the road to a floating collection—a collection in which materials borrowed from one library by patrons of another remain at the second library rather than being returned to the home library.

BACKGROUND

Denison University and Kenyon College are two small liberal arts schools located 30 miles apart. They are members of the Five Colleges of Ohio (Ohio5) consortium along with Oberlin College, Ohio Wesleyan University, and the College of Wooster. Four of the schools (Denison, Kenyon, Ohio Wesleyan, and Wooster) have shared an online catalog since 1996. All five college libraries are also members of OhioLINK, a state consortium of 88 academic libraries, including both public and private institutions, ranging from research universities to community colleges, as well as the State Library of Ohio. A statewide union catalog allows direct patron-initiated borrowing from any member library and delivery usually occurs within three to five days. Ohio-LINK libraries participate in a group membership in the Center for Research Libraries (CRL) and CRL-cataloged books may also be requested through the

OhioLINK central catalog, though delivery time may be slightly longer than for materials housed in member libraries. The OhioLINK central catalog provides access to more than 45 million items, including 13 million unique items. With renewals, students may borrow materials for up to 21 weeks, and faculty for 42 weeks. An additional union catalog interface also permits OhioLINK patrons to request and borrow materials from SearchOhio, a consortium of 21 public library systems. Some 9 million items are available through the SearchOhio collection. These consortial arrangements make an extensive number and wide range of materials available to Denison and Kenyon patrons within a relatively short time frame. This existing network of mechanisms for patron access was considered as part of the context within a floating collection might be implemented.

The Ohio5 schools have a number of consortial committees and the libraries have worked together on projects both large and small. During a consortial grant project 10 years ago, discussions about cooperative collection development among librarians at the Five Colleges included musings about the possibilities of floating collections among the libraries.[1] Materials would be shelved at the library to which they were returned, regardless of which of the five libraries actually owned the items. The same proposal has also been floated at the OhioLINK consortium level, but to date has not gained sufficient traction to move forward. One of the stumbling blocks identified during the Five Colleges' conversations was delivery time. Without the ability to provide next-day delivery, the proposal lacked the carrot necessary to bring everyone on board—a dramatic and tangible improvement in service for our patrons. After all, the libraries and their patrons already had statewide consortium borrowing and delivery within a few days. What the collection development librarians believed was that next-day delivery, combined with a floating collection, would help erase some more of the boundaries that continued to hinder cooperative collection development. With those two pieces in place, both librarians and patrons would begin to view the unified collection as a single unit rather than five individual collections. Unfortunately, at the time, the financial costs related to an improved delivery service were deemed too high when compared to the possible benefits.

Among the Ohio5 schools, Denison and Kenyon are located most closely to one another, and that small geographic distance has made even closer cooperation between these two libraries possible. In 2004 Denison and Kenyon received another grant from the Andrew W. Mellon Foundation, this one to plan a redesign of library technical services work across the two colleges. The goal of the project was to improve access to information resources and create value-added services for their patrons (Andreadis et al. 2007). As one part of the Denison–Kenyon technical services redesign process, a daily delivery service between the two schools was initiated in order to transport cataloged and processed materials from one library to the other. Although the delivery service was not intended specifically for the purpose of facilitating floating collections, it became clear that it could serve in that capacity in addition to fulfilling its role for the technical services staff and their needs. For these two schools in the Ohio5 consortium, one of the main obstacles to a workable floating collection had been eliminated. Certainly many libraries have successfully employed floating collections without next-day delivery, but in this instance, considering the proximity of Kenyon to Denison and the preexistence of OhioLINK, 24-hour delivery was viewed as a necessity to the project's success. In hindsight, as beneficial and convenient as it is, next-day delivery may not have been as crucial as it was once seen to be.

The two libraries did not conduct detailed surveys of other implementations of floating collections before moving forward, but it did seem clear that the idea had been undertaken more commonly in public libraries than in academic ones. This fact was perhaps daunting and exciting at the same time. By initiating a floating collection between two academic libraries, Denison and Kenyon would be moving into uncharted territory. In the end, the decision by the Kenyon and Denison library directors to move forward with a floating collection between the two schools was not based on an analysis of data. Rather, it was based on an instinctual and anecdotal opinion that the daily delivery of materials provided in the technical services redesign process created an opportunity to provide better service for their patrons by offering them immediate access to materials they have used and might need again. This rationale for implementing a floating collection is related but not identical to the reason often cited by public libraries—to reduce the time that materials spend in transit (Hilyard 2012, 16). The project also appealed to the love of experimentation that both directors possessed.

PLANNING

Although there seemed to be many advantages to the floating collection proposal, there was also a certain amount of apprehension about it. Five years later, it is difficult to remember the angst of that time clearly. However, the concerns were very real. Many of these same issues have been faced by other libraries undertaking this change in practice and procedure (Cress 2004, 49). One of the primary concerns was about a potential imbalance in borrowing. For example, would patrons at Denison request many more materials than patrons at Kenyon, resulting in an overabundance of materials at one location and empty shelves at another? A related issue was whether large numbers of titles in particular subject areas would be requested from one library, leaving patrons researching those topics at the other college with fewer resources immediately available. A third concern was about potential shelving issues. Neither library had an abundance of available stack space. What would happen if large numbers of books were requested in particularly tight areas of the stacks? Would difficult and time-consuming shifts of parts of the collections be required on a regular basis? Another issue was possible confusion for

shelvers and other staff at both institutions. Prior to the redesign of technical services, spine-label formatting and barcode placement were not uniform
at the two schools. How much training would be required for shelvers and
for circulation staff? And, as other librarians who have implemented floating
collection programs are aware, none of these questions can be answered in
advance. It is impossible to accurately predict how much and which parts of
the collection will be affected. It is possible, however, to train staff so they
are aware of the technical and physical processing issues. It is also possible
to maintain awareness of potential issues and to monitor implementation for
potential hiccups.

For Denison and Kenyon a critical question that required investigation was
whether the integrated library system (ILS) they shared with two other colleges had the capability to support a floating collection, and whether it could
be implemented by only two of the four libraries using the ILS. Since Ohio
Wesleyan and the College of Wooster, the other two schools sharing Denison
and Kenyon's catalog, had decided not to participate in the technical services
redesign grant and were not part of the daily delivery route, they also opted
not to participate in the floating collection project. In 2005, when the technical services daily delivery service began, Denison and Kenyon did not have
the necessary software within their shared ILS to make a floating collection
possible for only two of the four schools, although it was available from the
vendor. The decision to move ahead with the project was made and that software was acquired in 2006. Floating became a reality in the summer of 2007.

IMPLEMENTATION

To begin the process of floating collection implementation, an initial meeting of systems, circulation, and stacks management staff of both colleges oc-
curred early in 2007. Since the academic year for both Kenyon and Denison
runs from August to May, without a full academic summer semester, it was decided that beginning implementation during the summer months would be the
least disruptive. Instituting new procedures at a nonpeak period of lending and
borrowing activity would allow staff time to adjust. Check-in issues, shelving
concerns, and training could be resolved without the constraints of the school-
year endeavors. When checking in materials, circulation staff would need to
be aware of whether the materials were from the floating collections partner
library and thus meant to stay for shelving in that library, or if they would need
to be returned to their home institution via the courier service, since borrowed
materials come from many different libraries.

Both Kenyon and Denison have a number of collections (archives, multimedia, periodicals, reference, special collections, etc.) with limited, restricted,
or no circulation. It was decided at the outset that only the main monograph
collections would be part of the floating collection project, but at both Denison and Kenyon collections with restrictive circulation policies represent a

large percentage of each overall collection. Isolating them was not an issue, however, as these collections were also easily distinguished by item and location codes. A single combination of item and location codes at each institution identified the materials that would be part of the floating collection. Among the other circulating collections, government documents and folios (or oversize materials) were excluded, at least initially. With those choices made, implementation was not overly complicated. As part of a global update, a field indicating owning library was added to the item records of all materials slated to be part of the floating collection. Once the records were updated, the software was turned on that enabled floating as part of the circulation process. With the home library clearly listed in each record, floating books could easily be identified and returned to the owning library if necessary. For staff members familiar with barcodes, materials are also easily distinguished by the differing initial character string of each institution's barcodes. As a change to ongoing workflow, cataloging staff would need to add the owning location field when new records that fit the parameters of the floating collection were created. That field would automatically be added to batch-loaded records, which account for the bulk of items in the proposed floating collections. It was eventually decided to create an item type for materials in the general collection that would not be part of the floating collection. This item type has been used rarely, but having it available eliminated one additional cause of concern.

REVIEW

Neither Kenyon nor Denison tracked the floating collection at regular intervals, but periodically they created lists of what Kenyon materials are at Denison and what Denison materials are at Kenyon. Each report showed that the number of floating items at one institution was very similar to the number at the other library. The overall number of floating items has also remained relatively stable during the five years since floating was initiated. Currently, about 11,300 Kenyon items are at Denison and 11,500 Denison items are at Kenyon. This works out to about 3 percent of the materials made available for the floating collection.[2] In the end there has not been an appreciable imbalance of borrowing, nor has any particular subject area been more affected than any other. This is clearly different from the experiences at a number of public libraries with floating collections, where regular rebalancing of collection materials has been necessary (Canty et al. 2012, 68). To date, neither Kenyon nor Denison has undertaken any rebalancing projects. Perhaps this variance is due to the status of both Denison and Kenyon as undergraduate, liberal arts colleges, with similar collections and patrons. It could also be attributed to the inherent differences between academic and public library collections.

As expected, one of the real benefits to users has been next-day delivery. At the reference desk, the librarian can reassure patrons that the requested item will be available to them by a definite time depending on when the request was made—either the next day, if the request is made early enough in the day, or the day after, if the request is made in the late afternoon or evening. The floating collection has not been advertised per se at either school, but librarians do mention the delivery time during instruction sessions and in one-on-one interactions. Many patrons are also aware of the service, either from personal experience or through word of mouth.

The floating collection has also assisted with ongoing consortial collection development initiatives designed to reduce unnecessary duplication. Perhaps neither librarians nor patrons think of Denison and Kenyon's collections as a single entity rather than separate, but it is an easier sell to both librarians and faculty if one can say that the item does not need to be acquired because it can be sitting on our shelves tomorrow.

As with most projects, there have been a few unintended or unanticipated consequences. One must be more vigilant during the weeding process. Occasionally, items have been mistakenly pulled as duplicates when one copy actually belongs to Denison and the other to Kenyon. At other times, materials that fit the weeding criteria do not actually belong to the library doing the weeding, but these occasions are not so problematic as to overshadow the many benefits of this project. And, some of the common reported challenges in floating collections—shortages and overflows; lack of shelf space; and insufficient communication about redistribution (Hilyard 2012, 14)—have simply not been issues for either Denison or Kenyon.

CONCLUSION

The idea of the floating collection was initially billed as a pilot project, but after five years that label no longer applies. Anecdotally, it seemed clear early on that the project was working and formal assessment has never been deemed necessary. This decision is bolstered by the fact that no major issues developed and that the program is taken for granted by library staff. These are also signs that the pre-implementation anxiety was unnecessary and that the floating collection has been a valuable addition to the way that Denison and Kenyon provide access for patrons to materials.

Because of the different experiences reported by public library implementations, some questions remain. It would be interesting to know if other academic libraries implementing floating collections would also escape the public library overflow or shortage issues, as Kenyon and Denison have done. Would the type of academic library (research institution vs. community college) have any effect? What would be the results of floating among different types of academic libraries, as opposed to floating between two very similar institutions? The answers to these questions will have to wait for the implementation of more academic floating collections, but if the Denison–Kenyon experiment is at all indicative, this is a collection management strategy worth exploring.

NOTES

1. It is a three-year grant from the Andrew W. Mellon Foundation to foster cooperative collection development. The grant ran from 2001 to 2003. Additional information about the project may be found at: http://www.ohio5.org/web/default.html.

2. Denison University acquires approximately 4,800 volumes each year with a circulating monograph collection of 290,000 volumes. Kenyon College acquires approximately 4,000 volumes per year with a circulating monograph collection of around 340,000 volumes. In the past two years, Denison has circulated an average of 36,000 volumes from its collection and Kenyon 33,000 volumes.

REFERENCES

Andreadis, Debra K., Christopher D. Barth, Lynn Scott Cochrane, and Karen E. Greever. 2007. "Cooperative Work Redesign in Library Technical Services at Denison University and Kenyon College." In *Library Workflow Redesign: Six Case Studies*, ed. Marilyn Mitchell, 39–49. Washington, DC: Council on Library and Information Resources.

Canty, Adrienne Brown, Louise C. Frolek, Richard P. Thornley, Colleen J. Andriats, Linda K. Bombak, Christalene R. Lay, and Michael Dell. 2012. "Floating Collections at Edmonton Public Library." *Evidence Based Library and Information Practice* 7 (1): 65–69.

Cress, Ann. 2004. "The Latest Wave." *Library Journal* (October 1, 2004): 48–50.

"floating, adj." *OED Online.* Oxford University Press. Available at: [http://www.oed.com/view/Entry/71742?rskey=U8Lg4o&result=2]. Accessed December 5, 2012.

"floating, adj." *Visual Thesaurus.* Thinkmap. Available at: [http://www.visualthesaurus.com]. Accessed October 5, 2012.

Hilyard, Nann Blaine. 2012. "Take the Plunge, Implementing Floating Collections in Your Library System." *Public Libraries* 51 (3): 13–20.

24

FLOATING COLLECTIONS: PERSPECTIVES FROM A PUBLIC LIBRARIAN

Wendy Bartlett

To float a public library collection is to watch collection management Darwinism in action. The fittest items in the collection survive and float; the non-floaters scream "weed me." Popular items spin throughout the entire library system, never returning to a specific home branch, but catching hold after hold, traveling from one branch to the next. Selections made just in case are mercilessly left standing in place, a testimony to misspent collection development funds. Floating is dramatic, immediate, and for better or worse, serves to put collection issues squarely in everyone's lap from shelvers to the director.

Simply defined, floating collections are collections in which there is no owning location. Items may be started at a location that has a heavy interest in mystery, for example, but once that item leaves the branch at which it started, either from a patron request, or from being returned to a different branch, it stays there. It is not routed back to the starting location.

Over the past few years, floating collections have gained tremendous popularity in public libraries for several reasons. With reduced staffing and budget challenges making headlines across the country, administrators have looked to floating collections to provide instantaneous relief by cutting costs in delivery, labor (the items are handled half as often), and collection development budgets.

Because items no longer spend time traveling back to an owning location, hot items are more immediately available, causing a bump in circulation, and a savings on the collection development purchasing end. Patrons will universally exclaim that there are more new items available, when nothing could be further from the truth. The reality is that collection development has not spent any extra funds on materials whatsoever. Because delivery time is halved, the number of popular items needed can actually be reduced.. Because patrons perceive the collection as abundant and fresh, they spend more time browsing, often increasing circulation.

Much work goes in to preparing a collection to float, primarily in terms of weeding materials that have not earned their keep in terms of circulation. Again, depending on how rigorous or lax the weeding has been in the past (and there is often great variety within departments and age levels at the same branch or throughout the same library system), this is either a mind-bending all-out effort or a mere extension of good weeding practices. Once this pre-floating weeding is accomplished, the system will often get an increase in circulation simply because the stacks look better, shelvers find room for hot items languishing in the back room, and patrons can more easily find what they are looking for. It is a more pleasant browsing experience even before the floating materials reach the door.

But what is important to remember is that for every positive outcome, there can be major and permanent collection handicaps that impact the public librarian's ability to do his or her job well and to serve patrons, and while some of that impact can be lessened, the collection is always off once floating starts. This chapter addresses best practices that librarians have developed to get the most of their floating collection while attempting to ameliorate the negative effects that floating has on collections and collection management.

MAKE A GOOD DECISION ABOUT WHAT TO FLOAT

A recurring theme with floating is that one solution or method or practice does not by any means fit all. Systems with far-flung branches often decide to float everything to cut down as much as possible on delivery and fuel costs. Systems with a main library with a well-respected and highly trafficked research collection often decide to float branch materials and popular new materials, leaving main library's collection out of floating altogether. Sometimes funding plays a role. Some systems can only float those items bought with communal money, such as state funds, while being restricted in terms of where items purchased with local monies can go. In those cases, systems will frequently purchase popular movies and books and float those, keeping the rest of the locally purchased collections traditionally shelved and owned by a particular branch.

And remember the following maxim, because it is frequently forgotten in the what-ifs of planning to float. There is a direct correlation between circulation and floating. Popular items float more, no surprise. But what usually does come as a surprise is how little low-circulating collections actually float. Children's materials and the less-popular Deweys in adult nonfiction actually take a long time to float and refresh, while movies at a popular branch will float in and out almost immediately, creating an entire new selection.

Many systems float movies, music CDs, and best sellers, but do not float the regular collection. Others float everything except children's materials and adult nonfiction. And many systems float absolutely everything, save the odd special collection such as local history.

Determining how much and what to float is really a pretty simple decision. The more that is floated, the more money that is saved. Librarians who approach floating as a way to help a serious budget problem will want to float as much as possible, and deal with whatever collection disruptions and imbalances arise later. It is important to consider though, the hidden costs of floating the entire collection. Because the collection disruption is more intense—some branches are inundated, some lose a significant portion of their more popular materials—the time and labor costs involved in trying to even out the collection is not insignificant, and almost always involves higher paid staff. So while a savings is realized in delivery costs and at the circulation and shipping desks, branch managers and librarians spend a lot of time trying to contend with the uneven distribution of a floating collection. While the goal is never to try and restore a collection to the pre-float level, customers at the branches which lose materials will not be happy with a lesser selection, and librarians will have to try and adjust for that. Another hidden cost that the collection development department and librarians must work closely to control is the possibility of newer and highly desirable materials being weeded by the librarians at the inundated branches who are desperate to create more space for the materials that continue to float in. And finally, staff morale can be very challenged at both extremes of the floating spectrums. Librarians in branches with too much stuff feel as though they are working twice as hard as everyone else in the system just to beat back the tide. And they are right. And librarians in the branches with a net loss work twice as hard to provide something with which to please their patrons.

It is possible to have the best of both worlds. Many librarians have realized that floating brings wonderfully refreshed collections, which are highly desirable and help circulation. Librarians in that situation get the best of both worlds by floating parts of the collection, which help their budgets, while keeping large sections of their collections intact and balanced. There are as many scenarios as there are floating libraries. The advantage of only floating part of the collection initially is that the decision can be made piecemeal to float the rest, allowing for time to evaluate how disrupted the collection becomes. Clearly, a financially stressed organization (and how many libraries can claim not to be?) cannot be choosy, and floating as much as possible will help to ease that financial stress.

PREPARE, PREPARE, PREPARE

Whether the decision is made to float the entire collection, parts of it, or only popular materials, the more thorough the preparation of the collection prior to floating, the less negative the impact of floating will be. Weeding the collection, making sure that all branches are caught up on shelving (and stay caught up), measuring pre-float factors like book drops and hold shelves, knowing traffic patterns in the area of service, and communicating tirelessly with staff will go a very long way to making sure the float is as uneventful as possible. Needless to say, the degree to which these collection management and communication practices are in place as a matter of course in the library's daily life will determine how much time it will take to prepare to float.

A library with great communication in place will have little trouble with the rest of the preparation needed. A library where staff communication is a special event will have to gear up the communication piece before the tasks needed to get the collection floating can be farmed out and accomplished. Staff need to understand why floating is being put in to place, what parts of the collection are being floated, and how it will affect them and their patrons. And it is crucial that every staff member, from the shelvers (who play a critical role) to the branch managers and administrators understand floating. Librarians are sometimes guilty of communicating solely to other librarians and other staff members who work service desks, leaving circulation staff, delivery drivers and shippers, and shelvers out of the conversation. Floating is so granular, that it is impossible to overemphasize the necessity of bringing all employees into this conversation early and often. Staff will have many questions, and not a few fears about floating. Many of them focus around not knowing their collection; librarians worry that as the float happens, they will no longer be able to know what is on their shelves. This concern dissipates almost as soon as floating begins. It turns out that librarians do not give themselves enough credit. They hit the ground running after floating begins, and prove to be much more flexible and have better memory and sourcing abilities than they thought possible. The comfort zone is definitely gone, particularly if the entire collection floats, but librarians rise to the occasion. One way to help ease those staff concerns is to invite librarians from floating library systems to address the staff early on in the floating conversation. This goes a long way to dispelling concerns.

Weeding is an essential preparatory step to readying the collection to float, and again, if a collection has a history of being regularly and vigorously weeded, this is a simple step. But for many library systems, system-wide, regular weeding is unheard of. Weeding is something to do when it's slow. The problem with that approach is obvious to anyone who works in today's public library. It is never slow! Maybe back in the day when our mentor librarians were starting out, waiting for a slow period to weed was an effective tactic. With staff and budget cuts, most libraries are at staffing minimums. Add aggressive programming goals and the computer help needed by many patrons, and many library staff are lucky to get daily tasks accomplished. So what to do? Simply put, weeding needs to become a new daily task.

But to clear the decks and get floating going, most systems find themselves in need of a major weeding effort. The goal is pretty straightforward. If the shelves are full with very little wiggle room, at least 15–20 percent of each part of the collection that is designated to float needs to go in order to make room for the items that will float in. Fifteen to twenty percent of the collection is a lot with which to contend. But weeding aggressively will freshen the collection and prevent a huge workload later on. The average system needs to look hard at anything over three years old that has not circulated in a year. Getting that out will raise circulation instantly simply because patrons can find the more desirable items more quickly. It will also create room on the shelves for materials to come in and out. And librarians must make sure that every section that is going to float is weeded to this degree. If only nonfiction shelf sitters are weeded, fiction and music CDs will still be overcrowded when floating begins.

Librarians need to take a hard look at their backroom and see what and how much is waiting to be shelved. If all items are not back on the shelves within a day or two of being returned, not only is the library losing valuable circulation, but it will also be a catastrophe waiting to happen when floating begins, because more high circulating items will accrue in the backroom, particularly at branches with high call-in and drop-off rates. If there are branches in the system where shelvers struggle to catch up and stay caught up, that needs to be addressed and resolved before floating begins. Failure to do so will mean that the most desirable items brought in from the float will languish in the back room, defeating the purpose of refreshing collections for patrons.

The most common concern that librarians have about floating is that a smaller branch will be completely swamped by incoming materials. There are actually a couple of ways to predict what branches will feel an impact, and what branches will not. The first is simply location. If a branch is located near busy commuter routes, more items are dropped off there. But with floating, they stay there, and if the branch is not a top circulating branch, items may not leave fast enough to continue to absorb the drop-offs. Another excellent predictor is to analyze the morning book drop. What is the percentage of items that are owned by that particular branch, and what is the percentage of items that are being dropped off from other branches?

Looking at the hold shelf can also be very helpful. Staff is often convinced for some reason that their hold shelves will explode with floating. That's just not true. Hold shelves either stay the same or shrink a bit as better maintained collections mean customers more often can find what they need. But it is a good idea to record approximately how many shelves are being used, pre-float, in order to reassure staff once floating has begun. Staff will often maintain that they are a huge drop-off. Running actual metrics on a book drop and a hold shelf and then comparing them across the system will help staff understand where they are in the big picture, and will help them be a little more realistic about what to expect from floating.

THERE IS NO MAGIC BULLET FOR REBALANCING

One positive aspect about the effects of floating is that they are immediate. By the end of the first day, or possibly the second, it will be very evident which branches are hardest hit. It will take a few weeks to determine which branches are steadily losing materials with the float. Bear in mind, the vast majority of branches will not experience a noticeable difference at all. Floating works great for medium-sized, medium circulating libraries in low- to medium-traffic areas. It is the branches on the extreme end of the spectrum that catch the mega drop-offs or that feel the drain of resources. When this happens, don't make the mistake some systems make. The ostrich method, for example, is a popular but disastrous choice. Those directing the float maintain that the collection imbalances are not as drastic as librarians think they are, which is laughable, since the librarians are dealing with the fallout each and every day, and know precisely how drastic their particular situation is. Librarians are told that "imbalances happen" and are asked, essentially, to deal with it. Not good. This approach wastes resources, crushes morale, and most of all is a disservice to the customer who either finds a mess of overabundant resources or a scarcity thereof.

A better approach is to try and set up a central clearinghouse of some kind for librarians to communicate their needs. For those libraries with centralized selection, the collection development department is the logical choice. These librarians know all the branch collections, not just one. They also know who is truly experiencing hardship with floating, as opposed to others who may just need time to adjust to the change. Partnering between haves and have-nots can be very effective, in no small part because of the accountability engendered by having only a few people involved in rebalancing and exchanging materials. If the person in charge of the exchange at the sending branch sends materials that are old or are in poor condition, the receiver knows to whom he or she should address his or her concerns. Moreover, communication can flow on a more granular level, so that the sender is not sending just cookbooks, but slow-cookery cookbooks, or five-ingredient cookbooks, or whatever is popular at the receiving branch. The sender has more than enough to share, and the receiver ends up with a tailor-made collection for his or her patrons.

Beware of vendors claiming to be able to do rebalancing automatically. There is currently no vendor program that can rebalance a floating collection. Baker & Taylor's Collection HQ can swap old shelf sitters in to a new branch, for example, but that is precisely what floating does organically. Collection HQ is very promising, but has, of this writing, not caught up with the swift moving, daily needs of a floating collection. Other vendors try to rebalance by measuring linear feet of books and other items. A superb approach if one is leveraging inventory across several carpet stores, but a pretty blunt hammer to take to a library collection across several branches. A branch that needs medical books on diabetes can receive cookbooks. Or a branch needing cookbooks on Crock-pot cookery can receive books on Tuscan cookery. The collection may be balanced numerically with this method, but the gestalt of a well-balanced collection tailored to a particular community's needs cannot be achieved with the linear feet approach.

There is no magic bullet for rebalancing. There is no magic bullet for rebalancing. There is no magic bullet for rebalancing. Once librarians have repeated that to themselves often enough and internalized that mantra, they can stop looking outward for solutions to rebalancing and begin studying what other systems have done, and what they might effectively adapt for their own system. A workgroup composed of internal experienced librarians, circulation, and shelving staff will be best equipped for finding those rebalancing answers within their own organization.

MAXIMIZE THE BENEFITS OF FLOATING

Perhaps the best news about floating is that it is invisible to the customers. Staff have sometimes worried that their patrons will be disappointed somehow by floating, and the opposite is true. Patrons will claim that the library has bought more DVDs and best sellers, when in actuality, the system has bought the same number as always, or fewer. Why do patrons perceive it this way? Simple. Materials that used to be on trucks and in delivery bins simply pop right back out to the shelves. The patrons are not wrong; there is more to peruse because the hot merchandise is not on a truck or in a bin.

Workflow after floating has begun must include weeding as a daily task. Librarians will be stunned by the condition of items that arrive from branches that were not as fastidious about weeding. Shelvers and their supervisors will want to make sure that the shelving is kept caught up so that the hot and desirable materials are in front of the patrons as much as possible, and no time is lost in the backroom awaiting shelving. Merchandising is a much more dynamic process with a floating collection as a new browsing collection appears several times a day in a busy branch. Librarians will want to capitalize on that browsing collection to expand the selections that they want to point out to their patrons.

CONCLUSION

Floating is fast becoming a widely accepted best practice in many library systems across the United States and Canada. This popularity is due largely to two outcomes that floating produces: saving money and refreshing the collection, and increasing circulation. Floating lowers the cost of delivery because items are not returned to an owning location. For the same reason, it saves time and labor costs at circulation and shipping. Collection development can get more mileage out of popular titles because items do not spend down time on a delivery truck, but go out immediately to a new patron from wherever they have landed. Patrons love browsing the refreshed collections, and that is reflected in circulation.

But floating brings challenges and problems that become a permanent workflow issue. Floating materials will accrue unevenly at branches with high call-in and drop-off rates. Other branches where the book return is difficult to use, or that are farther off highly traveled routes, will lose more books to the float than they will accrue. This imbalance will become a constant issue for librarians at both extremes of the floating continuum as they work harder to have a balanced collection to offer their patrons.

Many library systems have opted for the best of both worlds by floating only a portion of their collection, often popular best sellers, movies, and music. Others include adult fiction. Many with large research collections at the main branch float everything except the main collection. No matter what the choice, frequent and two-way communication with all staff is critical to a successful float with the fewest possible negative outcomes.

Preparing for floating by having a well-weeded collection that is shelved in a timely fashion lessens the severity of collection issues created by floating. Impact can be predicted pretty accurately by monitoring traffic, and looking at the book drops and hold shelves. Once floating has launched, the imbalance in the collection has to be addressed. There is no single method to address this, but some kind of central oversight is ideal to maximize opportunities for getting the most out of materials, and because the busier branches will need a hand with rebalancing. There is no magic bullet for rebalancing, and librarians must stay open to the realization that they may have to change their approach to it from time to time as the collection demands will change. And remember, the fewer parts of the collection that float, the less rebalancing will rear its ugly head!

Once floating is underway, patrons will find new materials, which will enjoy a new life in a new setting. Librarians will also see the collection begin to change over time as materials float in and out, and will be able to add even more titles to the repertoire with which they help patrons. Browsing collections, particularly of new materials, movies, and music, thrive. Best of all, savings of delivery, labor, and material costs mean more money is available for administrators to infuse into other critical services. And if the library's budget situation is not in desperate straits, a mixed floating or nonfloating collection is often just the ticket to wake up and revitalize a traditionally housed collection.

SUGGESTED READING

Bartlett, Wendy K. 2013. *Floating Collections: A Collection Development Model for Long-Term Success*. Santa Barbara, CA: Libraries Unlimited.

Cress, Ann. 2004. "The Latest Wave." *Library Journal* 129 (16): 48–50.

Hilyard, Nann Blaine, ed. 2012. "Take the Plunge! Implementing Floating Collections in Your Library System." *Public Libraries* 51 (3): 13–20.

25

BEYOND MY PEOPLE AND THY PEOPLE, OR THE SHARED PRINT COLLECTIONS IMPERATIVE

Robert H. Kieft

As I began this chapter in the summer of 2012, a drama was playing out on Bryant Park.[1] It was a real-world, if not reality, show presided over by iconic lions, and it involved, for those viewers in the academic library collections business,[2] a by-now familiar cast of characters, plot elements, and dialogue, complete with *tirades* from important actors, production numbers for protesters, and a panoply of Brechtian commentary on the action from the press, bloggers, and miscellaneous fulminators and apologists. It potentially pitted the interests of some library users against those of others, rested on mission-shaping questions of asset allocation, and surfaced decisions informed by technological and resource-based change.

The script concerned plans announced by its president, staff, and board to send more of the New York Public Library's (NYPL) research collection to, from the point of view of Manhattanites, the desolate, remote, and savage plains of New Jersey and a facility operated, but not a collection held jointly, by NYPL and Columbia and Princeton universities. The collective protagonist Administration would then redevelop the space vacated by books for other traditional library functions taken into the leonine 42nd Street building from two buildings NYPL proposed to sell in order to support its research functions. This drama is emblematic of the tensions surrounding print collections on college and university campuses and particularly concerns itself with disputes over the allocation and functions of library space, disputes that not only reveal the needs, work practices, preferences, and turfs of different populations, but also a particular and powerful presence with which books, physical books, have become invested. Moreover, this very mythology of presence implicates the ethical status printed books enjoy as bearers of knowledge and identity and the workflows, interests, and cultures that surround them. The place of physical books in the future of libraries also evokes for many readers a larger set of tensions induced by the massive cultural shifts underway among the institutions of knowledge creation, publication, dissemination, use, and preservation, not to mention entertainment, communication, and community formation, in the wake of the 20-year commercial exploitation of the World Wide Web.

Libraries are what they collect, are they not? To think of a library is to think of what's on the shelf. The collection so conditions the connotations of library that from both popular and scholarly perspectives a library is institutionally as well as etymologically nonsensical without those shelves of books. Indeed, the commonsense connotation of library, especially of academic library, is stacks, endless and hushed stacks of books, the sounds of pages turning at remote desks hidden away among the ranges or at reading tables in well-proportioned, imperially high and preferably coffered-ceilinged rooms, the silence punctuated only by the occasional sneeze, whispered piece of advice, or, these days, the ring of a rogue phone.

Today, as the NYPL example demonstrates, common sense is tense with change in the service and materials interests of various groups with their several traditions of building use and their respective work practices and schedules: witness the complaints about lack of quiet space or the merry sounds of barely suppressed laughter among students working together, the conflicts about electronic versus print materials, open-stack versus remote high-density shelving, owned materials versus leased or borrowed, computers and cafes versus books. Academic libraries are adjusting with varying degrees of urgency and with emphases that depend on their local circumstances and mission to new information and education environments, and they are doing so in many aspects of their work by collaborating more closely than heretofore, deepening their dependence on other libraries and indeed restructuring their work strategically through these partnerships.[3] The shift for many libraries from retention on campus shelves to retention in off-site facilities is vexed enough, as is the case at NYPL; divesting of print volumes, especially of monographs, in favor of electronic or partnered, remote access falls for many readers and researchers on a continuum from worrisome to crazy. In a fundamental sense, academic librarians are rethinking the role of the local, open-stack collection—the very thing whose definition, composition, and service have constituted the idea of library—as libraries adjust to the several pressures and opportunities confronting them and as issues of the local versus shared approach to collections and materials management come to the fore. As libraries move beyond resource sharing to shared print[4] or, better, as resource sharing becomes shared print and as the materials to which libraries give access are increasingly electronic, librarians are asking questions about what in fact constitutes a local collection these days.

THE ELEMENTS OF COLLECTION DEVELOPMENT AND MANAGEMENT IN CHANGING TIMES

Since the chapters in this book propose to account for and contribute to the current rethinking of collections, my treatment of shared print begins with the traditions of collection development and management as they have been codified by textbooks and, presumably, as evidenced by their bibliographies, in the practices of local libraries.[5] As librarians have come to understand them, the activities and practices of collection development and management proceed from the assumption that the gathering, organization, and preservation of a group of materials are specific to an institutional context. For libraries in higher education, the mission and curriculum of the parent institution, the pedagogies its faculty employ, the kind of work it asks its students to complete, the programs and degrees it offers, the degree to which it emphasizes research, and the students it enrolls determine the kinds, provenance, and formats of materials the library collects, that is, owns and places on a shelf or a server or otherwise gives access to. These same institutional circumstances inform the depth and breadth of a library's collecting efforts, the criteria it applies to decisions to retain items, and the position it takes among other collections and in partnerships.

Whether understood as a prescriptive or self-study document, the collection development policy written by library staff and vetted with their constituents codifies an understanding of the library's place in the institution and in most cases explicitly states how the library identifies and procures materials, budgets for its collecting and preservation activities, gains knowledge of the needs of its constituents, analyses and makes decisions about the collections, staffs its collecting activities, houses materials, and relies on means other than purchase or subscription to provide materials to its users. These policy elements in turn imply, even if they do not explicitly name, a host of such other aspects of the library as user infrastructure (signage, circulation rules, communication lines, advisory services, space allocation), interpretation and promotion of collections, information systems for discovery of and access to materials, the quality and content of data about materials, staff roles and expertise, the creation and dissemination of knowledge, the legal and commercial relationships entailed by the processes of knowledge creation and dissemination, and, bringing the policy back to its reason for being, the mechanisms or criteria employed to assess the success of the library's contribution to the fulfillment of its parent institution's mission.

The library in its materials-provision dimension may function in a complex of such extra-institutional organizations as publishers, vendors, information systems, other libraries, and consortia, but its existence depends on and serves above all else the interests of the students and faculty, alumni, and citizens who constitute its parent institution's community. Elaborated and justified as the reasons for its collecting role have been by generations of how-to and best-practices advice and by reflection on how the tenets and traditions of collection development and management adjust to changing circumstances and contexts; the library's status as a local enterprise charged with the gathering and guardianship of (print) materials has become a cornerstone of librarians' sense of their professional identity.

The body of thought and experience that defines this collection development tradition incorporates, nonetheless, and contrary to the primacy of the local, the sense of a library's being a node in a network, one among many beasts inhabiting the ecosystem of the information jungle. The history and literature of cooperative collecting and interlibrary materials provision dates from the inception of modern librarianship in the United States in the later 19th century (Johnson, citing Melvil Dewey, 2009, 264; Burgett, Phillips, and Haar, 2004) and ranges from the passive, that is, allowing readers to know what is available elsewhere, to the more active stance of using knowledge of other libraries' holdings to inform local decisions about selection and deselection, to the yet more active, that is, agreeing to build complementary holdings of expensive items or agreeing to gather and house centrally or among partners segments of such bodies of material as newspapers or foreign governmental or commercial publications. Over the years, printed and online information systems and delivery strategies, in tandem with the sheer number of collectable publications and the space and fiscal limits that shape any given library's ability to amass material, have taken the cooperative impulses constitutive of modern librarianship and, in effect, made gathering or otherwise enabling materials access a collective activity.

Again, however, libraries are what they collect, are they not? Local library staff are proud of what they do for their students and faculty, proud to have anticipated reader interests by aggregating material, proud to be able to pull the rabbit of a new or oddball old book out of the hat with a trip to the shelf or the click of a mouse. Local library staff are proud to take care of their own and suspicious of the ability of other libraries' staff to do so; they are wary of entrusting their readers' fate to "that library over there" where, as everyone knows, staff couldn't muster a fully functioning brain or efficient workflow among them. Cooperation on collections may be in the DNA of libraries, but independence is as well. Librarians are, like other members of the species, territorial, hierarchical, and tribal beings, which means that institutional independence, whether grounded in mission, tradition, financial resources, governance and jurisdiction, or size and reputation, conflicts with common interests. At least for print materials, and in spite of their capacity for sharing, librarians will cite geography, delivery time, reader preferences and habits, and concerns about other libraries' commitments to collection management as reasons to gather and retain collections on campus. As the title of this chapter suggests, though, and as the changing information ecology requires, the local is sorely pressed these days to remain so.

A manifold of developments in higher education, publishing, the economy, and communication are prompting libraries to reconsider their several roles—collector, service and workspace provider, node in the network of collecting and cultural heritage institutions, site for learning, builder of academic communities, link in the chain of scholarly communication, and publisher. Per Richard Lanham, the library in its preservation aspect "has always operated with a digital, not a fixed print, logic. Books, the physical books themselves, were incidental to the real library mission, which was the dispersion of knowledge" (Fitzpatrick, 2011, 126, quoting Lanham). Put another way, staff who work in buildings called libraries are in the education business, not the library business, which means that the library and its collection are not the heart of the college, rather, the student–faculty and other learning relationships are. In an information-abundant world, libraries are entertaining, or are being asked to entertain by technological, fiscal, and social change, a series of cultural shifts that question the traditions governing the practices and relationships of gathering and organizing materials. The current age of digital reproduction and delivery severely stresses the concept of local collections as the aggregate or collective becomes the new local. At the very least from the point of view of the new information environment, and controversial though radical sharing of print collections is for many, an individualized collecting effort in a loosely federated, interlibrary-lending support system is insufficient for meeting the needs and expectations of a campus's user base of students and scholars. A library materials environment that emphasizes collective effort (Association of Research Libraries 2012), therefore, proceeds from several trends or assumptions, not the least of which is that convenience of access trumps all for readers (Connaway, Dickey, and Radford 2011). Libraries' readers and researchers want access to as much material as possible as quickly as possible, and the proliferation of information published on the open Web encourages them in this desire. Digitization greatly expands access to and the potential uses of information or text at substantially less cost than that of housing print (Courant and Nielsen 2012). Electronic delivery of journal content is now generally accepted (Schonfeld and Housewright 2009b), while print-on-demand shortens delivery time of remotely accessed text.

The maturation of these trends and circumstances has several consequences for the traditional practices of collection development and management and for the work of staff associated with them. If libraries are what they collect, then such changes to collection programs as those advocated by Atkinson (2005) and Lewis (2013) lead to a different model of library identity, one constituted as a collective, multisubjective entity whose identity is based, for the most part, not on collections, on things, but on relationships. As libraries consider different balances among the items in their service portfolio and as the value of their several assets of space, staff, collections, partnerships and affiliations, commercial relationships changes (Dempsey 2012; Lavoie and Dempsey 2010), the hard truth for many in this new information environment is that the value of the print collection as an asset for study and scholarship is changing relative to the value of other assets. On many campuses the space occupied by less-used print materials housed on open shelves has become more important for other purposes.[6]

TRENDS IN SHARED PRINT: FROM JOURNALS TO MONOGRAPHS

Advocates of shared print make their argument from several propositions. It saves costs of housing low-use older materials in expensive central campus real estate, allows for the reinvestment of that space, and, in the case of new publications, reduces the rate of unnecessarily duplicative collection growth. Especially for librarians concerned about maintaining the record of publication, large-scale collaborative approaches to managing print collections reduce the risk of loss of scarce and unique or even all copies through consortial collection assessments that systematize deaccessioning and retention. Moreover, shared print potentially increases preservation capacity by placing low-use materials in more secure environments, allowing the library community to concentrate preservation efforts on fewer copies, and encouraging greater access through digitization programs that run parallel to materials storage initiatives. Spending less on the maintenance of print collections also enables libraries to shift resources to other services and materials; through the kinds of institutional collaboration required for shared print and its electronic counterparts, libraries can strengthen the foundation for support of scholarship along other inter-institutional dimensions.

Major recent reports from OCLC Research (Lavoie, Malpas, and Shipengrover 2012; Malpas 2009, 2011; Payne 2007) have benchmarked the developing situation with respect to shared print and shared collections management. Other policy- and data-centered papers (Lavoie and Dempsey 2009; Lavoie and Schonfeld 2006; Lavoie, Connaway, and Dempsey 2005; Reilly 2004; Reilly and DesRosiers 2003; Schonfeld and Housewright 2009c), together with planning documents and reports from many consortia and organizations, support the argument for shared print and inform collective strategies that supersede libraries' familiar individual roles for gathering and maintaining the raw materials of scholarship.[7] Particularly as academic libraries and their parent institutions have responded to the technological and fiscal challenges of the past five years, shared print has become an important means for adjusting to local circumstances as new consortia have entered the picture and especially as existing partnerships or consortia based on materials housing, resource sharing, or eResource purchasing have built shared print onto their inter-institutional trust networks. The shared print movement has grown in variety and in the number of program implementations; it has been enlivened by the development of consulting practices and a community of interest, a rapidly diversifying multiplication of conference sessions and Webinars, and the establishment of an informal discussion group that meets at each ALA Conference under the auspices of the CRL (Kieft and Reilly 2009). Shared print has arrived at a point, in other words, where thinking about and incentives for it are sufficiently mature and abundant, and models for shared print agreements sufficiently numerous and well developed that groups of libraries may draw on a body of knowledge and experience to develop their own approach.[8]

THE CASE OF JOURNALS

In the past 5–10 years, the evolving practice of shared print librarianship has concerned itself largely with journal collections in regional configurations or state systems. In many cases, these journal programs rely on a decentralized housing model that promises long-term but not perpetual preservation of materials in access-oriented light archives with libraries absorbing their own costs of processing or donation and with relatively small amounts of money changing hands (Kieft and Payne 2012).[9] Such consortia as the Western Regional Storage Trust (WEST) (Stambaugh 2010) have thus adopted a pragmatic, lightweight approach, doing what they can relatively quickly with materials in place and setting a retention period at once long enough to satisfy conservatives and not so long as to impair the ability of partners to adjust archiving commitments. By the same token, keeping the lights on in the archive, relying on existing consortial resource-sharing or ILL protocols for access, and specifying exit requirements, these consortia have reduced the likelihood that an already complex planning process will bog down in persuading members to deposit items in a dark archive (and all that entails for designating service copies), or in creating new workflows and funding streams. In other words, they assemble components ready to hand rather than build something completely new.

In that such prominent examples of shared housing facilities[10] as the Five Colleges of Massachusetts, Washington Research Libraries Consortium (WRLC), and the Research Collections and Preservation Consortium (ReCAP) were designed for geographically proximate institutions, such distributed journal programs as WEST's (100+ members in 17 states), Association of Southeastern Research Libraries' (ASERL; 40 members in 11 states), and Committee on Institutional Cooperation's (CIC: 13 members in 9 states) expand the collective housing model to very large territories. Existing journal archiving projects also exhibit some tendency to consolidate and achieve extra-regional reach, for example, the members of the Consortium of Academic and Research Libraries in Illinois (CARLI) joining en masse in 2011 as affiliates of the Five College Depository for access to back files of journals collected there, or the partnership of ASERL and WRLC for journal archives.[11] In addition to geographical expansion, the past few years have witnessed the development of new organizational relationships for preserving and serving print collections, for example, that between the Linda Hall Library and CRL for scientific journals.[12]

Vital to all shared print programs, whether distributed or centralized and whatever the terms of or parties to their founding, are the emerging tools and services that enable individual and consortial collection management decisions based on an understanding of the composition, status, and use of titles in collections. For journal archiving projects, ASERL and CIC are using local methods for comparing holdings, assigning archiving responsibilities, and calling for volumes to complete archives. WEST ingests member holdings and uses Print Archives Preservation Registry (PAPR) (see later in this chapter) to process them into assignments for archiving and to identify members that have volumes to fill in holdings gaps. Chief among the new tools available is Sustainable Collections Services' (SCS) actionable collection intelligence analysis program for monographs. SCS has made rapid strides in the past couple of years in helping libraries and groups of libraries, including several of the monographic projects mentioned later, understand their collections and the potential for joint management of them with a variety of comparisons using holdings and circulation data supplied by libraries in conjunction with holdings data extracted from the WorldCat database. OCLC also promises a new version of its long-available and clumsy WorldCat Collection Analysis tool in 2013.[13]

In addition to being able to analyze holdings and use data, shared print agreements depend on specifying and disclosing the retention status and, ideally, condition of items in the shared collection so that partners as well as other libraries and consortia can deselect local materials in favor of the shared copies as they deem advisable. To meet this need, OCLC conducted a Print Archives Disclosure Pilot beginning in 2010. In 2012, it released a final report with draft metadata standards for the MARC 583 field, a preservation data dictionary patterned after the existing Preservation and Digitization Action term list, and resource-sharing test scenarios (OCLC 2012). In addition to this report and the practices it recommends, OCLC has established a staffed shared print management program for its members.[14] Beyond the print archiving data standards that OCLC is building into WorldCat, CRL has developed the searchable PAPR knowledgebase to support "archiving and management of serial collections by providing comprehensive information about titles, holdings, and archiving terms and conditions of major print archiving programs."[15] CRL's system thus not only includes retention and preservation data but also information about the consortial arrangements under which materials are kept. These two means for recording and disclosing archiving commitments contribute important decision-making tools for libraries as they shape local and regional collections under shared print agreements; they therefore serve as important building blocks of the developing community of interest and infrastructure of tools for shared print.

The Road from Journals to Books[16]

If work on journals has dominated the contemporary shared print agenda, projects for other classes of materials and in additional configurations of libraries expand the scale and scope of shared print activity, develop different cost-sharing options, and consider alternative means for sharing responsibility for the retention or purchase of print materials. Projects within and beyond consortia working on journals have taken, for example, a domain-based approach. With funding from the Andrew W. Mellon Foundation, CRL, in partnership with relevant national libraries and major collections, has undertaken collection preservation and access programs for agriculture[17] and law[18] materials. The area of U.S. government documents is ripe for shared print treatment in that a network of libraries is in place, collections are large and highly duplicative at the regional level, and digital versions exist or could be produced under such arrangements as those of the CIC with Google.[19] As discussions continue about the future of the Federal Depository Library Program and its retention rules,[20] a shared-print step in the direction of a different retention model for historical documents has been taken by ASERL with the establishment of a Collaborative Federal Depository Program,[21] which creates comprehensive collections of federal agency publications in Centers of Excellence throughout ASERL's region.

As journal sharing and other projects gain momentum, consortia are also turning their attention to monographs, which present the greatest challenges to shared print for a complex of reasons, not least because of their sheer number and the trivial amount of shelf-space gained per disposition decision (Kieft and Payne 2011). Local as opposed to collective sensibilities about books, the difficulty of easily gathering and using data about holdings and circulation, and the lack of business models for large-scale retention and serving of monographs, together with a corollary uncertainty about how many copies are needed to serve foreseeable demand, are significant impediments to program development. Sorting out roles among libraries for preserving copies and the shadow cast by e-text use experience, sales models for eBooks, and lack of full-text access to digitized orphan and in-copyright books also contribute their fair share of discouragement to the prospects for shared monograph collections.

Important though these financial, legal, and governance issues are, even more important are the affective dimensions of monographic shared print. Many librarians and faculty feel a sense of loss in what they see as the implicit devaluing of books in any program that draws down local, open-shelf print in favor of off-site housing or partnered access; they feel that (mere) administrators are forcing them to change their work practices and preferences, or even violating them, and are slighting their discipline by reducing its physical representation on the open shelves. Reading, teaching, and learning practices and text-use preferences are acutely in question in the monographic case, as is the place that print has come to occupy in culture generally and more specifically in the elaboration of library collections and services.

In addition to the controversy that surrounds books and reading, then, the monographic case exaggerates all the challenges that obtain in journal or domain-based shared print agreements. No recipe exists for making monographic shared print work, whether for older or new materials, print or electronic books, but several projects are bringing the requisite ingredients coherently together. Two stand out at this point, namely, the IMLS-funded Maine Shared Collections Strategy (MSCS),[22] which involves two public library systems and six public and private colleges and universities, and the Midwest Collaborative for Library Services' Michigan Shared Print Initiative (MCLS MI-SPI),[23] which involves nine publicly funded universities, including one ARL. MSCS' project began in 2010 and MI-SPI's in 2011; collection analysis and related consulting by SCS inform them. Both projects focus on identification and retention of a body of materials for 15 years, and both agree to retain those volumes in open or storage stacks under customary inventory control methods and the exercise of local preservation practices. Both factor into retention decisions parameters for acquisition date, recorded use, and the availability of the title elsewhere in the country. Neither places onerous burdens on participants, with the Michigan project's MOU emphasizing local library autonomy more often. Neither makes withdrawing from the agreement or deaccessioning retained volumes particularly difficult, and both rely on participant good faith and flexibility in maintaining the agreement as circumstances change.

The projects diverge, however, in the matter of identifying copies for retention. The Maine project focuses on unique and scarcely held titles and does not foresee, although it does not preclude, deselecting nonretained copies during its three-year course; moreover, as of May 2013, MSCS has yet to decide how to approach the roughly 2 million title-holdings with more than the (up to) two copies they want to retain. The Michigan project starts, conversely, by identifying titles with more than two copies that meet its deselection criteria. In other words, MI-SPI assumes from the beginning that libraries may divest of any copies beyond the two designated as retained in order to enable space reallocation, and it excluded from consideration copies uniquely held.

Both projects address older materials, but Michigan starts with the commonly held and unused and Maine with the scarce or unique. They are thus well down the road to retention commitments and deselection-based space management. Other consortia are at earlier stages. The six Los Angeles–based California state universities are in receipt of a collection analysis from SCS as an aspect of the work of the system-wide Libraries of the Future Taskforce (LOFT); they expect in 2013 to come to conclusions about shared print based on it.[24] Elsewhere, SCS is supplying an analysis and working on retention scenario development with 12 members of the ConnectNY group,[25] and in-process monographic collection analyses undertaken by the Greater Western Library Alliance (GWLA)[26] and the Council of Plains and Pacific University Libraries (COPPUL)[27] are contending with effectively using large OCLC-generated holdings data sets. Beyond these projects that are operational or are at the data gathering and review stages, several others are incipient. Beginning in the summer of 2012, Five Colleges of Massachusetts have served as the convener of discussions that may lead, with the encouragement of a grant from the Andrew W. Mellon Foundation received in the late winter of 2013, to the creation of a Northeast Regional Depository (NERD) (Five Colleges of Massachusetts 2012). They are launching a feasibility study to gauge interest among libraries in New England and are undertaking a research agenda that seeks to answer such questions about monograph archiving as how to qualify the differences among or uniqueness of copies, how many copies to keep, how to coordinate retention at different locations, how light the archive can be, what the right delivery time is, and how NERD would fit into the national or international picture.[28] Discussion is also beginning in California among representatives of the several segments of the academic library community about whether a regional approach to monographs might develop based on OCLC's mega-regions model, existing resource-sharing consortia, and collection studies undertaken by individual systems and groups.

The projects and initiatives discussed here begin to manifest a typical sequence, set of components, or decision points from which best practices are emerging. On the whole, it seems that where there is a history of resource sharing, reinforced by shared or linked library information systems, eResource purchasing, and rapid materials delivery, libraries find greater potential for collaboration on or federation of collections new and old. Conversely, in states or regions that lack a well-developed user-initiated system for resource-sharing or where, unlike the case of Minitex and the University of Minnesota, an ARL library in the state does not see its mission as including regional leadership for collections initiatives, colleges cite such absences to explain why they cannot think seriously about collaborative collections activities.[29] In cases where a consortium chooses to build a shared print program as an extension of their resource-sharing experience, partners start with a collection composition and use study so that members may understand the number of titles, items, and holdings overlaps in the partnership, the partnership's holdings with respect to those in specific other partnerships or geographical groups or in digitized collections, and an approximation of aggregate demand based on circulation history over the number of copies in the partnership. This analysis typically reveals a host of cataloging and record-matching anomalies that partners need to address in order to create greater confidence in the integrity of the data on which their retention commitments will rest. As a project develops toward recording and displaying retention commitments, it may also engage in systems development with the vendors of local and regional catalogs and OCLC so that the requisite data is adequately displayed as it moves among them.

In the case of journals, retention and archiving decisions are based on risk analysis (WEST), title (CIC), or nomination (ASERL). Only the first of these is practical for monographs in one of two ways, first, by assuming that uniquely held or scarce titles are at high risk and retaining them is therefore important for maintaining diversity in the knowledge ecosystem or, second, by assuming that for commonly held titles the risk of reducing the number of copies is low because the retained copies will be able to meet foreseeable demand. Whichever their focus, though, current projects appear to assume that (up to) two copies are sufficient when circulation is very low over a substantial period of time.[30] Thus far, Maine's is the first project for monographs that is registering a large number of retention commitments using newly created OCLC holdings symbols for shared print, although in the spring of 2013 ReCAP also decided to declare 5 million of the volumes held there as shared.[31]

Partners record their commitments in an MOU that defines the relationships among them, a governance structure, and decision-making protocols, exit clauses, and retention and agreement-review periods. In addition to relying on the relatively lightweight policy requirements in such MOUs as those of MSCS and MI-SPI that specify a 15-year retention commitment and do not demand item validation at the time of retention commitment, shared print agreements have tried to keep participation costs low through asking libraries to fund internally the costs of deselection and shipping of materials to archivers or through distribution of archiving responsibilities among member libraries that have already paid or in any case would have paid at least some of the costs of facilities construction and of processing and validating archived publications. In the WEST and CIC journal projects, for example, relatively small membership fees pay some of the costs for collection analysis services, for supporting the creation of archives, or for ongoing compensation to the archiving site for space use. The Five Colleges of Massachusetts charge an affiliate membership fee to libraries that want to rely on access to the journals they have archived, and HathiTrust foresees instituting a member fee to support the long-term storage costs that libraries which house monographs for its prospective Distributed Print Monographs Archive will incur. These relatively low-cost methods for participant support of journal projects have worked as projects are achieving early stability, but, given the cost of buildings, projects are well advised in the early stages to consider options for declaring materials already housed in storage as the base shared collection as ReCAP is doing and as WEST did with journals already held in Orbis Cascade's Distributed Print Repository and in the University of California system.

A major condition of possibility for large-scale collaboration on older monographs is the availability of a digital library that allows readers to perform many of the text-use functions that have in the past required printed books, for, if nothing else, the use of digitized text eliminates the need for some shipping of materials among partners. The replacement of print with e-text is controversial on several grounds,[32] but shared print agreements, as well as individual libraries, find it attractive to depend for public domain texts on digitized versions as they deaccession them or retain as a group a single copy. Shared print partnerships can certainly retain or deaccession large numbers of monographs without resort to digital surrogates on the assumption that less-used titles will continue to experience low use and can be delivered as needed to readers. The availability of e-text, however, just as certainly conditions the perceived role of print books and the demand for them. Such statements as "It's all on the Web, so why do we need libraries?" betray at the very least an incomplete understanding of what's on the Web and what libraries do, but in some quarters librarians and readers have to make an argument for retaining print at all these days. In that the demand for print will decline and the decline itself will affect the willingness of institutions to fund its retention; the rationales for print retention and business models for serving print have to account for and include electronic collections.

The approval by the members of HathiTrust in 2011 of a proposal to plan a Distributed Print Monographs Archive, in which "a group of print storage repositories will assume formal curatorial responsibilities for volumes that have a corresponding digital representation in HathiTrust's collection," is extremely important in this regard if only because OCLC Research has determined that approximately 33 percent and growing of any given academic library's print collection matches digitized copies in HathiTrust and 31 percent of Hathi's digitized texts are in the public domain (Malpas 2011). Members have not yet acted on this proposal; given, however, the distribution of Hathi's membership across the country and the size and importance of their print collections, given, too, the possibility that Hathi's millions of books could become a generally accessible digital library under an access agreement between rights holders and libraries, a Hathi-based archive of print would lend invaluable support to a national alignment of collections of print monographs.

Monographs and the End Result?

In summary, these projects for print titles are working on aspects of an ideal or facilitator state for monographic shared print in which,

- interoperable library information systems and data enable (1) accurate and easily actionable holdings and materials-use comparisons for judging aggregate traffic and demand, (2) consistent and clear communication about item condition and archiving status, and (3) user-initiated borrowing within and potentially across current groups and systems;
- a materials housing program combines archiving off-site and in place in both small and large repositories; in other words, a program creates a network of housing nodes based on natural or current alignments, a several-to-many cooperative;
- collectively funded and governed arrangements allow libraries to retain and serve scarce and unique copies and to serve as libraries of last resort, coupled with an understanding of how many partners or how large a collective collection needs to be in order to meet demand;

- an archiving collaborative balances current access with long-term preservation of copies and is nuanced enough as to allow for the changing needs of individual libraries; and
- linking digitized texts from the catalog, a digitization program, or including digitized texts in discovery services provides access without physical delivery.

The most important task before shared print programs, especially those for monographs and as suggested by the foregoing, is the development of business models that will allow some libraries to retain and serve the shared copies. Shared print projects may well predicate themselves on the existence of information and delivery systems that enable readers to easily discover, locate, request, and receive items from partners, but, as the Maine and Michigan projects make clear and as the NERD grant and incipient discussions in California are assuming, the success of shared print will depend on those libraries that will commit to playing the archiving role. As OCLC's several analyses of WorldCat holdings and SCS's more local studies show, all libraries have unusual or unique items that could be worth retaining; a relatively small number of libraries, however, can collaborate on archiving them for shared print agreements. In the past, the library community has relied on an informal or tacit understanding of the roles of college, research, public, and special libraries in preserving materials. Those roles and the relationships they define are probably still in place, but for shared print they must achieve a level of formality they have not heretofore enjoyed. As shared print formalizes libraries' collective roles, archiving libraries will need support from the library community on whose behalf they play the archival role, whether that support comes in the form of donation of materials under last- or scarce-copy policies, a fee for ingest, transaction fees for borrowing, or an annual membership charge like CRL's that funds the repository function. Shared print partnerships will have to contribute to the cost of building and maintaining the archive of retained copies in ways that give the host library more than the satisfaction of being a good citizen, and those costs are going to look like new money to libraries that divest of print in favor of depending on shared access.

The major hurdle to leap, then, in terms of the business of shared print under the roof of an increasingly digital library is less that of placing a price on the collective responsibility for maintaining the shared collection than it is of creating value from maintaining large collections of low-use items. Having made the argument locally that a library need not retain low-use materials on campus, the shared print librarian must turn around to argue for his or her library's helping fund a collective effort to do just that. Addressing the issues of inventory size and control will help that argument, but the argument for bearing the costs of collaborating on building and maintaining print archives, of recording and disclosing useful data about them, and potentially of creating digital versions of those texts has to be grounded in libraries' collective stewardship role for the record of publication and the way in which that record enables study, scholarship, and teaching. Shared print librarianship has much to do to develop business models for an environment where the number of copies is decreasing and the remaining copies concentrate in fewer libraries; the cost of serving those copies should decrease as the demand for print declines, but that decline will put all the more pressure on the shared print partnership to justify the costs of maintaining the archive.

At this point, it appears that shared print and the conditions required by shared print agreements will not result from designing a systematic, directed, or planned national-level program but from an additive, ad hoc series of local and regional projects proceeding on the same general precepts and values with respect to library collections. The virtue of this approach is, of course, its reliance on existing partnerships and it's not requiring the level of organization that a national approach would; that a national program will emerge from a series of local and regional programs conscious of each other is, moreover, consonant with the mosaic of jurisdictions, consortia, library systems, and partnerships that constitute the U.S. library community. In fact, the presence among local and regional projects of such funders as the Andrew W. Mellon Foundation and the IMLS, such research groups as OCLC and Ithaka S + R, such consultants as Samuel Demas, Lizanne Payne, and SCS, and such (overlapping) membership organizations as ARL, CLIR, CRL, and OCLC may well create a sufficiently integrated environment for communication and joint activity that the sum of local and regional projects will become a reasonably coherent national program in less time and with less effort than would be the case if libraries attempted to create an overarching national structure.

CONCLUSION

From all reports, marriage is a relatively easy status to attain but difficult, even arduous, to maintain successfully. In the case of libraries and their parent institutions, however, the contrary may be closer to the truth, for, unlike human beings, they never enter relationships willy-nilly as a Las Vegas lark, or for lack of anything better to do, and in no known cases at the wrong end of a shotgun in anticipation of the arrival of ill-timed offspring. Rather, like royal houses and empires, they enter into marriages grounded in equal parts guardedness and calculation of mutual territorial or dynastic advantage. In spite of the often-cited impediments to collections collaboration (Burgett et al. 2004, ch. 2), libraries have flirted since the beginning with professions of common interest, gone steady through a century of resource sharing, and shacked up in shared collections and facilities. The ways in which libraries and the colleges and universities that house them have heretofore in the world of print gained individual status among their kin have militated against the kinds of deep cooperation, even willed dependency, that economic and cultural forces abroad

today are encouraging. Since love is not the question, except perhaps for readers meeting in the stacks or cafe, the relationships articulated by the Janus
Agenda (Atkinson 2005), a host of MOU pre-nups, and the much-heralded
2CUL banns of Cornell and Columbia Universities are reconceiving funding
and institutional prestige on a very different, committed ground.

The topics that animate shared print discussions and the goals that define
the projects mentioned here at once mimic long-standing arrangements and
patterns and require new approaches to them. Although the sense of what a
library is remains local for many users and librarians, an appealing, if not universally agreeable, vision for shared print has evolved. The projects invoked
here make the case for shared print in its many dimensions and suggest the
contours of a collective future for print collections as programs take shape in
many parts of the country and among a variety of partnerships. In manifesting
a tendency to geographical expansion and toward interregional cooperation,
the evidence suggests an emergent national structure and an understanding of
the scale at which shared print can achieve critical mass. In the near future,
one size, one collection, could well fit all. Even if, and especially if, one thinks
"we are all weird," as collection analyses tend to indicate in terms of holdings
of unique items, the universal library of digitized and collectively archived
print text will level many of the distinctions among libraries in higher education, digital divides notwithstanding.

The collaborative futures adumbrated by the new civil unions among libraries affect all aspects of their relationships to each other and the roles they play
in the world. Those suggested by OCLC Research's proposed reexamination
of the library service bundle (Dempsey 2012; Lavoie and Dempsey 2010), by
Lewis for a new collections regime in 2020 (2013), and by the present author
and Payne (2012) for an "ideal state" of the print collections system in the
2020s are now becoming or soon will become concrete for a library community in which the tasks of collections staff will orient toward the collective
or network of users and materials more than to the local campus. The research and modeling published in OCLC's "Print Collections at Mega-Scale"
(Lavoie, Malpas, and Shipengrover 2012) provide a framework that enables
libraries to understand the regional and national implications of print holdings management and opens the way to establishing a more coherent program
than libraries now have for collective decision making, developing the bibliographic data needed for shared collections management, creating local and
regional collections policies that look beyond the present to the long term,
and communicating a narrative about the value of collections collaboration
for library constituencies.

Not all the lions guarding NYPL's imposing Fifth Avenue entrance may
soon lie down with the lambs of ReCAP in central Jersey, and libraries and
their consortia will continue to experience conflict as the largely local print
library gives way to the largely distributed print and electronic library. On the
way from resource sharing to shared print, librarians are finding their way

through many and dynamic uncertainties as they flesh out the ways and means for developing the shared collections inventory, a process involving substantial risk taking, experimentation with processes and relationships, research and data modeling projects, and cooperation not only among librarians but also the consortial groups, vendors, funding agencies, and service providers with whom they work. Shared print is the inevitable evolutionary outcome, however, of century-old programs of cooperative collection building and interlibrary lending as readers and researchers take advantage of new means for accessing and using the materials they need for their work. Shared print, together with such collective enterprises as CLOCKSS, HathiTrust, Digital Public Library of America, and the Digital Preservation Network, exemplifies the traditions of library cooperation as cooperatives become a true network, a system of mutual dependencies and potentials that makes sense of the endlessly proliferating similitude and differences among libraries. Although not easily and not until the library community and the organizations that fund it develop information and data systems and a sense of common purpose that dissolves some of the boundaries among current jurisdictions, shared print enables libraries collectively to ensure the availability of print publications in a systematic and orderly way. In a shared print environment, the collective becomes the local and the local the collective.

NOTES

1. Thanks to Victoria Steele, Brooke Russell Astor Director of Collections Strategy at the New York Public Library, for sharing her knowledge of the plans at NYPL. This chapter is especially indebted to Constance Malpas, Lizanne Payne, and Emily Stambaugh; colleagues in the Maine Shared Collections Strategy; and the many librarians and consortial staff who have participated in the Print Archiving Community Forum at ALA these past four years. The chapter discusses a number of recent projects; it does not cover, let alone do bibliographic justice to, the many other projects, influences, and published or presented work that have laid the foundation and provide context for them.

2. The chapter concerns academic library collection practices and the reconfiguration they are undergoing. Except in the Maine Shared Collections Strategy and in the Minnesota Library Access Center (MLAC), public libraries have not played a role in shared print agreements, but see the "Conclusions" drawn by Lavoie, Malpas, and Shipengrover (2012) for discussion of the importance of their holdings in the collective collections picture.

3. See the case made for libraries becoming a collective institution in Council on Library and Information Resources (2008, "Introduction"); Association of Research Libraries (2012); Demas and Lougee (2011); Gherman (2007); Kenney (2009); and Kenney (2012).

4. According to Kieft and Payne (2012), "A 'shared print' agreement (also called 'print archives' or 'shared collection management') is a formal program in which multiple libraries coordinate long-term retention of print materials and related services by one or more participants to support preservation and allow space recovery among campus collections. A 'shared print agreement' is not the same as a shared storage facility. Rather, it is characterized by an explicit commitment to retain materials for a specified time period (or indefinitely) in potentially multiple locations by multiple partners."

5. See Johnson (2009) and Evans and Saponaro (2012), textbook summae of the field that treat an array of historical, institutional, organizational, environmental, staffing, business, and procedural topics.

6. Today, the primary texts and practices of libraries' collecting role are being rewritten, even though to many librarians, faculty, and students that rewriting is controversial. The case for onsite, open-shelf access has been made most strongly by Andrew Abbott, University of Chicago, whose views on the scholar's need for very quick access to a large and heterogeneous corpus of sources were instrumental in the planning for the University's Mansueto Library (Abbott 2006, 2008). Conflicts over the downsizing or off-site housing of large portions of the print collection at Ohio State University (*Chronicle of Higher Education*, September 1, 2006, May 13, 2009), California State Polytechnic University, Pomona (*Chronicle of Higher Education*, July 10, 2007), Syracuse University (*Chronicle of Higher Education*, November 11, 2009), and Augustana College (*Chronicle of Higher Education*, July 25, 2011) reveal, as does the conflict at NYPL, assumptions about the role of the library and how the location of library print collections affects the work practices of readers. See also John M. Budd's discussion of physical collections and the role of their materiality in scholarly communication in his chapter, "The Collection(s)" (2012). In addition to these cases for maintaining open-stack, on-campus collections of printed works, especially of monographs, such writers as Carr (2010) make a case for print based on issues of cognition and the effects on learning of using networked devices and electronic text; Jabr (2013) summarizes the scientific literature on page and screen reading.

7. Interlibrary lending and resource-sharing programs have always positioned libraries as each other's off-site collection-housing facilities through a de facto distributed or decentralized model of archiving. Moreover, the establishment of CRL in 1949, the creation of such materials partnerships as those of the Triangle Research Libraries in the 1930s, and the implementation of the Farmington Plan and PL480 or of the Federal Depository Library System prefigure, as collections cooperatives, current shared print initiatives. Shared print takes such antecedents to higher levels of intensity and a difference in kind, however, by addressing not well-defined groups of specialized materials but garden-variety, general collections volumes.

8. See, for example, the Web site of the Print Archiving Community Forum http://www.crl.edu/archiving-preservation/print-archives/forum for reports on best practices and consortial activities; the record of such preconferences as "Shared Print Archiving: Building the Collective Collection, and a Print Safety Net" held at the Charleston Conference in 2011 at http://www.crl.edu/node/7488, "Shared Print Monographs: Making It Work" at http://sustainablecollections.com/weed-feed/2013/4/3/alcts-shared-print-monographs-preconference-detailed-program.html at ALA Annual in 2013, or the 2012 ALCTS "Local Collections, Collective Context: Managing Print Collections in the Age of Collaboration" at http://www.ala.org/alcts/events/ala/ac/12/collaborationage. See also issue 37 (3–4) (2012) of *Collection Management* at http://www.tandfonline.com/toc/wcol20/37/3-4, which, in addition to reports on specific projects, includes an especially useful essay on collection plans by Demas and Miller (2012). Rick Lugg and Ruth Fischer of Sustainable Collections Services (http://sustainablecollections.com/), which has emerged as an important member of the shared print community with its analysis service, offer a "Why Now" case for deselection and a "Knowledge-base" on matters related to print collections on their Web site as well as news about their projects and conference sessions. Samuel Demas began editing a column in *Against the Grain*, "Curating Collective Collections," in 2011, and Rick Lugg maintains a blog titled "Sample and Hold"

(http://sampleandhold-r2.blogspot.com/); both constitute a compendium of commentary on current issues in print collections management.

9. The CIC journal project mentioned in the following paragraphs operates with a centralized model in which members support a facility operated by Indiana University. It is also important to note the role that grants from the Andrew W. Mellon Foundation have played in the development of PAPR for CRL and WEST and from Mellon and IMLS in other projects involving shared print over the years.

10. See Clement (2012) for a literature review of the development of regional shared print initiatives based in the history of cooperative collection development. In addition to Payne (2007), see Murray-Rust (2005) and Kohl (2003) for historical and synoptic treatment of collaborative materials housing facilities. New purpose-built materials housing facilities continue to appear at individual institutions, for example, Colby College (http://www.colby.edu/colby.mag/issues/63/article/1396/new-storage-facility-to-be-boon-to-colby-libraries/) and the University of Pennsylvania (http://www.library.upenn.edu/libra/), or on behalf of consortia, as is the case with the Florida Academic Repository in Gainesville (see mention in http://lj.libraryjournal.com/2013/04/opinion/editorial/kudos-for-print-archiving/), even as such consortia as WRLC and ReCAP add modules to their facilities. The libraries of the University of California system have discussed building a third Regional Library Facility (RLF), and to delay the arrival of the day when they must do so they have established a nonduplication policy for materials housed in the two existing RLFs. The Orbis Cascade Alliance has yet to be able to fund a long-discussed shared housing project. OhioLink members are deduplicating their five regional housing facilities in an effort to avoid building more of them. It is increasingly unlikely that new collective housing facilities will allow housing of multiple copies, especially of journals.

11. See http://www.aserl.org/wp-content/uploads/2013/02/ASERL-WRLC_Shared_Archive.

12. See http://www.crl.edu/news/8113.

13. See http://www.oclc.org/collection-analysis.en.html and the OCLC presentation linked on the Print Archiving Community Forum under the January 28, 2013, posts from ALA Midwinter, 2013, at http://www.crl.edu/archiving-preservation/print-archives/forum.

14. See http://www.oclc.org/services/projects/shared-print-management.en.html.

15. See http://www.crl.edu/archiving-preservation/print-archives/papr for a full description of the PAPR registry.

16. As several consortia are preparing to manage older, less-used monographs collectively, some are seeking ways to slow the unnecessarily duplicative growth of print collections by reaching agreements on the acquisition of new books and to maintain resource-sharing capacity by developing collectively owned eBooks. Space constraints do not allow consideration of these important dimensions of shared print, nor do they allow consideration of the effects on the collective collection inventory of DDA practices.

17. See http://www.crl.edu/node/7371.

18. See http://www.crl.edu/node/7372.

19. See www.cic.net/Libraries/Library/CICDocumentsFramework.sflb.ashx.

20. See Schonfeld and Housewright (2009a) for an important study of a potential future for the FDLP and Ragains (2010) for a succinct journalistic treatment of the debate about paper-copy retention and digital publication in the FDLP.

21. See http://www.aserl.org/programs/gov-doc/.

22. See http://www.maineinfonet.net/mscs/ for thorough documentation of the grant through its project plan, meeting notes and decisions, conference presentations, and so forth.

23. See http://mlc.lib.mi.us/cms/sitem.cfm/library_tools/mi-spi/ for project documentation, their MOU, and work with SCS.

24. Unpublished report.

25. See http://www.connectny.org/. Fall 2012 Update.

26. See Goals 2 and 3 of the GWLA strategic plan (http://www.gwla.org/strategic2012/Strategic-Plan).

27. See http://www.coppul.ca/projects/SPAN.html for the COPPUL program description; see also their presentation linked on the Print Archiving Community Forum under the January 28, 2013, posts from ALA Midwinter, 2013, at http://www.crl.edu/archiving-preservation/print-archives/forum.

28. Unpublished grant proposal.

29. Unpublished interview and online survey results from 2011 and 2012 by the present author of print collections planning and campus attitudes toward shared collections practices at liberal arts college libraries.

30. Some consortia have set "unnecessary duplicate thresholds" as guidelines for purchase or, by implication, retention of copies, for example, CARLI's five copies for 140+ members in Illinois (http://www.carli.illinois.edu/products-services/collections-management/I-ShareNum-CopiesRe and the Orbis Cascade Alliance's three copies for three dozen members) (see link for November 3, 2010, under Threshold Project at http://www.orbiscascade.org/index/cdmc-current-work). These numbers, along with the retention policies of the several single-copy depositories and Ithaka's work on optimal copies (see, e.g., http://www.crl.edu/sites/default/files/attachments/pages/CRL%20webinar%202012%2001%2010%20Optimal%20Copies.pdf) are suggestive of movement toward, if not a consensus on, the smaller number of copies needed to satisfy collective demand or to archive the record of publication.

31. See presentation, "Shared Print Collections in North America: Going Main Stream and Picking up Steam," by Lizanne Payne, consultant to ReCAP, at the MSCS meeting of May 23, 2013, linked at http://www.maineinfonet.net/mscs/about/presentations/.

32. In addition to reader preferences and practices, dislike of screen reading, device and software deficiencies, lack of shareability, and so forth, scholars make the case against the use of digitized copies based on the artifactual evidence multiple copies of the same printed book can offer for several kinds of history and the inability of one digitized copy to represent variations in production.

REFERENCES

Abbott, Andrew. 2006. "The University Library." Internal report. Available at: http://www.lib.uchicago.edu/e/about/abbott-report.html. Accessed June 1, 2013.

Abbott, Andrew. 2008. "The Traditional Future: A Computation Theory of Library Research." *College and Research Libraries* 69 (6): 524–45.

Association of Research Libraries. 2012. "21st-Century Collections: Calibration of Investment and Collaborative Action." *Issue Brief.* Available at: http://www.arl.org/storage/documents/publications/issue-brief-21st-century-collections-2012.pdf; and http://www.arl.org/bm~doc/21stctfreport_11may12.pdf. Accessed June 1, 2013.

Atkinson, Ross. 2005. "Introduction for the Break-Out Sessions: Six Key Challenges for the Future of Collection Development." White paper. Available at: http://dspace.library.cornell.edu/bitstream/1813/2608/1/Atkinson_Talk.pdf. Accessed June 1, 2013.

Budd, John M. 2012. *The Changing Academic Library: Operations, Cultures, Environments*. 2nd ed. Chicago: ACRL, Publications in Librarianship.

Burgett, James, Linda Lucille Phillips, and John M. Haar. 2004. *Collaborative Collection Development: A Practical Guide for Your Library*. Chicago: ALA Editions.

Carr, Nicholas. 2010. *The Shallows: What the Internet Is Doing to Our Brains*. New York: Norton.

Clement, Susanne K. 2012. "From Collaborative Purchasing towards Collaborative Discarding: The Evolution of the Shared Print Repository." *Collection Management* 37 (3–4): 153–67.

Connaway, Lynn Silipigni, Timothy J. Dickey, and Marie L. Radford. 2011. *If It Is Too Inconvenient, I'm Not Going after It: Convenience as a Critical Factor in Information-Seeking Behavior*. Dublin, OH: OCLC. Available at: http://www.oclc.org/content/dam/research/publications/library/2011/connaway-lisr.pdf. Accessed June 1, 2013.

Council on Library and Information Resources, 2008. *No Brief Candle: Reconceiving Research Libraries for the 21st Century*. Washington, DC: The Council. Available at: http://www.clir.org/pubs/reports/pub142/reports/pub142/pub142.pdf. Accessed June 1, 2013.

Council on Library and Information Resources. 2010. *The Idea of Order: Transforming Research Collections for 21st Century Scholarship*. Washington, DC: The Council. Available at: http://clir.org/pubs/abstract/pub147abst.html. Accessed June 1, 2013.

Courant, Paul, and Matthew "Buzzy" Nielsen. 2010. "On the Cost of Keeping a Book." In *The Idea of Order: Transforming Research Collections for 21st Century Scholarship*, 81–106. Washington, DC: Council on Library and Information Resources.

Demas, Samuel, and Mary E. Miller. 2012. "Rethinking Collection Management Plans: Shaping Collective Collections for the 21st Century." *Collection Management* 37 (3–4): 168–87.

Demas, Samuel, and Wendy Pradt Lougee. 2011. "Shared Print Archiving and Formation of a National Trust: Will Your Campus Participate in a Collective Pint Preservation Strategy?" *Library Issues* 31 (6).

Dempsey, Lorcan. 2012, December 10. "Thirteen Ways of Looking at Libraries, Discovery, and the Catalog: Scale, Workflow, Attention." *Educause Review*. Available at: http://www.educause.edu/ero/article/thirteen-ways-looking-libraries-discovery-and-catalog-scale-workflow-attention. Accessed June 1, 2013.

Evans, G. Edward, and Margaret Zarnosky Saponaro. 2012. *Developing Library and Information Center Collections*. 6th ed. Santa Barbara, CA: Libraries Unlimited.

Fitzpatrick, Kathleen. 2011. *Planned Obsolescence: Publishing, Technology, and the Future of the Academy*. New York: New York University Press.

Five Colleges of Massachusetts. 2012. "Conference: Could the Bunker Be a NERD?" July 21, 2011, Mount Holyoke College. Unpublished Report. Available at: http://legacy.fivecolleges.edu/sites/libraries_council/documents/NERDConfSummary.pdf. Accessed June 1, 2013.

Gherman, Paul. 2007. "The North Atlantic Storage Trust: Maximizing Space, Preserving Collections." *Portal: Libraries and the Academy* 7 (3): 273–75.

Jabr, Ferris. 2013, April 11. "The Reading Brain in the Digital Age: The Science of Paper versus Screens." *Scientific American*. Available at: http://www.scientificamerican.com/article.cfm?id=reading-paper-screens. Accessed June 1, 2013.

Johnson, Peggy. 2009. *Fundamentals of Collection Development and Management*. 2nd ed. Chicago: American Library Association.

Kenney, Anne R. 2009. "Approaching an Entity Crisis: Reconceiving Research Libraries in a Multi-Institutional Context." Presentation, Distinguished Seminar Series, OCLC Research. Available at: http://www.oclc.org/research/dss/ppt/dss_kenney.pdf. Accessed June 1, 2013.

Kenney, Anne R. 2012. "From Product to Process: Collection Development in the 21st Century." Presentation, 2012 International Roundtable for Library and Information Science, Kanazawa Institute of Technology/Council on Library and Information Resources." Available at: http://staffweb.library.cornell.edu/system/files/Tsinghua-Nov%202012_ AnneKenney.pdf. Accessed June 1, 2013.

Kieft, Robert H., and Bernard F. Reilly. 2009. "Regional and National Cooperation on Legacy Print Collections." *Collaborative Librarianship* 1(3): 106–8.

Kieft, Robert H., and Lizanne Payne. 2011. "A Nation-Wide Planning Framework for Large-Scale Collaboration on Legacy Print Monograph Collections." *Collaborative Librarianship* 2 (4): 229–33.

Kieft, Robert H., and Lizanne Payne. 2012. "Collective Collection, Collective Action." *Collection Management* 37 (3–4): 137–52.

Kohl, David F. 2003. "Paper and Digital Repositories in the United States." *Library Quarterly* 13 (3–4): 241–50.

Lavoie, Brian, Constance Malpas, and JD Shipengrover. 2012. *Print Management at 'Mega-Scale': A Regional Perspective on Print Book Collections in North America.* Dublin, OH: OCLC. Available at: http://www.oclc.org/content/dam/research/publications/library/2012/2012-05.pdf. Accessed June 1, 2013.

Lavoie, Brian, and Lorcan Dempsey. 2009. "Beyond 1923: Characteristics of Potentially In-Copyright Print Books in Library Collections." *D-Lib Magazine* 15 (11–12). Available at: www.dlib.org/dlib/november09/lavoie/11lavoie.html. Accessed June 1, 2013.

Lavoie, Brian, and Lorcan Dempsey. 2010. "Rethinking the Boundaries of the Academic Library." *Next Space* 17 (December 15, 16–17). Available at: http://www.oclc.org/publications/nextspace/issues/issue017.en.html. Accessed June 1, 2013.

Lavoie, Brian, Lynn Silipigni Connaway, and Lorcan Dempsey. 2005. "Anatomy of Aggregate Collections: The Example of Google Print for Libraries." *D-Lib Magazine* 11 (9). Available at: http://www.dlib.org/dlib/september05/lavoie/09lavoie.html. Accessed June 1, 2013.

Lavoie, Brian, and Roger Schonfeld. 2006. "Books without Boundaries: A Brief Tour of the System-Wide Print Book Collection." *JEP: The Journal of Electronic Publishing* 9(6): dx.doi.org/10.3998/3336451.0009.208.

Lewis, David W. 2013. "From Stacks to the Web: The Transformation of Academic Library Collecting." *College and Research Libraries* 74 (2): 159–77. Available at: http://crl.acrl.org/search?author1=David+W.+Lewis&sortspec=date&submit=Submit. Accessed June 1, 2013.

Malpas, Constance. 2009. *Shared Print Policy Review Report.* Dublin, OH: OCLC. Available at: www.oclc.org/research/publications/library/2009/2009-03.pdf. Accessed June 1, 2013.

Malpas, Constance. 2011. *Cloud-Sourcing Research Collections: Managing Print in the Mass-Digitized Library Environment.* Dublin, OH: OCLC. Available at: http://www.oclc.org/research/publications/library/2011/2011-01.pdf. Accessed June 1, 2013.

Murray-Rust, Catherine. 2005. "From Failure to Success: Creating Shared Print Repositories." Paper presented at the 12th ACRL National Conference. Available at: http://www

.ala.org/acrl/sites/ala.org.acrl/files/content/conferences/pdf/murrayrust05.pdf. Accessed June 1, 2013.

OCLC. 2012. "OCLC Print Archives Disclosure Pilot Final Report April 2012." Available at: http://www.oclc.org/content/dam/oclc/productworks/OCLCPrintArchivesDisclosure PilotFinalReport.pdf. Accessed June 1, 2013.

Payne, Lizanne. 2007. *Library Storage Facilities and the Future of Print Collections in North America*. Dublin, OH: OCLC. Available at: www.oclc.org/programs/publica tions/reports/2007–01.pdf. Accessed June 1, 2013.

Ragains, Patrick. 2010. "Fixing the Federal Depository Library Program." *American Libraries* 41 (5): 36–38.

Reilly, Bernard F. 2004. "Preserving America's Print Resources: Toward a National Strategic Effort Report on the Planning Day Discussions." *Focus on Global Resources* 24 (1). Available at: www.crl.edu/sites/default/files/attachments/events/PAPReport. pdf. Accessed June 1, 2013.

Reilly, Bernard F., and Barbara DesRosiers. 2003. *Developing Print Repositories: Models for Shared Preservation and Access*. Washington, DC: Council on Library and Information Resources. Available at: www.clir.org/pubs/reports/pub117/contents.html. Accessed June 1, 2013.

Schonfeld, Roger, and Ross Housewright. 2009a. *Documents for a Digital Democracy: A Model for the Federal Depository Library Program in the 21st Century*. New York: Ithaka S+R. Available at: http://www.sr.ithaka.org/research-publications/documents-digital-democracy. Accessed June 1, 2013.

Schonfeld, Roger, and Ross Housewright. 2009b. *U.S Faculty Survey 2009*. New York; Ithaka S + R. Available at: http://www.sr.ithaka.org/research-publications/us-faculty-survey-2009. See also the 2012 survey results. Available at: http://sr.ithaka.org/re search-publications/us-faculty-survey-2012. Accessed June 1, 2013.

Schonfeld, Roger, and Ross Housewright. 2009c. *What to Withdraw? Print Collections Management in the Wake of Digitization*. New York: Ithaka S+R. Available at: http:// www.ithaka.org/ithaka-s-r/research/what-to-withdraw. Accessed June 1, 2013.

Stambaugh, Emily. 2010. "Heading West: Circling the Wagons to Ensure Preservation and Access." *Against the Grain* 22 (5): 18–22.

PART IV

PRESERVATION AND SPECIAL COLLECTIONS

26

Thinking About Collection Development in Special Collections

Steven K. Galbraith

THINKING OF THE FUTURE

Conventional wisdom tells us that special collections will play an increasingly important role in academic and public libraries. The idea is that as the content of general library collections grows more and more similar through eBooks, e-journals, research databases, and consortial sharing, the rare and unique content found in special collections will grow in stature. Eventually, special collections will define and individualize the content and personalities of libraries.

Essentially, this idea makes sense. The personalities of special collections will become increasingly distinct as most general collections grow ever more standardized. At the moment, libraries are in a multimedia hybrid state. However, as general library collections are digitized or acquired electronically and access grows increasingly virtual, special collection libraries and departments will remain vital physical locations for library users. They will be a key part of the on-site service mission of many libraries.

Digital access is an essential growth area in special collections, but artifacts held in these collections often demand hands-on research. This can occur when the nature of the object does not allow for a suitable facsimile or scholars are studying the artifact as a material object and a facsimile simply will not do. A recent rise in the study of material culture across many disciplines has benefited special collection libraries, as scholars study books and other historical objects not only for their contents, but also as physical artifacts that manifest important evidence of the cultures that produced them. This has brought an increasing number of researchers to special collection libraries.

This rise in interest in special collections has been a part of a larger shift in the field toward greater access to rare and unique materials. This has been done through efforts to catalog once-hidden collections, better outreach to users, and the adoption of user-friendly policies. Perhaps most significantly, special collections are finding their way into more classrooms across a number of disciplines as librarians teach with these materials, whether in an academic setting or through programming for the general public.

With all of this in mind, the future of special collection libraries does seem to be one of great promise and increased prominence. In order to actualize this future, however, special collections need to be built with care. In addition to describing and promoting current collections, special collection librarians must build their collections in ways that establish their libraries as vital centers of programming, teaching, and research.

What follows are thoughts regarding the role collection development can play in ensuring the vitality of special collection libraries. From seeking out utility players and unique objects to building a library of record in a fringe or local field of study, this chapter explores how shrewd collection development will help guarantee that the conventional wisdom regarding special collections will actually come to fruition.

THINKING UTILITY

The future of special collection libraries depends not only on current collections but also on how these collections are grown. In a time where acquisition budgets might be small and the demand for material high, librarians must critically assess potential acquisitions, asking: What role will the item play in the library? Who will use it and how? Will it be used for teaching, and will it add to an existing research collection? Does the item have immediate research value? Might this item be worth digitizing and adding to our digital library? Might it be used in an upcoming exhibition? Does my library have a custodial responsibility to preserve this item? In short, how does this item expand our library's mission?

Occasionally, an item expands a library's mission in many ways. It fits the bill for research, teaching, exhibitions, and digitization. Moreover, it might be used for these purposes across a number of disciplines. If an artifact has all of this going for it, it is what we might call a utility player, to lift a term from the world of sports. That is, a player who is able to play several different positions for a team.

As an example, the Cary Graphic Arts Collection at Rochester Institute of Technology has in its collection a copy of a book printed ca. 1470 titled *Incipit epistola lugubris et mesta simul et consolatoria de infelice expugnacione ac misera irrupcone et invasione insule Euboye dicte Nigropontus* or "a mournful and miserable and at the same time comforting letter of the unfortunate assault and lamentable breaking into and invasion of the island Euboea called Negroponte." This brief report describes the Ottoman Empire's siege of the island of Euboea from Venice in July 1470. The primary reason this book is in the Cary Collection is that it might possibly be the first instance of printed news and thus, in a sense, a very early newspaper. The overarching mission of the Cary Collection is to document the history of graphic communication and so the book is a strong fit. The Cary Collection has a custodial responsibility to preserve the book, while providing access to it for research and teaching.

Epistola lugubris is ideal to show a class of journalism students who visit the library to learn more about the history of printed news. But the book has much more to offer. Due to the copy-specific information that has been added to it as it has traveled through the centuries, the book is a strong example of a utility player. For example, like many books printed in the first decades of printing in Europe, *Epistola lugubris* is a hybrid of manuscript and print. Most of what appears on the page is printed, but manuscript embellishment in red ink has been added to emphasize all the capital letters that appear on the page, thus bringing the reader to proper nouns and the beginnings of sentences.

The book's second paragraph begins with a large space that has been left for someone to hand draw an initial letter "R" before the sentence beginning "—evere[n]dissimo i[n] Cristo patri ac clarissimo et spie[n]tissimo" If the "R" were added to the head of the sentence it would read "reverendissimo," Latin for "most reverend." Again, this hybrid of print and manuscript reflects the influence of manuscripts on early books. In other copies of *Epistola lugubris*, someone has added a manuscript "R" to the "—everendissimo"; the various previous owners of the Cary Collection's copy chose to leave it blank.

More evidence demonstrating the influence of manuscripts on this work includes the lack of title page, table of contents, and pagination or foliation. These are bibliographic elements that became standard in books as printing continued to develop. For students of the history of the book, *Epistola lugubris* provides many examples of the printed book in its developing stages. After all, books printed before 1501 are books in their infancy, as indicated by the term given them—incunabula—which is Latin for swaddling clothing or cradle.

The Cary Collection's copy of *Epistola lugubris* also features evidence of reader response, the kind of information that is crucial to the study of the history of reading. An early reader has marked many passages with brackets that look almost like grotesque faces. On two occasions, the reader has also drawn a hand pointing to a passage of some significance. Manuscript pointing hands, what bibliographers call manicules, are fairly common in early European books. Early readers often wrote in their texts, just as modern readers do today. Whereas we might use a highlighter or underline passages, a 15th-century reader might highlight important passages by drawing a manicule or some other mark. Manicules were so common in manuscripts that they became popular ornaments in wood and metal types, as well as in digital fonts (check your Wingdings). In this way, the discussion of *Epistola lugubris* could extend to the influence that manuscripts and printed books had on each other.

Another angle from which to approach the Cary Collection's copy of *Epistola lugubris* is from the point of view of the conservation and preservation of historical artifacts. The previous owner of this book displayed it with bands holding the pages open to those showing the manicule and other examples of reader response. It is clear that this book was displayed in this fashion for too long a period in an environment in which the climate was not controlled. The result is that the pages darkened, except for two light strips along the outside margins where the bands had once held the book open. The book must have been in direct light or in a harsh environment, because it now carries with it these signs of its mistreatment. While there is not really a positive side to damaging an artifact, at least this book can now be used to demonstrate the damaging effects of displaying a book improperly. Hence, this might be appropriate to share with a class of museum studies students or maybe students engaged in book conservation.

Epistola lugubris is a utility player for the Cary Collection: an artifact that meets the demands of the library's teaching, research, and custodial missions, while extending across a variety of academic disciplines. This kind of artifact is crucial to the future of special collection libraries. They are precisely what librarians and curators are hoping to find when they open bookseller and auction catalogs.

Accordingly, these are also precisely the kind of items for which antiquarian booksellers are looking. At a time when the growth of bookselling Web sites such as abebooks.com and alibris.com has made it easier than ever to find specific editions of books, utility players have become standout items for booksellers searching for something special to offer their customers. Booksellers and special collection librarians are also on the lookout for another very important class of items: those that are unique.

THINKING UNIQUE

The notion of rare has changed considerably in the digital age. In the opening of this chapter it was noted how most general collections are becoming more homogenous as libraries have more resources in common and are sharing more resources. A similar trend can be found in special collections, although to a much lesser extent, due to increased numbers of digitized artifacts.

One question that a librarian might ask before acquiring an item is "Do my users already have access to it?" In the past a special collections librarian would have rarely asked this question. Depending on the mission, scope, and resources of a library, this still might be a question rarely asked. But for librarians who need to think very carefully about how to allocate limited acquisition funds, this question is certainly a consideration. Never before have rare and unique materials been so accessible, and this access is only going to increase. In other words, expanding digital access has rendered these objects less rare, at least in a virtual way.

For example, a researcher wanting to view the 1611 first edition of the King James Bible can see a PDF facsimile through Early English Books Online (if their institution is a subscriber) or a free high-quality digitized version from the University of Pennsylvania Libraries' Schoenberg Center for Electronic Text & Image.[1] If a researcher just wants to read the text of the King James Bible translation, many different Web sites can accommodate.

Does this mean that a library should not acquire a 1611 King James Bible? Of course not. For some libraries this book is an essential item to have in the collection. But for most libraries the need to acquire this particular item may be diminished. There is already access to it. It is very important to note that for those of us who study artifacts as material objects, facsimiles will not do. We need to work with the artifact itself. But a great many researchers simply need to see the text, study the image, or hear the sound. Increasingly this can be accomplished digitally, and thus, from an access point of view, the actual object becomes, in a sense, less rare.

Rare may have become less rare, but unique is always unique. A great portion of modern history has been built on information found in printed books. Our understanding of earlier history is dependent upon analysis of manuscripts and archaeological artifacts—artifacts that continued to be produced after the invention of printing but are sometimes not studied to the extent of printed books. There is so much of the historical record waiting to be discovered in manuscripts and other realia (i.e., three-dimensional historical artifacts) that have not yet been examined. These entirely unique items belong in special collection libraries.

Manuscripts have always been a staple of special collections, though they are sometimes collected less frequently than printed books. At a time when printed books are less rare, manuscripts may rise in prominence. They contain information that might not exist in other media. They hold historical evidence that might have been overlooked as a consequence of the focus on print. Manuscripts are sometimes more difficult to use due to paleographic barriers that stand between the reader and the text, but these barriers cannot be broken if manuscripts are not preserved, described, and made accessible to readers.

Realia is even less frequently represented in special collection libraries. Traditionally, libraries tended to consist of books, not things. Yet things often contextualize the cultures that produced traditional library holdings; therefore, they can be used to enhance existing collections in exciting ways. The Cary Graphic Arts Collection, for example, houses not only a library of books and manuscripts, but also examples of the equipment used to create the books and manuscripts. From a 15th-century woodcut, to the matrices used to cast Bruce Rogers' Centaur type, to an Albion printing press that belonged to the American type designer Frederic Goudy, these materials not only make great teaching tools but also are themselves worthy of study. Moreover, under the right circumstance these materials could all be used again, replicating historical processes and, in turn, creating new examples.

The idea of unique extends to printed books, too. The most obvious case is when just one copy of a printed book survives. But there are other important ways that a printed book can be unique due to the distinctive cultural information it carries with it.

THINKING COPY-SPECIFIC

The notion of unique is not limited to manuscripts, realia, or single surviving copies of printed books. As books and other artifacts pass through centuries and decades, they absorb new information that later serves as evidence of the cultures that used them. For example, a book may carry with it important clues of its provenance indicating who used it and how. Association copies, or books formerly owned by someone associated with the book or by someone of note, are perhaps the most common example. For instance, 19th-century editions of Shakespeare's works are exceedingly common, but consider the 1832 copy of *Dramatic Works of William Shakespeare* owned and annotated by George Eliot and George Henry Lewes that survives in the Folger Shakespeare Library.[2] Such a copy clearly has a lot more to offer researchers than a clean copy of the same edition.

It is not just famous owners. Readers of all sorts leave historical evidence in the form of new bindings, bookplates, owners' marks, manuscript marginalia reacting to the text, and damage, both from use and censorship. Rather than acquiring simply another copy of an edition, librarians and curators are increasingly seeking out artifacts that have unique, copy-specific information.

Surviving copies of John Foxe's 16th-century protestant martyrology *Actes and Monuments* or *Book of Martyrs* sometime contain rich examples of reader response. A copy of the 1570 edition found now at The Ohio State University displays evidence of how one early reader inflicted intentional damage to the book in reaction to the often gruesome woodcut illustrations of executions.[3] On woodcut after woodcut, this reader blotted with ink the faces of executioners and other men depicted as villains. Finally, when the reader reached the most notorious image in the book, a woodcut illustration of Bishop Bonner scourging the bare bottom of a prisoner, the reader defaces Bonner by stabbing out most of his face, creating a hole in the page. Thus, this copy of the *Book of Martyrs* manifests distinct evidence of how one reader reacted to the book's inflammatory contents. Its contents are invaluable to researchers of the Protestant Reformation.

This sort of unique information is not only found in books (printed, manuscript, or otherwise), but also on most historical objects ranging from tools to machines to currency. Unique artifacts and artifacts containing unique information are of increasing interest to librarians and booksellers. For booksellers such items are more easily placed in new homes and often at higher prices. Consequently, prices may become obstacles to acquiring unique items and utility players, but special collection librarians must think big and work out ways to bring such items into their libraries.

THINKING BIG

In his *Taste et Technique in Book Collecting*, John Carter writes "be less afraid of paying a stiff price than of letting slip some book you know to be rare and which is important to you. You cannot tell when, at what price, or even whether, you will see another" (1949, 136). In short, whenever possible, price should not get in the way of an essential acquisition.

Okay, this probably sounds like an impossible way to approach acquisitions, particularly in a time of limited resources. Perhaps it is unrealistic, but the core of the idea is true. Libraries should not let big items slip away. A big item probably falls into the categories discussed earlier: a utility player, a unique item, or an artifact with immediate research value. Passing on such an item because of price means this item might never make it through your library's doors. Yet, librarians might pass on one major item because of its cost, and then spend the same amount on a handful or more other items. Although they might feel like they were thriftier with their budget, have they really gotten more value for their money? The question is whether the research value found in the handful of items equals the research value of the one big item. Has the library lost out on a critical opportunity?

Obviously there is value in purchasing certain types of materials while they are still affordable; many times it is a good way of building for the future. But this should not be done at the expense of items that belong in your collection but are simply more expensive. There is often a reason why big items are more expensive. Librarians should not be afraid to spend significant parts of their acquisitions budgets on a few major purchases. Say that if in a year you have bought only two new items for your collection, you might feel like you have not been doing your job completely or that you might have missed out on other potential acquisitions. But the greater question is whether you have truly enriched your collection.

Such important items might not even be purchased through the usual acquisitions budget. If budgets cannot get you what your collection requires, then creative solutions need to be found. High-end items might be enticing enough to whet the appetite of donors and friends of the library. Fundraising for such an item can be done prior to the purchase, but also afterward, through an adopt-a-book event. Looking beyond your local community, you may find a foundation or two to which you could apply for support.

Beyond budget challenges, librarians might also fear their administrators will look askance at the purchase of just a few items rather than what they might view as a more healthy number of items. This should not be seen as a source of potential conflict, but as an opportunity for education and outreach. Whenever possible, major acquisitions should be accompanied by outreach.

THINKING OUTREACH

Big items should not arrive at a special collections library without some amount of outreach. If the item was purchased because of its research value, then librarians should alert those scholars for whom the item will be helpful. If the item was purchased because of its relevance to various classes, then the librarian should reach out to the appropriate teachers. Joel Silver, the curator of the Lilly Library at Indiana University, recently wrote: "While previous generations of rare book librarians tended to focus on the building of their collections above all else, today it is access to and communication about the collections that occupy a greater portion of librarians' time" (Galbraith and Smith 2012, viii). This observation extends to all special collection librarians. The time of collection development independent of outreach has passed. In prior years the primary focus on collection building was extremely important, but it also led to major backlogs in processing and cataloging material. This, consequently, led to the growth of hidden collections. Hidden collections are effectively nonexistent collections: if your materials cannot be found in your online catalog, they do not exist to most users.

Over the past decade we have seen a movement to make hidden collections in special collection and archives visible. Building on this momentum and thinking beyond just backlog cataloging, librarians should view outreach as an essential part of collection development. Spending significant portions of a budget on materials demands the provision of support for getting these materials into the right hands. Time and resources needed to promote new acquisitions on places like Web sites, and appropriate listservs need to be a part of the acquisitions workflow. A portion of the acquisitions budget could be earmarked for the cost of promotional material or a welcome event. In 2008 when the British Library acquired a remarkable copy of Everard Digby's *A short introduction for to learne to swimme*, better known was the *Art of Swimming*, that had been hand colored and filled with humorous manuscript annotations, the library held an event to introduce this exciting new acquisition to its community.[4]

New acquisitions should also be defined broadly to include newly discovered or rediscovered items already in a library collection. Although it seems strange that a new item might be found in a library that has housed it for decades or longer, those in the field can testify to exciting discoveries within their own walls. These important discoveries require outreach to potential users. There are also times where known artifacts should be reintroduced to users through outreach. Researchers may not always know the extent of resources available to them.

In addition to simply doing right by the artifacts, bringing attention to acquisitions could also be a matter of survival. Your administrators need to know about the libraries and collections they are funding. They have to understand the mission of the organization and how new acquisitions support and expand that mission. Successful outreach regarding collection development will help build a library's reputation beyond its walls, letting the greater community know the library's value.

Eventually outreach supporting a library's holdings should serve to define its collection as a library of record in one or more fields. This sometimes means being creative—thinking beyond traditional collections and exploring the fringe.

THINKING FRINGE

The nature of what content constitutes special collections or archives has broadened. What was once a fairly traditional definition of what was archive-worthy has rightly expanded to include what might be considered fringe materials. The term fringe is borrowed from an excellent seminar held at the 2012 Annual Preconference of the Rare Books and Manuscripts Section of the Association of College and Research Libraries titled, "From Dungeons to Dragons: Collecting, Processing, and Accessing Fringe Formats."[5] The seminar examined the challenges of managing popular culture collections such as the Edwin and Terry Murray Collection of Role-Playing Games at Duke University, the UT Videogame Archive at the University of Texas at Austin, and the Eaton Collection of Science Fiction & Fantasy at University of California, Riverside. Each of these archives houses collections that might be considered nontraditional, though each represents a dynamic field of study.

In this way, they are not fringe collections at all, but important material that reflects the societies that created them. While role-playing and video games might seem trivial to some, they carry important cultural information. What will future generations learn about our present generation through the games we play? A great deal, if someone has the foresight to preserve our games for later study and use.

Foresight is key. Most collection development in special collections is guided by existing collections and the needs of local communities. Thus, most of the items that librarians acquire are predictable choices. They are often cultural touchstones. Exploring the fringe takes librarians in a different direction. It requires some degree of adventure and risk. Librarians must raise their cultural antennae and tune into the sort of artifacts that might be flying under the radar at the moment, but may have value further down the road and thus deserve to be preserved in an archive. Preservation is important. Often these types of artifacts are ephemeral and in danger of being lost.

Not only does building a fringe collection preserve what are often ephemeral materials for later study and use, but it also establishes a library of record for unconventional topics. In turn, the libraries that house them carve out a niche for themselves that distinguishes them from their peers. Unconventional libraries also make for interesting human-interest stories. When the University of California, Santa Cruz sought an archivist for its Grateful Dead Archive, the story was picked up widely by the mainstream news media and even landed on the desk of *The Daily Show's* Jon Stewart.[6] Mockery was made, though lighthearted, and in the process millions of Americans were introduced to the Grateful Dead Archive.

THINKING LOCALLY

Librarians do not always need to travel out to the fringes to find unconventional special collections. Traditionally, many simply looked to their communities to identify materials that reflected their own local personalities and histories. The New Bedford Whaling Museum in New Bedford, Massachusetts, for example, holds an amazing assortment of whaling artifacts, including the world's largest collection of American whaling logs and scrimshaw. These are natural fits. In the 19th century, New Bedford was a major center of the whaling industry in America. Thus, the artifacts preserved within the museum and its library document a significant and fascinating part of the city's history.

Thinking locally, however, does not always mean collecting a topic directly related to local history or culture. The Providence Public Library preserves the second largest collection of whaling logs, together with a group of manuscripts, scrimshaw, and other whaling artifacts. Providence was never a major whaling city and so these materials do not have the same sort of historical connection that they would in New Bedford. The Providence Public Library's focus on whaling and maritime history is built on a collection donated in 1956 by a Providence businessman named Paul C. Nicholson. In this way, a local benefactor's interest in whaling led his public library to become a research center for whaling history.

CONCLUSION: THINKING OF WHAT IS POSSIBLE

Building a special collection into a research-level collection in a subject or several subjects will define the library to its local community and beyond. Returning to the conventional wisdom regarding the increased prominence of special collections, there is no better way of defining the character of a library than establishing it as a library of record for exciting areas of study based upon its rare or unique holdings. The library may not make it onto *The Daily Show*, but it will attract the attention of teachers, students, and scholars, who will in turn come to that library for primary research material and teaching resources.

Primary research with special collections will continue to be conducted and taught as a methodology. Some of it will take place online, but a great deal of it will continue to take place in the reading rooms of special collection libraries and archives. Special collection libraries must continue to meet the needs of their users through smart collection building. This includes embracing utility players, seeking out unique items and other items with copy-specific information, being willing to find ways to acquire expensive materials so as not to pass up on artifacts that are vital to a specific collection, and establishing new collections based on material that might be considered unconventional or on the fringe. For all of these new acquisitions (and for those already in the archives), outreach is necessary to ensure they are visible to those who need them.

The most exciting part of all of this is that just about any library can build a special collection.[7] General research collections are very expensive to build and difficult to maintain. They are developed through commercial networks of vendors. Special collections certainly require funding, but they are usually built through the generosity of donors, whether individuals, corporations, foundations, or grant-funding agencies. They are established through creative and cooperative relationships among people with shared intellectual and artistic interests. This means that any library can help bring conventional wisdom regarding special collections to fruition. If we have all successfully done our share to make it so, more and more libraries and archives will continue to transform into vital intellectual centers.

That is something to think about.

NOTES

1. http://sceti.library.upenn.edu/sceti/printedbooksNew/index.cfm?TextID=kjbible.

2. http://shakespeare.folger.edu/cgi-bin/Pwebrecon.cgi?BBID=116816 and http://www.folger.edu/html/exhibitions/thys_boke/ordinarybooks.asp.

3. John Foxe, *The First [-Second] Volume of the Ecclesiasticall History Contaynyng the Actes and Monumentes of Thynges Passed in Every Kynges Tyme in This Realme, Especially in the Church of England* . . . (London: John Daye, 1570), 782. BR 1600 .F6 1570 vol. 2.

4. Everard Digby, *A Short Introduction for to Learne to Swimme. Gathered Out of Master Digbies Booke of the Art of Swimming. And Translated into English for the Better Instruction of Those Who Vnderstand Not the Latine Tongue* (London: James Roberts for Edward White, 1595). https://www.jiscmail.ac.uk/cgi-bin/webadmin?A2=lis-rarebooks;375bd8fe.0808.

5. http://www.rbms.info/conferences/preconfdocs/2012/2012docs.shtml.

6. http://www.thedailyshow.com/watch/wed-november-11-2009/want-ads---grateful-dead-archivist.

7. I need to thank my brother James Galbraith, the wiser of the two Galbraith librarians, for driving this vital point home for me.

REFERENCES

Carter, John. 1949. *Taste et Technique in Book-Collecting: A Study of Recent Developments in Great Britain and the United States.* Cambridge: University Press.

Galbraith, Steven K., and Geoffrey D. Smith. 2012. *Rare Book Librarianship: An Introduction and Guide.* Santa Barbara, CA: Libraries Unlimited.

27

COLLABORATIVE DISASTER NETWORKS

Thomas F. R. Clareson

INTRODUCTION

While libraries and cultural heritage collections have been struck by disaster for centuries—from the fire at the Alexandria Library to the Florence Floods of 1966, the onslaught of disasters affecting our written history and artistic heritage seem to have greatly intensified over the past 20–25 years, especially in the United States.

Beginning with Hurricane Hugo and the Loma Prieta Earthquake, both of which happened in 1989, and extending through the wide swath of devastation caused by Hurricane Sandy in late October 2012, our print and increasingly digital collections have faced many natural and manmade disasters, which affected large geographic regions.

Slowly but surely, the library and cultural heritage communities are creating institutional disaster plans. Many organizations are benefitting from working with local first responders such as police and fire departments, as well as emergency management agencies, in the development of their disaster plans. Once an institution has moved forward to complete its institutional plan, it can then turn to its community for additional support—and to provide additional support to its community. One way to combat large, city-wide, regional, state-wide, or multistate disaster events, and the widespread destruction in their wake, is through collaborative disaster planning among multiple libraries or across cultural institution types, working with local emergency managers.

THE TRIGGER POINTS

Beyond Hugo and Loma Prieta and their effect on libraries and museums, the 1990s saw flooding and wildfires, and the first decade of the 21st century included disasters causing tremendous amounts of damage to cultural heritage collections.

- Tropical Storm Allison, in June 2001, caused flooding in the greater Houston metropolitan area, which resulted in water damage to collections ranging from theater costumes to master film reels, from photographic collections to rare books and special collections materials.
- The terrorist attacks of September 11, 2001, in addition to a terrible human toll, destroyed materials from books and archival records to outdoor sculptures.
- In August 2005, Hurricane Katrina caused widespread damage to public libraries, municipal archives, museums, and historical homes in Louisiana, Mississippi, and Alabama.
- In August 2011, Hurricane Irene created a wide swath of damage to cultural institutions on the East Coast, from North Carolina to Vermont.
- October 2012 saw damages to library and museum collections in New York, New Jersey, and other East Coast locations due to Superstorm Sandy.

Unlike many manmade emergencies caused by building construction accidents and system malfunctions, these were large-scale disasters affecting multiple institutions or even whole regions of the United States. Although individual–institution disaster plans offered some assistance in these events, collaborative disaster planning among groups of institutions has proven to be even more effective. And, collaborative disaster planning is not just for catastrophic events, which actually happen very infrequently; this type of disaster planning approach can help when there is a disaster just at your institution. For example, if a pipe bursts over collections at your library, other institutions can help provide supplies to pack out wet materials, and can even provide trained people to assist, if previous collaborative work has included disaster response training.

NEW APPROACHES TO RESPONSE AND RECOVERY

Many national and regional organizations began to support the concept of collaborative disaster planning in the 1990s and 2000s.

Heritage Preservation, the leading preservation advocacy organization in the United States, led the charge by establishing the Heritage Emergency National Task Force in 1995. A collaborative effort of 42 cultural heritage organizations and associations, federal agencies, and national service organizations, the Task Force was a key collaborative in preparations for and recovery from incidents such as Hurricane Katrina and Superstorm Sandy, in part by offering a way in which affected institutions can communicate with organizations that could provide recovery information and assistance.[1]

The American Institute for Conservation of Historic and Artistic Works (AIC) developed its Collections Emergency Response Team in 2005, partially in response to Hurricane Katrina. This group provides assistance ranging from a disaster response telephone and email hotline to matching conservation professionals and specialists with organizations needing assistance to recover specific types of artifacts.[2]

Regional Conservation Centers such as the Conservation Center for Art & Historic Artifacts (CCAHA), Northeast Document Conservation Center (NEDCC), Midwest Art Conservation Center (MACC) and regional library networks such as LYRASIS (the merger of SOLINET, PALINET, NELINET, and members of BCR) and Amigos Library Services provide disaster assistance training and information as part of their preservation field services operations, funded in part by the National Endowment for the Humanities' Division of Preservation and Access. WESTPAS—the Western States and Territories Preservation Assistance Service—is another key group that primarily focuses on disaster assistance for many states west of the Mississippi River.[3]

On a local and regional basis, other approaches began to appear:

- Mutual aid agreements, where individual organizations signed memoranda of agreement, which pledge staff resources, supplies, and other support between member institutions in the event of a localized emergency or more widespread disaster.
- Multi-institutional circuit-riding recovery assistance where an expert within a state or region travels to assist organizations with disaster planning or recovery activities. Examples of this approach exist in Massachusetts, Iowa, and Missouri, as well as many other states.
- Disaster Supply Caches, where multiple organizations work together to develop stockpiles of disaster supplies. These caches save individual institutions' money through joint purchase and management of supplies. A further explanation of this disaster planning and recovery approach is described later.
- Libraries and cultural organizations that have a sister institution in another region of the country, which can provide communication support if your organization has to evacuate, and have even in some cases provided data backup support when there is an area-wide disaster.

These national, regional, and local multi-institutional disaster networks provide a wide variety of benefits to their members.

THE BENEFITS OF COLLABORATIVE DISASTER PLANNING

Ensuring that your library has an institutional disaster plan, which covers the specifics of your collection formats, collection storage, and building design, is the cornerstone preservation policy on which every library needs to build. Writing and practicing a plan, at least once a year, can protect your collections.

When disasters strike, especially those with the potential to damage a large number of buildings, such as hurricanes, wildfires, and tornadoes, a plan to protect multiple library buildings or branches, as well as neighboring cultural heritage institutions (e.g., museums, historical societies, and archives) should be in place and ready for activation.

The benefits of cooperative or collaborative disaster planning are many. An institution can save money, better utilize its resources, gain information and training, and deal with insurance and technical issues.

RECOVERY PLANNING

When disaster strikes, gaining access to your collections within the first 48 to 72 hours after they are initially damaged is important in allowing you to recover materials before water damage or mold causes further problems for the items.

Working on a local or regional basis and coordinating with other cultural heritage institutions can make recovery easier. Whether allowing you to offer services through reciprocal borrowing, shared service delivery, or other means, collaborative activity has meant speedier business resumption by libraries and other cultural heritage organizations. And in some cases, working with partners to find sites for relocation during long-term recovery can also help to leverage resources, resume service sooner, and deal with technical and insurance issues. Providing emergency preparedness information and disaster response and recovery best practices to a large group of organizations at the same time via group education and information puts participating collaborative members on a level playing field.

GROUP TRAINING

Educational efforts for a disaster collaborative can build familiarity in many ways. Planning needs to start with collaboration—getting to know your neighboring cultural heritage institutions—and first responders—in your community, and developing from there.

After developing their own disaster plans, organizations may want to consider sharing their disaster documents and floor plans, and storing them in a safe place in case their partner institution needs access because originals are lost or damaged.

Networking with peers on disaster plan development, demonstration and practice of wet material recovery, and tabletop disaster scenarios where group members assume recovery roles and work through a disaster timeline can be helpful in making sure all members of a disaster collaborative have baseline preparedness, response, and recovery skills.

Initial training, just as with initial disaster plan development, is an important activity. Just as important can be a novel opportunity to practice and update the plan. Pick a day each year for your group to learn about changes in each other's building collections and policies. One suggested time of the year to practice disaster plans on a group basis is MayDay, the date of a national campaign to promote emergency preparedness.[4] And, consider bringing first responders, emergency managers, and commercial disaster recovery vendors in for group meetings to demonstrate their services and answer questions (this approach also works with group insurance representatives).

SAVING MONEY

In this era of tight library budgets, saving precious library funds through coordinated disaster planning may allow those monies to be spent on other important programs and services.

An initial area where some collaborative disaster planning groups have saved money is through receiving group training and consulting. This might include an outside expert visiting each of the collaborative sites to assess disaster risks, and then providing training specifically designed to address the highest-ranked risks in the region.

Consortial contracting is another potential area of fiscal savings. Developing a coordinated contract with commercial disaster recovery vendors, which will make cost containment easier for you and capacity and coverage issues easier for the vendor, is one beneficial approach. Additionally, consortial or group insurance contracts (which many county, municipal, or higher education institutions already have) can help to spread costs over multiple organizations and may bring down prices on premiums.

Another tact which has shown demonstrable costs savings is the development of centralized disaster supply caches. Rather than individual cultural heritage institutions spending a large amount of money to develop kits of disaster recovery supplies just for itself, that may never be used, the development of a larger, shared cache of disaster supplies which can be accessed by any member of a collaborative disaster planning group is a proven money-saving approach for cooperative disaster planning. Examples of these caches are housed in locations from southern California to Pittsburgh/Western Pennsylvania. The caches are monitored and managed by collaborative groups, and available to members 24/7/365.

BETTER RESOURCE UTILIZATION

Collaborative disaster planning and recovery efforts can provide for efficient utilization of human resources as well as financial resources. Certainly the training mentioned earlier, if offered on a collaborative basis, can provide a greater number of trained responders from the cultural heritage community on a local, state, or regional basis who can group together to assist an individual institution or cultural organizations in a city or area struck by a disaster. In some cases, the responders from the library and museum communities may have specializations such as dealing with computer and technical equipment, or with difficult formats ranging from audiovisual materials to paintings and works of art on paper. Creating emergency response teams to aid other institutions requires specialized training and coordination, which is different from or in addition to writing and practicing disaster plans or conducting risk assessments. Ideally, the preparation for joint response would include local Community Emergency Response Team (CERT) training, a program developed by the Federal Emergency Management Agency and made available through many county Emergency Management Agencies (EMAs).

The other resource-based benefit which a number of disaster collaboratives have achieved is through touring each other's facilities to gain familiarity with other institutions in their consortia. Through these tours, you may be able to determine your partner institutions' collection strengths, staff strengths, and building weaknesses. Including facilities staff on these tours can be helpful in determining systems strengths or weaknesses, and having first responders involved in this process can ensure that they are familiar with your institution's building, floor plans, and contents before they respond to an emergency.

INSURANCE ISSUES

A number of insurance companies and customers within the cultural heritage industries have noted exponential growth in the levels of premiums during the 2000s. The 9/11 and Hurricane Katrina are key factors in these rate increases, and it is expected that Hurricane Sandy may cause price increases as well.

There are a number of things institutions and collaborative groups can do to potentially reduce premiums. Identifying high-probability risks—both inside your building and in the external environment (are there railroad lines, wooded or grassy areas, or industrial plants nearby?) is one way to determine disaster risk and probability levels. Then, determine what risks can be addressed. The Heritage Preservation's Risk Evaluation and Planning Program (REPP) initiative pairs representatives of individual libraries, museums, or other cultural heritage institutions with a local first responder to assess and rate the possibility of occurrence of disasters related to specific targeted risks due to the institution's building and geographic location. REPP began as a pilot program in 2008–2009; the tools to complete this assessment remain online.[5]

Additionally, having a current and complete collection inventory, and considering a collection valuation to determine the worth of your holdings are important steps. Finally, working within a disaster planning group may allow you to take advantage of consortial insurance policies and increase your buying power.

TECHNICAL ISSUES

In addition to becoming familiar with each other's collections, staff, and buildings, work collaboratively to review your disaster planning partner institutions' safety systems—such as smoke, heat, and fire detection, fire suppression, and building security systems. Individual libraries can note improvements they might want to make as a result of seeing other systems within their cooperative group.

The rapid growth of electronic records, electronic library resources, and digitized materials is another facet of cultural heritage collection stewardship that must be considered in disaster planning. Redundant, geographically separated sites for storage of digital collections and electronic records or resources have also grown in importance since the time of Hurricane Katrina. Shared, distributed digital preservation services such as the MetaArchive allow multiple copies of digital collections to be distributed and preserved among cooperating libraries.[6]

Finally, consider utilizing the concept of a computer hot site, where replica systems and services to what you currently have can be made available to allow resumption of service.

SERVICE RESUMPTION ISSUES

As mentioned earlier, reciprocal borrowing, where another library system can allow your patrons to borrow materials with their current library card or ID, has been a popular method for damaged libraries to resume service since the mid-1990s.

Another large issue to deal with in today's library environment is fulfillment of ILL requests. If your library is closed due to power outages, damage, or other concerns, you may not be able to locate and distribute ILL materials as usual. Working with collaborative disaster recovery partners and your ILL Service Provider may be a good way to keep up your lending and borrowing practices at a time of crisis.

A final area to consider may be thought of as too much of a good thing. Many libraries damaged by flood and fire have noted the generosity of other libraries and even patrons, in donating materials for these organizations to put back on their shelves. Having a strong collection policy that outlines what an institution is, or is not willing to accept as a donation is important in bringing your collection and services back to full strength. However, what if the materials you receive as a donation after a disaster are outside your library's normal collection development scope? An example is the Academic Research Library that received romance novels to fill its shelvesl after its collection was badly damaged by flooding. One solution is cooperative donation processing centers, which have been utilized to ensure that libraries are replenishing their shelves with appropriate materials.

ESSENTIAL PARTNERS—COLLABORATION AT WORK

One of the most important features of collaborative disaster networks, as they have matured, is the establishment of relationships between cultural heritage staff members and representatives of the emergency management and public safety communities.

It is extremely important to develop these relationships for a number of reasons. Local emergency managers and responders (fire, police, city or county emergency managers) are in charge during an event, and will take control of a fire, crime, or emergency situation until the immediate danger is controlled. Any response activities by a library, museum, or historical society must be coordinated and integrated with public safety and emergency management representatives. Before an emergency strikes, these partner organizations can assist cultural institutions with risk assessments, planning, and pre-disaster mitigation issues (such as suggesting how to secure or barricade windows if high winds are imminent). And, in recent years, more and more libraries are being designated as providers of essential services for their communities (e.g., computer and telecommunications centers for both responders and disaster victims), which means they can get recovery assistance sooner.

These relationships start at the local level, but there are also many important cooperative disaster planning relationships being built at the top national administrative levels. The Federal Emergency Management Agency (FEMA) was a cofounding member of the Heritage Emergency National Task Force in 1994. Through its Office of Environmental Planning and Historic Preservation, FEMA has a group of staff specialists who can focus on cultural heritage recovery when disaster strikes.

FEMA, as well as state and local emergency managers, interacts with cultural heritage staff on a local or statewide basis through the Alliance for Response initiative. This program, with active groups in more than 20 cities and regions, provides a way to build bridges between the emergency response and cultural heritage communities before a disaster happens. Following initial Forum meetings where the groups first meet together, continuing programs of education and information exchange have provided invaluable linkages in disasters such as Hurricane Sandy and the Colorado Wildfires of 2012.[7]

One of the products of the Heritage Emergency National Task Force and the Alliance for Response Initiative is a poster on working with emergency responders before, during, and after an emergency. Including steps such as identifying emergency responders, communicating and building a relationship with them, and providing them with the information they need to know, this publication can assist cultural heritage institutions in disaster preparedness outreach to the most important allies they can have in an emergency or disaster situation.[8]

Finally, a program which has been implemented in several states (Massachusetts, Rhode Island, and Connecticut as of late 2012) is the Coordinated Statewide Emergency Preparedness program, or COSTEP. A "planning tool designed to bring together cultural resource institutions with emergency management agencies and first responders," it provides "a blueprint for preparing for area-wide disasters and building alliances with federal, state, and local emergency management agencies" COSTEP "guides states through the process of planning for a disaster and fosters collaboration among a wide range of agencies" (COSTEP n.d.).

CONCLUSION

With all of the benefits and resources which collaborative disaster planning and recovery networks provide, libraries and cultural heritage organizations should definitely explore working together with other local cultural entities, emergency managers, and first responders. These resource groups can become allies that can help to save buildings, collections, and, most importantly, the lives of staff and patrons.

NOTES

1. For information on the Heritage Emergency National Task Force, consult the Task Force's Web site http://www.heritagepreservation.org/programs/taskfer.htm.

2. To learn more about the AIC Collections Emergency Response Team, consult its Web site http://www.conservation-us.org/publications-resources/disaster-response-recovery/aic-cert#.UnAFZBBGbl8.

3. More about these regional conservation and preservation centers can be found at the Web site http://www.rap-arcc.org/rap-members.

4. For additional information on the MayDay campaign, consult the Web site http://www.heritagepreservation.org/mayday/.

5. To learn more about Heritage Preservation's Risk Evaluation and Planning Program, consult the Web site http://www.heritagepreservation.org/REPP/.

6. More about the MetaArchive Cooperative can be found at the Web site: http://www.metaarchive.org/.

7. To learn more about these events, consult the Web site http://www.heritagepreservation.org/AFR/index.html.

8. This poster, "Working with Emergency Responders—Tips for Cultural Institutions," can be found at Web site: http://www.heritagepreservation.org/lessons/HPR_Emergency_Poster8.5x11.pdf.

REFERENCE

"COSTEP: Coordinated Statewide Emergency Preparedness." n.d. Available at: http://www.nedcc.org/free-resources/costep. Accessed May 17, 2013.

28

DIGITIZATION PROJECTS

L. Suzanne Kellerman

INTRODUCTION

This chapter discusses *digitization projects* as a collection development strategy, and according to the Penn State University Libraries' Digital Collections Review Team's Digital Toolkit, a digital project can best be defined as "a series of collaborative activities that transforms analog materials into a digital format. These activities include selection, organization and planning, preparation, description and access, production, digital preservation and assessment, evaluation, and publicizing the digital resource. A digital project may involve creating new content, organizing access to existing electronic content, or digitizing existing historic collections."[1] Possible items for digitization could include bound text, unbound sheets such as maps or works of art, still and moving images, data, and three-dimensional objects. The size of any digital project may range from several sheets, as in a single mining map, to upwards of thousands of pages or more, as could be found in a large archival manuscript collection, or it may be a single sound recording or a collection of oral histories found on reel-to-reel tapes.

The goal of digitization, and in this case a digitization project, is to improve sustainable access to the materials, to preserve materials by reducing the handling of originals, and ultimately for the digitized materials to be searchable on the Internet.

For decades now libraries have been in the forefront of using computer-based technologies to describe, manage, and enhance access to collections. Advancements in digital technology tools since the mid-1990s have revolutionized our thinking about collections—giving historic hidden collections new life and users the ability to discover them anew (Lynch 2009). In recent years libraries have turned to mass digitization partnerships with Google and other consortia such as the Open Content Alliance to cost-effectively digitize large portions of their collections—digitization that would be too costly for an institution to take on by itself (Conway 2010). Moreover, with each passing year new digitization vendors and service bureaus have emerged giving libraries a much improved competitive marketplace to purchase digitization services.

Regardless of the digitization approach, whether produced in-house, outsourced to a vendor, or partnering with a mass digitization agent, libraries and institutions of all sizes are either contemplating, planning for, or actively being engaged in some sort of digitization initiative. But before jumping on the proverbial *digital* bandwagon, there are many factors one needs to consider and decisions to make before scanning begins. In this chapter I will bring to light, through a series of questions, key decision points in the process that you will need to ask yourself before embarking on a digitization project. With 20 years of digital project experience, I will share resources, discoveries, and lessons learned along the way to successfully convert materials to digital form as a collection building strategy.

SELECTION

Choosing the right collection is the key to a successful digital project. Making good selection decisions at the outset of the project is time worth taking. The goal is to build an online product that is useful and useable. It is critical to keep the audience in mind, give them what they will use, and build a product that will bring something new to the collection by adding value. Remember digital projects are labor intensive and are a significant institutional investment. Once the content goes online, it requires perpetual care, continuing management, and periodic evaluation. System upgrades, the addition of new content, strategies for long-term preservation of the digital assets, content and system migrations, and the general housekeeping of the online site to keep it fresh and aesthetically appealing are all necessary ongoing activities for any digital project.

When selecting materials for a digital project, consider the following questions:

- What are the goals of the project? Does the project support your institution's mission or strategic planning goals and objectives?
- Who is the intended audience? Is there a specific user group targeted? Students, general users, researchers, scholars?
- How do you envision the final product? Are there value-added features to bring to the project such as incorporating teachers' guides to support classroom use, providing active links to similar collections, inserting geographic access reference points, adding blogging or other interactive publishing options, enhancing search capabilities or even adding crowdsourcing options for OCR (optical character recognition) text correction?
- Are the items in the collection scannable, or do they require preservation stabilization?

- Will the entire collection, a subset of the collection, or a sampling of the collection be scanned?
- Have you conducted a thorough Internet search of your targeted collection to determine if it has or has not already been digitized?
- Are there potential collaborations or resource-sharing partnerships with other organizations or institutions that have similar collection strengths?

COPYRIGHT

Copyright is the bane of most digital projects. It can derail a digital project instantly unless the necessary steps are taken to determine whether you have the legal right to make digital surrogates and disseminate the images. Whether the collections are published works or unpublished works hidden in your archives, carefully weigh the following questions as part of the selection- and decision-making process.

- Do you own or hold the legal rights to the content you want to digitize?
- Is there a donor's deed of gift document that you may need to review first to determine your rights?
- Is the content in the public domain, that is, pre-1923 imprint?
- Is it an orphan work, that is, works whose copyright holders cannot be identified or found?
- If you do not hold the rights, are you willing to seek the necessary permissions?

To help you make knowledgeable decisions regarding copyright issues and your rights to legally preserve published and unpublished works, arm yourself with the facts. Following are selected resources available to assist you navigate the legal implications of your digital project idea.

USEFUL LINKS

The American Library Association's digital slider (slide rule) for works published in the United States—http://www.librarycopyright.net/digitalslider/. Introduced in 2008, this tool allows users to select different date ranges and conditions to determine copyright status and permissions needed.

Columbia University Copyright Advisory Office—http://copyright.colum bia.edu/copyright/. This site offers a wide array of copyright information for libraries, including the fundamentals of copyright, fair use, copyright ownership, and permissions.

Stanford Copyright and Fair Use Center's *Charts and Tools*—http://fairuse .stanford.edu/charts_tools/. This Web page offers a variety of charts, tutorials, flowcharts, and tools to help you navigate your way through the legal issues of copyright.

Copyright Terms and the Public Domain in the United States by Peter Hirtle, Senior Policy Advisor, Cornell University—http://copyright.cornell
.edu/resources/publicdomain.cfm. This tool offers useful charts to determine if a work is in the public domain for published works, unpublished works, works first published outside the United States, sound recordings, and architectural works.

The Society of American Archivist's *Selected Copyright Resources*—http://www2.archivists.org/groups/intellectual-property-working-group/selected-copyright-resources. This Web resource provides a wealth of information on general introductory topics on copyright, fair use, orphan works, public domain, digitization, copyright law, and workshop information.

For further information on public domain works, see The Public Domain Review's *Guide to Finding Interesting Public Domain Works Online*–http://public
domainreview.org/guide-to-finding-interesting-public-domain-works-online/.

COPYRIGHT AND NEWSPAPER DIGITIZATION

When it comes to digitizing newspapers, there are two important and distinct rights issues to resolve before moving forward with the project. First, you must determine whether the newspaper you plan to digitize is in the public domain dating prior to 1923 and second, if the newspaper has been microfilmed, you must determine who owns the microfilm images regardless of the date. Housing a microfilmed newspaper in your library collection does not mean that you own the rights to digitize the microfilm. Permissions must be sought and granted from the rights holder of the microfilm before the holdings can be digitized. To determine ownership of the microfilm images you will need to check the microfilm box labels for a microproducer's name and address and view the reel of film. At the beginning of the reel, after the blank leader film and before the actual filmed contents, are a series of targets. Among these targets is the ownership target or copyright statement target listing the name of the contents owner or rights holder.

As an example, if you are considering digitizing historic newspapers that were dated pre-1923 and you found that by looking at the ownership target on the reel that it was microfilmed by the United States Newspaper Program, National Endowment for the Humanities in 1990, and the microfilm was held at a public institution, you would need permission from the public institution holding the microfilm.

If on the other hand the newspapers you plan to digitize were dated post-1922, meaning the holdings are not in the public domain, permission must be sought from the newspaper publisher if he or she is still in business or from whoever holds the rights to the paper. If the contents have been microfilmed, you must also seek permission from the microfilm rights holder.

To consider digitizing newspapers dated post-1922, the publisher would need to give you permission to use the content, and the microfilm producer would have to grant permission to digitize the microfilm. In some cases the publisher may own both the content and the microfilm rights; in other cases the publisher may own the rights to the content, while the microfilm rights belong to a commercial company.

Also with newspapers be careful to consider whether the paper contains service-produced news articles such as those from the Associated Press (AP) and Reuters, or articles produced by syndicated columnists. The publisher may not own this content and therefore cannot give you permission to redistribute it in digital form online. It is always best to seek guidance and permissions from the newspaper publisher first to determine what can and cannot be digitized.

PROJECT PLANNING AND ORGANIZATION

Now that you have carefully weighed the legality to digitize the collection you have in mind, and have determined that the collection has not already been digitized by another entity, the next step in planning your digital project is to determine whether you have the skill set, manpower, infrastructure, and funding to carry out the project. Whether you have many staff to call on for assistance or you are the only one in your organization assigned to carry out the project, your answers to the following questions will define the direction of your project and how the project will be managed.

- Who should be involved in the project? Possible stakeholders could include collection curators and staff, administrators, faculty or other subject experts, systems technicians, catalogers and metadata specialists, preservation professionals, scanning staff, Web developers, and financial officers.
- Is this a collaborative effort with another institution? If so, clearly define the roles and responsibilities for each party. Prepare a formal agreement outlining the agreed-to terms and meet regularly to discuss project goals, timelines, progress, and any changes needed to keep the project on track.
- Do you have the technical skills and knowledge needed to carry out the project? Will staff need to be trained? For instance, who will be responsible for inventorying the collection to determine its completeness, number of items or pages, condition, and structure? It is imperative to know your collection at the box-level, folder-level, and even page-level. Count and record the number of pages in the collection to determine its overall size. Fill missing gaps to ensure the completeness of the collection to be digitized.
- Will the collection require preservation stabilization of the originals prior to scanning? Will the materials need to be cleaned, unfolded, flattened and/or sleeved in Mylar sheets prior to scanning? Will the collection require additional or special housing after scanning now that it is unfolded?

- Will the project be produced in-house or outsourced to a vendor? What types of materials can you accommodate in-house? If outsourced, which vendors will you contact? Consider contacting peer institutions with known digitization programs to build a list of reputable vendors. As a financial steward of your institution's money, request project price quotes from several vendors to determine the best price for the desired service.
- What equipment and software will you need, whether produced in-house or outsourced? Will you need to purchase new hardware and software such as a dedicated computer and scanner for digitization, scanning software, content management platform software, image editing software, calibration software, or a color output printer?
- Will your current system architecture or infrastructure support the project? Where will your final product live? Does your institution have an existing locally hosted digital content management system you can use, such as CONTENTdm? Is there adequate long-term server storage space for Web delivery of the content and for the long-term preservation of the digital files you produce? Does your institution have a disaster recovery plan for electronic media? How will the project be sustained over time? Does your institution have a data migration plan in place?
- Is the collection cataloged in its entirety or partially? Is there a finding aid or an index to the collection that can be converted as part of the project to enhance access to the collection?
- How and who will gather the descriptive, administrative, technical, structural, and preservation metadata to create access points for the online collection? It is worth noting that catalog records may be created at various points of the workflow, depending on the origin of the metadata and project needs.
- What are your Web site requirements? Who will design and periodically review and upgrade the project Web site?
- How will others know what you digitized? What is your marketing plan?
- Is there adequate funding for the project? How much will it really cost? What are the direct costs and indirect costs? Are there internal or external grants available? Is there funding available from alumni or friends?

While these questions may appear daunting, it is important to take the necessary time at the beginning of the project, whether several weeks to several months, to seriously contemplate the various aspects of your project plan and its implementation. Also at this time consider establishing realistic time-specific project workflow goals and objectives. Setting measureable outcomes will help to keep the project on track and on budget. One way to master the digital project planning process is to develop a conceptual framework that will help stakeholders understand how the process works. One resource that I found useful in developing and implementing the digital project workflow at the Penn State University Libraries was the Northeast Document

Conservation Center's *Handbook for Digital Projects: A Management Tool for Preservation and Access*. This primer on managing digital projects covers the gamut of topics from the rationale for digitization and preservation, project management, selection, copyright, vendor relations, and end users' needs to a series of case studies on digital production best practices for various format types.

PRODUCTION DIGITIZATION STANDARDS AND BEST PRACTICES

The next step in the digital project progression is the capture process. Using either digital photography or digital recording devices, original source materials are captured in such a way as to not alter the information—meaning that the digital version represents the same information as the original analog version. While digital access to a collection can preserve originals through reduced handling, generally speaking, digitization is not yet a preservation medium; it is only a means of copying original materials that are stored on a stable medium. Digitization is all about improved sustainable access—the idea being that collections will be scanned only once and not rescanned.

Moreover, once the content has been scanned, management of the master image files and maintenance of the image database is essential; it is necessary to know what you have and where it is stored. Due to the relatively short life cycle of digital information, preservation of your digital content is an ongoing process. It is critical to have a backup plan for items mounted on local servers, but it is also important to have a preservation plan in place for the archival files. The Association of Library Collections and Technical Services (ALCTS), Preservation and Reformatting Section (PARS), Working Group on Defining Digital Preservation developed and issued the following definition of digital preservation: "Digital preservation combines policies, strategies and actions to ensure access to content that is born digital or converted to digital form regardless of the challenges of file corruption, media failure and technological change. The goal of digital preservation is the most accurate rendering possible of authenticated content over time" (ALCTS PARS Working Group on Defining Digital Preservation 2009).

To ensure the long-term accessibility of your digital assets consider the following questions:

- Does your digital project plan include a process to manage descriptive, administrative, technical, structural, and preservation metadata for digitized collections over time?
- Are processes in place to create and store backup copies on a stable medium for all master and derivative files produced for the project now and into the future?

- Who is responsible for maintaining the intellectual content of the collection over time?
- Who is responsible for maintaining the technical integrity of the collection over time?
- What process is in place to regularly check the files for corruption by use of a checksum to verify the integrity of the data?

Best practices for digital image production, digital preservation and quality control for capture, file management and maintenance and metadata standards abound. Following is a listing of some of the many resources available to assist you to follow current digitization project best practices.

USEFUL LINKS

Digital Project Resources

American Library Association's Association for Library Collections and Technical Services Preservation and Reformatting Section's *Minimum Digitization Capture Recommendations*—http://connect.ala.org/node/185648.

British Columbia Digital Library *Digital Library Construction Tools: How-To Manuals*—www.bcdlib.tc.ca/tools-manuals.html.

Cornell University's *Moving Theory into Practice, Digital Imaging Tutorial*—http://www.library.cornell.edu/preservation/tutorial/.

Digital Library Federation's *Digital Library and Standards and Practices*—http://old.diglib.org/standards.htm.

Howard Besser, "Introduction to Imaging: Issues in Constructing an Image Database." Getty Research Institute (2004). http://www.getty.edu/research/publications/electronic_publications/introimages/index.html.

Indiana University's Digital Library Program *Use of Digital Imaging Standards and Best Practices*—http://www.dlib.indiana.edu/education/work shops/lsta04/handout9.pdf.

Library of Congress' American Memory Technical Information, *Building Digital Collections: A Technical Overview*—http://memory.loc.gov/ammem/about/techIn.html.

National Archives and Records Administration's *Technical Guidelines for Digitizing Archival Materials for Electronic Access: Creation of Production Master Files—Raster Images*—http://www.archives.gov/preserva tion/technical/guidelines.pdf.

National Information Standards Organization, *A Framework of Guidance for Building Good Digital Collection*, 3rd ed. (2007). http://www.niso .org/publications/rp/framework3.pdf.

Northeast Document Conservation Center's *Handbook for Digital Projects: A Management Tool for Preservation and Access*—http://www.nedcc .org/resources/digitalhandbook/dman.pdf.

OCLC's *Best Practices and Planning for Digitization Projects*—http:// www.webjunction.org/documents/webjunction/Best_Practices_and_ Planning_for_Digitization_Projects.html.

Penn State University Libraries' *Digital Toolkit*—www.libraries.psu.edu/ psul/toolkits/digitaltools/standards.html.

Stanford University Libraries Digital Production Services *Quality Assurance— Cropping Guide*–http://lib.stanford.edu/digital-production-services/quality-assurance-cropping-guide.

Stanford University Libraries Digital Production Services *Quality Assurance— Image Defects*–http://lib.stanford.edu/digital-production-services/qual ity-assurance-image-defects.

University of Michigan's *Digitization Guidelines for Photographs and Tex-tual Documents*—http://bentley.umich.edu/dchome/resources/digitiza tion/20120719_digitizationguidelines_final.pdf.

Newspaper Digitization Project Resources

International Federation of Library Associations and Institutions (IFLA) Newspapers Section's *Digitization Projects and Best Practices*—http:// www.ifla.org/node/6777.

Library of Congress' National Digital Newspaper Program's *Guidelines and Resources*—http://www.loc.gov/ndnp/guidelines/.

University of Kentucky's *metalmorphosis*–http://www.uky.edu/Libraries/ NDNP/metamorphosis/resources.html.

Digital Preservation

Association of Library Collections and Technical Services, Preservation and Reformatting Section, Working Group on Defining Digital Preser-vation's *Definitions of Digital Preservation*—http://www.ala.org/alcts/ resources/preserv/2009def.

Cornell University's *Digital Preservation Management: Implementing Short-Term Strategies for Long-Term Problems*—http://www.dpwork shop.org/dpm-eng/eng_index.html.

Northeast Document Conservation Center's (NEDCC) *Surveying Digital Preservation Readiness: Toolkit for Cultural Organizations*–http://www .nedcc.org/resources/digtools.php.

University of Michigan's *Digital Preservation Management: Implement-ing Short-term Strategies for Long-Term Problems*—http://www.dpwork shop.org/dpm-eng/eng_index.html.

Metadata

Dublin Core—http://www.dublincore.org.

University of Denver's Collaborative Digitization Program's (CDP) *Dublin Core Metadata Best Practices*—http://www.mndigital.org/digitizing/standards/metadata.pdf.

WHAT MORE TO SAY? SHARING LESSONS LEARNED

In my 20 years of working with library curators and subject specialists to convert materials to digital form as a collection building strategy, I have learned some important lessons along the way. Some of these lessons were easy to grasp at the outset thereby averting potential problems later on; others resulted in redoing our work or even worse—ending up with unusable scanned collections. As an early adopter of digital technologies for collection development, we were motivated to try untested emerging technologies, but often uncertain as to where we were headed or what we might encounter. Initially it was a struggle. Each day was a challenge. However, over time and by gaining the necessary experience, the challenges and struggles became fewer; we righted our planning direction and focus and developed a vision for the foreseeable future. My hope is that by sharing what we have learned, you can avoid costly digital project pitfalls and experience success with your own digitization projects.

Lesson 1: Do not bite off more than you can chew; bigger is not always better.

A cool idea, enthusiasm, and ambition are a lethal combination and can easily distort reality. Our first digital project was to scan 350,000 archival pages. Needless to say, this project is still among our projects yet to be finished. Consider projects smaller in scope from 400 to 600 items in size, or in the case of newspapers, process batches of 10,000 pages at a time.

Lesson 2: It takes a team.

You need more than a single scanning technician to convert materials and build a digital collection. Subject curators, subject specialists and faculty experts, systems and information technology staff, preservation and reformatting staff, financial office personnel, and administrators each bring an important and necessary skill set to the digital planning and implementation process.

Lesson 3: It takes longer than you think.

How naive we were to think we could scan 350,000 pages in-house in two years. Today, our projects, albeit smaller in size, generally take 8–18 months from conception to public display. And regardless of the size of the project, the steps to digitizing a collection remain the same, although the time to inventory, stabilize, and scan the collections will vary.

Lesson 4: Quality is everything. Quality source materials *equals* quality searching results.

One important lesson we learned when working with microfilm is that poor film quality reduces the success in OCR processing and ultimately affects searching accuracy. With several of our historical newspaper digital projects we had to re-film portions of a newspaper due to the poor microfilm quality. Moreover, our need to re-microfilm resulted in additional project costs, increased time to locate and prepare materials for microfilming, a delay in the digitization phase of the project, and missed project deadlines.

Lesson 5: Garbage in—garbage out.

Just as important as having quality source materials is having quality description. High-quality description equals high-quality access and search navigation of collections. Metadata needs for different types of collections can be very different from what is supplied for traditional cataloging. With each digital project, it is necessary to work with the subject curator to determine access needs. The source of the metadata may be the cataloger, but depending on the project, it may also be supplied by a subject specialist, it may be purchased, or it could be converted from existing metadata such as MARC records, a finding aid, or a thesaurus.

Lesson 6: Build useful and useable Web sites that are intuitive to navigate.

Anticipate user needs first. Some of our first projects were all about production scanning with little attention paid to how users might access, navigate, or use the digital collection. With the eventual implementation of a team approach to digital projects, and the initial reference interview with the project curator to discuss scope, objectives, and expected outcomes of the project, we learned that user needs should be among the basic pieces of information that is gathered first. This also means building an intuitive user interface. Build search tip pages, provide derivative file formats for students to copy and paste into their research papers, add links to similar online content held elsewhere, and encourage use by incorporating interactive social media publishing options.

Lesson 7: Web sites should be forever.

Just when you think you're finished with a digital product you find out that your institution recently acquired another 50 items to be scanned and added to the online collection. Eventually, too, you will be faced with the need to enhance your Web site, upgrade and migrate your collection to the newest software platform, and more than likely you will need to move, add, or delete objects from the image database.

Lesson 8: Remember the original.

Build time into your digital project plan to stabilize and care for your original materials before, during, and after the scanning process. Whether microfilm reels, glass lantern slides, or paper copies, repairing, rehousing, or binding may be warranted. Also, remember to document the preservation methods and techniques used to prepare the collection on the Web site for future reference.

Lesson 9: Celebrate your accomplishments and let everyone know. Publicize.

Early on in our digitization program we were so focused on production and targeted completion deadlines that we did not record the names of the faculty, staff, and students who worked on projects. Today, not only do we record all participants involved in the project, but we also prepare an acknowledgment page on each project Web site and celebrate the launch of our new digital products.

To publicize our digitized collections, paper and email postcards are sent to donors and institutions with similar collections. We also use blog posts and other social media venues to spread the news. Keep in mind too that any promotional activities just might encourage future financial support for additional digital projects.

Lesson 10: Once you build it, they will come—to your Web site and to your library.

Never underestimate the power and potential of worldwide access. Users will find your products quickly, so be prepared for inquires, requests for physical access to originals, and especially requests to purchase images and/or print reproductions.

CONCLUSION

Despite the scores of challenges that you may encounter in your digitization project—from handling fragile materials in less than ideal conditions to the countless computer files that will need to be preserved over time, digitization as a collection development strategy in building online research collections *is* achievable.

To recap, a summary of the steps for you to follow are included in the following.

1. Select materials
2. Clear rights

3. Locate and retrieve materials (annex, branch location, other campus locations)
4. Inventory, collate, and stabilize the materials (disbind, mend, repair, deacidify, encapsulate)
5. Determine digital content management platform for display and access
6. Determine file naming convention (OCLC# or barcode, folder/box or title/date/volume/issue number), for example, 3465879_R102_A_0001.tif
7. Collect metadata in a spreadsheet (bibliographic information, such as author, title, date of publication)
8. Scan (color, grayscale, or black/white)
9. Collect structural metadata (size, dpi, etc.)
10. Assess and treat original materials (rebind, box, etc.)
11. Return original materials to home location
12. Upload scanned images and metadata
13. Create user interface Web page giving context for users
14. Request MARC tag 856 link be added to the bibliographic record in your online catalog—link to the online product
15. Request digitized collection be added to your main portal Web page for your digitized collections
16. Generate publicity or marketing plan for the digitized collection
17. Update all internal spreadsheets of the collection going live online; report collection status to project curator or subject specialist and other project stakeholders; calculate costs incurred, and so forth
18. Add e-copy sticker to the physical analog item or collection container to alert users that the content has been scanned and is available online

Libraries have embraced digitization as a means to convert analog collections to digital. Each year hundreds of digitization projects are launched and presented online thereby exposing collections to users worldwide. I hope that the information presented in this chapter equips and encourages you to consider project digitization as a feasible and vital collection development strategy for your institution.

NOTE

1. "Digital Collections Review Team Digital Toolkit," The Penn State University Libraries. https://www.libraries.psu.edu/psul/toolkits/digicoltoolkit.html (accessed December 30, 2012).

REFERENCES

Association of Library Collections and Technical Services, Preservation and Reformatting Section, Working Group on Defining Digital Preservation. 2009. "Definitions of Digital Preservation." Available at: http://www.ala.org/alcts/resources/preserv/2009def. Accessed December 30, 2012.

Conway, Paul. 2010. "Preservation in the Age of Google: Digitization, Digital Preserva-
    tion, and Dilemmas." *Library Quarterly* 80 (1): 61–79.
Lynch, Clifford A. 2009. "Special Collections at the Cusp of the Digital Age: A Credo."
    Research Library Issues 267.Available at: http://publications.arl.org/9ishf/prvp3/4. Ac-
    cessed December 7, 2012.

29

PRINT AND DIGITAL PRESERVATION

Jacob Nadal

INTRODUCTION

Terry Sanders' film *Slow Fires* (Sanders, Maddow, and MacNeil 1987) defined the challenges facing library and archives preservation efforts in the 20th century. Throughout the stacks, acid hydrolysis was constantly breaking down the cellulose fibers of paper, rendering the collections unusable. The problem was inherent to the media itself, and the only way to keep the information was to reformat it to new media. Microfilm was the technology that carried the day. Libraries adopted microfilm because it allowed for more compact storage, but it was repurposed for preservation because of its physical durability and chemical stability. By the time *Slow Fires* made its debut, the characteristics were nearly synonymous: microfilm was compact and eternal. It turns out though, that longevity is a minor consideration in libraries compared to storage space and ease of use.

Ironically, *Slow Fires*, a film about microfilming, concludes with a scene of an early digital library project that used optical discs to store images and text files. The filmmaker seems to have intuited the obvious narrative arc of ever-denser storage media, each generation one step further removed from physical presence and implicitly, from physical harm. This is the promise of ubiquitous computing: the data is fixed in no one place in particular, but can be delivered to many places simultaneously and every place potentially. Something is going on here at a deeper level than simply putting information on smaller or more durable media, and a better framework is needed to understand this. The Function Requirements for Bibliographic Records (FRBR) and the Open Archival Information System (OAIS) serve well in this role. In this chapter, I use these frameworks to explore way that preservation is accomplished across the domains of digital libraries and cloud computing, and printed or paper-based collections.

These two models, already widely used in their practitioner communities, are useful for harmonizing activities across the library and archival enterprise. The remainder of this chapter is in four sections. The first section gives a brief review of FRBR and OAIS with particular reference to how they work conceptually outside of their original spheres. The second and third sections discuss the state of digital preservation activities with particular reference to cooperative efforts, and examine the management of print storage in cooperative and consortium arrangements. Finally, these elements are unified into a preservation strategy that incorporates both print and digital preservations, each one supporting the other to ensure that libraries can reliably accommodate many types of use.

FRBR AND OAIS

FRBR[1] and the OAID[2] are two of the key theoretical developments in the evolution of library collection management and technical services. FRBR is an ontology that shows how a Work can be Expressed in a variety of ways that are Manifested in particular media and mediums that are managed as individual Items by the library.

The FRBR hierarchy—Work, Expression, Manifestation, Item—was developed as an aid to describing collections but is highly effective for evaluating preservation as well. Indeed, engaging in preservation without clear reference to the level of the hierarchy where preservation should be targeted can create substantial problems. Work-level preservation efforts can succeed while Manifestation-level efforts fail. This type of confusion is at the heart of the ongoing conflation of digitization and preservation. Digitization can be an effective strategy at the Work and Expression levels, while simultaneously failing at the Manifestation and Item levels.

Deriving an alternate version of a Work at any level of the FRBR hierarchy is an important test for preservation. At a certain point, a work may be so greatly modified on its way to becoming an Expression that it is better to call it a new work entirely. Take the case of something like *Heddatron*, a version of *Hedda Gabler* with a half robot cast, wherein Ibsen is repeatedly thwarted by a kitchen maid and August Strindberg while trying to write *Hedda Gabler*. In parallel, a Michigan woman is abducted by robots and forced to perform Ibsen's masterpieces over and over again. If every printed copy of Ibsen's *Hedda Gabler* was lost—eliminating an entire chain of Expression, Manifestations, and Items—but a recording of a theatrical performance survived, we could use that recording to derive new scripts to create new Expressions, Manifestations, and Items. If the theatrical recording was subsequently lost, but the new scripts retained, the Work would have still been preserved throughout. However, if every Expression, Manifestation, and Item representing *Hedda Gabler* were lost, but we still had *Heddatron*, we could achieve at best a fragmentary and confused version of Ibsen's work. The Expressions, Manifestations, and Items of *Hedda Gabler* are sufficient for preservation of the Work called *Hedda Gabler*. The Expressions, Manifestations, and Items of *Heddatron* are not.

This brings us back to *Slow Fires* and the subsequent debate over microfilming that Nicholson Baker launched in *Double Fold* (Baker 2001) and the articles that preceded it in the *New Yorker*, such as "Deadline" (Baker 2000) and "The Author vs. the Library" (Baker 1996). Baker excoriated librarians for microfilming newspapers and discarding the originals in the name of preservation. Librarians were preserving the Works and their Expressions, but were not preserving the Manifestations and Items. This observation is not meant to resolve the discord, but rather to facilitate debate. Accepting the concept that preservation plays out at different levels of the FRBR hierarchy, and that preservation at one level can occur in parallel with loss at another level, is necessary in harmonizing print and digital preservation strategies. Baker was objecting to a failure to preserve Manifestations and Items; librarians were rejoicing that they had preserved Works and Expressions.

There are numerous methods available to care for and repair items. These should be called conservation techniques, to clarify that they are a distinct class of activities related to preservation. Conservation techniques need to be deployed within a larger strategic framework of preservation and curation. The OAIS describes three main function of an archive: Submission (S), Archival Storage (A), and Dissemination (D) (CCSDS 2012). Each function is coupled to an information package (IP) and a method of transforming the IP between each function. The Submission Information Package (SIP) becomes and Archival Information Package (AIP) as it is Ingested into Archival Storage, and the AIP becomes a Dissemination Information Package (DIP) to give consumers Access to Information.

In terms of preservation theory, it is important to recognize that the SIP, AIP, and DIP may be nearly identical to one another. This would not be the norm in digital archives, where there are likely to be different formats for Archival Storage and Dissemination, as well as substantially different metadata at each stage in the OAIS reference model. For a print library, however, a book and its catalog record can be traced through this whole process and except for adding a few labels on ingest and providing a local call number, the object and metadata in the various Information Packages will be nearly identical.

Although the impetus for developing the OAIS was the recognition of digital preservation challenges, OAIS itself is fairly agnostic about the type of materials that the "Archive" might contain. As we attempt to develop strategies for managing preservation across different media, it is important to emphasize the media-independence of the OAIS model. Therefore, I make reference to the OAIS Functional Entities of Archival Storage and Preservation Planning in the discussion of print and digital preservation systems that follow, to emphasize the similarity of concepts across both media and by contrast, to emphasize where digital and artifact-specific traits present preservation advantages or risks that can be offset by one another.

COOPERATIVE DIGITAL PRESERVATION

Digital preservation efforts have had a long collaborative and cooperative tradition. E-journal preservation (and increasingly, eBook preservation) is the area of digital preservation most widely encountered by libraries and most closely coupled to the decisions libraries make about managing their print holdings. E-journal preservation occurs predominately through the Lots of Copies Keeps Stuff Safe (LOCKSS) (http://www.lockss.org) and Portico (www.portico.org) projects. LOCKSS and Portico both have strong records for preservation, but substantially different approaches. Alongside LOCKSS and Portico, HathiTrust (www.hathitrust.org) and the Internet Archive (www.archive.org) are the most important eBook preservation efforts at present, containing works digitized by Internet Archive and Google's large-scale digitization projects. Finally, it is important to note that the digital preservation efforts discussed here are chosen because they are closely coupled to libraries' general research collections, rather than library and archives special collections. Special collections are increasingly important to library services in the 21st century and are one of the major drivers of digital library projects, but almost by definition, special collections are not managed in a cooperative fashion as a shared resource.

The LOCKSS software has a substantial and successful record of maintaining content over time and has developed into several related projects that build on the same core preservation engine. The Global LOCKSS Network (GLN) has subsumed the original e-journal preservation function of the LOCKSS project. Private LOCKSS networks are being established as cooperative arrangements of digital libraries to share the costs of preservation. There are 10 or more now in operation, including MetaArchive (http://www.metaarchive.org) and Controlled LOCKSS (CLOCKSS) (www.clockss.org). MetaArchive is an international membership organization run by the Educopia Institute, a 501(c)3 organization. MetaArchive "caters to cultural memory organizations that are collaborating to preserve very high value locally created digital materials" and is reported to be among the largest Private LOCKSS Network implementations. CLOCKSS provides a dark archive of scholarly journal content, kept in a network of 12 LOCKSS boxes across Europe, Asia, and North America. When content in CLOCKSS is no longer available from a publisher, it is copied from the CLOCKSS Archive and made available at no cost to the library community.[3]

Critical to understanding the role of LOCKSS, and distributed preservation strategies generally, is the idea of storing many copies of identical objects in discrete locations. In FRBR terms, distributed preservation assumes many Items and, by preserving them, ensures the continued existence of a Manifestation, preserving in turn an Expression and thus a Work. Damage can occur to an Item in one node of the network without affecting the existence of the rest of the WEM chain.

Portico is the other major e-journal preservation system in use in the United States. Portico bears many similarities to CLOCKSS in the way it acquires and releases content, but uses a substantially different approach to preservation. LOCKSS receives materials from publishers and replicates them as ingested. Originally this meant that LOCKSS harvested the Web-delivered versions of the articles, generally HTML or PDF files. In OAIS terms, LOCKSS harvests the publisher's DIP and treats it as the LOCKSS SIP. With minimal changes, this as-published content becomes the LOCKSS AIP. There is a potential problem if the publisher's DIP, the content that is actually delivered to library users, is substantially different from the publisher's own AIP, which lives in its proprietary content management systems, especially if they were to contain metadata or higher-quality data than the publisher released through its AIP (McCargar et al. 2009). The degree to which this is a real problem has not been well quantified, though. CLOCKSS may also mitigate this potential problem by acquiring files more directly from the publisher than the original LOCKSS system.

Portico, by contrast, was established to take publisher's source files and normalize them for preservation. This allows Portico to mitigate several potential problems related to format obsolescence as Portico fully controls its own preservation formats. There is still some question as to when in the chain of production the publishers create the package of content that is received by Portico, and it is fair to assume that the answer differs between publishers. However, by working with publishers directly, Portico has the potential to get at production source files instead of distribution files. The loss of data through the digital publishing chain has received some attention, especially in the area of news preservation (Center for Research Libraries 2011). Although this is an emerging issue in digital preservation, production files potentially contain data and metadata that are valuable for long-term preservation.

Portico stores its archive in several on- and off-line versions and on different hardware platforms. The master copy of the archive in Princeton, New Jersey, is maintained using the Documentum content management system and Oracle database platform, and the Portico content storage area for publisher content is backed up to tape. One online replica of the archive is located on a file system in Ann Arbor, Michigan, and a second in commercial cloud storage. Both replicas are stored in a file system rather than a database/CMS and are self-describing and boot-strappable, so that the archive can be rebuilt from either replica. An off-line replica of the Portico archive is stored off continent at the National Library of the Netherlands, for preservation in their secure vault. Incremental backups of the archive are shipped to the National Library of the Netherlands on a quarterly basis and a full backup of the archive is created and shipped to the National Library of the Netherlands annually.[4]

Despite their different technical approaches, both LOCKSS and Portico achieve good results in preserving their holdings. HathiTrust and the Internet Archive do not represent radically different models for storing and managing digital content, but they are distinctive and important collections of material. Like the e-journals in LOCKSS and Portico, the digitized books in HathiTrust and the Internet Archive are closely coupled to libraries' printed and general research collections, in contrast to digital versions of library special collections.

HathiTrust and the Internet Archive preserve huge amounts of data. There are about 475 terabytes of data representing nearly 10.6 million volumes in the HathiTrust.[5] The Internet Archive hosts over 3.8 million texts, more than 1.1 million videos, and over 1.4 million audio files, totaling some 1.7 petabytes (1,741 terabytes) as of December 2010.[6] Both repositories use a fairly conventional datacenter model to store and replicate their content. In the case of HathiTrust it stores its data in a file system managed using California Digital Library's Pairtree micro service (University of California 2008), on two Isilon storage systems, one in Michigan and the other in Indiana. These are replicated on a frequent, periodic basis, usually daily but with some alteration depending on the amount of data in play on any given day. The two systems are mirrored and load-balanced, as well, so that a user may be served data from either system at any time, an important disaster mitigation technique.

The Internet Archive stores its data on its Petabox systems (Internet Archive 2004). The Petabox uses commodity hardware to provide 650 terabytes of storage in a single rack with low power consumption level of 6 kilowatts per petabyte, plus little need for air conditioning. Indeed, Internet Archive uses excess heat from its Petaboxes to help heat its building in San Francisco. At present, it reports having four datacenters in operation and has also used Bibliotheca Alexandria as a mirror site for its Web archive (Bibliotheca Alexandrina 2002).

All of these systems have good records in preserving their digital content, with no notable failures or loss of content to date. Although they represent different philosophies and levels of mitigation and risk-tolerance, they collectively make a strong case for the position that large-scale digital collections are reliable and available in the present. And, because these digital collections have a strong relationship to library print collections, they can be an important element in library preservation planning when used in conjunction with appropriate print storage strategies, discussed in the next section.

COOPERATIVE PRINT PRESERVATION

Shared collection practices, from ILL to large-scale digitization, have always mixed economic necessity with service aspirations. The development of purpose built high-density storage facilities (Payne 2007) that bring together sharing functions such as digitization and ILL (Seaman 2003) with preservation through environmental controls, preservation imaging and on-site conservation laboratories has opened the way to a new era in library collaboration around the management of the printed record (Malpas 2011).

Cooperative collection management allows access to a greater variety of material by distributing the costs of some resources across a network of partners. In many cases, there is a convenience cost for some users, as they wait for materials to be delivered. There are also outright and overhead costs to the library as they pay fees for using and maintaining the delivery system, but costs and delays often trump no access at all. Some libraries are electing to purchase materials outright rather than use ILL, an interesting network effect related to online booksellers making materials more discoverable for purchase and shared cataloging lowering the cost of metadata creation for new acquisitions.

Although the problem of scarcity is inherent in print collections, it plays out in digital libraries as well, with a key difference. In print collections, shared resources overcame a problem of scarcity. There were either very few items to begin with, as in the case of museums and special collections, or there were limits on the funds available to acquire items. In digital collections, scarcity is deliberately imposed.

Scarcity still persists in the experience of using digital resources, but it occurs at a different point in the supply chain. Print collections may suffer from a shortage of actual items to read and have to balance access versus the preservation needs of a particular physical object, whereas digital collections may be made scarce from a lack of usage environments; they are a metaphorical print library that has neither chairs nor light bulbs. Sometimes these constrains are rooted in available infrastructure. In 2012, 100 percent of public libraries reported that they offer Internet access, but in the same study 41.7 percent of report that they lacked sufficient broadband access to meet patron needs, and 69 percent report speeds lower than 10 megabytes per second (Bertot et al. 2012). The digital divide is a systematic barrier to access, but it is shrinking, and should be strongly contrasted to intentional constraints such as pay walls and systems that limit the number of simultaneous users for a particular resource. In the early 20th century, an argument that limited processing power and bandwidth-required restrictions on usage was believable, but it is harder to sustain in the 21st century, when most publishers, academic libraries, and public libraries have connected to very high-speed networks, and computation resources are available as a commodity service from many vendors.

Usage restrictions in the digital library are increasingly driven by license terms that are tied to a particular business model, not to an inherent characteristic of digital information. These restrictions are solutions to fiscal problems, not intrinsic characteristics of digital information (Farb 2006). The potential for ubiquitous digital access has enabled libraries to pay more attention to the economics of shared print storage and to bring preservation concerns to the forefront of that picture.

One of the most germane examples of distributed print storage is the U.S. Government Printing Office (GPO), which was from its inception intended to couple preservation and access functions and keep the nation's records safe through "such a multiplication of copies, as shall place them beyond reach of accident," rather than through "vaults and locks which fence them from the public eye and use in consigning them to the waste of time."[7] The GPO Depository Library Program was a direct inspiration to LOCKSS and has served well to keep government publications widely available since 1813. Today, the same core concept is driving a reinvestigation of shared collections and alluding to digital terminology to cloud-source the print collection.

Other programs are not as long established, but equally venerable. The Five Colleges created a shared collections system and depository in 1951, as the Hampshire Inter-Library Center (HILC). Since 1949, CRL has acquired resources that are difficult to for an individual library to acquire—for reasons of cost, scarcity, or both—and provided them to the CRL member libraries. In addition to maintaining objects in storage facilities, CRL has been involved in microfilming and digitization, and tellingly, was one of the early service providers for the Trusted Repositories Audit and Certification process (TRAC) (Center for Research Libraries 2007). OhioLINK (www.ohiolink.edu) was established in 1987, the same year the University of California system also created a shared collections program operated out of the Southern and Northern Regional Library Facilities (SRLF and NRLF). NRLF (www.srlf.ucla.edu) was developed in 1982, and SRLF (http://www.lib.berkeley.edu/NRLF/about .html) in 1987. Together they hold over 12 million items and served as the foundation for the Western Regional Storage Trust Program (WEST) (http:// www.cdlib.org/services/west/). As of July 2007, as least 68 high-density storage facilities existed in the United States and Canada, holding more than 70 million volumes in total (Payne 2007, 6).

Throughout the 20th century, these programs have primarily served an access function by overcoming the scarcity problems of print collections. Preservation has always been an important secondary element in their missions, but has come to the fore recently. Access to adequate digital versions of the works kept in shared print networks has enabled a shift in focus, from preservation as a beneficial effect toward preservation as an intentional good. This change is playing out for two reasons. The first, discussed earlier, is the ability of digital libraries to provide Manifestation- and Expression-level access to a vast collection of materials that is large enough to dwarf all but a few American research library print collections, and accessible in a format that is intrinsically able to be ubiquitously available, even if law, economics, and policy proscribe use. The second, less discussed here, is the renewed attention to library collections as artifacts and the implicit requirement that these receive appropriate conservation treatment.

Several major developments in core preservation practice have likewise moved the preservation function of collaborative storage to the forefront. One is the development of a number of new conservation labs in conjunction with collection storage facilities. The other is the development of a more sophisticated system for the evaluation of preservation environments. The final element is an emerging effort in the preservation community to adapt risk management frameworks that deal with scarcity and endangerment to library networks.

Conservation lab construction was stimulated by several factors in the 21st century; in particular by the Andrew W. Mellon Foundation's support for new lab spaces coupled with the economic advantages of constructing new high-density storage facilities (Teper and Alstrom 2012). For our discussion, the critical outcome is the close coupling of collections in need of services with the service providers. At the UC SRLF, for example, the preservation-imaging unit has been colocated with the existing storage facility since its inception, and plans for that facility include relocating the conservation laboratory into the expanded storage space. Indiana University and the University of Illinois Urbana-Champaign both constructed new storage facilities with integrated conservation labs in the 21st century. The New York Public Library has developed what may be the rule-proving exception, a conservation facility located not at the collection storage location, but at the central logistics point, which is still a hub for collections on their path from storage to use. Preservation and conservation facilities and expertise are at a key point of flow for library collections in all of these models, providing built-in opportunities to utilize preservation services, especially for general research collections.[8]

The cornerstone of preservation environment research is Donald Sebera's (1994) work on isopermanence. Sebera's key observation is that any given rate of deterioration can be caused by many combinations of temperature and relative humidity, and likewise, multiple combinations of temperature and relative humidity are capable of producing preservation benefits. James Reilly and other researchers at the Image Permanence Institute (IPI), William Lull, Tim Padfield, and others developed Sebera's work in the interest of determining if there were a better path to conservation than the traditional effort to maintain a flat-line, constant temperature, and relative humidity environment (Tedone, Pavelka, and Becker 2008). From this, IPI's Time-Weighted Preservation Index (TWPI) was developed and used as the basis for a series of field trials and research projects that led to the creation of hardware and software for monitoring and evaluating preservation environments. At the same time, the introduction of direct digital controls (DDC) into facilities management enabled more fine-grained, programmatic control of systems.

Adoption of DDCs is another variation on the theme: a change adopted out of fiscal concerns, but providing the opportunity for better preservation as a secondary benefit. A key collaborator on the IPI field trials, and the environmental optimization portfolio that developed out of them, is Herzog/Wheeler Associates, consulting engineers concerned with energy efficiency. Coupling Herzog/Wheeler's process for energy efficiency with IPI's metrics for preservation environments has led to multiple benefits: collections receive a better storage environment, energy usage and concomitant expenditures are reduced, and oftentimes (due to better review and understanding of mechanical systems in a storage facility), relatively inexpensive preventative maintenance makes catastrophic mechanical system failure far less likely. While this final utopic outcome is highly dependent on institutional priorities and politics, the dual benefit of reduced energy use for better preservation environments is compelling on its own, and intrinsic to the optimization process.

As technology has altered the usage of print collections, a delightful irony has emerged. The development of the Internet was predicated on the robustness of packet-switched networks, and, preservation models that effectively treat printed volumes as packets are now being developed. A working paper by Candace Arai Yano's IEOR group at UC Berkeley, commissioned by JSTOR, is the foundation for this model. Yano, Shen, and Chan (2008) adapted models from manufacturing to develop risk of loss curves for print journals. Their basic argument was that the question of how many printed items were needed to ensure the existence of a single perfect item at the end of a given period of time was in essence the same question as asking how many spare parts needed to be produced during a production run to ensure sufficient supply to cover repairs for the life of a manufactured device.

Based on Yano's adaptation of this line of thinking to the library environment, Nadal and Peterson (2013) developed a framework for evaluating risk in shared print collections that incorporates a greater degree of preservation information and library-domain-specific information. The results are notable. In many cases, 12–24 copies in usable condition are sufficient to satisfy a century-long planning horizon. For many items fewer than 12 copies are extant, which calls for significant preservation effort. However, in many cases these are already held at institutions with some level of preservation capability. More significantly, for a vast collection of materials, well over 50 copies are extant, making it possible to think of preservation as a service that focuses on a defined subset of the volumes in libraries. Preservation capacity still may not be robust enough across the system to meet that need, but being able to define the need is a critical step toward developing a viable strategic plan for preservation.

UNIFIED PRESERVATION STRATEGIES

In the emerging scenario of large-scale digital collections backed by reliable digital preservation systems and equally large-scale shared print collections supported by reliable artifact preservation systems, FRBR and OAIS can be valuable ways of talking about unified preservation strategies that are more economical in capitalizing on the benefits of different formats and use cases.

For strategic preservation planning in research collections, Expression-level preservation is the goal. Work-level preservation is too abstract for useful policy making, while Manifestation- and Item-level preservation is more clearly the province of special collections. As an example, a researcher may want to consult different editions of a work (Expressions), but can use these in either print or digital form (Manifestations), yet does not specifically require the copy in the Rare Book Division with a Nobel Prize acceptance speech written on the flyleaves (Item).[9]

Print and digital collections play different and complementary roles in achieving Expression-level preservation. Conservator Gary Frost has made a compelling argument that print collections play a role in verification of digital resources, coining the term leaf-master to refer to a printed work kept for this purpose (Frost 2008). The adoption of the concept of managed scarcity in WEST attests to the necessity of this role for print collections. JSTOR's studies also provide some information about how often this function is required, noting that half of its error reports occur in the first two years of posting an item online, and 92 percent within five years (Schonfeld and Housewright 2009). So far it appears that needs are minimal, which attests to the overall quality of digital collections and should give some comfort to anyone who cannot quite trust the math in the scarcity risk-management frameworks.

In fact, this dimension of trust may be one of the key coming-of-age challenges to librarians in the early 21st century. There is substantial data and information available to suggest that digital collections are reliable and usable and that shared print preservation can be effectively risk-managed. These assertions warrant healthy skepticism, but they are often subject to a chauvinism toward tangible objects that is harder to defend. It is important to differentiate between a few concepts that are sometimes misunderstood in our contemporary information environment: downtime as opposed to loss, and obsolescence versus decay.

Downtime is possible in a digital environment for a variety of reasons having nothing to do with the integrity of the underlying data. Momentary interruptions in access are independent of preservation outcomes, which are hedged against by processes for detecting and mitigating risks of obsolescence, data corruption, and physical damage and decay. All of these strategies work in tandem to preserve an Item that is sufficient to accomplish Manifestation-level preservation, and in turn keep at least one Expression of a Work available. Simultaneous failures of all these systems are required for the complete loss of any Work that exists in both a print and digital Manifestation. For a research library community concerned with preservation of Works and their Expressions, maintaining both print and digital Manifestations are critical elements of preservation strategy, but there are clearly diminishing returns on maintaining dozens or hundreds of redundant Items across the system.

Print and digital preservation do not exist in a zero-sum relationship, but instead, they should be treated as elements of a balanced preservation strategy. Many libraries will weight their efforts strongly toward print preservation. This is a primary function in rare book and manuscript collections. The Othmer Library at Brooklyn Historical Society where I work, for example, is a National Interior Landmark where place-based and primary-source research and education are intended to come together. A recent visit from architecture students at the New York City College of Technology involved viewing George Post's architectural drawing for the library and then making their own measurements and drawings within the library itself. There is no digital equivalent. Artifact preservation is intrinsic to our services.

For other libraries, print collections are all but irrelevant. For example, the engineering libraries at Stanford and Cornell have made news by moving away from print collections (Sydell 2010), yet both universities are central players in e-journal preservation efforts. Indeed, Stanford hosts the LOCKSS project and Cornell both hosts arXiv (http://arxiv.org/) and was the original developer and site for the Digital Preservation Workshop and Tutorial (http://dpworkshop.org) that has been one of the primary venues for training and education in digital preservation.

Most libraries fall between these extremes. (Stanford and Cornell both maintain substantial book collections beyond their engineering libraries, of course.)[10] A review of the membership lists for LOCKSS and Portico will turn up dozens of libraries that also maintain print storage facilities. Print collections and digital collections serve different functions and perform complementary roles. Taken together, a hybrid print and digital preservation strategy supports a wider range of use-cases and presents a lower risk of loss than either type of collection can provide on its own.

CONCLUSION

I have argued that physical artifacts and digital resources have complementary roles in preservation, and that the FRBR and OAIS models are complementary frameworks for managing stewardship efforts across these two domains. There are some types of inquiry that are essentially artifactual and others that are essentially digital, but for supplying a document to a reader, for the core function of libraries and archives, either type of resource can serve well enough. Some may prefer reading a text on screen and others on the page, but reading occurs in either case.

The ALA's definitions of digital preservation state that "[d]igital preservation combines policies, strategies and actions that ensure access to digital content over time." Remove the word "digital," and this could be a workable definition of preservation of any sort, describing a goal of "access over time" that is achieved through "policies, strategies, and actions." In this chapter, I have described two sets of high-level actions and a strategy for evaluating them. Print preservation is enacted through environmental controls, conservation, and agreements to limit risk and control scarcity. Digital preservation is enacted through replication of copies and encoding digital objects in well-understood formats that are tailored to their user-community's needs. These actions can support a strategic preservation effort when FRBR entities are used to decide when print and digital resources serve the same need and when the OAIS is used to evaluate the viability of each preservation approach.

NOTES

1. IFLA Study Group on the Functional Requirements for Bibliographic Records. 1998. Functional requirements for bibliographic records: final report. München: K.G. Saur.

2. Open Archival Information System. http://www.iso.org/iso/home/store/catalogue_ics/catalogue_detail_ics.htm?csnumber=57284 (accessed July 18, 2013).

3. "Who Gets Access to Content Impacted by a Trigger Event?" https://www.clockss.org/clockss/FAQ (accessed July 18, 2013).

4. "Portico Replication and Backup Policy, v. 1.1." http://www.portico.org/digital-preservation/wp-content/uploads/2011/03/Portico-Replication-and-Backup-Policy.pdf (accessed July 10, 2013).

5. "HathiTrust Statistics and Information." http://www.hathitrust.org/statistics_info (accessed July 10, 2013).

6. "Internet Archive PetaBox." http://archive.org/web/petabox.php (accessed July 10, 2013).

7. Thomas Jefferson to Ebenezer Hazard, Philadelphia, February 18, 1791. In *Thomas Jefferson: Writings: Autobiography, Notes on the State of Virginia, Public and Private Papers, Addresses, Letters*, edited by Merrill D. Peterson. New York: Library of America. (1984)

8. There is more work to be done on the costs of preservation, especially the balance between direct costs for services and the overall costs across a collection or a library's portfolio of service. For instance, some of these libraries had special collections adjacent spaces that were replaced or reconfigured in response to the construction of new lab spaces. The direct cost per special collections item treated may be higher, in these cases, even though preservation services overall may be having greater impact at lower cost. For an introduction to these issues, see Calvi, Elise. 2006. *The Preservation Manager's Guide to Cost Analysis*. Chicago: Preservation and Reformatting Section, Association for Library Collections & Technical Services.

9. I owe this particular example to Michael Inman, Rare Books Curator at the New York Public Library, who showed me an exceptional inscribed presentation copy of John Marquand's *Thirty Years, from Ernest Hemingway to Lee Samuels*, with Hemingway's holograph draft of his Nobel prize acceptance speech on two blank leaves at the end. http://nypl.bibliocommons.com/item/show/13127997052_thirty_years (accessed July 18, 2013).

10. Cornell is actually one of the most notable examples of the genealogy of print and digital preservation. Anne Kenney, now Cornell's university librarian, was associate director for Cornell's Department of Preservation and Conservation from 1987 to 2001, and then transitioned into a leadership role in digital libraries and preservation.

REFERENCES

ALCTS Preservation and Reformatting Section, Working Group on Defining Digital Preservation. 2007. "Definitions of Digital Preservation." ALA Annual Conference, Washington, D.C. (June 24). Available at: http://www.ala.org/alcts/resources/preserv/defdigpres0408. Accessed November 4, 2013.

Baker, Nicholson. 1996. "Letter from San Francisco: The Author vs. the Library." *The New Yorker* (October 14): 50.

Baker, Nicholson. 2000. "Deadline." *The New Yorker* (July 24): 42.

Baker, Nicholson. 2001. *Double Fold: Libraries and the Assault on Paper*. New York: Random House.

Bertot, J. C., A. McDermott, R. Lincoln, B. Real, and K. Peterson. 2012. *2011–2012 Public Library Funding and Technology Access Survey: Survey Findings & Report.* College Park, MD: Information Policy & Access Center, University of Maryland College Park. Available at: http://plinternetsurvey.org/sites/default/files/publications/2012_plftas.pdf. Accessed July 11, 2013.

Bibliotheca Alexandrina: Internet Archive. 2002. Available at: http://www.bibalex.org/internetarchive/ia_en.aspx. Accessed July 10, 2013.

Center for Research Libraries. 2007. *Trustworthy Repositories Audit & Certification: Criteria and Checklist.* Available at: http://www.crl.edu/sites/default/files/attachments/pages/trac_0.pdf. Accessed July 10, 2013.

Center for Research Libraries. 2011. *Preserving News in the Digital Environment: Mapping the Newspaper Industry in Transition.* Available at: http://www.digitalpreservation.gov/documents/CRL_digiNews_report_110502.pdf. Accessed July 11, 2013.

Consultative Committee for Space Data Systems (CCSDS). 2012. *Reference Model for an Open Archival Information System (OAIS).* Washington, DC: CCSDS. Available at: http://public.ccsds.org/publications/archive/650x0m2.pdf. Accessed July 11, 2013.

Farb, Sharon E. 2006. "Libraries, Licensing and the Challenge of Stewardship." *First Monday* 11 (7). Available at: http://firstmonday.org/htbin/cgiwrap/bin/ojs/index.php/fm/article/viewArticle/1364. Accessed July 11, 2013.

Frost, Gary. 2008. "BookLab: Verging on the Future of the Paper Book." *BookNote* (20). Available at: http://cool.conservation-us.org/byauth/frost/frost1.html. Accessed July 11, 2013.

Internet Archive. 2004. *Petabox 4.* Available at: http://archive.org/web/petabox.php. Accessed July 10, 2013.

Malpas, Constance. 2011. *Cloud-Sourcing Research Collections Managing Print in the Mass-Digitized Library Environment.* Dublin, OH: OCLC Research. Available at: http://www.oclc.org/content/dam/research/publications/library/2011/2011-01.pdf?urlm=162949. Accessed July 18, 2013.

McCargar, V., J. Nadal, H. Snyder, A. Vanek, and F. Zarndt. 2009. "Newspapers, Data Formats, and Acronym Stew: Preservation and Distribution of Born-digital Newspapers Using METS/ALTO, NITF, and PDF-A." Proceedings of the IFLA International Newspaper Conference. In *Newspapers: Legal Deposit and Research in the Digital Era,* ed. Hartmut Walravens, 115–24. Berlin/Munich: De Gruyter Saur

Nadal, Jacob, and Annie Peterson, "Scarce and Endangered Works: Using Network-Level Holdings Data in Preservation Decision Making and Stewardship of the Printed Record" (Preprint, accepted for publication in ALCTS Monographs). Available at: http://www.jacobnadal.com/162. Accessed July 10, 2013.

Payne, Lizanne. 2007. *Library Storage Facilities and the Future of Print Collections in North America.* Dublin, OH: OCLC Programs and Research.

Sanders, Terry, Ben Maddow, and Robert MacNeil. 1987. *Slow Fires: On the Preservation of the Human Record.* DVD or VHS. United States: American Film Foundation. Available at: http://www.americanfilmfoundation.com/order/slow_fires.shtml. Accessed July 18, 2013.

Schonfeld, Roger C., and Ross Housewright. 2009. *What to Withdraw? Print Collections Management in the Wake of Digitization.* New York, NY: Ithaka S+R. Available at: http://www.sr.ithaka.org/research-publications/what-withdraw-print-collections-management-wake-digitization. Accessed July 10, 2013.

Seaman, Scott. 2003. "High-Density Off-Site Storage: Document Delivery and Academic Library Research Collections." *Journal of Interlibrary Loan, Document Delivery & Information Supply* 13 (3): 91–103.

Sebera, Donald K. 1994. *Isoperms: An Environmental Management Tool.* Washington, DC: Commission on Preservation and Access.

Sydell, Laura. 2010, July 8. "Stanford Ushers in the Age of Bookless Libraries." *National Public Radio.* Available at: http://www.npr.org/templates/transcript/transcript .php?storyId=128361395. Accessed July 10, 2013.

Tedone, Melissa, Karen Pavelka, and Snowden Becker. 2008. "From Gray Areas to Green Areas: Developing Sustainable Practices in Preservation Environments: Symposium Papers." Austin, TX: Kilgarlin Center for Preservation of the Cultural Record, School of Information, The University of Texas at Austin. Available at: http://www.ischool .utexas.edu/kilgarlin/gaga/proceedings.html. Accessed July 18, 2013.

Teper, Jennifer Hain, and Eric Alstrom. 2012. *Planning and Constructing Book and Paper Conservation Laboratories: A Guidebook.* Chicago: Association for Library Collections and Technical Services, a Division of the American Library Association.

University of California. 2008. CDL Pairtree, Version 0.1. Available at: https://confluence .ucop.edu/display/Curation/PairTree. Accessed July 10, 2013.

Yano, Candace Arai, Z.J. Max Shen, and Stephen Chan. October 2008. "Optimizing the Number of Copies for Print Preservation of Research Journals." IEOR Department and the Haas School of Business.

EPILOGUE

As this book makes clear, libraries of all kinds are actively building collections in ways that could not have been predicted even 10 years ago. The economics of publishing, unanticipated changes in funding for libraries of all kinds, technological advances, and rapidly changing patron expectations have come together as interconnected forces to forge a new landscape. However, this new landscape is unfinished and it is difficult to anticipate what collections and collection management will look like in another 20 years. What we can be certain of is this: the need for collections (in the broadest sense of the word) is not going away and there is plenty of room to shape collections and influence their use.

What can we expect as the most significant sources of change in our work? We offer the following points as a guide:

1. All libraries must balance local needs for materials in a variety of formats with the budgets they have at hand. Stretching collections dollars will mean more shifts in decisions about how access to materials is provided (buy, rent, borrow, etc.)
2. Libraries will become more collaborative on many levels—from local to international. As libraries increasingly share collections and the responsibility for preserving materials, there will be a shift in how decisions are made with more emphasis on interdependencies.
3. The variety of materials libraries provide access to will increase. New formats and new genres are emerging. Libraries of all kinds will increasingly be portals to rich special collections worldwide.
4. Shared storage of print and digital collections will become the new normal. Questions of how to store materials, how many copies to preserve, and so forth, are moving toward resolution.

5. Librarians associated with collection development and management in all types of libraries will be increasingly involved in promoting use of their collections and assisting with discovery of collections worldwide.

In summary, while there will be much about collection development that will be immensely surprising in the next 20 years, we feel confident exciting developments will prevail. With an engaged profession committed to ever wider access to the contents of the world's libraries, what could inspire more wonder?[1]

NOTE

1. The thoughts expressed here owe much to the deliberations of the Association of Research Libraries Task Force on 21st Century Research Libraries Collections.

INDEX

About the Editors and the Contributors

ROBERT ALAN was appointed head, Serials & Acquisitions Department in 2004 after serving as head, Serials Department (2000–2004) at Penn State University. He held previous positions in technical services at the University of California Davis and the University of California, San Diego. Mr. Alan has worked extensively in the areas of serials cataloging, acquisitions, and electronic resource management. He received his MLS from the University of Arizona.

BECKY ALBITZ is associate college librarian for Collection Management at Bates College, Lewiston, Maine. Previously, she was the media services librarian at the University of Iowa and NYU, head librarian, Penn State Shenango (Sharon, Pennsylvania), and most recently electronic resources librarian at Penn State University. Her published works include *Licensing and Managing Electronic Resources* and a number of articles on media librarianship and licensing. Albitz holds an MA in film from Penn State, an MLS from the University of Pittsburgh, and a doctorate in higher education from Penn State.

KIM ARMSTRONG is currently deputy director of the Center for Library Initiatives at the Committee on Institutional Cooperation (CIC) (www.cic.net). The CIC is an academic consortium of the universities of the Big Ten athletic conference and the University of Chicago. Her current responsibilities include management for the Google book scanning project, the CIC Shared Print Repository and support for working groups on resource sharing, content licensing, and scholarly publishing. Kim has been an academic librarian for over 20 years, holding positions in both academic libraries and consortia.

CHRISTINE AVERY is the director of Commonwealth Campus Libraries within the University Libraries at Penn State University and for several years was also collection development coordinator for Commonwealth Campus Libraries. Avery joined the University Libraries at Penn State in 1990 and was previously Head of Reference and User Services at the University of Wyoming. In her work at Penn State she manages 20 campus libraries located across the Commonwealth of Pennsylvania. Avery was an ARL Visiting Program Officer from 2010 to 2012 assigned to the Task Force on 21st Century Research Library Collections, which produced the issue brief "Calibration of Investment and Collaborative Action." She is an active member of Educause. She received her MLS from the University of Texas, an MS in applied social research from Texas Christian University, and a BS in sociology from Texas A&M University.

CHISTOPHER BAKER is the training manger in charge of Staff Development for Gwinnett County Public Library (GCPL) in Metro Atlanta. His interest in eBooks in public libraries grew during his work as a collection development librarian for GCPL. Baker holds both a BA in English and an MLIS from Valdosta State University in Southern Georgia. He has been featured in *Library Journal's* NextGen column and has presented at Digipalooza, OverDrive's User Conference, PLA's Virtual Spring Symposium, and the Georgia COMO Conference. Baker lives in the historic Northwoods neighborhood of Doraville, Georgia, with his rat terrier, Tweed.

WENDY BARTLETT is the collection development manager for the Cuyahoga County Public Library system located near Cleveland, Ohio. Opinions expressed in this article belong to the author and do not necessarily represent the opinions of the Cuyahoga County Public Library. Before joining the Collection Development Department, she was the branch manager for the Beachwood Branch of the Cuyahoga County Public Library, and prior to that was the assistant director of the Kent Free Library in Kent, Ohio. She is the author of *Floating Collections: A Collection Development Model for Long-Term Success*, forthcoming from ABC-CLIO in Fall of 2013.

ANNE BEHLER is information literacy librarian and instruction coordinator for Library Learning Services at the Pennsylvania State University Libraries. She began the leisure reading collection at the University Park Campus in 2007, and continues to serve as the collection's selector. In addition to her collection development activities, Behler coordinates library instruction initiatives for Penn State's first-year English Composition program. She is an active member of two divisions of the American Library Association (ACRL and RUSA), and is an inaugural class member in the Penn State University Libraries' Leadership Program.

ROBERT W. BOISSY is currently manager of Account Development for the publishing house Springer Science+Business Media. He has served in various roles at Springer in licensing and marketing since 2003. Prior to his work in publishing, Robert spent 15 years at a subscription agency in training, support, and technical jobs involving data exchange and implementation of standards. He has served as chair of the International Committee for Electronic

Data Interchange for Serials (ICEDIS), president of the North American Serials Interest Group (NASIG), and as a member of various committees for the National Information Standards Organization (NISO). Robert holds a BA from Middlebury College, an MLS from SUNY Albany, and a Certificate of Advanced Study in Information Transfer from Syracuse University.

SIAN BRANNON is the Assistant Dean for Collection Management at the University of North Texas. Prior to this post, she worked for a decade in public libraries in various positions. She graduated from Texas Woman's University with her PhD in 2013, with a concentration in public library management. Her professional involvement includes many years of service to the Public Library Data Service Statistical Report of the Public Library Association, and serving on the editorial boards of *Reference & User Services Quarterly, Public Libraries*, and *Library Resources & Technical Services.*

JOHN M. BUDD is a professor in the School of Information Science and Learning Technologies at the University of Missouri. He has also been on the faculties of Louisiana State University and the University of Arizona. Throughout his teaching career he has taught collection-management-related courses. Prior to his work as a faculty member he was the head of Collection Management at Southeastern Louisiana University. He has served as Chair of the Collection Development and Evaluation Section of the Reference and User Services Division of ALA. He has also served as president of the Association for Library and Information Science Education and Beta Phi Mu and chair of ALA's Library Research Round Table. He is the author of 10 books and more than 100 journal articles.

JEFFREY D. CARROLL is director of Collection Development at Columbia University Libraries. He previously served as the head of Serials Acquisitions, also at Columbia. He holds an MLS from Syracuse University and an MA in creative writing from the City College of New York.

THOMAS F. R. CLARESON is senior consultant for Digital & Preservation Services at LYRASIS, the largest library and cultural heritage network in the United States. He consults nationally and internationally on preservation, disaster preparedness and recovery, digitization, special collections/archives, remote storage, funding, and advocacy issues. He has served as a lead consultant on 17 Institute of Museum and Library Services "Connecting to Collections" statewide preservation planning grants, and six implementation projects. He is also coleader of the annual "Digital Futures" five-day workshop series, sponsored by King's College London in the UK and Australia. With more than 20 years' experience in preservation and digitization services, Clareson was previously Program Director for New Initiatives at PALINET and global product manager at OCLC Online Computer Library Center, Inc.; he also served in various capacities at Amigos Library Services, Inc. He holds an MLS from Kent State University, an MA from Ohio State University, and a BA from Ohio Wesleyan University. Formerly a representative from the Society of American Archivists to the Joint Committee on Archives, Libraries, and Museums, he currently serves on the Board of Trustees of Heritage Preservation, the national institute for preservation and conservation advocacy. He has taught graduate-level preservation courses for the University of Texas at Austin, University of California-Los Angeles, and the University of Illinois Urbana-Champaign.

NADINE P. ELLERO is the serials acquisitions librarian at Auburn University Libraries, in Auburn, Alabama. Prior to coming to Auburn, she was the intellectual access/metadata services librarian at the Claude Moore Health Sciences Library at the University of Virginia, in Charlottesville, Virginia (1990–2011). She is a member of the American Library Association (ALA) and chair of the Association for Library Collections & Technical Services (ALCTS) Cataloging and Metadata Management Section (CaMMS) Research & Publications committee. She has published articles in *Library Resources & Technical Services*, *Journal of Electronic Resources in Medical Libraries*, and *Journal of Library Metadata*. Ellero presently serves on the editorial board of *Library Resources & Technical Services* (LRTS). Her professional interests include resource acquisition, metadata, standards, and all avenues of information resource discovery. From the University at Buffalo, the State University of New York, she holds an MLS and BA in Linguistics.

JODY CONDIT FAGAN is associate professor and director of scholarly content systems at James Madison University Libraries & Educational Technologies. She is the founding editor of the *Journal of Web Librarianship*, and holds a master's in library science from the University of Maryland; a master's in history from Southern Illinois University Carbondale, and is currently a PhD candidate in the School of Strategic Leadership Studies at James Madison University. With Meris Mandernach and others, she implemented EBSCO Discovery Service at James Madison University in 2010.

DEG FARRELLY has worked with academic media collections for nearly 40 years. As the media librarian for Arizona State University his primary responsibility is selection and management of quality media content to support teaching and research across the university's four campuses. He now focuses on streaming approaches to video collection development, including consulting for major media distributors and library publishers. Also the subject librarian for the Communication and Film & Media Studies programs on the Tempe campus, deg recently transitioned to a new role as administrator of ASU Libraries' ShareStream implementation. deg presents frequently on matters of academic media at national conferences, including CCUMC, the Charleston Conference, Electronic Resources & Libraries, the National Media Market, the American Library Association, and highly attended Webinars for *Library Journal*. His national on academic streaming video (with Jane Hutchinson) provides seminal data on this emerging library trend. Outside of professional activities, deg is an avid Scrabble player, collects mid-20th-century pottery, glass, and aluminum, and manages the lending library for the nonprofit group OrigamiUSA. Some of his original origami designs have been published internationally.

STEVEN K. GALBRAITH is curator of the Cary Graphic Arts Collection at Rochester Institute of Technology (RIT). Prior to coming to RIT, he was the Andrew W. Mellon Curator of Books at the Folger Shakespeare Library in Washington, DC, and visiting professor and curator of Early Modern Books and Manuscripts at The Ohio State University. He is the author of books and articles on English Renaissance literature, printing history, rare book librarianship, and book conservation and digitization.

KAREN E. GREEVER has been collection development librarian at Kenyon College since 2006. Previously she served as technical services librarian and acquisitions librarian, both at Kenyon, and as authority control/catalog management librarian at Ball State University. She holds an MA in Classical Archaeology from Bryn Mawr College and an MLS from the University of Kentucky.

MERLE JACOB was Director of Library Collection Development at the Chicago Public Library, where she purchased materials for the main library and the 80 branch libraries, trained librarians in collection development, readers' advisory, and reference, and helped set up the book discussion groups in the branches. As a member of the American Library Association (ALA), she was part of a group of librarians who set up CODES (the collection development section) in RUSA, a division of ALA. When she was president of CODES, she established the Readers' Advisory Committee. Throughout her career Merle has spoken at numerous ALA programs and state library programs on collection development, weeding, readers' advisory, and the mystery genre. She helped found the Adult Reading Round Table, the oldest readers' advisory group in the country. She has written articles for *Library Journal, Reference & User Services Quarterly, Booklist,* and other journals, and is the coauthor of *To Be Continued: Fiction in Sequels.* In 2002, she was awarded the Allie Beth Martin Award by the Public Library Association in recognition of her extraordinary knowledge of books and the ability to share that knowledge with others. Since her retirement, she has been busy doing consulting work for publishers and libraries. She is the mystery column writer for NoveList, the electronic library database for readers' advisory, and reviews reference books for *Booklist.*

L. SUZANNE KELLERMAN is Judith O. Sieg Chair for Preservation and Head of the Digitization and Preservation Department at the Penn State University Libraries. She earned her master's in library science from the University of Pittsburgh. She joined the Penn State University Libraries in 1985 serving as the field cataloger for the Pennsylvania Newspaper Project. From 1988 to 1990 she served as an acquisitions librarian at Penn State and later in 1990 she became Penn State's first preservation librarian. In 1998 digital library initiatives were added to her department's core services. Preservation and access of information resources in all formats remains her core professional commitment and research focus. She has given numerous presentations and published on a wide array of topics including deacidification, disaster planning, response, and salvaging, electronic theses and dissertations, and digitization project planning and production. Preservation, microfilming, and digital conversion of historic Pennsylvania newspapers, including collegiate newspapers, are her current research interests. She is currently serving as the principal investigator of Pennsylvania's participation in the National Digital Newspaper Program and serves as the chair of the Pennsylvania Digital Newspaper Project's Advisory Committee. In 2007 she was elected to the Standing Committee of the IFLA Newspapers Sections and is currently serving as its secretary/treasurer.

ROBERT H. KIEFT is college librarian at Occidental College. Prior to this appointment in 2008, he worked for 20 years at Haverford College, where he was most recently director of college information resources and librarian of the college. From 1974 to 1988, he worked at Stanford University in circulation, reference, and collection development. He earned his MLIS from the University of California, Berkeley, and a PhD from Stanford University. A member of the Collection Development and Evaluation Section of the Reference and User Services Association, he has held a number of positions in that section, including chair (2000–2001). He has published articles and reviews in *Choice*, *Collaborative Librarianship*, *Collection Management*, *College and Research Libraries*, *Reference Services Review*, and *Reference & User Services Quarterly*. Dr. Kieft developed his interest in shared collections during his Haverford years in the TriCollege Consortium and as a board member of the Pennsylvania Academic Library Consortium, Inc. (PALCI), and the Philadelphia Area Consortium of Special Collections Libraries (PACSCL). He is currently on the board of the Western Regional Storage Trust (WEST) and is an adviser to the Maine Shared Collections Strategy.

JAMES (JAMIE) LARUE was director of the Douglas County Libraries, headquartered in Castle Rock, Colorado, from 1990 through 2014, during which the Douglas County Libraries Model was launched for library managed e-content. He is the author of *The New Inquisition: Understanding and Managing Intellectual Freedom Challenges* (Libraries Unlimited, 2007).

MICHAEL LEVINE-CLARK is the Associate Dean for Scholarly Communications and Collections Services at the University of Denver Libraries. With colleagues from the Colorado Alliance of Research Libraries, he founded the open access journal *Collaborative Librarianship*, and serves as coeditor for scholarly articles. He has been a member or chair of many committees within the Association for Library Collections and Technical Services (ALCTS) and the Reference and User Services Association (RUSA), and has served on a variety of national and international publisher and vendor library advisory boards. He is currently serving as the cochair of a NISO working group to develop recommended practices for Demand Driven Acquisition of Monographs and as the coeditor of the *Encyclopedia of Library and Information Science*, fourth edition. He writes and speaks regularly on strategies for improving academic library collection development practices, including the use of eBooks in academic libraries and the development of demand-driven acquisition models.

LOGAN MACDONALD is the Collection Development Director for Anythink Libraries in Adams County, Colorado. In 2008, Logan helped develop WordThink, Anythink's BISAC-based classification system that was implemented district-wide in 2009. Prior to joining Anythink, Logan worked for the Montrose Regional Library District in Montrose, Colorado, and University of Washington Libraries in Seattle. He is frequently introduced by colleagues as "The Man Who Killed Dewey."

MERIS A. MANDERNACH is associate professor and head of research services at The Ohio State University. She was previously the Collection Management Librarian at James Madison University. She holds an MS in library and information science from the University of Illinois at Urbana-Champaign. Her scholarship encompasses topics of discovery tools, usability studies, and the evolving nature of reference and research services.

VICTORIA MORSE has taught medieval and Renaissance history at Carleton College since 1999. After receiving her PhD from the University of California, Berkeley, she had a postdoc with the History of Cartography Project at the University of Wisconsin, Madison. Since being at Carleton she has been a co-director of the Medieval and Renaissance Studies Concentration and of the "Visualizing the Liberal Arts" grant funded by the Andrew W. Mellon Foundation. Her research interests include cartography and political and religious understandings of space in late medieval Italy.

LINDA R. MUSSER is a distinguished librarian at the Pennsylvania State University where she is head of the Fletcher L. Byrom Earth and Mineral Sciences Library. She received her BS in civil engineering and worked in industry prior to receiving her MS in library and information science from the University of Illinois. A former cataloger, she has published numerous papers related to technology in libraries and the literature of the sciences and engineering.

JACOB NADAL currently serves as Director of Library and Archives for Brooklyn Historical Society. Since receiving his MLS from Indiana University in 2001, he has led preservation efforts at Indiana University, New York Public Library, and UCLA, and served on the boards of the ALA/ALCTS Preservation and Reformatting Section and the California Preservation Program. He holds an appointment as a visiting assistant professor at the Pratt Institute School of Information and Library Science, teaching digital preservation and curation, and serves as an adviser to the Library of Congress Office of Strategic Initiatives Digital Preservation Outreach and Education and National Digital Stewardship Residency programs.

SUE O'BRIEN is the Assistant Director for Support Services at the Downers Grove Public Library in Downers Grove, Illinois. She graduated from Rosary College with an MALS degree. She started her career at the Chicago Botanic Garden library, and she has worked as a reference librarian, a readers' advisor, and manager of the Literature and Audio Services Department at the Downers Grove Library. She especially enjoys sharing books with library patrons, family, and friends.

BONNIE REID is currently Assistant Director for Public Services at the Downers Grove Public Library, Downers Grove, Illinois. She graduated with an MSLS degree from the University of Illinois at Urbana-Champaign and has worked in several public libraries in Illinois. Prior to becoming an assistant director, she served for many years as the manager for the Reference and Information Services Department at Downers Grove, where she enjoyed weeding the nonfiction collections as well as encouraging and directing other staff in weeding.

JULIET T. RUMBLE is a reference and instruction librarian and the philosophy and religion subject specialist at Auburn University Libraries in Auburn, Alabama. She is a member of the American Library Association (ALA) and has served on various committees in the Association of College and Research Libraries (ACRL) Instruction Section (IS). She has contributed articles to *Technical Services Quarterly, Journal of Business & Finance Librarianship, Journal of Interlibrary Loan, Document Delivery & Electronic Reserves,* and *Scandinavian Studies.* Her research interests are in the areas of information literacy, assessment, and collection development and management. Rumble holds an MSLS from the University of North Carolina at Chapel Hill and a PhD in philosophy from Vanderbilt University.

MARK SANDLER is the Director of the Center for Library Initiatives at the Committee on Institutional Cooperation (CIC). He is interested in how libraries, publishers, and users are managing the transition from print to electronic resources, with particular focus on the collaborative efforts of libraries to extend their mission to include content creation. Dr. Sandler was among the founders of the Text Creation Partnership—a working group that partners with libraries and commercial publishers to create accurately keyboarded and encoded editions of early texts. He has also worked closely with the Google/library mass digitization project, and has written and presented widely about how mass digitization initiatives are affecting local collection development strategies.

Prior to assuming his current role at the CIC Consortium, Dr. Sandler was the collection development officer at the University of Michigan University Library, and has taught collection development and research methods at the University of Michigan School of Information. He holds a doctorate in sociology from Michigan State University, and an MLS from the University of Michigan.

KATHLEEN SULLIVAN has worked in public libraries for 40 years, where her primary responsibility has been as a collection management specialist. She has served on many local and national library committees and has taught workshops on collection maintenance and analysis. For the past 15 years, she has been the Collection Development Coordinator for the Phoenix Public Library.

LAUREL TARULLI received her master of information management from the University of Alberta in Edmonton, Alberta, Canada. A member of the faculty at Dalhousie University's School of Information Management, in Halifax, Nova Scotia, Ms. Tarulli's research areas include readers' advisory services, information management, cataloging and classification, and social discovery tools. In addition to teaching, Laurel is the editor of *Reference & User Services Quarterly*'s readers' advisory column, contributor to NoveList and author of numerous articles and chapters. She is the recipient of ALA's Esther J. Piercy Award and the 2010 Distinguished Alumni award from the University of Alberta.

KATHY TEZLA is the Head of Collection Development at the Laurence McKinley Gould Library at Carleton College in Northfield, Minnesota. Prior to her position at Carleton, Kathy was involved with the evolution of academic collections at the University of Michigan and Emory University as a selector, social sciences coordinator, and as a government documents librarian. Since 1984 she has served on numerous ALA committees and task forces within RUSA and ALCTS: Collection Development and Evaluation Section (CODES) and Collection Management and Development Section respectively (CMDS). She has served as Chair of the Government Documents Roundtable (GODORT) and ALCTS Collection Management and Development Section (now Collection Management Section). She was a Fulbright Scholar in Budapest, Hungary in 1991.

DAVID A. TYCKOSON is the associate dean of the Henry Madden Library at California State University, Fresno. He regularly teaches an online course through Infopeople on Rethinking Reference Collections. He has also written a number of articles on various aspects of reference services and teaches the Reference and User Services Association's (RUSA) online class on the Reference

Interview. David served as president of RUSA in 2007–2008 and won the Mudge Award for distinguished contributions to reference librarianship in 2005.

CHRISTOPHER H. WALKER has been serials cataloging librarian at the Pennsylvania State University Libraries since 2005. Past chair of both the ALCTS Continuing Resources Cataloging Committee and the Ulrichs Serials Librarianship Award Jury, he represents his institution on PCC/CONSER's Operations Committee. While catalogers generally have a reputation for being inflexible and narrowly focused on their own work, he has made a career out of letting the needs of the user occasionally trump the Rules. When not writing about cataloging, his research interest is in the history of information services, with a current project on the 16th-century Paris book trade.

NEAL WYATT is a collection development and readers' advisory librarian in Virginia and is the author of *The Readers' Advisory Guide to Nonfiction* (ALA Editions, 2007) and coauthor of the forthcoming third edition of *The Readers' Advisory Guide to Genre Fiction*. Active in the American Library Association, Wyatt has served as president of the Reference and User Services Association (RUSA) and as chair of RUSA's Collection Development and Evaluation Section (CODES). Committed to helping librarians discover the most notable resources for their collections, she founded the Reading List Award for Genre Fiction and the Listen List Award for Outstanding Audiobook Narration and was part of the team that created the Sophie Brody Award for Outstanding Achievement in Jewish Literature and the Andrew Carnegie Medals for Excellence in Fiction and Nonfiction. Wyatt writes *Library Journal's* "RA Crossroads" column and edits its "Reader's Shelf" column, is the immediate past editor of *Reference & User Services Quarterly's* "The Alert Collector" column, and is the coeditor of ALA Editions readers' advisory series. She is the 2012 winner of the Margaret E. Monroe award, the 2013 winner of the Isadore Gilbert Mudge Award, and was named a *Library Journal* Mover and Shaker in 2005. Wyatt is currently a PhD candidate in the Media, Art, & Text program at Virginia Commonwealth University.

DIANE ZABEL is Louis and Virginia Benzak Business Librarian and Head of the Schreyer Business Library at the Penn State University Libraries. She is an active member of the American Library Association (ALA). Zabel served as elected president of the Reference and User Services Association, one of the divisions of ALA, for the period 2005–2006. She was elected to the ALA Council and served a three-year term as ALA councilor-at-large (2009–2012). In 2011 she was the recipient of the Isadore Gillbert Mudge Award, an ALA award that recognizes distinguished contributions in reference librarianship. Zabel is the immediate past editor of *Reference & User Services Quarterly* (2006–2012). She is the editor of *Reference Reborn: Breathing New Life into Public Services Librarianship* (Libraries Unlimited, 2011). She holds a master of urban planning degree (1980) and a master of science in library and information science (1982) from the University of Illinois at Urbana-Champaign.